Creative Industries and Developing Countries

How can culture and the market be married in a way that is favourable to developing countries? This book pushes the frontiers of the new development paradigm by arguing that developing countries can use their creative assets and energies as a source of economic growth – if they can better position themselves in the global economy. It turns on its head the polarised debate about commerce and culture, by taking a fresh look at some traditional activities whose intrinsic cultural value has for too long hidden their economic worth. By bringing together new theoretical ideas, country case-studies and policy analysis, this book aims to show how developing countries can benefit from the emerging opportunities in global creative industries.

With new approaches in mind, Barrowclough and Kozul-Wright commissioned essays from economists, lawyers and industry experts on global trade trends, digital technology, film in West Africa, audio visuals in India, the music industry in Brazil and the Caribbean, the copyright industry in Arab countries, and policy lessons from developed countries – including sources of finance, subsidies and the role of incubators and intermediaries. They aim to guide debate, clarify new themes and illustrate how the cultural resources of the developing world can become a new way of integrating into the global economy – helping to raise the voices of developing countries, widening our range of creative choices, and promoting cultural diversity and economic and human development.

This book will be of major contemporary interest to economists and policymakers alike, as well as those with an interest in industrial organisation, development policy, evolutionary economics and the creative industries.

Dr Diana Barrowclough and **Dr Zeljka Kozul-Wright** are economists at the United Nations Conference for Trade and Development, Geneva.

Routledge studies in contemporary political economy
Edited by Jonathan Michie
University of Birmingham, UK

This series presents a fresh, broad perspective on the key issues in the modern world economy, drawing in perspectives from management and business, politics and sociology, economic history and law.

Written in a lively and accessible style, it will present focused and comprehensive introductions to key topics, demonstrating the relevance of political economy to major debates in economics and to an understanding of the contemporary world.

Global Instability
The political economy of world economic governance
Edited by Jonathan Michie and John Grieve Smith

Reconstructing Political Economy
The great divide in economic thought
William K. Tabb

The Political Economy of Competitiveness
Essays on employment, public policy and corporate performance
Michael Kitson and Jonathan Michie

Global Economy, Global Justice
Theoretical objections and policy alternatives to neoliberalism
George F. DeMartino

Social Capital Versus Social Theory
Political economy and social science at the turn of the millennium
Ben Fine

A New Guide to Post Keynesian Economics
Steven Pressman and Richard Holt

Placing the Social Economy
Ash Amin, Angus Cameron and Ray Hudson

Systems of Production
Markets, organisations and performance
Edited by Jonathan Michie, Jill Rubery, Brendan Burchell and Simon Deakin

New Economy, New Myth
Jean Gadrey

Hollywood Economics
How extreme uncertainty shapes the film industry
Arthur de Vany

Bilateral Trade Agreements in the Asia-Pacific
Origins, evolution, and implications
Edited by Vinod K. Aggarwal and Shujiro Urata

Creative Industries and Developing Countries
Voice, choice and economic growth
Edited by Diana Barrowclough and Zeljka Kozul-Wright

Creative Industries and Developing Countries

Voice, choice and economic growth

Edited by Diana Barrowclough and Zeljka Kozul-Wright

Routledge
Taylor & Francis Group
LONDON AND NEW YORK

First published 2008
by Routledge
2 Park Square, Milton Park, Abingdon, Oxon OX14 4RN

Simultaneously published in the USA and Canada
by Routledge
711 Third Ave, New York, NY 10017

Routledge is an imprint of the Taylor & Francis Group, an informa business

First issued in paperback 2011

Typeset in Times by Wearset Ltd, Boldon, Tyne and Wear

British Library Cataloguing in Publication Data
A catalogue record for this book is available from the British Library

Library of Congress Cataloging in Publication Data
A catalog record for this book has been requested

ISBN13: 978-0-415-39138-2 (hbk)
ISBN13: 978-0-415-51246-6 (pbk)
ISBN13: 978-0-203-08670-4 (ebk)

To the memory of my father, Z.K.W.
To my family, D.V.B.

Contents

Illustrations

Figures

Tables

Boxes

Part I

Voice, choice and growth

1 Voice, choice and diversity through creative industries

Towards a new development agenda

Diana Barrowclough and Zeljka Kozul-Wright

Creative industries and the new development agenda

This book explores ways in which developing countries may take greater advantage of the opportunities that are emerging in global creative industries markets. The sector is one of the newest and most dynamic of the global knowledge economy, where creativity, knowledge and other intangibles serve as the basic productive resource. It is already presenting significant benefits to some developing countries.

It is also a sector in which the appropriate policy framework is even more than usually necessary; because sources of comparative advantage are created as much as they are inherited, and because markets, left to their own devices, are not very good at providing the optimal environment for creating them.

Creative industries are difficult to generalise about, as they are so heterogeneous, but they are essentially dualistic industries, consisting of two key components: the intangible and the tangible. They are underpinned by intangible creativity and ideas (symbolic cultural expressions, musical ideas, visual images, products of the intellect) as well as a tangible mode of delivery, embodied in so called 'delivery channels', such as TV transmitters, film, radio, sound recordings, PCs, books, journals and magazines. Creativity is a lot like innovation, it comes with high risk, uncertainty, transactions costs, network externalities, spillovers and public good effects that imply that markets alone will not be sufficient to create an adequate resource base. This volume therefore uses the insights of economic and related theory, as well as lessons from the hits and misses of selected developing and developed countries, to describe policy measures that can help developing countries to harness their advantages in this sector and to redress their disadvantages.

Our perspective implies a new way of looking at what are essentially ancient and traditional activities. Culture and creativity – embodied in modern tradable forms – are increasingly being valued as an economic activity, rather than as a purely cultural activity. This has come about, in part, as the liberalisation and globalisation of service markets has opened up whole new areas for production, consumption and export. Increasingly, in developing countries, creative industries are valued not only for their cultural and social functions – such as social cohesion, nationalism, preservation of common values and collective institutions – but also as an economic tool for development, i.e. for their potential to create employment, generate incomes, earn export revenues and alleviate poverty (UNCTAD, 2004a, 2004b; Throsby, 2001). They are beginning to be seen as a way of regenerating local communities and catalysing entire cities; of diversifying and re-positioning traditional or regressing economies; of boosting human capital, skills levels and innovation; and of opening a door to the global knowledge economy (see Florida, 2002). This book does not suggest they are a panacea, but rather aims to draw attention to their untapped potential. Numerous governments in both the developed and the developing world have identified the sector as a high-growth target and there has been a mushrooming of creative sector-mapping and creative industries conferences and workshops. Creative activities are still valued as a form of cultural expression and diversity, but this is increasingly not the sole focus.

The creative industries defined

The creative industries include a set of interlocking sectors that produce symbolic goods and services which rely on creativity and knowledge more than other activities. They have been described as 'industries that have their origin in individual creativity, skill and talent with a potential for wealth and job creation through the generation and exploitation of intellectual property.'[1] This encompasses a wide range of activities dealing with the production and distribution of creative content that includes advertising, architecture, art, crafts, design, fashion, film and video, interactive leisure software, music, performing arts, publishing, software and computer services, television and radio (DCMS, 1988). This vast array of interrelated activities lie at the crossroads of arts and commerce and cover diverse areas ranging from the recording industry; the motion picture industry; publishing; computer software; the radio, television and cable industries; photography; video games and new multimedia products and services; Internet sites.

This book focuses in particular on the audio-visual creative industries (film, television, music and so on), in part because of their economic value but also because they share similar economic characteristics in their production and distribution (see the section, 'What is special about creative industries?'). It therefore excludes creative activities pertaining to textiles, design and handicrafts which are also important, but for which a different analytical approach is more appropriate.

The concept of 'creative industries' is a relatively recent one that links together ancient and traditional skills of creativity and communication with the latest IT and digital technologies and IPRs. Creative industries use market mechanisms for valourising their production and distribution. These include, but are not restricted to, IPRS, and tensions are intensifying over the way to best stimulate and reward creativity. These characteristics distinguish them from more traditional cultural industries whose primary function is the creation of cultural or social value. While there are obvious overlaps with traditional 'cultural' activities, such as performing arts and handicrafts, the underlying concept behind the creative industries as a new cluster of interrelated activities emphasises the commercial over the cultural dimension of such activities.

The diverse creative activities that fall under the creative industries umbrella are situated in the so-called 'creative economy': implying the knowledge-based activities that produce and distribute goods and services based on texts, symbols, images and experiences. The creative economy refers to the cycle of creation, production and distribution of goods and services that use knowledge, creativity and intellectual capital as their primary productive resource (UNCTAD, 2004a, 2004b). The creative economy demonstrates the growing power of such intangible assets as primary determinants of international competitiveness. By means of digitalisation and related technological advances, the creative economy has been pushed to the forefront of global economic development. This perspective is not universally accepted, and there is some controversy and debate (e.g. Larry Elliot's "Talk is cheap," *Guardian*, 18 May 2007).

The creative industries are sometimes referred to as 'copyright based industries', indicating the critical role of intellectual property and copyright laws as the economic evaluation of the intangible nature of this creativity, although the term 'copyright-based industries' is far broader than 'creative industries' (Siwek, 2004).

The term 'industries' is also important, because it moves the perspective away from the traditional vision of creativity existing at the level of the individual artisan, such as giving live performances, or the cottage-activity making one-off crafts pieces, and places it in the frame of a distinct economic sector that accounts for a rapidly expanding share of the global economy, and that deserves the far greater attention of policy makers. For example, it has been estimated that these industries produced intellectual property in the form of patents, copyrights, trademarks and proprietary design worth $2.24 trillion dollars in 1999 (Howkins, 2001), with the US contributing approximately 40 per cent of the global total. The point to make is that in advanced market economies, creative industries are modern industries, based on principles of mass production, whereas others are post-industrial, based on the model of flexible specialisation. However, in developing countries (with the exception of Brazil, China and India) they are for the most part still post-industrial, based on the model of flexible specialisation. Most creative industries, particularly in developing countries, tend to remain craft-based or art-based cottage industries (or as music is called in Jamaica: no more than a 'scene').

Box 1.1 Creative industries and the development agenda

- Creative Industries offer a new source of exports, investment and economic growth for developing countries. Growth in trade and in export revenues in creative industries is faster than in older, more conventional, goods and services.
- Creative industries offer new opportunities for employment growth, including jobs with a high degree of creativity and skills.
- The indirect employment effects in complementary sectors, such as ICTs, multimedia and tourism, may even outweigh direct effects. The

upstream stages of the industry chain tend to be rather labour-intensive, which can be especially important in countries with high youth unemployment.

- Creative industries can become a portal into the global knowledge economy and a shortcut to move up the global value chain. There are also synergy effects that will impact upon other sectors of the economy, such as tourism and ICTs.
- There is a new institutional energy for the topic, as manifested in the establishment of national and international agencies, intermediaries, and advocacy groups.
- Succeeding in this sector requires an enabling policy environment. Without the appropriate policies, institutions and capabilities to stimulate and promote finance, production and consumption of domestic creative industries, they will not thrive.
- Central to the issue of an enabling policy infrastructure is support for entrepreneurship, especially in the SME sector.
- Equally critical is the legal and regulatory infrastructure, the IPR regimes (in particular the role of copyright) and its implementation; the regulatory environment, including competition policy, the technological infrastructure and mobilising finance for creative industries.
- Regional arrangements in distribution, marketing and advertising along with increased role for regional markets should also be considered.

This new way of looking at creative industries adds a new element to older, more traditional 'public good' perspectives. Boosting local production will help ensure that local communities hear their own 'voice', through home-grown music, screen and television products that would not otherwise have been produced. It will also, in this approach, contribute to a countries' ability to export through regional and global markets, which can add further to diversity, based on the creation of an increased range of consumer 'choice'. Cultural diversity is a valuable public good, providing benefits to all.

Creativity as commerce: the economic value of the sector

The economic value of this sector may greatly surprise readers who are new to this debate. For example, World Bank estimates have placed the global value of the creative industries at as much as 7 per cent of world gross domestic product, and industry forecasts typically predict growth rates of 10 to 20 per cent per annum. Other estimates have varied depending upon whether software and general scientific research and development are included, indicating that it is important to define carefully the composition of the creative industries cluster. For the most part, this book is focused on the narrower definition of copyright industries – a major component of creative industries, but one which excludes, for example, patent-industries, which would be more R&D in *sensu stricto*, oriented.[2]

The commercial potential in this sector is enormous. For example, the most recent estimate for the entertainment and media industry is some $1.3 trillion in 2005 (Pricewaterhouse Coopers, 2006). Table 1.1 below presents a selection of the activities in which many developing countries could participate – including films, television, television distribution, recorded music, radio, internet, video games and publishing. Given that the latest figures for global GDP are $41,290.4 billion (World Bank, 2006), this suggests a share of around 2.8 per cent just for the activities indicated in the table. This is clearly a market that should not be ignored by developing countries.

Not least, the employment potential in these sectors is significant. In the United States, for example, it has been estimated that the creative industries employ some 1.3 million people. This, in addition to the revenues cited in Table 1.1, demonstrates that the sector is more valuable than, for example, automobiles, agriculture or aerospace. In the United Kingdom (where it was estimated that the sector generated revenues of over £112.5 million), the sector employed 1.3 million people (DCMS, 2003). These effects may spread beyond the immediate economy of creative industries, through spillovers, into other sectors of the economy that have a less direct connection, such as tourism.[3]

At present the shares of these global markets are still very uneven, and even the developing countries described in the chapters of this book that are participating fairly fully in the market have a long way to go before they capture a significant share. However, the widespread diffusion of new technologies is helping to make the distribution of global market shares more fluid. For example, in 2005 the United States alone accounted for $489 billion, or 42 per

Table 1.1 Global market value for selected creative industries ($ millions)

	2001	*2005*	*2010*[a]
Films	64,169	80,473	104,060
Television distribution	109,953	154,351	230,282
Television networks	127,048	164,222	226,577
Recorded music	39,008	37,123	47,927
Video games	20,631	27,054	46,462
Magazine publishing	92,758	98,453	117,585
Newspaper publishing	167,775	178,760	208,129
Book publishing	103,419	112,953	130,533
Sports	68,427	86,298	120,900
Internet advertising	65,617	144,513	265,561
Business information	71,112	78,022	101,226
Total	929,917	1,162,222	1,599,242

Source: Derived from Pricewaterhouse Coopers LLP (June 2006).

Note
a Estimated.

Table 1.2 World imports of audio-visuals, from source countries and regions (1989–2004) (ranked in descending size)

World imports from:	*1989 ($ m)*	*2004 ($ m)*	*Rate of change 1989–2004*		
			Change by a factor of:	*% change*	*% change in 'all imports'*[a]
World	6,105	24,973	4.1	309	200
Developed world	5,793	21,825	3.8	277	153
Europe	3,429	15,897	4.6	363	184
North America	2,158	4,974	2.3	130	139
United Kingdom	625	2,002	3.2	220	128
Developing world	293	2,953	10.1	905.6	320
Developing Asia, including:	412	3,304	8	701.5	269
(i) India	30	265	8.7	774.6	368
(ii) Malaysia	6.3	58	9.3	826	405
Latin America, including:	39	410	10.4	942.3	264
(i) Brazil	3.7	20	5.4	437.4	180
Africa	3.9	12	3.1	207	192

Source: Barrowclough and Kozul-Wright (2006), derived from COMTRADE database.

Note

a All imports include all agriculture, all manufacturing, etc., in addition to audio-visual imports.

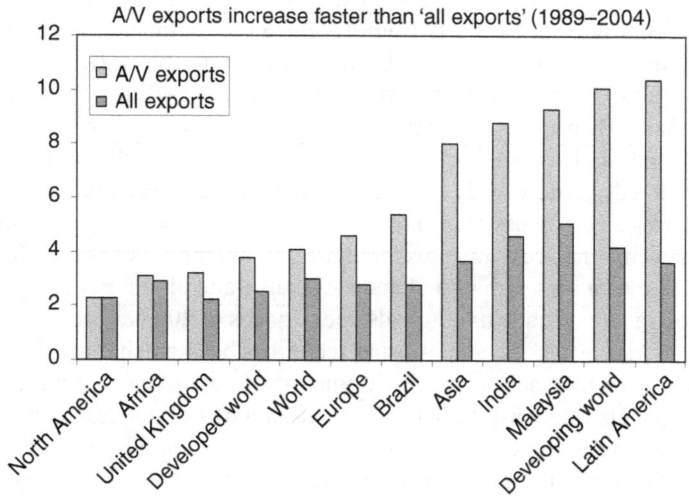

Figure 1 Exports of audio-visuals from developing countries increased faster than exports of general goods and services (1989–2004) (source: derived from COMTRADE database).

cent, but the share accounted for by Asia in general, and China in particular, along with other developing countries is growing rapidly (Table 1.2 and Figure 1.1).

Recent trends and their implications for developing countries

We have cited recent estimates on the overall size of the creative industries economy world-wide, and in a number of developed countries, but data on current trends is at best patchy, especially with respect to developing countries. Countries such as China, India and Brazil have experienced rapid growth in exports, while many other countries, particularly in Africa and Latin America, appear to have lost market shares, including smaller players such as Burkina Faso, Senegal, Tunisia, Morocco, Egypt and others (UNESCO, 2006a).

Data is generally lacking however, and this has been highlighted by UNCTAD and others, leading to the call for the collection of accurate and comparable trends data and analysis of policy information for developing countries.

On the basis of the limited information currently available, the most recent COMTRADE data[4] offers a valuable picture of recent trends in imports and exports of audio-visual goods and services (film, music and so on) that confirms the expectations that are widely held of this new and dynamic sector. The audio-visuals sub-sector is one of the most important under the entire creative industries umbrella (excluding ICTs and software). Trends over the last 15 years, for example, suggest that this new sector is growing faster than more conventional economic activities (Figure 1.1). Also, exports of developing countries are growing at a faster rate than exports from developed ones, including the global giants such as the United States and the United Kingdom (Table 1.2).

According to the COMTRADE data, trade in audio-visuals has grown significantly faster than trade in general over the last 15 years. World trade of audio-visual goods and services[5] increased four-fold from $6.1 billion in 1989 to $25 billion in 2004, while world trade of all goods and services increased only three-fold (the figures are less than those cited in the Pricewaterhouse Coopers study, which were final consumer expenditure, including advertising). In per cent terms, this meant a growth rate of audio-visuals trade of 309 per cent, compared to a growth rate of trade of all goods and services of 200 per cent.[6]

As shown in Figure 1.1, the audio-visual sector has been much more dynamic than traditional economic activities. World imports of audio-visuals from developing countries increased ten-fold, whereas world imports of goods and services in general from developing countries increased only four-fold (Figure 1.1). The implication is that the audio-visual sector is much more dynamic for developing countries than the other, more traditional, sectors.

The potential in the audio-visual sector is especially marked for some developing countries. India, for example, saw world imports of its audio-visual products increase eight-fold while world imports of its products in total increased only five-fold; Latin America saw world imports of its audio-visual products increase ten-fold compared to a four-fold increase in world purchases of its total goods and services. It is notable that audio-visuals growth exceeded growth of all exports for every country and region, with the exception of the United States, for which the rate of growth in audio-visuals was the same as the rate of growth of exports of all goods and services (this rate was also considerably lower than the other countries and regions).

Clearly, the absolute magnitudes give a different perspective in that audio-visuals are still a very small proportion of total trade. COMTRADE estimates that total global trade was worth some $2.9 trillion in 1989 and $8.8 trillion in 2004, and audio-visuals are therefore only a very small part of this. But the point is that trade growth has been very much slower in the other sectors. The share attributed to audio-visuals is therefore rising and it is not surprising that so many countries have identified this sector as a key growth prospect.

Related to this rapid growth by developing country exporters, the share of developing countries in global trade in this sector is increasing sharply, in relation to the developed world. The fact that there is an eager market awaiting the creative industries' products of developing countries is suggested by trends shown by the data of world imports of audio-visuals from developing countries, which increased more than three times as quickly as audio-visual imports from the developed world (Table 1.2). World imports from the developing world increased ten-fold over a period, while in the same period imports from the developed world increased only four-fold. The developing world's markets were therefore growing twice as fast as the developed world's.

The implication of the trends is that, although in absolute terms, the lion's share of the trade is still held by the developed world, the developing countries' share is increasing very quickly. In 1989, world imports of audio-visuals from developing countries accounted for only 4.8 per cent of total world imports in the sector – but by 2003 this had risen to 12 per cent of total world trade. This is a rapid rate of change that merits more attention, not least because of what it could mean if the current trends continue. Some areas benefited much more than others – with Asia virtually doubling its share to 8 per cent of total world trade and Latin America also increasing, although to a smaller level of 1.6 per cent of the global total. Europe increased its share from 56 per cent to 64 per cent, as did Oceania, up from 0.72 per cent to 0.89 per cent. In contrast, North America was down almost half, from 35 per cent of the total to only 20 per cent; and Africa remained low, having fallen from 0.6 per cent to 0.5 per cent. Some important reasons for this disparate performance are described in detail in the policy and case-study chapters in this book.

Finally, it is also worth noting that while the sector is generally considered to be a volatile one, with growth rates varying significantly from year to year, in aggregate terms the volatility was no higher than for trade in general.

The COMTRADE data therefore supports the country case-study picture that is given in the chapters of this book. In India, in particular, for example, the audio-visual services sector has been one of the fastest growing areas of the economy and forecasts are for it to continue apace. As described in Chapter 7, it is already estimated to employ more than five million people directly, both in domestically-owned and in foreign-financed audio-visual productions. A new and growing trend has been the development of regional clusters that specialise in particular sub-sectors of the creative industries, such as film post-production or animation, in addition to India's success as the world's most prolific producer of feature films.

The prognosis is not, however, the same for all developing countries, and as shown in the case-studies the performance has been uneven. A few African countries have a foothold in the audio-visual sector, such as the Republic of South Africa (film), Nigeria (film), Senegal (music), Mali (music) and Burkina Faso (film). However, for the most part, this sector remains marginal and others are being left completely behind. Africa's exports of audio-visuals were markedly lower than the average for all developing countries. The Arabic countries, in particular Tunisia, Morocco and Egypt, have also fared much less well than might have been expected.

These findings are important because being left out matters; not least because of the role that creative industries play in the global knowledge economy. Skills that are developed in creative industries tend to be generic, i.e. they can be readily directed or transferred into other high value-added activities and vice-versa. Over the last two decades most developing countries have lost their share in world trade, and in particular they have lost place in terms of high value-added and service exports and have become increasingly dependent upon exports of commodities (UNCTAD, 2006). It is not only because of poor technology and enterprise development, but also because they lack the infrastructure, skills and complementary services that are needed to develop into the new and dynamic activities. Failing to participate in the creative industries boom is part of this falling-behind phenomenon.

A second reason that being left out matters is that unless developing countries start producing their own films, music and other creative products, they will increasingly find themselves importing them. This is of course not without some benefit, in the sense that consumers are offered international products previously unavailable and at low prices. However, increased dependence on cultural imports is likely to have an adverse impact on domestic production that will in turn increase these countries' cultural trade deficit with the developed countries. A steady decrease in domestic film production for example, has been noted in many African and Latin American countries (UNESCO, 2006a). Hence there is not just the danger of missing out on valuable export opportunities – they may also lose their own distinctive 'voice' amidst the content imported from the cultures and industries of other countries, especially from northern developed ones. Lost opportunities associated with low level of production of domestic cultural goods and services have been noted elsewhere (UNCTAD, 2001; UNESCO, 2006a, 2006b).

Moreover, it has been argued that the threat of cultural homogenisation and standardisation associated with the spread of western-dominated, highly concentrated media structures, leads to reduced consumer choice and welfare losses (e.g. see Barber, 1995; Appandurai, 1990; Tomlinson, 1994). These influential writers posit that cultural homogenisation, an unfortunate by-product of globalisation, is facilitated by an absence of strong local creative industries and the presence of western-dependent media structures, resulting in the inability to resist the external media monopolies. This trend of gradual 'McDonalidisation' poses a threat to vibrant, independent local cultures in favour of uniform *pensamiento unico* that leads to a narrowing of choice, voice and opinions. The real and/or imagined dangers of a serious backlash to such tendencies can no longer be ignored.

What is special about creative industries?

We examine the creative industries cluster primarily through an economic rather than cultural lens, but this does not mean that they are the standard or conventional goods and services to which mainstream economic theory – including its branches relating to asymmetric information, imperfect competition and market failure – is usually applied. These models of market failure are intrinsic to our approach, but there are also other additional ways in which creative industries are special and different, and which pose new challenges and opportunities for policy makers in developing countries.

One of the most special features of creative industries is that they produce symbolic goods that are explicitly based on the manipulation and use of ideas and creativity, and investment in knowledge creation via investment in R&D, to a far greater degree than conventional sectors (Drucker, 2000; Howkins, 2001;

Florida, 2002; UNCTAD, 2004). Intangible content can be as important as its tangible manifestations, in the forms of film, television or recorded music, for example. Creative industries display a high level of product differentation, based on intense innovative activity, both in products and processes. Indeed, while innovation is central to creative industries, it tends to be predominantly non-technical in nature as it is embodied in networks and clusters. This implies that most innovation is of non-technical nature (i.e. innovations are rarely patented, except those in delivery channels).

In terms of industry structure, the sector tends to be characterised by the co-existence of a small number of very large firms alongside a large number of small, sometimes extremely small, firms, often located in the informal sector. There is also a high degree of self-employment, with individuals working on a project-by-project basis and often in precarious financial conditions. The number of part-time, self-employed workers would far, far outweigh the number of those in permanent employment. Much learning is by doing, on-the-job; although in some countries formal schooling in various forms of creative industries (notably the film sector) exist. Many workers flip in and out of employment, often supplementing their creative industry work with regular employment in other, more conventional, activities. Not least, these effects can make it very difficult to get a clear sense of the size and scale of the sector. Distribution of the finished product is highly concentrated and remains largely in the hands of the major players, although this picture is changing, for example in the music industry, with the growing role of the independent sector (in 2005, 25 per cent share of the global market was held by independents (IFPI, 2006)).

Another marked characteristic is that creative industry clusters emerge frequently and appear to be particularly important in both formal and informal levels. Clusters tend to arise because most firms are so small. The benefits that such clusters spillover into other 'non-creative' aspects of the economy has lead to a growing focus on what are called 'creative cities', with many cities in East Asia, for example, aspiring to become the creative hubs of their regions (Wu, 2005; Florida, 2002). Clustering can also take place between countries, as well as within them, in a virtual form through the use of collaborative arrangements between firms, investors and creative individuals who are highly mobile and travel from one location to another in search of opportunities. More formal collaborations are increasingly taking place, both at the inter-firm level and between countries through the signing of bilateral co-production agreements. Finally, at the corporate level, strategies focus on protecting rent, especially copyright, but also through other ways of organising the value chain, such as control of the distribution network. This is very different, therefore, from more traditional forms of economic activity.

This heterogeneity and diversity of the creative industries sector pre-empts a uniform industrial structure. While some industries are characterised by monopolistic and oligopolistic competition (recorded music), others are almost natural monopolies (especially in cultural heritage such as opera or cable TV). The large majority of firms in creative industries are small SMEs, often in the informal sector, and marked by intense entrepreneurial activity (Holzl, 2005). Recent literature indicates that labour markets in creative industries are distinct from those in the manufacturing sector. They are marked by high degrees of fragmentation and uncertainty. Since the degree of uncertainty in creative industries is generally higher than in more conventional industries, employment is sporadic and is dominated by part-time workers and multiple-job holders (Throsby, 2001). Career choices are strongly non-pecuniary in nature and a number of studies indicate that informal learning or 'learning-on-the-job' plays a more important role than formal learning. Owing to distinct characteristics of labour markets, there is a chronic excess supply of labour and self-employment ratios are high (Wassall and Alper, 1992; Throsby, 2001; Holzl, 2005).

Traditionally, the highly concentrated, vertically integrated oligopolies that dominate the industry (all OECD-based) have posed high barriers to market entry (see Caves, 2000), particularly in certain segments of the value chain, such as distribution. Suppliers of audio-visual services in most developing countries are continuing to lose market share to products supplied through major distribution channels (for example, in the film industry). The trend is often aggravated by the poor state of cinemas and the growing presence of multiplex theatres, which are often foreign owned and vertically integrated in the supply chain of audio-visual products, excluding largely local products. At the same time, even successful producers of audio-visual products, such as India or Brazil, can find it hard to market their products abroad, penetrate the existing distribution chains and set up their own distribution networks. The United States, by comparison, built up export competitiveness in audio-visual products through control of the distribution networks, where its major companies were even more important in convergent markets. Economies of scale enabled the United States to become the most competitive supplier, offering inexpensive and attractive products.

But there are signs that this may be changing (Kozul-Wright and Jenner, 2007). In other segments of the value chain, barriers are far lower and the structure is relatively fluid, especially in areas dominated by digital technologies (the latest phases in production and digital distribution). The average size of most firms in creative industries is very small in developing countries (fewer than ten employees). However, it is unclear whether the standard industry life-cycle pattern in industrial competition holds in creative industries (Holzl, 2005). This is especially questionable as regards the oligopolistic large-sized firms that dominate the sector in terms of output. The hypothesis that digital technological paradigm reduces barriers to entry remains to be tested.

There are also other, less tangible, ways in which creative industries are special. First, there is a profound mixing of the state and the market in many creative industries that does not exist in other industries. This is most apparent in the context of broadcasting media, but it can also exist in the worlds of film and music. Because the audio-visual creative industries play an important social, political and cultural role, there has long been an argument that the state should support the production and consumption of a diverse and far-reaching range of media services, without going so far as to lead to state control. The state's role should, for example, ensure that a country's citizens have universal access to a broad range of informational, educational and entertainment media services, including a range of choices and a level of quality that would not necessarily be provided by the market alone. This can include broadcasting in minority languages; providing programmes suitable for children; religious broadcasting documentaries and an independent and neutral news service. Many different modes of financing exist, ranging from full state support for an arms-length broadcaster (the British Broadcasting Corporation model), to competitive funding of 'gaps' in the content that would otherwise be provided by broadcasters that depend on the sale of advertising or subscription (the New Zealand On Air model). Different financial models have profound implications for the nature of the service that is provided (see among others Coase, 1966; Peacock, 1986; Barrowclough, 1998, 2001). The concerns about the role of public intervention to improve market outcomes have existed since the invention of radio, film and television, and are an indicator of the extent to which the creative industries have always been considered to be 'special'.

Related to this, there is a tension between 'commerce' and the 'commodification of culture' that also does not usually exist in other chains of production and consumption. The cohabitation of commerce and culture need not necessarily be a contradiction, but it can be. One question concerns how an artist can benefit from markets and transform culture and cultural products into tradable, and particularly, exportable goods, whilst at the same time ensuring that authentic cultural value is preserved and that cultural integrity is not abandoned. A frequently discussed example is the challenge of creating film or musical products that will appeal to international tastes without diluting the products' value and meaning to local or national consumers. Some themes appear to be both local and universal – as witnessed by the versions of Bizet's opera, Carmen, that have emerged from Senegal, South Africa and other countries – but it is still a challenge to appeal to both global and local tastes at the same time, without becoming de-contextualised and meaningless to both audiences. In some cases, this has been the raison d'etre of state cultural financing institutions (for example, in New Zealand the publicly financed subsidiser of some kinds of television sees its role as helping New Zealanders to 'hear their own stories').

This may sound philosophic, but it can have very concrete ramifications: for example, is a film about country X, written and produced in country X, but with star actors and a conclusion that will appeal to country Y, still an expression of culture from country X? Such questions have arisen, for example, in the context of music in Brazil, and arise frequently with respect to film subsidies in Europe. One aspect of the international collaborations mentioned above for example, can be that producers in signatory countries are eligible for each country's domestic initiatives for public support, including for example, subsidies to film makers and access to venture capital. The implications of this for public policy, especially in the context of financial support for domestic production, are discussed in the chapter by Verena Wiedeman (see Chapter 10).

Another reflection of the tension between culture and commerce is that artists (in general, although there are of course always one or two famous exceptions) tend not to be fond of markets, nor to be proficient in dealing with them and it could be argued that it would be counter-productive to their productive capacity to become so. It does not contribute to their creativity or innovative capacity to also be chief executive, accountant, lawyer or public relations agent. For this reason, most developed countries have set up intermediary agents or agencies to act as an interface between the artist and the market – be it financiers or consumers (e.g. as described in the chapters in this volume). This in turn sets up principal-agent challenges of the sort that exist also in the health and education sectors and which require a nuanced policy touch and clear objectives and criteria.

Some of the most important challenges that emerge in these various policy responses are described in the various chapters of this book.

Why is the sector growing so rapidly?

The rapid growth of this sector stems from a multiplicity of supply and demand-related features, which are in turn related to trends of structural change in the global economy. In particular, this includes the way that services and knowledge-based activities have gained in importance in advanced market economies over the last two decades, following a massive increase in investment in ICTs (see Florida, 2002). The link to creative industries reflects the fact that they are to a large extent ICT-based and have benefited from high investment and R&D in the ICT sector. One of the most recent manifestations of this, for example, is seen in the convergence of complementary technologies and the emergence of digital and multimedia technology. Even the very notion of the 'creative industries' reflects this blurring of the ground between ICT, knowledge and entertainment – leading to the renewal or revival of old and traditional cultural forms into something new, that can be traded on global markets (Kozul-Wright, 2002/2003).

A related factor has been the opening up of markets, stemming from the deregulation of national cultural and media policy frameworks that has characterised most countries from the 1990s onwards. Markets that were previously closed were opened, creating new incentives to boost production and trade, coupled with an increase in private sector investment, as many country governments sought to maximise their national broadcaster's abilities to earn their own market revenues rather than rely on public finance. Private investors were encouraged into industries that had previously been the hallmark of the public sector. In New Zealand, for example, this contributed to the creation of an independent production sector that had not existed beforehand. In India, it helped to improve production standards and to widen the market appeal of Indian films. On the other hand, liberalisation has also brought with it threats to nascent domestic industries through the effect of low cost, low-risk imported content.

Technological change and technical innovation has also dramatically increased the number and range of products that are available, for example, changing formats for product delivery, which has had a profound effect on the value chain of many creative industries, opening up new opportunities for smaller firms and for newcomer countries. The effect in particular of digitalisation cannot be exaggerated, because it implies a dramatic reduction in production costs and production lead-times and other forms of barriers to entry that creates a real opportunity for smaller producers and for late-comers. With the new digital technologies, film and recorded music, for example, can be produced and distributed at a fraction of the historical costs. Peer-to-peer distribution mechanisms, for example, where consumers download products via the Internet, can offer new ways of gaining access to global markets and developing countries can – if they have the right copyright and collection mechanisms in place – generate significant revenues from this sector.

In addition, the creative industries have benefited from the general rise of the services economy, in the way that a rising tide can lift all boats. International trade in services more than quadrupled between 1980 and 2002, from approximately $400 billion to about $1.6 trillion. Most of the increase is still dominated by developed countries but developing countries' share of global services trade has been rising. Creative industries have contributed to this general rise in services trade, and have also been affected by it, in the sense that many newly traded services activities also required a creative industry input, such as novel design or innovative marketing.

Demand side effects have also been significant – in particular, the growing affluence of many developing as well as developed countries. This leads to an increase in the consumption of income-elastic goods such as film and music. These were previously luxuries, but are now increasingly within reach of the emerging middle classes, especially young consumers. This is particularly noted in the experiences of India and China, for example. Reinforcing this effect was the fall in prices that has been marked in many of the creative industries products, which has further boosted demand. Home videos and DVDs, for example, have fallen dramatically in price over the last decade to the extent that in many countries people keep a 'library' at home rather than hiring from rental stores. The rise of Internet usage has further contributed dramatically to the growth of creative industries over the last two decades. Direct downloading and digital delivery have contributed significantly to increases in demand for audio-visual content.

These various influences affect the creative industries in two important ways. On the one hand, as liberalisation and technological change opened new possibilities, there was a natural imperative to global trade. This stems from the fact that many creative industries are characterised by economies of scale, especially in downstream activities such as marketing and distribution, where the participation of developing countries is still marginal. When per unit costs are either the same or falling as the scale or production and distribution rises, producers will aim to spread their costs over a larger and larger market – moving from domestic consumers to global ones. Adding to this is the fact that the industries rely on novelty and faster production cycles. Scale economies reduce entry barriers, which encourages the entry of new producers and new consumers but also makes for a riskier investment climate. A supply response to this is to increase scale, often through concentration and oligopolistic structures. This has been most pronounced at the financing, distribution and marketing end of the value chain. However at the same time, the new technologies signify that there are new possibilities opening up for small and nimble firms to enter global markets as never before – offering highly niche services. This can occur at the regional as well as the national level, and tends to be associated more with the creative sides of the industry than distribution or marketing (Kozul-Wright and Rayment, 2004). In the Indian audio-visual sector, analysed in this book, it has also included benefiting from new markets in creative industries-related outsourcing and computer animation (see Chapter 7).

The less regulated markets and a more open trading system have implied not only more competition, but also a different kind of competition that has further contributed to the speed of its growth. The leading sources of comparative advantage are in knowledge and information, product quality and originality, speed of delivery and customisation. These may be more important than the traditional cost-based factors, although these are still important. Increasingly, for example, it is argued that human capital 'software', such as an experienced workforce, was more important than physical capital or 'hardware' such as studio and post-production facilities. This can be an important incentive for developing countries with a large or relatively low-cost creative labour force, but it also poses problems because it is not easy to ensure that a labour force gains in skills without having the opportunity to exercise them and to learn by doing tasks that still require a certain degree of hardware for production to take place in the first place. Finally, in terms of production, the new economy implies new forms of international inter-firm collaboration especially in trade and technology-intensive industries.

Why enabling policies are so important

Throughout the 1960s and the 1970s, most activities in developing countries that we now call 'creative industries' were marked by strong state involvement. The following two decades saw a retrenchment of the state that included the disentangling of their supportive regulatory framework. This process has taken place largely under pressure from Bretton Woods's institutions, as noted by UNESCO, in the case of several West African countries such as Burkina Faso, Senegal, Nigeria and others (UNESCO, 2006a: 229). With the exception of some incipient policies in the ASEAN region, most developing countries now have neither any specialised nor general policies for the development of this sector. Increasingly, a consensus is emerging that the Washington consensus-led model has not delivered on its promises, witnessed by increased interest in industrial policy in the developing world and a critique of the 'one size fits all' model (UNCTAD, 2006; UNIDO, 2005). This includes the sphere of IPRs (e.g. the WIPO Development Agenda (CIPR, 2002)). Disregard of the demand side and excessive concern with exports has resulted in poor economic performance for a large majority of non-Asian developing countries over the last two decades, with the least developed among them falling further and further behind (UNCTAD, 2006).

In most of these countries, cultural and creative industries are largely dominated by the informal economy, operating without regulations that would help the sector to raise finance, improve labour conditions or upgrade the industry. Moreover, the audio-visual sector in Africa, for example, suffers from almost complete absence of linkages amongst its different components, e.g. the TV channels do not buy distribution rights for domestic films (UNESCO, 2006a: 220), and the systematic approach to building capabilities in the creative industries sector that could provide demand stimuli and unleash a growth dynamic for this sector.

Why are policies important for the development of the creative industries sector in developing countries? Policy is essential to this sector, largely owing to the special characteristics of the cultural goods and services described above. As noted by Baumol (Baumol and Bowen, 1966; Baumol and Baumol, 1984) and others, a free market framework is unlikely to generate a propitious environment for the growth of this sector. Nor is the supply response likely to emerge in response to weak market incentives and serious market distortions. That policy matters has been demonstrated by all successful case studies, whether in Ireland, New Zealand, Republic of Korea, Canada, Australia, and Sweden.

But in order to be effective, specialised sectoral policies for the development of creative industries need to be situated within the broader framework of capital accumulation policies that could play a crucial role in development process. These policies should also be linked to structural and technological change that would stimulate inter-sectoral linkages aimed at sustaining a steady increase in productivity and incomes. The policy challenges are not confined to the domestic level. In some respects, those challenges at the international context (the dominant role of the majors) pose additional predicaments as their resolution will most likely entail international coordination and concerted action.

Successful experiences of policy support for the development of creative industries suggest that overcoming domestic constraints, in areas related to information, low levels of absorptive capacities, policy vacuum, supply bottlenecks and distorted market incentives should become the priority. The state should accelerate the fledgling private sector to speed up the private capital accumulation process, support human capital development and facilitate resource mobilisation with a view to closing the productivity gap between their creative enterprises and those in more advanced developing countries. Policies for creative industries should focus on mobilisation of domestic resources in the enterprise sector, encouraging expansion of domestic demand, overcoming of supply constraints and realigning distorted incentives. Increasing domestic consumption and public investment should be a priority.

Foreign investment, in the appropriate settings, may also offer growth opportunities. For example, the employment created for countries hosting large-scale foreign film production can help to boost domestic skills that may, in turn, help drive domestic production. However, domestic policies that target domestic investment are usually considered far more important than merely attracting FDI in terms of building up domestic resources and local cultural and technological capabilities, as well as domestic institutions aimed at closing the institutional hiatus, as well as adopt policies aimed at strategic integration with the global economy. This might include, for example, policies to facilitate transition toward digital economy and to build technological capacities in favour of adoption and widespread diffusion of new technologies; this includes training and investment in human capital in specialised skills such as entertainment law, design, film making, music production and publishing, contracts and so on). Consequently, governments in developing countries would be well advised to consider the use of active and strategic trade policies in supporting the growth of this promising but fledgling sector (UNCTAD 2004a, 2004b, 2006):

> While the economic and employment-generating potential of these industries is vast and many developing and transition economies have great potential in this area, most are still marginal players, despite their rich cultural heritage and pool of talent. That position reflects a combination of domestic policy weaknesses and global systemic biases.
>
> (UNCTAD, 2004a)

It is clear, from both economic theory and the examination of country case-studies, that for creative industries to thrive, the appropriate policy framework is critical – more so than in many other economic activities. Many countries, ranging from large and well-known global exporters such as the United Kingdom to newer entrants such as New Zealand, have targeted the sector as a key priority for economic growth. They have a sophisticated menu of policy tools and regulations promoting production in this sector. In these countries, the debate has moved on from whether the sector is a valuable one or not, to which policy tools are best adapted to participating in it or which are most acceptable given international policy commitments. Few developing countries have given the industry the same level of attention in terms of the supportive or promotional policies that exist in most developed countries, although for some the sector could become more valuable than their traditional low value-added, commodity-based industries (see for example the experiences of India and Brazil, described in Chapters 6 and 7).

The greatest policy challenges for developing countries in this sector are in fact the opposite side of a coin that also gives them the most opportunities. The sector's inherent propensity to scale, for example, is the incentive, the carrot that offers developing countries the chance to earn significant export revenues. On the other hand, scale is difficult to achieve, especially for newcomers. This will particularly affect small countries and newcomer countries – a definition that includes most developing countries (see for example Chapter 4 on the experience of Burkina Faso).

However, it is clear that country size – a factor that cannot be affected by policy – is important but it is not the whole story. Latin America, for example, has a long production history in creative industries, dating back to the early twentieth century, sizeable markets and a large population over which to achieve significant economies of scale, stemming from advantages linked to language and cultural affinities at the regional level and with the large North American market. However, it has not realised its full potential. In 1996, for example, Brazil was the world's sixth largest music market, but five years later it had fallen to twelfth place. Indeed the situation has seriously deteriorated over the last decade (see Chapter 6). Owing to the special characteristics of creative industries described above, the absence of an appropriate policy framework has frequently been detrimental to the development of this sector. Many of the previously existing policies in support of this sector, for example, in Latin America, had been abandoned as result of the neo/liberal policies of the 1980s and 1990s, to the detriment of their growth and development. This is certainly the case of the audio-visual sector in Brazil and many other Latin American countries (Katz, 2006).

The fact that even countries with large populations are not immune from the policy challenges that the industries embody stems from the character of the sector. As described earlier, it tends to have high up-front capital costs (including sunk costs) and very low marginal costs. Even with the new technologies and an integrated distribution network, it is not easy for new or independent producers to find a foothold in the industry. The product cycle is incredibly fast and short, and even successful products can have a very short shelf-life. Not all 'experience goods' are consumed time and time again. The drive for scale simply further exacerbates the risk that is inherent in this intangible and 'experience' good. It is not easy to predict whether a project will prove to be a failure or a success, although the odds are that failures far outweigh successes, and this adds a risk element to the difficulties of financing production on a large scale. Co-productions across countries and across firms can reduce risk, but this also dilutes the national flavour of music or a film and hence brings the tension described earlier, of marrying culture with commerce.

Similarly, chasing mass market tastes rather than niche or enthusiast tastes – in order to increase the size of the market – is a feasible strategy to reduce risk as well as to increase the profits that come from scale. However, this will also lead to a menu of products offered that are increasingly homogeneous and lack diversity. These sorts of economic arguments can be further augmented by more traditional 'public good' type arguments that show why markets alone will not produce the range or amount of creative products that are optimal and why some form of public support is required – to provide goods and services that can benefit all, but for which none would pay.

Such arguments of non-rivalness and non-excludability, for example, have long been used to justify the role of state finance of public television or public radio. The new economic arguments related to exports and trade simply add an extra dimension to traditional rationale for a public policy role to augment and supplement the markets in these sectors. Lack of diversity of television or radio produced by commercial markets has, for example, long been cited as a reason for public support of national television or radio, and when this argument is carried – through trade – to international markets as well, one can see there is a kind of global diversity argument that can now be made. Traditional calls for public policies to ensure 'choice' exists in national markets, in the sense of these being a wide and diverse range of products on offer, can now be expanded to global ones. If there is a lack of 'voice' in national markets because of the many forms of market failures that exist in creative industries, then this will lead to a lack of 'choice', because we can only choose from the (narrow) range of what we are offered. This lack of diversity can then spread from the national dearth of different voices and choices, to the global level.

The economic history to these arguments has been well described elsewhere and is for the most part now well accepted. Here is not the place to revisit it.[7] Rather, the focus is on 'what to do about it'. Our goal therefore is to explore some of the key policy options that are available to address the challenges faced by developing countries. Of course, it goes without saying that the appropriate supportive regulatory and economic and institutional framework needs to be elaborated in line with the particular needs and the level of development of each particular country.

A final area in which policies are particularly important concerns intellectual property rights, or in the case of audio-visual sector, copyright. It is worth remembering that IPRs are a market based mechanism whose purpose is to transform intangible ideas into monies. They are a market device that aims to ensure a return to artists, creators and the investors who have helped to bring their creative product to the market. There is now a fairly wide-spread agreement that the current IPR system does not serve well the creative individuals in developing countries. There is, however, less agreement on what to do about it. As with the more general policy issues described above, no 'one-size-fits-all' approach is appropriate and each country needs to adopt and adapt its own sector policies on IPRs, as with other more general policies, in view of its own level of development and its own institutional needs (CIPR, 2002; Boyle, 2004; Maskus and Reichmann, 2005) (See Chapter 2).

Technology shift and creative destruction and the role of IPRs

In economic literature, ideas are considered non-rival goods. The economic rationale for IPRs for non-rival goods are unclear, as property rights involve trade-offs between incentives (appropriability) and monopoly distortions (Landes and Posner, 1989; Romer, 2002; Towse, 2005). There is much controversy whether IPRs work as incentives or barriers to entry that may even be counterproductive for innovation in cultural and creative industries (Holzl, 2005; Johnson, 2005; Gana, 1995; Cohen *et al.*, 2002; Cohen, 2006). Information, ideas and knowledge are not conducive to the same economic and legal treatment as physical property due to their status as quasi-public goods (Johnson, 2005).

The question of 'piracy' in the context of discussion of creative industries in developing countries is a highly complex one, namely it is difficult to distinguish who are the biggest pirates, or to distinguish the good guys from the bad. The entire system of IPR, especially the copyright, is perceived as institutionalised piracy by many players. There is a growing perception that the rights holders, mainly a handful of major corporations that control over 85 per cent of the world's copyrights, are not sharing the monies from copyrights equitably with all the players, least of all with the creators of original works. Many creators, performers and smaller players in creative industries feel unjustly treated by the whole system and are looking for alternative models. This widely shared perception causes major difficulties in legitimising the current structure of the IPRs in creative industries, with on the one hand, the handful of majors making high profits, while on the other the creators being unable to make a even a basic living wage. In Jamaica, for example, despite the worldwide record sales of reggae, very little money filtered back to the Jamaican economy (Kozul-Wright and Stanbury, 1998). The large discrepancies between the revenues of the creators and the corporate rights holders in the creative industries have produced major tensions and discontinuities in the current system of industrial organisation (see Kozul-Wright and Jenner, 2007). Much of the current literature is marked by controversy regarding the impact of IPRs on this sector; is it an incentive or a barrier to innovation? (Gana, 1995; Okediji, 2003, 2006; CIPR, 2002; Towse, 2000, 2001, 2005; Andersen *et al.*, 2000).

The export and sales revenues cited for the creative industries in the previous pages of this introductory chapter were based for the most part on traditional – or what will soon become conventional – technologies of production and distribution. They showed that developing countries can participate in global creative industries markets even when they are characterised by high entry costs, long-lead times and complex distribution and marketing structures marked by vertical and horizontal integration which do not favour newcomers. But what is really promising is the new prospect that lies ahead in the world of digital technology and multimedia and Internet market distribution. Many observers are questioning whether the traditional copyright is still valid in the digital paradigm (Anderson, 2002; Johnson, 2005; Kozul-Wright and Jenner, 2007). This creates what could be called a classic Schumpeterian moment of creative destruction when clusters of new technological innovations threaten the prevailing order, and opens new doors to new entrepreneurs and newcomers, including those from developing countries. The opportunities that have been described in the old system still exist, but the new techno-economic paradigms will offer lower costs of production, easier means of distribution and even the smallest independent producer in the smallest developing country will be able to meet major markets.

New Web technologies, new formats, new processes and new business models present many opportunities for the independent, new and small players in the creative industry. In music, for example, digital studios and software programmes have significantly reduced production costs. The Internet has enabled increased sales opportunities in the global marketplace. For example, global digital sales in 2005 tripled to $1.1 billion, as the new digital market took shape

(IFPI, 2006). Currently there are 300 legal music online services available in over 20 countries, and more than two million songs are already available online. In Europe, paid-for downloads increased ten-fold in 2004 to over 200 million downloads, worth some $330 million. Music industry analysts predict that digital sales could reach 25 per cent of total sales in the next five years. Reflecting this, 50 million portable players were sold in 2004. The point is that developing countries can potentially earn money from sales in this medium, where costs are low and revenues comparatively high. (The iTunes music store is now available in 21 countries, and offers users a selection of over 3,000 music videos, for sale at $1 each. Costs are estimated at about five cents each (IFPI, 2006)).

Currently, in the music business for example, the majors' strategy for battling piracy are DRM technologies (encryption) and costly and often disputed litigation against unauthorised downloading sites – in 2005 there were nearly 2,000 cases against illegal file sharing in 17 countries,[8] and the music industry is enforcing its intellectual property rights through litigation, education information campaigns and increased use of highly controversial, proprietary DRM or digital management technologies and rights management technical systems that impose a 'digital lock up' and thereby restrict access. However, these trends are changing. Most recently, EMI has announced that starting in May 2007, it will offer its catalogues online DRM-free, i.e. without copyright protection.[9] IFPI research (IFPI, 2006) indicates that already more music fans are legally downloading music than illegal file swapping, as consumers are increasingly willing to pay for downloads. And the market is increasingly finding new means of capturing payments from Internet downloads or peer-to-peer exchanges. Independent labels have flourished and some from the larger developing countries are emerging as serious global players. The majors' strategies however, despite much resistance, are beginning to change and embrace P2P innovations; for example, recently NBC Universal has struck a deal with technology and commerce specialist Wurld Media that will make selected movies available for on-demand downloading via peer-to-peer distribution early next year – the first time that a major studio has licensed content to a P2P service. But this is just the beginning. Similar attempts at rapprochement are being undertaken by a growing number of majors. A recent study by the European Commission predicts that in Europe, the revenue from online content will reach €8.3 billion by 2010, equivalent to growth of over 400 per cent in five years (European Union, 2007).

For developing countries, this means that a new door is opening online. Similarly, in advanced market economies, independent producers ('the Indies') now collectively represent 20 to 25 per cent of the global market in both recorded music and publishing, and they include 90 per cent of all the music companies. This is the context in which most developing country producers will find themselves. They have not, as yet, developed legitimate online markets as so far the major's account for around 80 per cent of the global market, but this is one road where many new opportunities will lie.

Critical to this will be that they find new business models with regard to collective licensing – the means through which copyrights are registered and consumption of the artists' work; is it through downloads or traditional means these are paid for. If developing countries do not have the appropriate IP structures, regulatory and collection mechanisms in place, they will not be able to benefit from the technological transformation and the associated market opportunities.

This is not necessarily a question of having 'stronger' property rights. The particular IPR regime chosen must be sensitive to a country's level of development, its factor endowments and its openness to trade (e.g. CIPR, 2002; Falvey *et al.*, 2004). Moreover, the situation is still very fluid with respect to the new digital technologies and new systems of collecting property rights revenues and different relations between artists and vendors are still being designed. But at a minimum, it will be essential that developing countries acquire some degree of access to knowledge and creative works and a fair system of inducement and remuneration of creativity and risk management associated with high risk ventures. This is most likely to entail some type of realignment of the current copyright structures toward fair, rather than free, copyright structures and open sources of property rights (see Kozul-Wright and Jenner, 2007).

Copyright revenues represent the incomes paid to creative workers and, if realigned, can become an essential part of moving from a cottage industry where people are creative for pleasure, to a creative economy where artists can make a living from their creative assets and efforts. New business models are being proposed to remedy the current situation, such as the blanket license model, aimed at monetising the unauthorised use of music on the Internet and other mobile platforms for the benefit of creators and consumers (see Oksanen and Välimäki, 2005).[10] There is an urgent need for legitimate licensed services to be adopted by developing countries to deal with the abuses provoked by rampant unauthorised P2P activities. As many developing countries do not enforce copyright regulations even under conventional technologies, it is clear that a large step forward is needed if they are to succeed in the digital world, and this is complicated by the fact that new forms of licensing and copyright payment models are still being formed to adapt to the new technology. The transition to digital is still in its incipient stages in even the most advanced countries, but it is here to stay and developing countries should not passively wait for the appropriate new business models to emerge. The development of independent copyright structures, new business models, including defining, enforcing and collecting copyright revenues need to go hand-in-hand with the development of digital technological capabilities.

It is important to note that the IPRs should not become the end but the means to a fair and more efficient system of incentives and inducement and reward for creativity. However, the current copyright system is largely perceived as being unfair and ineffective in meeting its original functions, new business models, including the reform of the copyright are actively being sought to remedy this situation (Canada, Australia and the UK, for example). Whichever model is chosen, the essential point is that if domestic producers and investors are to benefit from the flow of revenues associated with sales of their creative products, then they need to own the copyright to their work. Failure to own, or to enforce, copyrights can be extremely costly not just from the point of view of the individual artist involved, but it can also be very costly for a country – as in the Senegalese case described in this volume (see Chapter 5).

However, one cannot so simply say that all artists in all developing countries should never sell their IPRs. There may be a trade-off to consider. For example, selling one's copyright to a recording studio or a financier will necessarily reduce your earning potential, but it also reduces risk. Many public sector institutions that offer preferential loans or grants to struggling artists may require full or partial transfer of the IPRs, using the argument that this is how they create the pool of investment finance with which they fund their subsidies. Obviously some sustainable and equitable means of sharing risk and return between the investor and the creator needs to be agreed. Similarly, some countries have targeted foreign investors in their domestic creative industries, arguing that at the least a large-scale internationally-financed production will offer a chance for local people to learn new skills and perhaps to take the financial risk of ownership next time. In New Zealand, the foreign-financed 'Lord of the Rings' and 'Narnia' productions are a case in point. More generally however, what is needed is a careful appraisal of the costs and benefits of each case, and moreover, artists need to have a range of options from which to choose.

The specific case of the copyright or creative industries rests within the wider question of the impact of different IPR regimes in developing countries. Facilitating access to new knowledge, through simplification of access to IPR, and also ensuring that the holders of knowledge are appropriately recognised and rewarded for their contribution, is an important element in designing a framework that will lead to increased investment and productivity. This will include the simplification and improvement of the regulatory business environment and improvement of the legal infrastructure, flexible copyright laws and new business models adapted for digital distribution.

Ten key policy steps

Countries cannot begin to think about exporting creative industries if they do not produce them in the first place, and hence the first policy challenge is to ensure the existence of an enabling framework that encourages their domestic production. This means strengthening domestic supply capacities. This process will require a coherent, integrated use of strategic policies. Key to this is the fact that in many ways the sources of comparative advantage in these markets are both inherent – stemming from a country's endowments of people, creativity, history and culture – but they are also manufactured, in the sense of being able to be nurtured and encouraged, with the right policies. The same could be said of course for most areas of the knowledge economy, and it is this that offers the potential, as well as the challenge, for developing countries.

The second challenge is to produce goods and services that global markets value and will want to purchase, and bring them to the market. Again, the policy responses to this are not self-evident, and the volume describes a number of different paths that have been tried and tested in both developing and developed countries (as described by Verena Weidemann in Chapter 10). The third challenge is to do this in a way that does not fall victim to the tension that exists between culture and commerce – between the creative process, with its roots in domestic culture and experience, and the production of tradable creative commodities, that reach out beyond domestic tastes and earn export revenues by appealing to global markets (see Jaguaribe in Chapter 12).

The ten top policy tools described below are a minimum check-list – a more detailed description is given in this book. Moreover, of course they will need to be sensitive to the tension that exists between culture and commerce, to the promotion of national and international diversity and to the seeking of markets, revenues and profits. It is not easy to retain the authentic value of culture whilst seeking global markets. The point is, however, that while these ten fundamental points tend to be covered by all the developed countries that are successful in this sector, they have not been addressed to the same extent by developed countries. There is, however, no one-size-fits-all policy approach and each country will need to find the particular menu of policies that suits their own sources of advantage and disadvantage, and their national and international policy goals. The policies appropriate for a large developing country, with a sizeable population base on which to achieve sales before venturing globally, for example, will be very different from those appropriate for a small country that cannot achieve the same economies of scale. Similarly, countries speaking a global language will face a different mixture of threats (low price imports from market leaders) and opportunities (a new market for their exports) compared to those speaking a language that exists primarily only within their national borders.

Box 1.2 Ten key policy steps

What are the most important steps to take? Experience in the more developed market economies, reinforced from the case-studies of the developing economies described in this volume suggest that the main areas requiring policy intervention include the following:

1 Investment in human capital – promotes creativity and the attainment of creative technical skills and builds local skills and capacities in this sector. For example, IT, training and education policies to help bridge the knowledge divide.
2 Facilitate transition to the new digital paradigm in all phases of the value chain – to lower production costs and access new global markets.
3 Realign copyright and intellectual property rights structures to promote more fairly the rights of original creators, and strengthen national copyright collection and licensing agencies. Facilitate fair distribution of the returns to copyright, not free exploitation of the

copyright – adopt alternative collective licensing schemes based on more coherent economic logic than the current ones.
4 Provide incentives and build capabilities, both monetary and non-monetary systems to promote innovation and creativity.
5 Facilitate access to finance for new and small producers, or innovative products and ensure access to capital for creative industries participants.
6 Adopt strategic trade policies – including boosting co-productions.
7 Provide incubators and business support to small businesses and new entrants; facilitate SME and independent producers to hook into global distribution networks.
8 Create dynamic cities and creative clusters to benefit from spillovers and linkages.
9 Promote products internationally to reduce information failures and to introduce domestic producers to the world stage.
10 Explore strategies of linking to independents production and distribution structures in more advanced economies.

Data issues

The lack of accurate data in this sector is one of the main problems that have contributed to its long-held lack of profile. Few governments or policy-makers have been fully aware of the current size and scale of the sector. This is now starting to change – in developed countries at least. This recognition of the need for systematic collection of data represents a major step forwards to providing the reliable, accurate and consistent data that will help to inform better policy-making.

There are many reasons for the poor data until this moment: not least, the fact that the 'creative industries' do not readily fit into the most commonly accepted industry and employment categories. Adding to this the fact that there are so many different individuals and companies involved, that many are part-time, freelance or otherwise informally employed in the sector; the fact that much of the costs and revenues that stream from the sector are in the form of licensing agreements that can have a very long life-span and may be complicated or confidential; the role of 'angels' and other philanthropic funders who may wish to remain anonymous; and the fact that the sector is characterised by such a high frequency of intangible or poorly defined networks and ancillary services that corporate reporting structures, let alone national ones, may not identify them, let alone account for them fully. It seems likely that information will improve markedly in the coming years, given the focus that is being given to this sector by developed countries, and it is to be hoped that the various mapping exercises and other activities being conducted in so many countries of the world will help to add the empirical evidence that will support advocates of the sectors in developing countries.

One of the outstanding areas for research that remains, with respect to the availability of data, is to better understand the complex global value chain of creative industries. Special attention needs to be given to the organisation and geography of the value chains and how new entrants in general, and developing countries in particular, can participate more in their more valuable parts. For example, what will be the impact for developing countries, of the diversification of content providers and inputs that is taking place among the large international media firms that still occupy a dominant position in these chains? Similarly, more research is needed on how countries can take advantage of FDI-supported development (e.g. the combined effects of FDI and public policy in New Zealand, described in Barrowclough, 2004). What strategies are needed to help investors, producers and skilled individuals in developing countries create beneficial linkages with foreign firms, in terms of learning, or moving up the value chain into higher value-added processes and products? Exploring the benefits of linking to the independents should also be an important part of the agenda. The fiscal, trade, financial and competition policies that are needed to act coherently in order to strengthen the interactions between local and international partners cannot emerge until there is a better source of data and information on what is currently occurring, and how it could be improved.

UNESCO's recent Universal Declaration on Cultural Diversity (2005) can be seen as another international agreement in support of domestic creative industries that has further contributed to a better resolution of many of these data issues, in addition to its broader achievements. It has spearheaded a great deal of policy interest in many developing as well as developed countries, through its identification of domestic creative industries as repositories of local knowledge that are to be valued and promoted. Cultural diversity has been highlighted as one of the key pillars of sustainable development, not least because of its contribution to the richness and complexity of the human experience. The initiative has strengthened many of the traditional public good arguments that have long supported the sector, and in so doing add another plank to the argument for better evidence-based research and policy analysis. Further details about what the international community can, and are, doing in this sphere can be found in the annex.

Summing up – voice, choice and diversity

The word 'voice' used in this title has two distinct but interrelated meanings. In the first instance it stems from the traditional public good perspective of the creative industries – seeing film, music or the arts as a way of ensuring that communities have a means of expressing themselves and their cultures – i.e. a way of hearing their voice. Through enabling many different voices to express themselves, with different messages or through different media, there is also more diversity and ultimately more choice. These kinds of arguments have traditionally been used to justify public support for the production and consumption of creative activities that markets would not, on their own, produce even though they may be desired by all. Public broadcasting is the classic example.

For example, if there is no local production, such as public broadcasting with locally produced content, then local consumers will not have the chance to 'hear their own voice' or to tell their own stories. Given the increasingly globalised world driven by economies of scale and increasing returns, where domestic consumers can import the voices and stories from other countries at very low prices, it is easy to see how one ends up with a situation where there may be few choices other than to consume products that have been made for other markets. For example, why would a film maker in a small developing country deliberately choose to make a film that will attract an audience of 500,000 people, when for a similar cost she can try for the mass market of hundreds of millions of people? Even getting only 1 per cent of the mass market would be greater than getting the entirety of the former. And turning it the other way around, why would a television broadcaster choose to invest in producing a new and original programme when it can import a programme that has been tried and tested, even advertised in advance, and which costs a fraction of the price? Similar challenges inherent in the process of trade liberalisation should be seriously considered in the design of an enabling policy framework.

Aiming for the mass market is not necessarily a bad thing per se, unless quality suffers unduly and if production and trade delivers products and services that are valued by consumers, and at prices that are low. However, if it also means that there are no domestic products on offer, because domestic producers could not compete in terms of price or scale, then there has clearly been a reduction in choice. Moreover, that will then mean there is no local product to export – and hence international markets are also denied the possibility of choosing a product from that country, over the other products that are on offer. Thus the traditional argument that public policy is needed to ensure that local creative industries exist at the national level can be extended to the global level – a kind of 'global public goods' argument, in the sense that there are benefits to us all from having more from options which to choose. The more choices that are available, the greater is the likelihood that more of us will be able to select our 'first best' choice, rather than simply accepting the least-worst of the various goods that are on offer. This argument therefore adds an economic reinforcement to more traditional arguments for diversity – against homogenisation and duplication.

However, the concept of 'voice' can also be used in a more political way. Borrowing from Albert Hirschman (1970), 'voice' includes collective-action, policy-making and other non-market means of expression. 'Voice' is defined as:

> any attempt at all to change ... an objectionable state of affairs ... through appeal to a higher authority with the intention of forcing a change ... or through various types of actions and protests, including those that are meant to mobilize public opinion.
>
> (ibid.: 47)

Voice becomes important when markets cannot be guaranteed to provide the desired outcome. The voice option therefore includes boosting awareness of the potential economic contribution of the creative industries, and second, elaborating the appropriate policy framework that is required to realise it.

Strengthening the role of 'voice' seems to us an appropriate metaphor for articulating the challenges facing creative industries in developing countries. In most cases, these are still infant industries with massively untapped potential. Slowly, at the domestic level, policy-makers are beginning to grasp this potential and are seeking ways to offer support to creative industries in the context of diversifying into more dynamic and higher value-added activities (e.g. China, Singapore, Hong Kong). This effort will require building a good dialogue between the creative and the business communities, overcoming social differences between the creators and the business community, addressing the marginal status of key players, diminishing the dominance of big, corporate players and of intermediaries in the supply value chain, altering the highly uneven power distribution within creative communities and recognising the economic contribution of the sector.

The challenge for policy-makers is to rethink their policy priorities and identify potential growth opportunities of this sector and position it at the centre of the new development paradigm within the knowledge economy. This rethinking implies a shift in the policy focus toward creative industries, seeing them as a portal into the new knowledge economy rather than a traditional craft or cottage activity with little economic potential.

Under the described circumstances, creative industries in low income countries have found it increasingly difficult to escape their marginal or niche status and become more reliable engines of economic diversification. But the consequences of this failure are not confined to economic consequences within developing countries. These are industries which feed off each other, through experimentation, imitation and cross fertilisation of ideas. Diversity describes the economic environment in which creative industries can really flourish. However, where a combination of first-mover advantages and market forces dictate the pattern of industrial development, diversity is likely to be victim.

In developing countries, where market mechanisms either do not function or operate effectively, the 'voice' instrument, in the form of collective action, carries a greater weight than the 'exit' mechanism as an instrument for change. But exercising voice effectively is a political choice that can only be made based on informed views, reliable data, documented information and knowledge. We hope that this book will fill some knowledge gaps in that area by sharing some successful experiences from more developed countries and suggest new paths for articulating voice, as well as some strategic orientations for the policy-makers in developing countries aspiring to benefit from integration into the global economy with their cultural resources and creative industries.

A united 'voice' for creative industries is emerging at the international level, led by UNCTAD, the UNDP, ITC, ILO, EU, World Bank, UNESCO and WIPO. Already creative industries have become established players in rich countries and have very quickly acquired a strong international presence. Indeed, given the dynamics of these industries, first mover advantages have been particularly pronounced making it all the more difficult for newcomers to gain a foothold. However, new technologies provide a window of opportunity to competition in global markets, even for smaller players, provided an enabling policy framework is designed to offer the much needed support.

National policy measures need to be dovetailed at the international level, by a provision of a supportive regulatory policy framework governing knowledge creation and use by means of improved IPR regulatory regimes that could buttress, rather than hinder, the creative process. Support measures for cultural diversity are essential. In the area of financing, the international community needs to improve its aid effectiveness (and orient aid toward sectors with higher value-added activities, such as creative industries); enable country-level learning experience; target the right kinds of FDI; facilitate financing to creative industries and provide policy support and technical assistance with a view to filling in the knowledge gaps and overcoming learning constraints to development.

Striking the right balance between exit, voice and diversity is the challenge facing local policy-makers in the developing world, the international development community and the developed world alike. We hope that this book will make a contribution to finding that balance.

Notes

1 Definition adapted from DCMS, 1988.
2 However, with recent digitisation, the music industry is becoming more R&D-intensive.
3 For example, in Scotland, it has been estimated that current tourism expenditure related to the nineteenth century poet Robbie Burns, alone is worth £100 million per annum (Scottish Enterprise, 2006).
4 COMTRADE – the United Nations Commodity Trade Statistics database.
5 Measured here using COMTRADE imports data where the recording partner is 'world', thereby measuring exports from individual countries and regions as indicated.
6 This was particularly marked at the beginning of the period as growth rates slowed down relative to trade in general in 2003 and 2004, but this was more evident in the developed world than in developing countries – for which the audio-visual sector almost always grew faster than trade in general.
7 The path to justify public support can be traced intellectually from, for example, Samuelson on non-rivalness and non-excludability; Pigou on externalities; Arrow on culture and information asymmetries; Coase on broadcasting; Stiglitz on asymmetric information and market failure; Teece on transactions costs. More recent writing specifically on the subject of creative industries includes Caves on the role of contracts in creative markets; Kozul-Wright on music and copyright; and Barrowclough on market failure and diversity in creative industries.
8 Including the infamous litigation against a 12 year old girl in the USA.
9 Application of DRM technologies recognises iTunes songs only on Apple's iPod and not from other online stores, such as Napster.
10 In some countries, for example, new legislation concerning a 'blanket' payment for music downloads has been seen as a promising start. Consumers pay a flat fee, usually monthly, irrespective of the amount of music downloaded, and this is distributed to musicians on a sliding scale depending on the number of times their music

was downloaded. Advantages of the model include its simplicity of administration and low cost. Disadvantages include the fact that high-users are subsidised by low-users.

Bibliography

Andersen, B. (2002), 'The performance of the IPR system in the new economy', *DRUID, Mimeo.*

Andersen, B., Kozul-Wright, Z. and Kozul-Wright, R. (2000), 'Copyrights, competition and development: the case of the music industry', UNCTAD Discussion Papers 145, United Nations Conference on Trade and Development, Geneva.

Appandurai, A. (1990), 'Disjuncture and difference in the global cultural economy', *Theory, Culture and Society*, 7, 295–310.

Barber, B. (1995), *Jihad Versus Mcworld*, Times Books: New York.

Barrowclough, D. (1998), 'Public television quasi-markets in New Zealand and the United Kingdom', in W. Bartlett, J. Roberts and J. Le Grand (eds) *A Revolution in Social Policy. Lessons from the Development of Quasi-markets in the 1990s*, The Policy Press: Bristol, UK.

—— (2001), 'Spilling over and crowding out: public/private sector convergence and competition in the provision of public goods', CESifo Working Paper 569, Centre for Economic studies and IFO Institute for Economic Research, Germany.

—— (2004), *Not only the rings: promoting screen production and recent experience in New Zealand*, UNCTAD/Brazil Connects.

Baumol, W. and Baumol, H. (1984), 'The mass media and the cost disease', in William S. Hendon, Douglas V. Shaw and Nancy K. Grant (eds) *The Economics of Cultural Industries*, Association for Cultural Economics: Akron, Ohio, pp. 109–123.

Baumol, W. and Bowen, C. (1966), *Performing Arts, the Economic Dilemma*, Better World Books: New York.

Boyle, J. (2004), 'A manifesto on WIPO and the future of intellectual property', iBRIEF/International, Duke Law and Technology Review, 0009.

Caves, R. (2000), *Contracts between Art and Commerce*, Harvard University Press: Cambridge, MA.

CIPR (Commission on Intellectual Property Rights) (2002), 'Integrating IPRs and Development Policy', September, 2002, C/O DFID, London.

Coase, R.H. (1966), 'The economics of broadcasting and government policy', *American Economic Review* 65 (2): 440–447.

Cohen, J. (2006), 'Copyright, commodification and culture', in *Locating the Public Domain: Identifying the Commons in Information Law*, Kluwer Law International; Alphen aan den Rijn.

Cohen, J. *et al.* (2002), *Copyright in a Global Information Economy*, Aspen: New York.

DCMS (Department of Culture, Media and Sport) (1988), *Creative Industries Mapping Document*, DCMS: London.

—— (2003), *Creative Industries Mapping Document*, DCMS: London

Drucker, P. (2000), 'Managing knowledge means managing oneself', *Leader to Leader*, spring, 2000.

Durham, M. and Kellner, D. (eds) (2001), *Media and Cultural Studies: Keyworks*, Blackwell Publishers: Malden, MA.

European Commission (2007), *Interactive Content and Convergence: Implications for the Information Society*, Brussels: European Commission.

Falvey, R., Foster, N. and Greenaway, D. (2004) 'Intellectual property rights and economic growth', *Internationalisation of Economic Policy Research Paper 2004/12.*

Florida, R. (2002), *The Rise of the Creative Class and how its Transforming Work, Leisure, Community and Everyday Life*, Basic Books: New York.

Gana, R. (1995), 'Has creativity died in the Third World? Some implications of the internationalization of intellectual property', *Denver Journal International Law and Policy*, 109.

Hamelink, C. (1994), *Trends in World Communication*, Southbound: Penang.

Hirschman, A. (1970), *Exit, Voice and Loyalty*, Harvard University Press: Cambridge, MA.

Holzl, W. (2005), *Entrepreneurship, Entry and Exit in Creative Industries: An Exploratory Survey*, Mimeo, WIFO: Vienna.

Howkins, J. (2001), *The Creative Economy*, Penguin Books: London.

IFPI (2006), *The Digital Music Report*, International Institute of Phonographic Industries: London.

Jassawalla, A.R. and Sashittal, H.C. (2002), 'Cultures that support product-innovation processes', *Academy of Management Executive*, 16 (3), 42–54.

Jeffcutt, P. and Pratt, A.C. (2002), 'Editorial: managing creativity in the cultural industries', *Creativity and Innovation Management*, 11 (4), 225–233.

Johansson, F. (2004), *The Medici Effect*, The Harvard Business School Press: Cambridge, MA.

John-Steiner, V. (2000), *Creative Collaboration*. Oxford University Press: New York.

Johnson. W. (2005), 'Creative pricing in markets for intellectual property', *Review of Economic Research on Copyright Issues*, 2 (1), 5–10.

Katz, Jorge, (2006), 'Tecnologia de la Informacion y la Comunicación e Industrias Culturales. Una Perspectiva Latinoamericana', CEPAL, UN, LC/W.92, Santiago de Chile.

Kamoche, K.N., Cunha, M.P. and Cunha, J.V. (eds) (2002), *Organizational Improvisation*, Routledge: London.

Kao, J. (1996), *Jamming*, Harper Collins: New York.

Kern, P. (2006), 'The future digital economy', presentation to the OECD, 31 January.

Kozul-Wright, Richard and Rayment, Paul (2004), 'Globalization Reloaded: An UNCTAD Perspective', UNCTAD Discussion Paper, 167, Geneva, UNCTAD/OSG/DP/2004/1.

Kozul-Wright, Z. (2002/2003), 'From culture to cultural industries – policy challenges for cultural industries in developing countries', Culturelink, Special Issue 2002/2003, Cultural Diversity and Sustainable Development, pp. 141–152.

Kozul-Wright, Z. and Jenner, P. (2007), 'Creative destruction in the music industry and the copyright', Dynamics of Institutions and Markets in Europe (DIME) Working Papers on Intellectual Property Rights (IPR) Birkbeck College, University of London.

Kozul-Wright, Z. and Stanbury, L. (1998). 'becoming a globally competitive player: the case of the music industry in Jamaica,' UNCTAD discussion paper 138, United Nations Conference on Trade and Development.

Landes, William and Posner, Richard (1989), 'An economic analysis of copyright law', *The Journal of Legal Studies*, 18 (2), 325–363.

Landry, C. (2000), *The Creative City*, Earthscan: London.

Livingstone, L.P., Palich, L.E. and Carini, G.R. (2002), 'Promoting creativity through the logic of contradiction', *Journal of Organizational Behaviour*, 23, 321–326.

Lubart, T.I. (1999), 'Creativity across cultures', in R.J. Sternberg (ed.), *Handbook of Creativity*, Cambridge University Press: Cambridge, UK, pp. 339–350.

Maskus, K. and Reichman, J. (2005), *International Public Goods and Transfer of*

Technology Under a Globalised Property Regime, Cambridge University Press: Cambridge, UK.

Reese, R.A. (2001), 'Copyright and Internet music transmissions: existing law, major controversies, possible solutions', *Miami L. Rev.* 237.

Moglen, E. (2003), *Freeing the Mind, Free Software and the Death of Proprietary Culture.*

Nemeth, C.J., Personnaz, M., Personnaz, B. and Goncalo, J.A. (2003), 'The liberating role of conflict in group creativity: a cross cultural study', Institute of Industrial Relations, University of California, Berkeley, Paper 090-03.

Netzer, D. (2004), 'The subsidized muse: the government and the arts in western Europe and the United States', *Journal of Cultural Economics.*

Okediji, R.L. (2003), *The International Relations of Intellectual Property: Narratives of Developing Country Participation in the Global Intellectual Property System.*

—— (2006), 'The international copyright system: limitations, exceptions and public interest considerations for developing countries', UNCTAD/ITCSD Project on IPRs and Sustainable development, Issues paper No. 15, Geneva.

Oksanen and Välimäki (2005), 'Copyright levies as an alternative compensation method for recording artists and technological development', *Review of Economic Research on Copyright Issues*, 2 (2), 25–39.

Paulus, P.B. and Nijstad, B.A. (eds) (2003), *Group Creativity: Innovation through Collaboration*, Oxford University Press: Oxford.

Peacock, A. (1986), *'Making sense of broadcasting finance'*, reprinted in R. Towse (ed.), (1997) *Cultural Economics: the Arts, the Heritage and the Media Industries*, volume 1, Edward Elgar Publishing Inc: Cheltenham UK.

Pricewaterhouse Coopers (2006), *Global Entertainment and Media Outlook 2006–2010*, London, United Kingdom.

Romer P. (2002), 'When should we use intellectual property rights?', *The American Economic Review*, 92 (2), 213–216.

Siwek, S. (2004), Copyright industries in the US economy', Report prepared for IIPA, International Intellectual Property Alliance, Washington, DC.

Throsby, D. (2001), *Economics and Culture*, Cambridge University Press: Cambridge.

Tomlinson, J. (1994), 'A phenomenology of globalization? Giddens on global modernity', *European Journal of Communication*, 9 (2), 149–172.

Towse, R. (2000), *Economic Aspects of Limitations and Exceptions to Copyright, Erasmus University.*

—— (2001), *Creativity, Incentive and Reward: an economic analysis of copyright and the information age.* Edward Elgar Publishing: Cheltenham.

—— (2005), 'Alan Peacock and Cultural Economics', *The Economic Journal*, 115 (June), 262–276.

Tschmuck, P. (2003), 'How creative are the creative industries?' *Journal of Arts Management, Law and Society*, 33 (2), 127–142.

UNCTAD, *Trade and Development Report*, UNCTAD: UN, New York and Geneva, various years.

—— *The Least Developed Countries Report*, UNCTAD: UN, New York and Geneva, various years.

—— (2001), 'Intellectual Property Rights and Development', Policy discussion paper.

—— (2004a), 'Creative industries and development', 11th session, Sao Paulo, Geneva.

—— (2004b), 'Creative industries and development', TD (XI) BP/13, 4 June, 2004, Background document prepared for UNCTAD XI, Sao Paulo, Brazil.

—— (2006), 'developing productive capacities', *The Least Developed Countries Report*, United Nations: New York and Geneva.
UNESCO (2005), Convention on the protection and promotion of the diversity of cultural expressions, Paris, October, 2005.
—— (2006a), *Trends in Audio-Visual Markets, Regional Perspectives from the South*, UNESCO: Paris.
—— (2006b), *International Flows of Selected Cultural Goods and Services, 1994–2003*, Institute of Statistics: Paris.
UNIDO (2005), *International Comparison of National Policy Instruments and Innovation Systems for Technology Development*, UNIDO: Vienna.
Wassall, G. and Alper, N. (1992), 'Towards a unified theory of the determinants of earnings of artists', in R. Towse (ed.), *Cultural Economics*, Springer Verlag: Berlin.
World Bank (2001), 'Intellectual property: balancing incentives with competitive access', in *Global Economic Prospects*, World Bank: Washington, DC, pp. 129–150.
—— (2006), *World Development Indicator*, World Bank: Washington, DC.
Wu, Wiping (2005), 'Dynamic cities and creative clusters', World Bank policy research working paper 3509, February, World Bank: Washington, DC.

Part II

Prospects and perils

2 Opportunities presented and threats posed by the digital production/distribution revolution

Roger Wallis

Introduction

The nature of creativity and rights, as exemplified by the music industry

Creativity starts at home, but nothing comes out of a vacuum. The domestic environment must encourage and protect creative, educational and entrepreneurial efforts. The extraordinary international and local success of the Swedish music industry in recent years is a perfect example of this. Creative individuals with basic skills in music, IT knowledge, performing talent and encouragement in the area of entrepreneurship have created hubs of expertise that can compete with the major resources of traditional music industry centres (London, Los Angeles). A functioning copyright environment with efficient supporting institutions (collection societies) was also a prerequisite for exploiting this potential.

Artistic and creative talent is abundantly available, everywhere. Modern information and communication technology allows creative persons to interact across genres, and document the results. Modern technology provides opportunities for this talent to spread globally, and, above all to interact with other cultures, thereby constantly developing new hybrid forms. The ease with which distribution is facilitated by digital technology provides both opportunities and threats. This chapter seeks to concentrate on maximising the positive aspects, and exerting a reasonable level of control over potential threats. We will also note that many highly publicised 'threats' to parts of the entertainment industry – e.g. those from Internet 'piracy' – can in actual fact provide subtle, indirect advantages for those experimenting with new business models.

Much of the following analysis will reflect conditions in the music industry. This approach is supported by two arguments. First, the music industry is the cultural industry which historically shows an early uptake of new technology for performing, producing, reproducing and distributing cultural goods. Second, experiences in the music industry can provide an indication for likely developments in other related audio-visual cultural industries. Whether or not the latter supposition will be proven is another matter, but the spread of technologies which allow for higher bandwidth connectivity, at lower prices, suggest this could be the case.

Traditional problems experienced by creators of cultural products in developing nations

There are many examples on record of cultural products emanating from developing nations and being commercially exploited in the industrialised world. In general little of the revenue generated has returned to the country of origin. Sometimes creators have physically moved away from their home country to enjoy better control over their copyrights. Others have registered their works with representational bodies such as copyright collection societies in Europe or the USA because they lack faith in equivalent institutions as home. Bob Marley was an example of the latter. Others who have stayed in their home countries have often seen little of the proceeds. The Kenyan composer Fadhili William, who first registered the copyright for the song *Malaika* in the 1960s, died in 2000. He was hardly a rich man, despite the global success of this East African song. A search of copyright society databases shows many different individuals and firms (music publishers) claiming part or the whole of the rights to *Malaika*. He discovered that it was hard to fight for his rights globally, without financial resources, and without a strong local copyright regime and institutions, integrated into the international system of copyright revenue flows.

Is this to be seen as yet another case of developing nations functioning as primary exporters of raw materials, where the materials (in this case musical talent) flow into a value chain where rents are captured by others who manufacture, market and sell in a global market? Can digital production and distribution technology allow for easier and more direct access to a truly global market, with more value being added in the countries of origin of cultural goods and services?

The key to a positive future will be a combination of new, accessible, high quality technology supported by local infrastructures, together with the implementation of principles of fair treatment of exporters of cultural goods. A serious threat could be the growing collective dominance of a few global entertainment conglomerates. These control both huge numbers of Intellectual Property Rights (IPRs) for different products, as well as the means of their exploitation (production, reproduction and distribution). The digital revolution, on the other hand, has allowed new players to enter the market for distribution of cultural products, whose interests are not directly related to achieving global sales of a very limited number of heavily marketed cultural products. The computer manufacturer Apple and its launch of the downloading service iTunes is one such example.

The traditional music industry value chain for physical products

Let us consider the traditional music industry value chain, producing and selling physical products such as CDs. A breakdown of an average price of a CD sold in Europe is as follows:

	Euro
Consumer price (excluding tax)	16
Retailer	6
Wholesaler	3
Manufacturing	1
Production/marketing	3
Artist	1
Composer/Publisher	1

The very rough figures above show that manufacturing and distribution account for over 60 per cent of the cost of a CD. It is hard to say exactly how much a record company receives from each sale of a CD because of the many different contractual relationships that can exist with artists and publishers. Many artists receive a fee in advance of the recording, but never receive any more royalties if the product does not generate considerable sales. Their contract might stipulate that costs for recording and even some marketing (e.g. production of a video) are deductible from royalties. More recently some record companies have begun to demand a share of performance royalties as a contractual condition (reflecting the shift of consumer spending from CDs to concerts).

Vertical and horizontal integration in the entertainment industries has also resulted in elements of collective dominance which further cloud the picture. The major record company might control wholesale distribution. The composer might have transferred his rights to a publisher owned by the record company – this would give the same publisher a share of up to 50 per cent of all copyright earnings. Above all, if the works in question originate outside the territory in question, then artist and composers' royalties can diminish by up to 50 per cent or more.

This complex picture can seem like a minefield for creators in developing nations, however rich their talent. In general such creators are both composers and artists, or they base their works on elements of traditional folklore, where the notion of 'individual ownership' of a composition is somewhat illogical. Practices such as 'bundling of rights' and 'one-off payments' are not uncommon. The creator sells all rights, for example publishing, artist or even performance rights to a local firm or a local subsidiary of a global conglomerate. A lump sum payment can mean that no further royalties are ever received. This can have considerable economic relevance if one considers that such rights can then be exploited by the new owners for decades. The record companies control the recordings for up to 50 years, and in some countries can claim revenues when recordings are performed in public, for instance when they are played on radio stations.

A small local record company, in say Kenya, which seeks a global distribution deal, might well have to accept what is know as a 'lease tape deal'. A recording is supplied, and the local record company would receive a fee in the region of 9 per cent of the local sales price, possibly after various deductions. One such is the 10 per cent deduction for 'breakage' which was introduced at the time when music was distributed on Bakelite 78-rpm discs, and has still not totally disappeared despite the introduction of the non-breakable CD.

The lease tape deal provides the following approximate breakdown of revenues:

	Euro
Consumer price (less taxes)	16
Retailer	6
Wholesaler	3
Manufacturing	1
Record company (country of sale)	3.50
Publisher (country of sale)	0.50
Record company (country of origin)	1.50
Composer (received at home)	0.25
Publisher (country of origin)	0.25

This breakdown assumes that the creator (as a composer) is registered with a local copyright collecting society, and that this society has functioning reciprocal arrangements with an equivalent organisation in the country of sale. The latter would then have details of the composer, works registered, etc. and should be able to identify to which parties, at home and abroad, copyright dues received from the record company selling the products should be distributed. The local creator's artist royalties would, in theory, come from the local record company's 1.50. With a typical 5 per cent royalty and a 50 per cent deduction for foreign earnings, this would result in as little as 3 euro cents per sold CD. If the contract with the local record company was a 'one-off payment' type, then it is likely that no further royalties would be received by the artist.

This traditional structure of the value chain for physical products can be briefly compared with the Apple iTunes initiative, where a download of a work costs 97 US cents. Of this sum, over 60 per cent is paid out to the record company, artist and composer/publisher. On this basis, if direct deals could be done globally with such a distributor, i.e. if there were easy open access to this part of the US market, then the download of an album with ten songs, would generate 6.50 US dollars. This is over €5 for this combination of rights holders, as compared with €2 in the traditional value chain.

The current IPR regime, as exemplified by the music industry

Income from the traditional physical value chain is far from being the only source of revenue for record companies, composers, publishers and performers. As early as 1990, over half of the total music industry revenue in Sweden came from other sources than sales of physical products (Malm and Wallis 1992).

Let us consider the current regime for copyrights, via an analysis of where they arise in the value chain and who controls them (Figure 2.1). The traditional model involves a lengthy value chain that has hardly changed over decades,

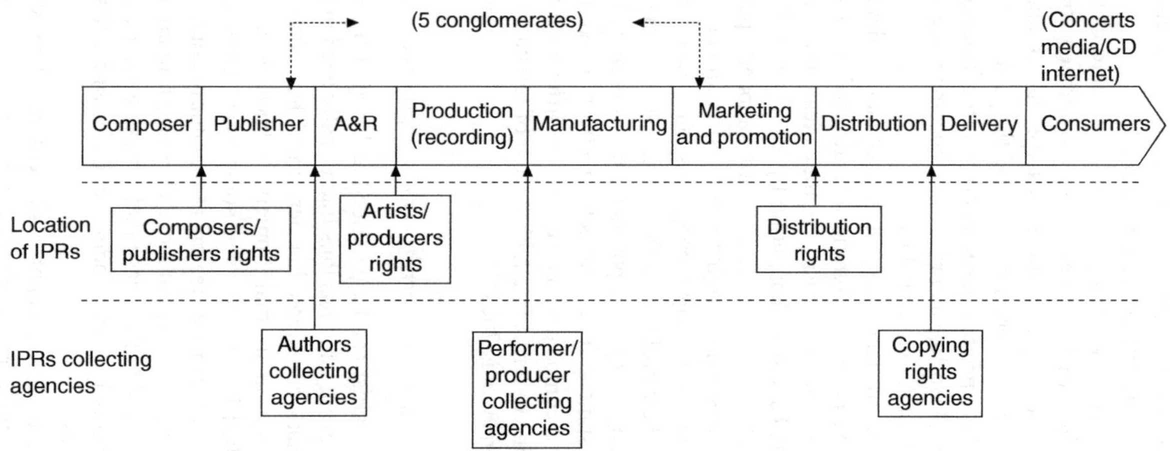

Figure 2.1 The traditional music industry value chain, including points at which various rights appear.

despite the roles of players becoming very different. A composer creates a work and transfers the right to exploit it to a music publisher. The publisher, in theory, seeks to 'pitch' the work with an artist or a record company; this involves getting a promise from an artist/record company to record the work. The record company then manufactures physical product, markets them via other media such as radio, and distributes products to retailers.

Various rights appear at various points in this value chain. Over the past decades, new areas where rights holders can claim compensation for usage have appeared. These include neighbouring rights (producers and performers can claim compensation for different forms of public performance), and copying rights (particularly where printed music is copied, for instance, in schools). As we move into the digital world, such rights can become more significant and are generators of revenue for copyright holders.

There have been many technological and economic developments which, somewhat surprisingly, have not significantly affected the traditional business chain. Many composers are also artists, i.e. they create their own compositions. Most major publishers have been bought up by leading record companies. What is an income for a publisher (e.g. the fees record companies pay to include songs on CDs, or so-called mechanical rights revenues) is an equivalent cost for the record company. With both major publishers and major record companies seeking to maximise their profit, then this models leads inevitably to increased pressure on diminishing fees to composers (at the bottom end of the chain) and higher costs for consumers. The interlocking effects of combined ownership (publishers and record companies) as well as the different forms of rights revenues seem to combine to result in a high degree of resistance to change in this traditional value chain (Wallis 2001).

The different types of composers', performers' and producers' rights

The composer and the artist can be described as being at the bottom end of the music industry 'food chain', and has thus traditionally been in a vulnerable position. The desire to hear one's creation performed has often encouraged composers to sign away their Intellectual Property Rights (IPRs). That this desire has also frequently resulted in poor or even non-existent contractual relationships has further made it hard for many creators to monitor or control what happens to their work in the course of its exploitation. There are a multitude of sad tales of composers seeing very little of the cash their works generate (Wallis and Malm 1984: 163–215), particularly in developing countries where few institutions exist to protect their interests.

Individual holders of IPRs cannot easily enforce their statutory claims to exclusive usage and remuneration. Since the middle of the nineteenth century, composers (and occasionally publishers who represent them) have responded by creating collective bodies, so-called collecting societies which monitor music activity in a given territory, and collect and distribute fees accordingly. As described in Chapter 5, the first European composer's collection agency was

SACEM in France, founded by 13 composers and lyricists in 1851. Its stated aim was 'to defend the common rights of all composers and lyricists, with or without the co-operation of their publishers, in relation to the owners of public establishments where their literary and musical works are performed'.

The rise of the global media corporation combined with new digital production and distribution technologies has seriously undermined these early principles (Wallis *et al.* 1999).

Getting a song recorded traditionally involved the publisher contacting a record company's Artist and Repertoire (A&R) department. Once the A&R staff had decided on a combination of composition and artist, the recording process would be instigated. Record companies would then manufacture, market and distribute the work. They would promote the record on radio and in concert, initiating public performances to generate further revenues (from the exploitation of *performance rights*) for composers and publishers via agreements between collecting societies and broadcasters and venues (between 5 and 8 per cent of box office receipts would be the normal rate of return from the latter). Examples of established collecting societies which collect and distribute performance rights revenues are the PRS in the UK, STIM in Sweden, IMRO in Ireland, ASCAP and BMI in the USA.

Many attempts have been made to establish equivalent organisations in developing nations, but these have been fraught with problems. As a condition for representing and collecting revenue for repertoire from developing nations, rights holders in the developed world via their established copyright societies have traditionally demanded reciprocity via equivalent payments for use of 'Western repertoire' in the poorer nation. With foreign currency in tight supply and heavy foreign loan obligations, it has been hard for poorer nations to prioritise such payments. The fact that much of the world's popular music is based on elements and influences borrowed from developing countries is not considered in this equation. Some limited funds have been made available by CISAC (the international umbrella organisation for copyright societies) to assist in the establishment of local collecting societies, but the results have not been impressive.

Record companies, too, pay copyright revenues to composers/publishers for the use of their works on physical discs (LPs, CDs etc.) via the exploitation of their *mechanical rights*. This refers to the mechanical process of reproduction. Returns to composers/publishers here are in the region of 8–9 per cent of the wholesale price of the recording. Such incomes are collected and distributed by mechanical rights collecting societies. These are often closely related to performing right societies in the same territories. The MCPS in the UK is part of the MCPS-PRS Alliance. NCB, which collects mechanical rights in the Nordic and Baltic area, is owned by the performing rights societies in Sweden, Finland, Denmark, Norway and Iceland.

The future for 'mechanical' reproduction rights in the digital world

As more music is distributed on-line, the notion of 'mechanical reproduction rights' needs to be redefined. There is no better illustration of this than the industry debate over mobile phone ring tones (MPRTs). Initially monophonic (i.e. a melody without harmonies) these personalised ring tones have begun to generate considerable sums for distributors, mobile phone companies and rights holders. This is a small but growing business area worth an estimated US$71 million in the USA (2002). Does the downloading of a ring tone involve the exploitation of performance rights, mechanical rights or both. Negotiations between publishers, mechanical and performance collection societies have resulted in a temporary compromise. Revenues are split 75/25 (mechanical/performance).

The significance of this debate is considerable. We will probably see an integration of these two traditional forms of copyright revenues, as well as the institutions that collect them. This in turn may well lead to conflicts between major publishers (keen to retain and extend their control over the handling of mechanical rights) and creators keen to defend their traditional influence over the administration of performing rights.

Mobile phone technology now allows for terminals (the mobile devices) to include polyphonic ring signals (creations with rhythms, sound effects, melodies and harmonies) and 'real tones' or excerpts from recorded musical works. As mobile phones spread over the world, often providing a cheaper infrastructure alternative than fixed line solutions, then this could become an important source of revenues for creators/producers. This assumes, once again, that works are registered in some form of database, that their use can be identified and that revenues can be distributed to the rightful owners.

Other types of rights expand as the importance of intangible revenues grows

Over the course of the twentieth century the recording industry discovered both new sources of income and new areas in which revenue could be lost. On the one hand, 'neighbouring rights' allow performers and producers (record companies) as well as composers and publishers to claim fees when recordings are performed in public (generally via broadcasters). And there are by now numerous intangible sources of revenue from recordings, sources arising from the exploitation of rights rather than from sales of physical products (Malm and Wallis 1992). There are collecting societies distributing revenues from sources as diverse as photocopying, cable re-transmission, blank tape levies and synchronisation rights. On the other hand, consumer electronics devices have made it increasingly easy for consumers to copy music and share it via physical cassettes, CDs and digital files – the battles to restrict these practices are fought in the name of copyright (Frith 1992).

The importance of publishing for the global music industry

Publishing revenues in North America have been estimated at US$1,200 million for the year 2002 (*Music and Copyright* 2003a). This can be compared with a trade value of almost $1,600 million for shipments of physical carriers of recorded music during the same year. Music publishing is clearly of considerable importance for the global music companies. EMI is the only 'major' which supplies details of the financial contribution of publishing to its results. These show that publishing income accounts for around 20 per cent of turnover, but contributes over 60 per cent of net revenue.

The major publishers have accumulated huge numbers of rights. A scan of the comprehensive Norddoc database developed by collection societies in Scandinavia and Finland shows that the five major publishers control almost 70 per cent of a total of 3.5 million registered works. If one considers that a large number of the 3.5 million are 'manuscript' registrations (i.e. works without a publisher where the writers have retained all rights), then the Big 5 publishers' share of all published works is clearly even higher than 70 per cent. The Big 5 will now become the Big 4, after regulatory authorities in Europe and the USA approved the merger of Universal Music Publishing and BMG Music Publishing in 2006/2007 – despite the size and influence of the new giant publisher.

This illustrates another important fact. The key for creators to realise more added value lies in their degree of control over their rights, as the importance of intangible sources of revenue grows. One of Sweden's wealthiest music creators, Per Gessle of the duo Roxette, proudly states that there is only one song he ever wrote where he does not control the publishing. Such a goal is easier to state than to achieve, especially where practices such as bundling of rights require a creator/artist to sign away publishing rights as a condition for being given a recording contract. The chapter will now analyse current changes and trends in the media landscape, noting the emergence of new business models and their potential for new forms of revenue generation by those seeking access to different markets.

The media landscape, locally and globally

The media landscape globally is the result of the interaction between different factors: technological, economic and social/cultural. These will be considered in turn.

Technological and business factors

Uptake of music industry technology

1. History teaches us that the music is generally the first sector in the entertainment field to assimilate new technology. The amazing spread of analogue cassette technology for recording/production and distribution in the 1980s to every corner of the world is but one example.
2. The digital development has seen a steady spread of accessibility of high quality equipment and carriers at a decreasing price. Stand-alone CD and DVD recorders ('burners') will soon cost less than $60 and have also become standard components in most home computers.

Effects of digital technology on production/distribution of audio and multimedia products

The following trends can be observed in the developed nations – they will inevitably spread to LDCs (a process which can be enhanced by government policies). The significant trends include:

THE PRODUCTION PROCESS

Input to manufacturing is in a digital form from studios where products are stored on high capacity hard discs. There is a steady shift from analogue technology to digital equivalents.

PRODUCTION TECHNOLOGY

High quality digital recording technology has become ubiquitous, with wide availability and price reductions.

IT EXPERTISE

Musicians/composers and even video producers in many countries have their own studios, or easy access to studios. Such access to resources and expertise is no longer restricted to the major national or international media companies.

PEER-TO-PEER OR P2P SOFTWARE (FILE SWAPPING)

This relatively new type of 'overlay' network technology is truly global. It can replicate the establishment of groups of fans/sub-cultures in the physical world, in a way that knows no national boundaries. P2P networks can provide access to diversity in contrast to the trend towards more uniformity in range of choice offered by traditional media such as radio and television. On the other hand, the development of such networks has caused problems, particularly for international owners of copyrighted materials.

A SHIFT FROM TANGIBLE TO INTANGIBLE REVENUE STREAMS

This is most notably in the music industry. As various services offering 'legal' download services become more internationally available, this shift will become more intense, with the physical aspect, previously in the form of a CD or a cassette, being replace more and more by live performances. New players such as computer companies selling music to market their appliances – Apple's iTunes is an example – could result in control over global distribution getting a new power structure.

SHIFT IN REVENUE ALLOCATION IN EXISTING VALUE CHAINS

'Digital Piracy' leads to some traditional revenue generators making losses whilst having a marketing function for other related revenue sources (e.g. Internet music and live concerts)

Peer-to-Peer activities via the Internet

The development of the unmanaged Internet, however, produced a major, if somewhat anarchistic, distribution network for audio and audio-visual products. File swapping activities (Peer to Peer or P2P) between Internet users have led to millions of files with music, games, other software and even films being copied and spread from individual to individual. This represents a high level of interactivity, with curious consumers looking for new cultural products and experiences. The significance becomes clear when one observes that one of the most popular file-sharing applications (Kazaa) and its software program Fast Track had been downloaded over 340 million times by December 2003. This is an all time high world record.

P2P also causes considerable problems for traditional entertainment industry business models and modes of digital asset protection. Most P2P users have been branded as pirates by the established music recording industry. Sales of physical products have certainly suffered, but the exact causal relationship to P2P activities is not totally proven. Some studies suggest that avid P2P users buy more physical products such as CDs than non-P2P users (Jupiter 2000). Figure 2.2 summarises a result from a study of P2P Napster users in Germany carried out by the media analysts Jupiter in 2000.

More recently a UK study, financed in part by a major record company, found that regular P2P network users bought far more 'legal' downloads from

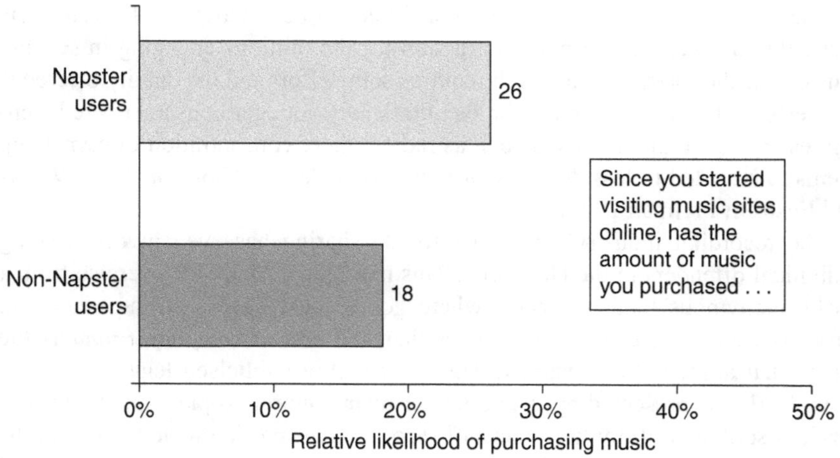

Figure 2.2 Napster users and purchases of CDs (Jupiter 2000).

new services such as Apple's iTunes than non-P2P users. The study concluded that turning such fans into criminals was not a wise industry strategy. (BBC News 2004). Other studies suggest that the price of CDs and general economic conditions could explain much of the shortfall in major markets such as the USA.

P2P activities spread globally as the Internet spreads. One of the most extensive studies of file sharing in the USA, carried out by researchers from Harvard Business School and the University of North Carolina and released in 2004, concluded simply that 'file sharing does not reduce record sales' (Oberholtzer and Strumpf 2004). Most people who downloaded files appeared to be individuals who would not have bought the albums they downloaded. Another interesting conclusion was that over 55 per cent of all files downloaded in the USA come from computers in other countries. This focuses once again on the international potential for marketing of cultural products provided by overlay networks such as Kazaa and Gnutella.

The Internet has also allowed small radio stations anywhere around the world to become globally available via 'streaming'. This provides a new global marketing opportunity where the range of choice can be controlled by those selecting the music that is performed.

'Legal' music industry alternatives to 'illegal' digital distribution of audio and audio-visual products

The established recording industry has been slow to start initiatives involving the 'legal' selling of digital files of audio or audio-visual products over the Internet. The main reason has been a fear of losing control over digital assets in the 'unmanaged' Internet environment. Those initiatives that were launched by the major record companies in 2000/2001 have more or less collapsed. Whilst seldom offering more than a few hundred thousand recordings, they could not compete with the range of choice in global Peer-to-Peer networks. This suggests that cultural diversity is a major attraction for the millions engaging in seeking music over the Internet (the search requires some effort and the quality offered is not perfect). It can also explain the fact that many younger consumers are listening less to conventional media such as radio, where concentration of ownership seems to have led to less diversity of output (Dicola and Thomson 2002; Wallis and Edström-Frejman 2004).

The recording industry's response to file sharing has even involved suing individual offenders in the US courts. This has been a tricky PR exercise from a fairly anonymous industry sector where goods must have a strong emotional attraction, and where the *artist*, rather than the *record company brand* is the image that attracts the consumer. The most highly publicised legal alternative from 2003 was presented by the computer manufacturer Apple. Apple's iTunes services sold over 50 million tracks of recorded music (via downloading) in the USA during the period April 2003 to January 2004. Compared with the total number of tracks sold on conventional CDs in the global market – probably over ten billion – then this is a relatively small number. However, compared with the diminishing numbers of singles being sold, it is highly significant.

The selling price in the Apple offering was set at 99 cents per recorded work, with the record company retaining 47 cents (excluding artist royalty). This is a much higher margin than in traditional sales of physical phonograms (where manufacture and distribution account for 60 per cent of the consumer price), and leaves only a very small margin for the company offering the service. An analysis of the breakdown of the 99 cents made by the US trade paper *Billboard* (reprinted in the trade paper *Music and Copyright*, December 2003b) showed the following breakdown:

	Cents
Bandwidth costs	2
Record company	47
Artist	7
Producer	3
Composer/publisher	8
Service provider (ISP)	17
Distribution affiliate	10
Credit card fees	5

This shows that artists and composers receive no more remuneration than in the traditional physical world, despite the absence of the need to manufacture, store and distribute. One also notes that a significant share goes to those involved in the digital transport and financial transaction aspects, notably telephone companies/ISPs and other affiliates.

If the recording industry can maintain this revenue share (as a condition for offering distribution rights) then the ability to compete on price for different digital distributors will also be limited. This in its turn suggests that popular tracks of popular artists could become commodities (rather in the same way that popular banking services such as deposit accounts became commodities when banks introduced Internet banking in the industrialised nations). Such initiatives comprise a paradigm shift in control over the functioning of the distribution channel. Record companies still control the rights to their records, and can thereby dictate conditions for the distributor. But new distributors are entering the field. They include computer manufacturers, retailers (Wal-Mart) and it is likely that we will even see soft drink manufacturers selling music physically and digitally to market their wares.

A key point to note with the 'new' types of music distributors is that they have taken control of the last slice of the value chain to the consumer – the price they have paid is a high percentage of their income to the record companies controlling the rights to recordings. The significance of this will be the subject of further scrutiny later.

Traditional and alternative new business models in the digital environment

The global music companies have, understandably, not been keen to depart from established business models, and move into uncharted areas. On the other hand, many creators working with niche genres, start-ups and various forms of SMEs have embraced the Internet more warmly, using it to market their existence, and then seeking revenues later after establishing a consumer interest. Amongst this category, one can find managers, artists and concert promoters, who can benefit from a shift from producer-led marketing to consumer-led marketing. This involves a shift away from a business model, which first produces a physical product (a CD or a DVD), then markets it heavily through various channels such as traditional radio and TV and proceeds to sell via physical retail outlets. New emerging models start with a digital recording, make it available over the Internet, use the interest which can be generated to promote physical experiences such as live concerts, and then derive revenues from sales of physical products (CDs, T-shirts etc.) at a later stage. In this way what is often branded as 'illegal Internet piracy' (i.e. downloading of music without being absolutely sure that all rights holders have given the consumer their permission, which is highly impractical at present), becomes a valid marketing tool.

The development of different music industry business models

The advent of the Internet and the spread of digital technology led many to predict that the traditional model would speedily disappear and be replaced by a very direct, short business chain, linking creators who produced their own materials, via some intermediary, to consumers. There are few examples of this on record. One was My MP3.com, which allowed anyone to enter recorded materials where they controlled all the rights. Consumers could search for such materials over the Internet and down load 'for free'. My MP3.com income came from banner advertising and was split 50/50 with those uploading materials.

My MP3.com also spread copyrighted materials and was sued by the major record companies. Universal Music Group ended up taking over what was left of My Mp3.com. The service for unsigned acts – those without record company contracts – was discontinued in Europe in the autumn of 2003.

Some smaller players in the music industry, notably groups which own their own record companies and/or publishing, have developed the use of the Internet

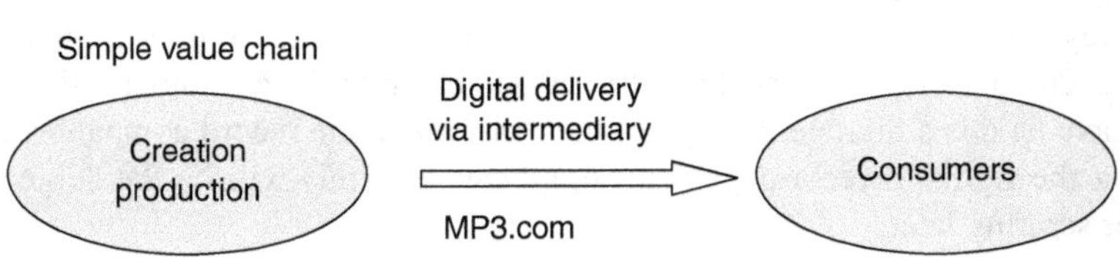

Figure 2.3 The dis-intermediated vision.

as a marketing tool. The aim is to attract a potential audience specifically to concert performances, that is by offering material over the Internet to create a demand to 'experience the real thing live'. This model reverses the traditional approach of manufacturing a CD, promoting it via radio/TV, and then at some later stage, if it sells, arranging for a concert tour. In the new model, the revenues stem from the creation of a demand for live performance. Often records are sold primarily in conjunction with such concerts. A further likely development, which is technically possible, will involve concertgoers being given the opportunity to purchase a CD recording of the very concert they have just experienced.

The lower model in Figure 2.4 illustrates a related development involving concert promoters. Many concert promoters have integrated the marketing of concerts with 'one-click' sales of tickets via the Internet. That potential concertgoers who download music to find out about the artists in question is an anathema for the record industry is hardly surprising. But for the concert promoter, this allows their own marketing to be integrated with the ability to search and listen, and then decide on the spot to buy a ticket. Such models will certainly be further refined in the near future. It is interesting to note in this context that music publishers (firmly lodged in the traditional music business chain) have seen their performance revenues increase, partially through increased revenues from concerts, whilst income from works released on CDs (mechanical rights revenues) has decreased.

Relevance for other cultural products (films, books, games, etc.)

The experiences gleaned so far from the music sector will also apply in many ways to the dissemination of other cultural products. It is highly unlikely that file sharing can be prohibited via legal means (as some global content owners believe). With over 340 million copies of the file sharing program Kazaa downloaded, and an estimated 100 million engaging in some type of P2P activity, then the notion of 'policing' this area becomes impractical. Actions against

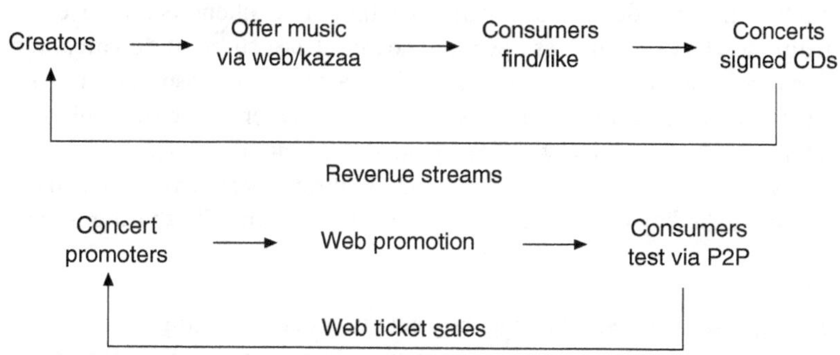

Figure 2.4 New models involving promotion via the Internet and later revenue streams from live performances/sales of CDs.

individuals or actions aimed at making such technology illegal will probably encourage the development of even more anonymous systems, for instance, where the user is not even aware of what is on his/her hard disk. It is also interesting to note that the same type of technology, albeit under a different name, GRID, is being heavily promoted by the European Union for improving collaboration between scientists via sharing computer resources. A general observation from the area of business studies is that perceived business problems caused by disruptive technologies cannot be solved by either introducing a counter technology or by trying to block such technologies.

Legal moves to limit file sharing of copyrighted works have been implemented or are under way. Many nations have already introduced or are in the process of implementing the spirit of the 1996 WIPO copyright treaty. This has resulted in the Digital Millennium Copyright Act in the USA, and the 'Infosoc' copyright EU directive from 2001. These regard the act of linking a personal computer with copyrighted music stored on its hard disc (together with a file-sharing program) as equivalent to making copyrighted materials available to the general public. As such this is illegal without the expressed permission of all relevant copyright holders. On the other hand with new business models emerging involving copyright owners offering their materials for free over the Internet as a marketing device for other revenue sources, then the current legal moves against P2P could become an obstacle to the development of these new types of value chains.

File sharing involving audio-visual products such as films has been limited up to now by bandwidth consideration – downloading via a slow modem takes far too long. But as broadband spreads both in the industrialised world, but also in countries such as China, then this is likely to expand. On the other hand, much current research enforces the view that the availability of illegal copies of cultural products via the Internet seems to enhance consumer needs for other related experiences (concerts, viewing the movie in a social context at a cinema, etc.). Anecdotal evidence suggests that piracy of DVDs with films in some markets can be correlated positively with an increase in demand for associated merchandising (sales of T-shirts, games, etc. related to characters in the film, etc.) The film, albeit pirated, whets the appetite for 'the real thing'.

Even in the music industry, one can note the same phenomenon. Recent research from the Harvard Business School showed that a surge in downloading of a popular recording was generally followed by a surge in consumer purchasing, as reflected by its position on the US sales charts (Oberholzer and Koleman 2004). On the other hand, many who downloaded the song, the report concludes, would not have bought the record, even if they had not taken it from the Internet. Here we have the key to much of the confusion regarding file sharing of cultural products.

1 It encourages some to buy the legal physical product (marketing function).
2 It encourages others to buy related goods or experiences (merchandising, concerts).
3 It allows some who would not buy it anyway to enjoy the product.

It is interesting to note that record companies in the USA, even those that are officially dedicated to stamping out file sharing, actually buy marketing data from firms such as Big Champagne, tracking file sharing requests over the Internet.

There is emerging evidence that consumers in the industrialised world would be willing to pay a fixed surcharge on their telephone/broadband bills to be allowed to engage in P2P legally. A 2003 survey of European households found that 63 per cent if broadband users downloaded music, 41 per cent wanted streamed film clips and 32 per cent were interested in playing games with other PC users. Significantly, 55 per cent said they would be willing to pay up to €15 a month to legally download music files to their PCs (Strategy Analytics 2004).

More recently the French organisation Spedidam, representing over 12,000 artists, has sponsored a bill in parliament to make P2P legal via a so-called 'global licence', which consumers could pay together with the telephone/ISP bill (Spedidam 2006). The proposal is violently opposed by producer interests.

There was a general belief in the late 1990s amongst technology prophets, consultants and the IT industry as a whole that any physical product or service that could be digitised would more or less disappear from the physical world. No more CDs, no more bank branches, travel agents, cinemas, etc. All consumption would occur via computer devices at home or in some type of hub (e.g. an Internet cafe). More recently researchers have come to realise that the Internet should be viewed as an addition to existing media channels, rather than as a replacement channel (DiMaggio *et al.* 2001)

The physical products have not disappeared. Cinema visits in Sweden enjoyed an all time high during the latter half of 2003. Global sales of CDs fell by 11 per cent in the first half of 2003, but still amount to some one billion copies worldwide with a trade value of almost €13 billion (source: International Federation of Phonogram Industries). CD sales even increased in some countries, for example Finland (+6 per cent) and in the UK during 2003. It is interesting to note that this is occurring in territories where domestic music (as opposed to international hit music) is strong.

An ongoing research project, TIDE, at the Royal Institute of Technology in Stockholm is studying the relationship between tangible and intangible products/services and experiences in the digital environment. This cross-industry study compares developments in a selection of different industries where it has been possible to digitise traditional products and services – newspaper publishing, the music industry, retail banking, travel, healthcare and distance learning. Results so far suggest that intensive access to virtual products/services (i.e. via the Internet) seems to create new consumer demands for physical equivalents. The increase in demand for live music concerts in Europe and the USA is but one example.

This suggests there should be considerable potential for the international distribution of music from nations with a strong tradition of live music. Those that will suffer are music forms created solely within a studio environment, where the ability to present a physical experience such as a concert is not relevant.

Copyright and copyright institutions

Copyright and related institutions are not made redundant via the shift towards a digital distribution environment. The need for reliable international registers of creators and works, based on collaboration between national institutions, is essential in a world of global digital networks. Nations that do not establish such institutions will be at a disadvantage if their citizens' intellectual property is spread in an international marketplace. In practice this means that nations which desire to exploit home-grown cultural products locally and globally must have efficient, reliable copyright societies which register audio- and audio-visual works, matched with their creators, and also collect and distribute revenues from local public performances. It is important that the creators themselves are involved in these organisations – they are the best local ambassadors for creating credibility for their organisation. Without their support and involvement it is very hard to establish this credibility in the local market.

These organisations must collaborate regionally and internationally. They must also demand similar terms in their bilateral agreements with other nations as those enjoyed by more established organisations in the developed nations. There has been a tendency for societies representing repertoire from the USA and the UK to refuse embryonic collecting societies in 'new' countries the right to deduct 10 per cent from local collections for cultural purposes, as a condition for representing their foreign repertoire in the country in question. This is standard in agreements between European societies. The Swedish collection society, STIM, for instance, has traditionally deducted up to 10 per cent from all moneys collected in Sweden and uses this for various promotional and cultural purposes, many of which serve to promote respect for creativity and copyright. Even for an established music industry nation such as Sweden, these sources of cultural support could dwindle in the future – major publishers are demanding that no such deductions for cultural purposes are made from future revenues derived via online (Internet) sales.

International trade agreements

There is a lively ongoing debate in many smaller nations about demands in current rounds of international trade agreements about the status of cultural products. This has mainly concerned the future of support measures for local cultural industries, which in strictly trade terms are viewed by some international players as giving local producers an unfair advantage. Measures that are seen as trade barriers by some are regarded as essential forms of support for cultural diversity by others. The latter argue that many local cultural products that only have small potential markets would not survive without extra support.

The conflict of interests is best illustrated in the context of competition between an international blockbuster film and a small local production supported by local subsidies. In a typical major film budget of over US$100 million, up to 40 per cent of this could be used for marketing. Local producers would argue that there is no way they could compete fairly with such imports in the absence of local support measures. Large conglomerates also enjoy the benefits of various forms of cross-subsidisation between different types of areas of activity.

Once an initial investment has been recouped in the gigantic US market, then costs for global distribution become marginal. Sales of merchandising, related music products, etc., add to the potential revenues. The soundtrack for the film *Titanic* in 1998 sold 25 million copies worldwide. Collective dominance in the entertainment field gives such global players huge advantages. Collectively it can be argued that these far outweigh any negative trade effects of local subsidies for local cultural products such as music, film and books.

The jury is still out on the extent to which TRIPS (Trade related issues of Intellectual Property Rights) and other trade discussions will affect the world of cultural products. Various NGOs and countries are lobbying for a 'cultural products exception'. This was a major focus in negotiations leading up to the recently established UNESCO convention on cultural diversity.

The entry of new players such as Apple computers providing the last lap of the distribution chain between production and consumption should be carefully monitored. If such players can offer unlimited scalability, i.e. the capacity to offer any number of different products, then entry barriers should become lower. According to the spirit of TRIPS and other WTO principles, then any producer, anywhere in the world, should be able to claim access to such distribution channels, without being forced to go through various intermediaries. One can speculate that the major copyright owners may attempt to extend their control over share of revenues to access such channels. UNCTAD should monitor this with care.

Summary of findings and recommendations

This section seeks to summarise the opportunities and obstacles for LDCs to use new technology and new business models to profit from international exploitation of their cultural products.

Digital distribution technology – the relevance of the Internet

The growing importance of global digital networks for making a wide diversity of cultural products available to millions (albeit sometimes 'illegally') has been described above. This consumer privilege, of course, is mainly reserved for those in the industrial world. Internet penetration in the poorest nations will be low for the foreseeable future (the same applies to mobile phone penetration). On the other hand, the same model that brought television to remote or poorer communities, via the 'one TV set in the local cafe' solution, could apply.

International statistics of Internet usage show that, although figures are still low in many developing countries, the rate of increase is considerable (Table 2.1). Internet cafes providing hubs are the first sign of the Internet equivalent of the 'one TV set in the village' – the difference being that they offer an opportunity for interactivity, where materials can be uploaded and downloaded. Low capacity telephone lines limit the extent of this spread of technology, but new

Table 2.1 Estimated numbers of Internet users

Country	*Estimated population (million)*	*Users December 2000*	*Users January 2004*	*Growth (%)*
Kenya	34	200,000	400,000	100
Egypt	71	450,000	1,900,000	322
Morocco	31	100,000	700,000	600
Turkey	75	2,000,000	4,900,000	145
Ghana	20	30,000	170,000	466

Source: Internet World Stats 2004.

Table 2.2 Estimates of number of mobile phone users

Country	*Mobile phone users*			
	1999	*September 2000*	*June 2002*	*January 2003*
Ghana	22,240	132,000	NA	NA
Ivory Coast	134,560	342,000	NA	NA
Morocco	150,000	1,530,000	5,000,000	6,000,000
South Africa	2,500,000	6,100,000	13,000,000	14,000,000

Source: African Cellular Statistics 2004.

wireless alternatives (e.g. EDGE solutions) could provide for improved communication potential.

Mobile phone uptake is also increasing at a fast rate all over the world, even if the percentage of the population involved is still minimal compared with many industrialised nations. Statistics are not as up to date as in the case of Internet users, but Table 2.2 gives some indication of the trend.

As regards telecommunication infrastructure in poorer nations, one can discern two different approaches to wireless alternatives. Either one builds a smaller number of large capacity base stations, where services provided start at a very simple level (e.g. for consumers using very elementary mobile voice terminals). If and when demand for more sophisticated service emerges, including more bandwidth, then such facilities can be added. Systems such as GPRS, HSCSD (High Speed Circuit Switched data) or EDGE (Enhanced data rates for GSM evolution) all use small bits of spare capacity that exist in current GSM mobile networks for increasing communication speeds and capacity.

Developments in the global music industry – opportunities for smaller players to find international markets?

The five major record companies have been hard hit by falling sales of CDs by international stars. Sales of DVDs (where sound, pictures and text are available) are rising rapidly, but have been unable to cover revenue losses from sales of CDs (minus 11 per cent globally during the first half of 2003). The majors, as we have noted, claim that the reason is simply P2P activities over the Internet.

We can expect to see further examples of consolidation within the recording industry. Sony and BMG merged their recording activities in the autumn of 2004. This merger, based on arguments of scale, is only one response to the current overall drop in CD sales. All the five major record companies have announced a series of actions aimed at cutting costs and returning to profitability. These include terminating contracts with numerous smaller and middle ranking artists, releasing staff from their contracts, and re-writing contracts with major artists to include shares of other incomes than those from CD sales (e.g. concert revenues, merchandising, etc.). Many local subsidiaries have been closed or had their activities with local repertoire and artists scaled back. The major companies are also concentrating more and more on a handful of proven global stars. Risk taking with unknown quantities is no longer on the agenda.

With publishing, the picture is very different. Publishing, as we have noted, still remains more lucrative than profits from sales of physical products such as CDs. This is particularly true of those publishers controlling large numbers of copyrights dating from the 1960s and 1970s that include many evergreens, i.e. works that are regularly performed in some public context, on radio or TV, etc.

It is important to emphasise the point that much of publishers' income in the developed world comes from long-term contracts written in the 'golden age' of publishing. Up to and including the 1970s retention percentages of up to 50 per cent, and means of limiting returns from success abroad were features of contracts with authors and singer-songwriters. The 'life of copyright' contract lives on for 70 years after the composer's death. A leading UK entertainment lawyer, Charles Law, has written:

> of course, publishers today have a problem compared with publishers 30 or so years ago … the days have long gone when publishers can hope to acquire a song for the duration of copyright, let alone keep half the revenue generated. In fact a publisher retention of 35 per cent was criticised by the Court in the Stone Roses Vs. Zomba case in 1993 and following that case in 1993 it is unusual to see a publisher retention of more than 30 per cent in a long-term exclusive contract. Those publishers lucky enough to own copyrights on the old basis are amongst today's wealthiest publishing houses.
>
> (Law 2004)

The fact that authors have not been able to extract themselves from such old contracts can be found in the vague wording of such contracts as regards the publishers' contractual obligations. Unfortunately such contracts, often bundled with other contracts (e.g. regarding recording) are still common outside the more mature music exporting markets.

These observations are of critical importance for creators from poorer nations who are offered deals with international publishers, based on promises to provide international promotion. It is important to be aware of the developments described by Law in the quote above. There is a need for a minimum level of music industry education of creators and local producers. A primary focus should be on issues such as:

Life of copyright In most nations, composers' rights are protected up to 70 years after their death. Signing a 'life of copyright' contract with a commercial publisher gives that publisher the right to a share of all incomes from the exploitation of the work almost indefinitely (lifetime of the composer plus 70 years). In most mature music export markets, composers (and their legal advisers) now only sign such contracts for a limited period of time, usually between 5 and 15 years. Alternatively, they start their own publishing company which does administrative deals with international publishers (who then retain a fee in the region of 15 per cent).

'Receipts' or 'At source' publishing contracts Previously it was common for publishers to require composers to sign 'Receipts' contracts. These gave the composer a share, usually 50 per cent of what was actually returned to the publishing company in the composer's home territory. What happened to moneys collected abroad was not covered by the contract. In some cases composers ended up receiving less than 15 per cent of what had been collected by the publisher's agents abroad. The 'At source' system was introduced in the 1970s and 1980s in the UK, after a legal case involving Elton John and his publisher. This type of contract specifies the percentage a composer will receive of moneys at the point of collection (at source). Successful composers can expect anything up to 70 or 80 per cent of collections according to this principle. Only in the last few years have 'At source' contracts become commonplace in Sweden. They are rare in the developing world.

Bundling of contracts, or even 'buy-outs' Where a sum is paid to the creator to relinquish all rights, or as a condition for, say, getting a record release, or the inclusion of music composed for an audio-visual product. These must be avoided (in some cases they are illegal) both for the sake of the creator's commercial potential and for the sake of a functioning market where publishers and record companies can compete for talent.

Some publishers, even those that are owned by the major record companies, are starting to move into areas of activity traditionally controlled by record companies. Examples are running their own recording studios for composers who are also artists (singer-songwriters).

Even some established artists have managed to extend their control over their own copyrights by using the Internet for personal promotion when their record companies have showed signs of losing interest. Examples include inviting fans to make advance purchases of the artist's next recording (even before it is recorded), thus using the fans to provide the necessary capital for the planned investment (Tuomola 2004).

Areas requiring national policy formulation and related support measures

INFRASTRUCTURE

- Telecommunications (see above). The operators' claim to enjoy a lack of conduit responsibility supported by the WIPO copyright treaty and legislation in Europe and the USA might well have to be re-appraised. As already noted, there is currently no distinction between the moral aspects of this absolution (e.g. the difficulty to hold operators responsible for the nature of the content) and the economic aspects where an activity such as P2P is driving network and revenue streams.
- Production facilities (studios). Here one can assume that a system of loans and training (IT literacy) will encourage entrepreneurs to establish resources where local cultural products can be produced. A focus should be on mobile resources, e.g. for recording live concerts (see next point). This also involves some resources for training.
- Support for live concerts with local performers that can be documented in audio and audio-visual format.
- Support for actions which can raise the status of local music, locally and internationally. Make sure that local music gets exposure both physically (through local stores, concerts) and via different communication media (traditional such as radio, and Internet via streaming).

LOCAL TRADITIONAL MEDIA POLICY

Studies from the USA and Sweden suggest that a greater degree of concentration of ownership of radio and television stations leads to a diminished range of choice in their output. Their output tends to reflect an international repertoire from the major record companies, rather than local repertoire. This has become a serious problem in many nations. It has been hotly debated in South Africa where quota systems supporting local music are being introduced. In Australia, a system which encouraged the airing of local music on local radio stations is under threat from demands in a new bilateral trade deal being discussed with the USA (such rules being regarded as unfair trade barriers).

Figures from both the USA and Sweden suggest that younger listeners are leaving radio and using the Internet to find music (via P2P or streamed radio stations). Local music needs to be available on local media if it is to enjoy local status, and thereby develop.

Experience from countries such as France, which employ content quotas for French-language music, suggest that rules concerning 'volume' are not sufficient. A high percentage of French music can be attained by airing one artist one hundred times, or each of ten different artists ten times. This illustrates the need for a focus on range of choice and to include goals of diversity in any quota regime aimed at giving publicity to domestic cultural products. These rules apply specifically to radio stations, but also to a certain extent to television.

MAKING LOCAL RADIO AVAILABLE OVER THE GLOBAL INTERNET

Local stations that do promote local music should also be encouraged to make their output available over the Internet via streaming. This allows anyone anywhere in the world, in theory, to discover new music (even if streaming technology, in contrast to traditional broadcast transmission technology, has limitations as regards the maximum number of simultaneous listeners). Such stations must naturally have an agreement with the national copyright society(ies) so that some revenues for this service can be collected and distributed to local rights holders. Since local advertisers can hardly be expected to fund such activities, then some form of support will be required from state or other sources.

EDUCATION, BUSINESS ACUMEN AND REASONABLE CONTRACTS PROTECTING THE CREATOR IN THE GLOBAL MARKET

Over the decades there have been any number of tales of cultural artefacts, traditions and products being 'stolen' from countries which are poor in financial terms, but rich in heritage, talent and modes of cultural expression.

In the area of music, many Third World creators and performers have suffered from poor contracts or no contracts at all. Where both artist and composer are one and the same person, recording and publishing contracts have often been 'bundled', giving the producer great power over exploitation of the work, and the creator a correspondingly weakened position.

There is a widespread need for elementary knowledge about such matters. Such knowledge should be made available via simple educational tools, as well as by initiatives allowing composers with different experiences and knowledge of the industry to interact. State, inter-state and regional cultural support should be made available for different types of 'creative workshops', where creators can meet, interact and literally create new works (whilst jointly retaining the rights to all that is produced). This would also give them an option to exchange experiences of the industry, and learn about potential problems as well as opportunities.

Final thoughts

The world of digital technology and digital networks is fraught with hurdles and hindrances, but also offers numerous opportunities for global communication. The music industry has traditionally been the sector within the entertainment industry that has first taken up and assimilated new technology. The same applies to new digital developments. Fighting new technology to solve problems in old business models has never and will never work. The opportunities can be grasped. But they can only be realised where creativity goes hand in hand with understanding, knowledge and a fair measure of controlled risk-taking.

For this to happen, decision-making must consider very carefully the policy issues enumerated above, and act in accordance with a holistic view of the relevant technological, financial, legal and cultural parameters.

Bibliography

BBC News (2004) 'Downloading myths challenged', available at news.bbc.co.uk/1/hi/technology/4718249.stm (2006–02–19).

Becker, E., Buhse, W., Günnewig, D. and Rump, N. (2003) *Digital Rights Management, Technological, Economic and Legal and Political Aspects*, Springer Forlag, Germany.

Dicola, P. and Thomson, K. (2002) 'Radio deregulation – has it served citizens?' Report from the Future of Music Coalition, Washington DC, USA.

DiMaggio, P., Hargittai, E., Rusell Neuman, W. and Robinson, J. (2001) 'Social Implications of the Internet', *Annual Review of Sociology*, 27: 307–336.

Financial Times (2004) 'Skype's free calls attract masses', 3 September, London.

Frith, S. (1992) 'The industrialisation of popular music', in J. Lull (ed.) *Popular Music and Communication*, Beverly Hills: Sage, pp. 53–77.

Kretschmer, K., Klimis, G.M. and Wallis, R. (2001) 'The global music industry in the digital environment: A study of strategic intent and policy responses, 1996–2000', in S. Janssen, M. Halbertsma, T. Ijdens and K. Ernst (eds) *Trends and Strategies in the Arts and Cultural Industries*, Barjesteh van Waalwik & Co, Rotterdam, pp. 419–441.

Jupiter Research (2000) Beavillain, O. 'Selling Music On-line', speech to Pop Com conference, Cologne, August 2000.

Law, C. (2004) 'The development of the music publishing industry', in S. Horsfall (ed.) *Back to the Future, IAEL yearbook 2004*, London: Five Eight/Frukt, pp. 66–77.

Malm, K. and Wallis, R. (2002) *Media Policy and Music Activity*, London: Routledge.

Music and Copyright (2002) 'EMI reports an 83% rise in EBITA to US Dollars 124m', No. 240, November 27.

Music and Copyright (2003a) 'Gross retained revenues of music publishers fell 20% to 1.2 billion in 2002', No. 243. January 22.

Music and Copyright (2003b) 'On-line music market expands but high costs and increased competition threaten standalone web retailers', No. 265, December 24.

Oberholzer, F. and Koleman, S, (2004) 'The effects of file sharing on record sales – an empirical analysis', research paper, Harvard Business School/UNC Chapell Hill, March.

Oberholzer, F. and Strumpf, K. (2004) 'The effects of file-sharing on record sales: an empirical analysis' working paper. Online, available at: www.unc.edu/~cigar/papers/File_Sharing_March2004.pdf.

Rosenblatt, B. (2002) *Digital Rights Management, Business and Technology*, M&T Books, New York.

Spedidam (2006) 'France-Peer-to-Peer', www.spedidam.fr/actu/actu.htm#peer.

Strategy Analytics (2004) 'On-line music – Europe's sounding great', quoted in *Music and Copyright*, March 31.

Tuomola, A. (2004) 'Disintermediation and reintermediation of the sound recording value chain', *Journal of Media Studies*, 1 (1): 27–47.

United Nations (2003) 'Music Industry Workshop', Youth Forum Brussels, May 2001, Geneva.

Wallis, R. (2001) 'Business as usual or a real paradigm shift in the value chain? The example of the music industry's response to e-commerce technology and ideology', in B. Stanford-Smith and E. Chiozza (eds) *E-work and E-commerce*, Amsterdam: IOS press, pp. 998–1005.

Wallis, R. and Malm, K. (1984) *Big Sounds from Small Peoples – the music industry in small countries*, London: Constable.

Wallis, R. and Wikström, O. (2002), 'Re-visiting the Dot.com fallout in search of lessons learned and values created', in B. Stanford-Smith, E. Chiozza and M. Edin (eds) *Challenges and achievements in E-business and E-work*, Amsterdam: IOS press, pp. 1441–1448.

Wallis, R. and Edström-Frejman, A. (2004) 'Can diversity be a profit-maximising strategy? The apparent incompatibility of deregulation policies, media concentration and audience access to range of choice', in R. Salaverria and C, Sadaba (eds), *Proceedings of the 2003 COST A20 conference on New Media Paradigms*, Pamplona, pp. 571–587. Ediciones Eunate.

Wallis, R. *et al.* (1999) 'Globalisation, technology and creativity: current trends in the music industry', final summary report from the ESRC study at City University Business School, London. Online, available: www.city.ac.uk/multimedia.

WIPO (1996) Copyright Treaty or WCT, adopted in Geneva on 20 December 1996.

3 Financing creative industries in developing countries

Stuart Cunningham, Mark David Ryan, Michael Keane and Diego Ordonez[1]

Introduction

In the past decade there has been a great deal of attention focused on the role of ICTs as enablers of development (Preston 2001). As returns are eroded on lower-end manufacturing, countries are seeking technological innovation as a means of capturing markets higher up the value chain. Governments have responded by investing heavily in national information infrastructures that will bridge the manufacturing economy and the services economy (see Chin 2003). Along with this shift in priorities, there is increasing acknowledgement of the global knowledge-based economy and associated *economies* such as the new economy, the online economy, the network economy, the learning economy and the information economy.

The value of the creative economy – and in particular the economic rents that are derived from intellectual property – has been heralded in industrialized and newly industrializing countries. The harnessing of creativity brings with it the potential of new wealth creation, the cultivation of local talent and the creation of creative capital, the development of new export markets, significant multiplier effects throughout the broader economy, the utilization of information-communication technologies and increased competitiveness in an increasingly global economy. The core creative industries, which include the value-added services that accrue with digital technologies, are now increasingly attractive to governments outside the developed world. However, optimism that these advanced services can provide a way forward is tempered by the knowledge that basic services are not universally available outside of large cities in developing countries.

While creative industries are considered to be new growth areas, in developing countries the output of creative industries barely figures in the reckoning of productivity. Creative industries in developing countries are at a competitive disadvantage due to a more pressing need for financial aid to be directed at problems of education, poverty alleviation and institution building. Likewise, the optimism that developing countries can leap-frog, itself a neo-classical economic paradigm, needs to be evaluated from the perspective of geography, social institutions and lack of effective innovation systems (Sachs 2000).

This does not imply, however, that creative industries cannot accrue capacity and value in developing countries. The dot.com crash of 2000 and the Asian financial crisis of 1997–1999 have caused governments and business to be more cautious about business models. While the former dampened the fervour of entrepreneurial service providers and start-ups, the Asian economic crisis demonstrated that the state–industry nexus, whereby powerful corporations and state-owned enterprises monopolized the market, had actually worked against innovation, and in particular the formation of competitive creative industries that could generate export earnings.

In this respect the most pertinent lessons about redundant development models in the creative industries have come via South Korea where prior to the Asian economic crisis much of the economy was controlled by *chaebols* (sprawling conglomerates). Short of cash following the Asian meltdown, the *chaebols* were forced to divest cultural industry assets, among which were large advertising agencies. Occurring during a period when Korea was moving from an export-oriented economy to a consumer service economy along with a concomitant increase in spending on advertising, this divestiture precipitated the growth of new competitive enterprises (Yoon 2001: 22). In the same time frame – and in response to the dot.com crash – creative ventures such as SM Entertainment and record label YBM Seoul went public while other start-up entertainment businesses took advantage of government largesse towards culture industries and venture capital seed money. According to Suh-kyung Yoon, 'Money has allowed the industry to prosper, but competition has sparked its creativity' (Yoon 2001: 2).

This focus on the dual role of competition and creativity is relevant for our discussion of the financing of creative industries in developing countries. While start-up finance is a factor input often lacking in creative industries, the marriage of finance with creativity is (and has been) fraught with risk (see Ryan 1992). Many creative projects remain within the realm of ideas because there is inadequate finance to facilitate their development and a lack of support mechanisms such as marketing, distribution and promotion to add value. In this context, forms of micro-finance have potential (for some creative *micro-enterprises*) to 'kick-start' or develop ideas to a level where they can be taken further. Moreover, in some newer and investment-heavy creative sectors, such as the video games and digital animation industries, there is reluctance from investors to commit 'sunk' funds to develop what might be seen as 'risky business models'. This deficiency in funding mechanisms is linked to the unclear relationship between cultural capital and economic capital. Returns on investment in culture increasingly need to be quantified, whether positive public good externalities such as contributing to a peaceful and multicultural environment, or actual profits to shareholders.

In the words of Throsby (2001), cultural value is 'various and variable' (29). While he argues that the measurement of cultural value is difficult, it can be disaggregated into several culturally valued components: aesthetic, spiritual, social, historical, symbolic and authenticity (159). Thus cultural value permeates myriad issues including cultural identity, diversity, creativity, cultural life of the community, regional development and heritage tourism (148).

Cultural value in developing countries is often embedded within national cultural and folkloric contexts. Where there is a long cultural history, the creation of products for the marketplace is both constrained and aided by tradition. While many elements of traditional culture have contributed to the development of contemporary creative industries such as video gaming, design and cinema, the maintenance of traditional aesthetic forms often requires that the aesthetic code remains intact. This can be illustrated by debates over the commercialization of tradition. In portraying these separations, we provide the following segmentation in developing countries based on the nature of markets for cultural products.

This chapter is organized as follows. First, we introduce some key issues in relation to financing creative industries in developing countries, including a basic value chain framework. The first section also provides a typology of the cultural sectors in relation to developing country contexts. This is followed by a snapshot of the kinds of markets that currently exist. The second section is a discussion of barriers to development and modes of finance currently being utilized or contemplated.

In the third section we examine specific case studies (from China, Latin America and Indigenous Australia) that illustrate the following:

- shifts from a state-centred to a mixed financing model (China);
- reliance on foreign finance leading to weaknesses in the value chain and how private partnerships can overcome systemic distribution barriers (Latin America); and
- hurdles facing micro-financing models and lessons for developing international niche markets (Indigenous Australia).

This is followed by a synthesis of the findings of this study.

The breakdown of cultural production and consumption into the four categories in Table 3.1 is useful in identifying impediments to marketization. However, it does not imply that cultural production is necessarily trapped within these 'boxes'. While elite and popular cultures exist as critical discourses, research into consumption patterns shows that high culture users are increasingly eclectic in their tastes, becoming 'cultural omnivores' – that is, they consume both commercial and subsidized forms (O'Regan 2001: 9). Cultural consumption is not confined to the cinema, the museum or the art gallery. In contrast to a conservative predisposition to argue that there is not enough elite culture, or too much popular/commercial culture, there is a view that culture is ubiquitous and value-adding. In fact, culture is a vital element of economic value chains and it constitutes a way of life. It is also expressed in polyvalent forms from public art to folk festivals, from urban design to the design of web sites.

It is important to recognize therefore that the globalization of cultural production and governmental support of cultural policy are breaking down the divisions between what is elite and popular, and between what ought to be subsidized and what ought to be subject to market forces. Arguments, such as

Table 3.1 Cultural segmentation in developing countries

Segments	*Examples*	*Investment and models*	*Returns/markets*
Traditional elite This segment most reflects aesthetics, authenticity, spirituality and inherent historical cultural identity	Indigenous (traditional) art, Chinese classical poetry	Static aesthetic forms with low capacity for hybridisation; low value-adding and level of investment except in training of practitioners	High value in original form in elite markets; some traction in tourism markets; Symbolic capital for national identity but often meets uninterested national markets
Traditional popular This segment reflects social, historic, and mythical forms	Folkloric legends and myths e.g. *Romance of the Three Kingdoms* (China); Dreamtime stories (Indigenous)	Evocative folk culture capable of commercialisation and hybridisation across mass media	Cross-cultural acceptance high, public domain IP but has capacity for transition and commercialisation into contemporary popular segment and breakthrough markets. Example of traditional motifs in video gaming
Contemporary elite Often prestigious cultural troupes; high social capital	Ballet and symphony, high-end performing arts	High costs of production with patronage and business sponsorship; low capacity to commercialise due to consumer resistance	Discriminating markets but low economic returns; prestigious cultural capital
Contemporary popular Most closely correlated with the creative industries	Music, film, anime, video games, TV formats and series, advertising design, interactive content	Consumer driven; high value added upstream and downstream	National and international consumer markets, as well as linking to content-seeking business markets

Source: adapted from Richard Kraus, 1995.

Throsby's (2001), about the 'intangible' attributes of culture, which have long been the premise for public support of traditional classical, traditional contemporary and elite segments remain pertinent, especially in developing countries, but the capacity of these segments to be repurposed via the medium of heritage and tourism for example, means that they are not insulated from the marketplace. Traditional forms of culture, aside from its role as maintaining cultural identity, now targets niche markets in innovative ways. In China, for instance, it is possible to download a classical Chinese poem on a mobile phone. This issue is pertinent if we consider that domestic creative industries in developing countries are still predominantly sourced from traditional culture.

Creative industries and location

In confronting the question of financing it is important to point out the fact that difficulties and barriers to raising finance for creative industries development are not limited to developing countries. A lack of start-up finance, capital for expansion, a scarcity of venture capital, the knowledge and inflexibility of commercial financial institutions, as well as the monopolization of international markets by a few multinationals are problems faced by creative industries across the developed world. Barriers to financing creative industries in developing countries are exacerbated by information asymmetry, weak institutional and political support, low levels of entrepreneurial capability, a dependency on foreign firms and foreign investment, inefficient or non-existent copyright regimes and piracy.

The question is one of how to proceed in this environment. Michael Porter, well-known for his work on competitive advantage, asserts that the productivity of nations and regions depends on the value of products and services, their quality and uniqueness, and on the efficiency with which they are produced. In short, productivity depends on how firms (and nations) compete (Porter 2000: 16). While the issue of competitiveness has been critiqued in relation to developing countries (UNCTAD 2003), the creative industries do not replicate characteristics of industrial sectors. The discussion of China provides an instance where national investment in the video games industry is designed to create a base for the development of skills and expertise that will enable China to compete with Korea in this lucrative value-added field. Likewise, the involvement by the All China Sports Federation in the development of e-sports (national video gaming competitions) shows that competitiveness in such new sectors is contingent on national demand. China hopes to leverage its advantages of low cost Internet access and massive demand to develop an industry champion. The same applies in the broadcasting industries where state-directed agglomeration is aimed at increasing national competitiveness in response to the perceived threats of cultural imperialism by transnational media and communication companies (see Keane 2004). Moreover, there is overwhelming evidence to suggest that creative industries – and the networks that enable them – cluster in networked cites and regions in the developed countries, and increasingly in big cities in East Asia (see Yusuf and Nabeshima 2004).

The inability to raise finance for start-ups is just one reason for the lack of sustainability of creative businesses in developing countries, in comparison with resource-rich regions in developed countries. It also illustrates why places such as Hollywood in the USA and Tokyo (Japan) have assumed leading roles as exporters of cultural content: the former for its film industry, the latter primarily for anime and video games. The quality and uniqueness that makes these products exportable depends on financial investment being readily available. The fact that multinational producers of creative content are cognisant of the role of breakthrough cultural movements (rap, 'world' music) provides some solace for developing countries and impoverished regions within developed countries, from where such breakthroughs and innovations are often incubated. However, the development of the quality and uniqueness of creative industries is also contingent on having a large consumer market available to test and feed back quickly into the product innovation cycle. In this sense knowledge of where markets lie for products is essential in the development process. This is clearly illustrated in the Indigenous Australian case study.

An emerging trend in the developed world is that creative industries (and creative practitioners) are needing to recognize the limits of purely grant-driven public funding due to both the limited availability of such funding and, also, the culture of grant dependency that it can generate. In the process, innovative activity is occurring, with a focus on establishing private and community partnerships. The report *Banking on Culture* illustrates European responses to the difficulties in obtaining funding through traditional means and how this is leading to new ways of obtaining finance and indeed how public and financial institutions finance creative industries. The issue of financing creative industries cannot be viewed in isolation from other integral issues that underpin the successful economic development of these industries. *Banking on Culture* illustrates three key issues that need to be considered in conjunction with issues of financing the creative industries. These three issues are:

- creative enterprises and business require highly specialized business support delivered alongside finance;
- other forms of business support for marketing, management development and innovation are equally important; and
- creative industries need specific help to access effective and expanded protection for intellectual property rights.

(Hackett *et al.* 2000: 4)

In short, the quality and the uniqueness of the product – as well as the efficiencies of production – may be comparable within developing economies, but middle value-adding factors in the value chain, namely promotion, branding, and distribution, as well as protections against piracy, are underdeveloped. In fact, it is worth drawing attention to where value is lacking and ask if finance is being directed appropriately.

What we note from the case studies in this study is that there are many vari-

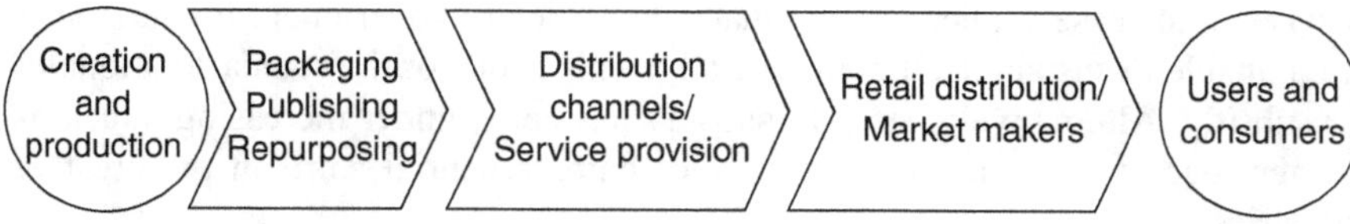

Figure 3.1 Basic value chain model (source: Adapted from Cutler (2002) and Caves (2000)).

ables and no general rule of thumb for where finance is best directed in the creative industries. It may not be simply a case of providing more finance to the creation and production stage of the chain, but instead to target the distribution or marketing segments (see Figure 3.1). If, for instance, there is a perceived weakness in branding or distribution, then mergers and acquisition activity, or joint ventures between international companies (with technical expertise, R&D and distribution networks) and independent creatives (with local knowledge) may provide a better recipe for development. Moreover, while branding and distribution are problems for small producers, increasing interactivity between users/consumers and creators/producers means that the latter have a better idea of how the marketplace is responding to new developments. In relation to export markets the Internet can provide a means of getting ones ideas to a wider market. This disintermediation reduces the role of the 'market makers': gatekeepers such as reviewers, festival curators and the media promotional circuit. Most calls for funding, however, still come from the initial 'creation and production' segment in the value chain; for instance, funding to mount operatic productions or to finance a movie.

Types of markets

Dynamism of markets (i.e. demand) impacts directly upon the financial bottom line. The characteristics of markets also provide a barometer to measure export potential. The typology presented below is an attempt to represent the limitations and potential of markets for developing countries.

The uninterested (domestic) market

Producers of elite forms of traditional culture such as Beijing Opera (China) or Australian Indigenous culture often meet with consumer apathy within domestic markets. The problem of disinterest in national cultural treasures is often seen by supporters of such forms to be simply an effect of lack of finance, but could be as much a result of discount due to ready availability and domestic everydayness.

The grants 'market'

This is where cultural producers compete for a limited supply of government and foundation funds for approved activities and projects, including those that enhance national or regional identity, and increasingly multiculturalism. As we observe in the case studies, culture that is beholden to government for support is often unable to sustain itself commercially. This is one of the standard rationales for subsidy. Alternatively, straight subsidy has come under increasing attack as it often leads to dependency and stymies entrepreneurial spirit in the creative industries.

The tourist market

Tourists seeking to purchase authentic cultural relics and experiences represent an important market for local creators. Cultural theme parks provide outlets for sale of Indigenous and national cultural goods. Tourist markets act as outlets for the work of creative producers, often independent producers or micro-businesses. Little product differentiation is required because tourists often seek artefacts identifiable with their tourist destination. The darker side of this trade is the high incidence of opportunistic copying and cloning, with value not being returned to the producer.

The diaspora market

National and culturally specific cultural content can be successfully targeted at buyers located at a distance from the homeland. Diasporas often seek out authentic homeland culture. By way of contrast, pockets of production exist within first world countries that service Diasporas and often squeeze out the authentic cultural production of the homeland. An example is the huge production centre for Vietnamese culture in California that is distributed internationally through diasporic retail outlets (Cunningham and Sinclair 2001).

Breakthrough markets

International elite markets such as Sotheby's auctions are an example of breakthrough markets. Product from the developing world finds itself occasionally celebrated as unique and valued. The market for Indigenous art (see case study below) represents a breakthrough into this narrow but lucrative market. Similarly, where the creative product or service from a marginal location is unique and distinctive it can inspire or kick-start a new mainstream fad, for example reggae in the 1970s, hip-hop in the 1980s, world music in the 1980–1990s.

Financing creative industries in developing countries: barriers and modes of finance

Barriers

There are numerous barriers to the development of export-orientated creative industries in the developing country contexts examined in this study. The tables illustrated below represent the primary financial, public support, distribution and piracy barriers restricting creative industries development in key sectors such as film, television, audiovisual/multimedia, publishing and performing arts. While many specific barriers are discussed in some detail in the respective case studies, this section presents an illustrative overview.

China

The process of starting a creative business in China is not straightforward. Funding is just one of the impediments. Another significant hurdle to navigate is the intractability of the regulatory system that oversees particular creative industries sectors. In new and potentially profitable industries such as streaming content, firms need to obtain multiple licences in order to operate. Over-bureaucratization is endemic to China's cultural sector and works against implementation of long-term business models. In television drama production, licences are given to new entrants for short-form productions. Joint venture productions, moreover, are permitted on a case-by-case basis. The necessity of obtaining multiple permits to produce creative content, often from different industry regulators (Ministry of Culture, The State Administration of Industry and Commerce, The State Administration of Radio, Film and Television, Ministry of Information Industry), can act as a deterrent to entry into creative industries. This entry barrier is further exacerbated by dependency on relationship maintenance as a means of achieving success. This leads to uncertainty and fosters a huge grey market where permits are not required. There are some notable start-up exceptions in the ICT sector such as Netease (Internet portal) and the Hunan Television consortium in southern China (broadcasting), but in most cases, these success stories have been supported by foreign investment and early entry into the marketplace.

Survivability of start-ups is thus endangered by regulatory agencies getting out of synchronization. This has the effect of creating systemic weaknesses in business models. Other difficulties facing start-ups include the high transaction costs associated with copyright and rights management, technology input costs and the shortage of working capital and skill sets. In fact, the most pressing problems facing investment are copyright and revenue sharing. Lack of copyright protection in film, television and interactive software constrains investment. Investors in these industries are likely to see their profits dispersed via DVD pirates, or in the case of television their programme ideas are copied without permission (Keane *et al.* 2003). Likewise, revenue from rights management is yet to be systematically regulated although the Chinese government is making concerted efforts in this area.

The necessity of conforming to governmentally prescribed forms and genres is complicated by distribution bottlenecks. These factors, in combination with existing conventions within the marketplace, notably a propensity to rely on relationships, make it difficult for cultural enterprises to generate start-up capital. Product innovation is therefore more likely to be incremental and

Table 3.2 China: barriers to export-orientated creative industries

Barriers	*Film*	*Television*	*Audio-visual*[a]	*Publishing*	*Performing arts*
Start-up capital	✓		✓		
Working capital	✓	✓	✓		✓
Lack of business expansion capital	✓	✓			✓
Distribution barriers	✓	✓		✓	
Intellectual property regime	✓	✓	✓	✓	
Piracy	✓				
Institutional support framework				✓	✓

Note

a Audiovisual production in China is video games, multimedia content and Internet-based content.

imitation is favoured over innovation. The focus on imitation has led to the success of Japanese and Korean creative industries. Whereas these countries have managed to move to the next stage (innovation), China remains locked into a cycle of dependency. Table 3.2 summarizes the barriers to export-orientated creative industries in China.

In short, the kind of reflexivity that is needed to ensure innovation and creativity, particularly in industries such as media, music and entertainment software that operate in an environment of uncertainty, is stymied. While people working in creative industries often need to find creative solutions to problems such as bureaucracy and censorship, the solutions are often pragmatic and exemplify low risk-taking. In some respects, therefore, China's cultural sector embodies many aspects of developing countries. In other instances, it typifies a marketplace where there is a large enough domestic market to allow a multitude of small players to make money. The fragmentation of China's massive market is itself an impediment to the growth of brand equity.

Latin America: music

Latin American countries, notably Brazil and Mexico, have large and significant local music industries. Latin American music sales account for 5 per cent of total world music sales. As illustrated in Figure 3.3 (below), domestic consumption of local music is also healthy. With the emergence of new music genres such as World Music, New Age Music and Latin Music since the early 1990s, new international markets and opportunities have opened up for Latin American music production (Gauthier and Yudice 2002: 10). As music is deeply rooted in local Latin American cultural traditions there is an abundance of naturally skilled local talent. There are low barriers to entry and no restrictive start-up capital requirements (artists generally draw upon personal savings or loans to purchase equipment) with artists beginning with live performance for payments, then moving into broadcasting before embarking upon recording for the local market (Throsby 2002: 14). The Latin American music industry has an established live music practice, a local and national broadcasting system, a domestic recording industry and in some instances access to international markets.

However, the primary barrier to development of Latin American music is the domination of national and international commercial distribution channels by the 'major' transnational music corporations (EMI, BMG, the Warner Music group, Sony Music Entertainment and Universal/PolyGram). As one study has noted, 'if a recording produced by an independent company is successful, it is quite likely that big scale revenues from a newly discovered artist are not earned by the company. Rather, they generally are overtaken either by the majors who offer lucrative contracts to successful artists or they are pirated' (Gauthier and Yudice 2002: 10). As a result, talent is effectively 'poached', companies lose control of the distribution of their product and economic returns are siphoned away from the country of origin. Throsby (2002) argues that independent firms act in ways that suit the 'majors' as they develop music outside of the mainstream, and if they generate new audiences, begin to become successful and pose a threat to the 'majors' dominance, they are simply absorbed by the 'majors' (10). The combined lack of working capital and the lack of capital for business expansion stunt the growth of local companies and their capacity to compete against the majors.

Latin America: film

Public support for the Latin American film industry is characterized by an over-reliance on foreign investment, which is reflected through a wide range of available tax breaks for foreign film-makers; in comparison negligible public financial and funding support are available for local production. The lack of public funding for local production is largely the product of an over-emphasis on regulatory and tax incentives. As a result, combined with low levels of private investment, there is a scarcity of start-up and working capital. Endemic piracy and copyright barriers stunt the commercialization and diffusion of Latin American film products, and restrict opportunities for the development of economically sustainable regional markets. The strengthening of copyright laws and the control of piracy may open up new economic markets throughout Latin America. Table 3.3 summarizes the barriers to export-orientated creative industries in Latin America.

Table 3.3 Latin America: barriers to export-orientated creative industries

Barriers	*Music*	*Film*
Start-up capital		✓
Working capital	✓	✓
Lack of capital for business expansion	✓	✓
Distribution barriers	✓	✓
Piracy	✓	✓
Institutional support framework (subsidy, grants, etc.)	✓	✓

Finance

The modes of finance examined in this study have been grouped into three primary categories: 'public subsidy/support'; 'private partnerships' and 'private investment' (Table 3.4). Each category consists of a wide range of different finance types. While many of the 'types' of finance in the 'private partnerships' category are not strictly monetary, they add value to a creative enterprise through untraded interdependencies such as skills, knowledge, resources and branding.

A number of primary trends emerge from analysis of the modes of finance examined in this study. First, organizational/institutional networks and informal people networks are extremely important in levering financial support and developing connections to financial sources. Second, most modes of finance are aimed at the creation and production stages of the value chain. However, private partnerships such as joint ventures, collaboration and other untraded interdependencies such as skills and branding are becoming an important means in overcoming distribution and other market barriers (see Storper 1997). There is also a significant lack of large-scale capital investment in the regions and creative industries examined. New technologies, and in particular partnerships with technology firms (ISPs, telco's, etc.), provide avenues for firms to enter global markets and to overcome distribution barriers. Nevertheless, despite the trend towards the commercialization and privatization of public cultural resources, there remains a strong role for governmental support mechanisms in sectors that are deemed to embody national or regional cultural value.

Models of public financing

The financing of the creative industries has an uneven legacy across the globe. Developing countries have often tended to fund culture more in the cause of national development and less as a means of economic development. One way of characterizing the spectrum of public support for creative industries is through variations in what has sometimes been called 'the arm's length principle' (For a discussion of this see http://www.culturaleconomics.atfreeweb.com/arm's.htm).

The arm's length principle describes cultural policy models that allow degrees of involvement for government. It is a useful model because it preempts a shift towards commercialization as a more viable and less dependent and politicized model of financing.

At one end of the spectrum is the *engineer* state model, suggesting a direct and often intrusive public intervention into the domain of cultural production. The governments of the former Soviet Union and the People's Republic of China favoured this model in order to control the output. Management was centralized, product was standardized and autonomy was low. The *architect* state model is typified by a Ministry of Culture dispensing funds to creators and producers who meet national cultural objectives. The funding of flagship performing arts companies can often be linked to their role in supporting a national vision of excellence. Likewise a *patron* state model implies financial support administered through arm's length councils, a model that has the advantage of promoting excellence without compromising the process of creativity. Grants, however, are often subject to risk preferences of grantees. Awards and prizes disbursed by councils are often distributed based on criteria that are directed towards specific rationales, which may not be linked to business development. However, an example of 'aid' that is linked to productivity is the Creative Capital Foundation (http://www.creativecapital.org) where marketing and other 'non-artistic' aid is provided. This model is more indicative of *facilitation*, which has increasingly been seen as the best means of assuring a mix of public–private support. Mechanisms including provide tax deductions for donor contributions to the creative industries and incentives for export-oriented creative industries. This model has a high uptake in the USA.

Models of public–private funding: micro-finance

Micro-finance is a mode of financing already employed in a large number of developing countries as a means of poverty alleviation and as a way of financing micro-enterprises across a number of industries. The most common micro-finance models are: village banking, credit unions, self-help groups and rural financial systems (McGuire and Conroy 2000: 5–6). The most notable institutional examples of successful micro-finance programmes operating in developing countries are *Grameen Bank*[2] in Bangladesh, the Bolivian *BancoSol*,[3] and *PlaNet Finance*[4] sponsored micro-finance institutions operating in a number of countries. However, from preliminary analysis and evidence available, the majority of these micro-finance programmes are generally aimed at financing micro-businesses in primary industries, retail and marginalized social groups who may not have access to credit. Micro-finance programmes of this sort have seldom been directed specifically at creative industries – at least in relation to enabling creative inputs. There are two sides to this lack of uptake of micro-credit. While there may be a clear lack of financial assistance available for creative industries, there may also be a lack of awareness of available assistance measures on the part of the creative producers, especially in the case of generic financial models.

Nonetheless, micro-credit offers a viable model for financing *micro-business* in the creative industries – especially in terms of developing or 'kick-starting' ideas. *Banking on Culture* foregrounds micro-credit as a loan instrument with significant potential in developing micro-enterprises in the cultural sector (Hackett *et al.* 2000: 'Section 5.3'). These findings are based upon a case study of the UK Full Circle Loan Fund established in 1997, a successful generic micro-credit fund supporting female entrepreneurs modelled on a Grameen Bank model of micro-finance.

The Grameen Bank micro-finance model is generally structured as follows. Loans are lent at either start-up or growth phases of the business cycle and initial

Table 3.4 Modes of finance and private partnerships

Category	*Type*	*Sector*	*Country/ example*	*Description*
Public subsidy/support	Entertainment levy/tax	Performing arts	China	China has a 3% tax on popular entertainment venues with funds being invested back into supporting the Arts.
	Funding body	Art	Chile	The FONART fund is administered by the Ministry of Education and is the primary form of Public Art funding
	Tax breaks/tax incentives	Film	Colombia	Foreign film producers tax will be calculated at 60% of generated income/local film investment is 100% tax deductible and others
	Tax exemptions	Film	Peru	Tax exemptions on local film production revenues
	Film funding	Film	Venezuela	A percentage of a Government body's budget is invested in local movie production
	Movie levy and rental levy	Film	Argentina	Percentages of movie tickets, movie sales, rentals and all income received by the National Radio Broadcasting are collated to form the 'Motion Picture Fund' which funds local production
Private partnerships	Attracting International professionals through co-productions	Film	China	The idea of luring international professionals to a local industry with links to 'majors', finance, technology and skills
	Publishing partnerships with online content providers	Publishing	China	Publishers sell their rights to online content providers attached to Internet portals to ensure wide distribution
	Collaborative venture: art and real-estate	Art	China	Artists pay a nominal fee to use the 798 space which the owners are attempting to develop into a residential development project

	Private incubation	Music	Colombia	Kankano Laboratorio Cultural has effectively become a private incubation centre providing artists with a live venue, and a recording and rehearsal space
	Utilisation of institutional networks	Art	Aboriginal art	The success of the *Dreamings* exhibition was in part through levering the international network, consultants and individual actors of the Asia Society
	Bundling of an audio CD with a mobile phone package deal	Music	Brazil	The album 'Arepa 3000' became part of a pre-paid mobile package from Movilnet, with 80,000 units purchased by the telephony company
Private investment	Philanthropic reciprocal investment	TV	China	Producers negotiate investment deals through personal contacts/networks or with private enterprise
	Direct private investment	TV and film	China	A direct investment is made in return for publicity, such as programme naming with products, and featuring of products on-screen
	IPO	TV and Internet	China	Chinese companies raise finance through public listings on both the Chinese and NASDEQ stock-exchanges
	Foreign investment through informal people networks	Media	China	Informal investment arrangements circumvent regulatory barriers prohibiting foreign investment; investors often are foreign businesses
	Commercial patronage	Cultural arts	China	Arts companies are sponsored by local companies
	Philanthropy	Art	Aboriginal art	Philanthropic funding has contributed to the development of Aboriginal art communities and a primary form of investment

loans are restricted to income-generating activity. High repayment rates are achieved through peer group systems/group lending, social pressure and legal measures. Transaction transparency is an essential component and savings can be associated with credit to act as an additional safe-guard.[5] The Full Circle Loan Fund adapts this model to suit female entrepreneurs with poor credit ratings. The Fund adopts its lending practices, its peer group and social pressure system, and its repayment structure. An added condition is the provision and approval of a workable business model. Although this fund is a generic mode of finance with a broad focus on financing micro-enterprises generally, it has financed a range of creative micro-enterprises such as clothes designers, a book publisher, artists and a web-page designer (Hackett *et al.* 2000). There is potential for the development of similar models that can be used to provide either specific or generic finance for creative industries in developing countries contexts.

Micro-finance has potential for several reasons. First, it is already a proven and effective model of financing micro-business in developing countries. Second, it makes available amounts that are suitable for both start-up and working capital within some sectors (the average BancoSol loan is US$1,390).[6] Third, it has the potential to develop micro-enterprises to a level where they become more attractive to investors, and eligible for other forms of credit (Nazirwan 2003: 1). Micro-credit models are flexible and can be regionally or locally adapted, thus making it a suitable model for most (and the poorest) developing country contexts. Finally, as safe-guard mechanisms are a standard feature of this financial model, many of the systemic problems in obtaining finance from commercial institutions – risk-management concerns, the intangible nature of creative assets, a lack of institutional specialization – are to an extent mediated.

However, micro-credit is only really an appropriate instrument for small enterprises and certain creative activities such as photography, independent music, publishing and similar forms of small-scale production. As *Banking on Culture* notes, micro-finance is not an effective form of finance in areas that require high levels of grant funding or in larger commercial sectors requiring large capital injections such as venture capital and equity investments.

Emerging characteristics of finance models: parameters and safeguards

An emerging trend for creative industries-specific finance models is the development of unique parameters or safeguards to cater effectively for the intangible nature of creative assets and outputs, manage risk and to ensure the robustness of business models. The development of these parameters varies and depends on the type of finance being allocated. The following parameters are developed from findings in *Banking on Culture* and micro-finance models being applied by Grameen Bank and BancoSol.

Examples of emerging creative industries financing parameters are the following.

Loans, credit and funding

- Loans are lent to entrepreneurs at either start-up or growth phases of the business cycle.
- All applicants must provide a workable business model.
- In some cases potential borrowers must agree on becoming a member of a lending circle or a 'peer group' scheme consisting of small groups of borrowers who meet regularly, effectively providing a collective guarantee to the lender.
- High repayment rates are achieved through the peer group systems/group but also through innovative techniques such as group lending and social pressure, legal measures and economic sanctions.
- Specialized knowledge including an understanding of the respective sector, the market and pricing is becoming pertinent to the development of creative industries specific loans, the assessment of loan applications and the management of risk. To use the music sector as an example, the lending institution requires an informed and specialized knowledge of:

    i the music market;
    ii income flows (regular gigs, potential merchandizing, royalties structures, etc.);
    iii pricing issues (gigs, likely CD sales, etc.); and
    iv the nature and value of assets (guitars, amplifiers, mixers, etc.).

Organization and institutional parameters (building the capacity of organizations to deliver loans)

- The provision of a business plan.
- Careful analysis and acceptance of the business plan.
- Innovative guarantee mechanisms.
- Different ways of accessing risk.
- Local and specialist knowledge to assess market trends and proposed business models.
- Methods to measure product or service effectiveness such as conventional impact assessments.
- Assessments of transparency or disclosure.
- Social accounting and auditing.
- Monitoring through management information.
- Legal frameworks.

Case studies

Financing creative industries in China

Introduction

China is presented as a case study for the principal reason that it exemplifies a transitional environment (Curran and Park 2000: 13), in which many cultural institutions that were previously funded directly from the public purse are adopting a mixed model of enterprise and subsidy. This is often typified by unusual (and sometimes irregular) forms of financial investment. From an industry development perspective China is endeavouring to add value to its cultural economy by learning from creative industries' management models utilized in developed nations.

From the outset, however, we need to point out that the term creative industries has only recently been officially recognized in China. Discussions of how creativity functions as an input into economic development are relatively rare, apart from international business literature translated into Chinese. The more familiar term used in China is, in fact, 'innovation' (in Chinese *chuangxin*), being part of the government's broad reform agenda promoting the concept of social renewal and progress (Yi 2000). The slogan 'innovation is the spirit of a nation's progress' is widely propagated and 'innovation centres' are to be found in Chinese universities, including cultural industries innovation centres at Shanghai Jiaotong University and Beijing (Peking) University. While innovation is widely touted, there is an acknowledgement among many critics and industry professionals that China needs to re-assess its cultural industries development approach due to a tendency to favour imitation over innovation. In short, while innovation is a theoretical catch word, it has yet to be transformed into practice. Innovation without creativity means that the pressure is on business to produce products and services that capture markets. As markets are fragmented, there is a tendency to borrow creativity from elsewhere (see Keane 2004).

The importance of creativity is now coming into finer focus in China. The reluctance (until recently) to see creativity as a crucial ingredient in relation to innovation can be explained to some extent by the tendency to equate innovation with science and technology, and as an antidote for China's non-innovative manufacturing sectors. Another important reason for the lack of focus on creativity is the role of culture in socialist China, where cultural output was considered superstructural and intangible – rather than an economic commodity. In short, culture's role was to reflect the economic reality, a role that did not privilege the creator in the sense understood in liberal democracies. Until the early 1990s China's cultural sector produced standardized cultural goods and commodities, which were distributed to a national community, namely 'the people'. Output was largely organized around quotas and prescribed forms; and those who were charged with the responsibility of determining production criteria were in most cases bureaucrats with little real sympathy for the autonomy of creative artists.

While this description presents an industrial model of production, it did not mean that culture was an industry in the commercial sense. It was a state administered industry, one where the costs were born by government and business models were conspicuous by their absence. Cultural production was not about diversification, product differentiation and profits. This 'engineer state' model receded in the wake of economic reform and gave way to a market model of production in the mid-1980s and early 1990s. In this transitional period central government moved away from direct administration and encouraged enterprise and local initiatives partly in order to amortize the cost of cultural production. The term 'cultural institution' (*wenhua shiye*) became the preferred term, at least until 2000, when the national government officially endorsed the concept of 'cultural industries' (*wenhua chanye*). Whereas the former designated publicly funded culture and included state-funded troupes such as musicians, dancers, opera troupes, etc., the contemporary cultural industries are directly associated with the notion of enterprise (see Keane 2004).

Statistics pertaining to the cultural industries in China can not be directly correlated with international benchmarks and are therefore best read as indicators of sectoral growth. According to the Chinese Ministry of Culture, the value of the cultural sector increased from 1.21 billion yuan (US$146 million) in 1990 to 8.37 billion yuan (US$1.01 billion) in 1998, representing a sixfold increase. Meanwhile the number of registered organizations associated with culture increased from 68,000 to 92,000 – an increase of 35 per cent. Employment in the cultural sector increased 46 per cent, from 495,000 to 721,000 during the same period. Most significantly, the number of private enterprises engaged in some form of cultural activity increased rapidly. In 1990 the private cultural sector numbered less than government cultural units. By 1998 private enterprises constituted 2.7 times the number of public units and the level of employment and the value of output was 1.5 times that of the official public cultural sector (Ministry of Culture 2003). When one takes into account that all of China's media are state owned, the dynamism of the surrounding or non-core enterprises is evident.

Despite impressive growth statistics and activity within the private sector, China's cultural consumption lags behind international benchmarks. Whereas cultural industries have become mainstay contributors to GDP in developed countries, the value of the (national) cultural economy in China in 1998 occupied just 0.26 per cent of GDP and 0.8 per cent of the services sector. By comparison the cultural economy of the USA contributes an estimated 7 per cent to GDP. In 1997 the consumption of culture and entertainment services per resident was 2.35 per cent of total consumption, far below the level of developed countries and less than other developing countries (Ministry of Culture 2003). While these figures tell a less than impressive picture it should be noted that the majority of China's population are classified as peasants, despite recent trends suggesting massive urbanization. Moreover, if we look at mega-cities such as

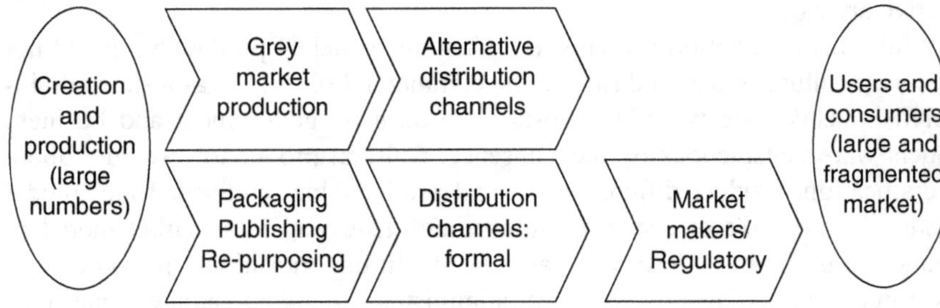

Figure 3.2 Basic value chain of Chinese creative industries.

Beijing, Shanghai, Guangzhou, Chongqing and Tianjin we find a strong level of cultural consumption. According to a recent report, the consumption of knowledge-based services by Beijing residents comprised more than 4 per cent of expenditure (Luo and Zhao 2003). It also needs to be noted that there is also a high degree of elasticity inherent in these figures taking into account the grey economy and the high incidence of pirated cultural goods. In other words, much cultural consumption is not registered as market sales.

The basic value chain of Chinese creative industries/cultural industries is impacted upon by numerous impediments in the distribution channels segment (see Figure 3.2). In this sense it demonstrates unique characteristics that allow products to reach consumers more directly than the formal commercial route of prescribed distribution outlets, venues and galleries. However, the high incidence of informal distribution of products (such as pirated DVDs and music CDs) and the frequent barter of services and content has seriously impacted upon the capacity to grow creative enterprises. Informal relationships based on *guanxi* (networks) further hinder the implementation of professionalism and best practice. Moreover, the large numbers at either end of the value chain (creators and end-users) mean that a great deal of importance is focused on the middle segments, which are stymied by institutional rigidities; for example, the role played by market makers – in many instances, officials who preside over allocation of book numbers, television production licences and permits.

Dominant sectors, targeted markets and export potential

The dominant cultural sectors are here defined by China's own industry classification system. As the term cultural industries has recently evolved there is still no absolute line on what is included, and there is a tendency to add more sectors to the cultural economy, particularly with China now coming into contact with the concept of creative industries, which is favoured by Hong Kong, Singapore, Taiwan and Korea, as well as Australia and New Zealand. Probably the most useful attempt to correlate the cultural industries with creative industries comes from the Chinese Academy of Social Science, which designates *core* industries such as media (publishing, broadcasting and digital content) and *non-core* performing arts industries. However, consensus among academics is that the broad cultural sector includes film, television, audiovisual, publishing, cultural arts, sport and education. It is noteworthy that the cultural industries (as defined) in China do not as yet include architecture, advertising, design and heritage (although these elements are indeed embedded within the current categories).

The following is a snapshot of business models, investment models and export potential in these industries (with the exception of education) with particular emphasis on new financing models.

FILM

The success of China's film industry and the capacity to create exportable content is contingent on unleashing creativity as much as stimulating finance. The film industry is currently in a state of crisis, despite the endorsement by Quentin Tarantino of China as an ideal location for production. Tarantino has undoubtedly been impressed by the willingness of the Chinese to work enthusiastically for low salaries in contrast to the spiralling costs in other international locations. The most salient points to note, however, are that low levels of capital investment, combined with an unwillingness to embrace risk and flawed distribution segments in the value chain, are retarding the competitiveness of China's film industry. Ten years ago China's fifth-wave generation of film makers, such as Zhang Yimou, Chen Kaige and Tian Zhuangzhuang, were acknowledged internationally. As China's film fortunes wane the Korean film industry is achieving international recognition. Can China learn something from Korea where money has poured into film making from a range of private investors? The success of the Korean new wave has seen film financing models going online, allowing ordinary people to buy into the movie business (Kim 2002). *Netizen funds* are a way by which (mostly) young Koreans invest in film projects for a return based on the movie's success after release.

In China, international directors with links to majors are likely to be seen as folk heroes bearing money, technology and skills. Of these money is the most crucial. In 1995 the Chinese government promoted the development of non-state investment by allowing investors (both individuals and non-state enterprises) whose outlay was more than 70 per cent of budget to be regarded as producers. The following year this was reduced to 30 per cent (Chu 2002: 46). However, the government stipulation forcing studios to produce a quota of approved 'mainstream melody' films (that is, propagandistic films echoing China's reform) has meant that exhibitors have turned to foreign productions for box office revenue. Investor unwillingness to support the film industry has opened the door for foreign investment. Since 1997 the partial privatization of China's leading film studios (Beijing Forbidden City Film Corporation, Xian Film Corporation, Ermei Film Corporation and Shanghai Film Corporation) has stimulated private investment and co-productions with most of the capital coming from Hong Kong, Taiwan and Japan. Return on investment is however stymied by a lack of enforceable copyright regime that sees pirated copies widely sold on city streets.

TELEVISION

Television is a creative industry that employs an army of people in China. Television stations are still technically owned by the state, but they are now allowed to apply for licences to operate as corporate entities responsible for their profits and losses. A stimulus to market competition has been the growing advertising spend as China's consumer market develops. The market for prime time television has acted as a barometer for assigning value to productions. The increasingly competitive nature of television production has forced production units to countenance a range of financing options. Often a producer or a 'middle man' is engaged to raise funds. This person might be a cultural entrepreneur with connections in the corporate world. The producer (or alternatively someone in the production company) may approach an old school friend or army comrade of high rank and ask for financial favours. This is not straightforward philanthropy, however, but investment based on *guanxi* (reciprocal) relationships. Direct investments are also negotiated with profitable enterprises that stand to gain on their outlay or simply wish to have their name and/or product associated with the programme or placed within the screenplay.

The recent consolidation of China's television broadcasters into mega-conglomerates (echoing the formation of film corporations) has seen the emergence of new business models, including increased outsourcing to new independent companies and the subsequent trading in programme rights in China's evolving multichannel marketplace, which is enhanced by digital television roll out (Keane and Donald 2002). The development of independent creative production, however, is constrained by the need to establish relationships with regulators in order to secure licences. An additional means of investment that has become common in China's television and new media (Internet portals; broadband) sectors is listing on the Chinese stock exchange and Nasdec, respectively. The most successful commercial venture to utilize this model of raising finance has been the Hunan Television network in southern China. Hunan TV, a provincial station, controlled 75 per cent of in-province advertising revenue by the late-1990s and subsequently used this advertising base to set up a shell company and list on the Shenzhen stock market.

AUDIOVISUAL

The audiovisual industries sectors (in China categorized as music CDs, DVDs, VCD, Internet-based content and video games) vary in degrees of innovation and in their capacity to target export markets. While the domestic mass market for audiovisual products is large in terms of actual consumers, there exists a high degree of parasitic imitation that constrains returns on investment. There is also massive copyright infringement and pirating, particularly in the popular music

(CD) and film (DVD) industries. Problems replicated in the publishing industry (see below) pertain to the start-up of music operations. Record companies in China can only release albums through a music publisher/distributor, which by definition is a government entity. These music publishing houses recoup the bulk of profits, approximately 60 per cent (see de Kloet 2002).

There are some notable exceptions in the audiovisual sector, however, that do allow substantial profits; these manage to cut out the grey markets and the rake-off by publishing houses by linking directly to a subscription model. For instance, the video games market demonstrates potential growth and presents a model for private investment. Most of the Internet portals in China currently derive from 15–30 per cent of their revenues from gaming (other significant earning derive from the SMS boom). For instance, a leading Internet portal, NetEase, draws up to 38 per cent of total revenue from gaming (Fong 2003).

PUBLISHING

Publishing in China is typified by the relative cheap costs of reproduction and the relatively difficult process of getting product into the marketplace. China has its best sellers and its popular magazines, but most publishing loses money due to the necessity of distribution through state outlets. Successful manuscripts are often duplicated and distributed on the grey market. As in the music publishing sector there are constraints imposed by the need to obtain a book number (licence) in order to publish. These are allocated by government. A publishing house in China generally has several studios in which editors work. Editorial studios and publishing house have an internal commercial relationship. However, the editorial studios are not autonomous from publishing houses, although they may venture into the marketplace under their own imprint – a kind of semi-commercial arrangement. These independent commercial ventures still depend on publishing houses for the book number, which allows them to publish. They cannot form a business without this. At present, publishing is a controlled economy that is regulated by the book number system.

Greater financial autonomy exists in the magazine market although a proprietor of an independent magazine needs to be associated with a publishing company to obtain a licence. While foreign investment in content publishing is prohibited, there are a number of models to circumvent this bottleneck. A foreign publisher may not invest directly in a Chinese magazine start-up although it may obtain a licence to form a joint venture and distribute a Chinese version in China after content has been vetted (for instance *Elle* and *Cosmopolitan* magazines). Alternatively, money is made available to magazine proprietors by informal investment mechanisms, that is, where the magazine proprietor has *guanxi* (relationship of trust) with a foreigner investor. Another model of publishing that typifies a model of disintermediation is online publishing whereby the author sells the rights to an online content provider linked to an Internet portal.

CULTURAL/PERFORMING ARTS

The varieties of cultural arts are many, as would be expected in a country with such history and depth of tradition. These include Beijing opera and kunqu (a form of high opera), modern classical opera and ballet, traditional and folk songs, acrobatic troupes, visual arts, calligraphy, spoken theatre, puppetry and multimedia performance art. The cultural arts remain heavily reliant on government funding and are constantly faced with the dilemma of how to adopt new business models and to adapt their aesthetic practices to nurture younger audiences increasingly lured to interactive forms of performance and media. For some years now the Chinese government has levied a 3 per cent tax on karaoke parlours and other popular entertainment venues with funds being returned to support the cultural arts (Kraus 2004). The reform of the cultural performing arts sector has recently entered a new phase with the setting up in April 2004 of the China Arts and Entertainment Group, which consists of nearly two dozen enterprises, including China Performing Arts Agency and China International Exhibition Centre. The two core companies will be State holding enterprises and will derive investment from all sectors of society, including individual and foreign capital. Two core companies will be China's sole agencies for running the global art performance and exhibition business sectors.

An interesting example of the avant-garde in China's cultural arts sector is the 798 Space in the Dashanzi Art district in north-east Beijing. The 798 Space is based upon a simple business proposition. Artists contribute a nominal fee for use of the space to the land owner, Hongkong Land Holdings, which has an eye to create an upscale environment for a residential development called Central Park. This instance of urban redevelopment it is not about heritage, but rather the future. The developer has reportedly spent massive amounts of money on refurbishing the premises. It is unclear, however, what will happen to the artist studios, cafes and bars when the factory is demolished in 2005, but in the interim the space provides a creative milieu for the development of avant-garde and experimental culture. The space operates via a collective management company in order to oversee the studio space, the products and its activities. The area that houses this community (independent filmmakers, photographers, designers, video and visual artists, musicians and theatrical groups) is an old switching factory, no. 798, from which the space derives its name. In April 2004 the organizing committee representing the studios housed in the 798 Space are planning to organize the Dashanzi International Art Festival, which will incorporate contemporary Chinese and international art and performance.

According to the developers this collaborative venture between art and real estate will cultivate wealthy buyers. It is estimated that 30 per cent of the traffic that passes through is non-Chinese, including many tourists. It is also estimated that 90 per cent of the buyers of property at Central Park have the minimum of a bachelor's degree and 70 per cent are employed by multinationals (Collier 2003). George Yudice (2003) has described similar sites of 'extracting cultural capital' in Mexico. His point about artists being 'service providers' is relevant:

return on investment in such projects accrues to the land developers, the sponsors, curators and artists. The district also benefits from the availability of low wages in the service sector, which paradoxically make the site attractive for international investors while at the same time making the district too expensive for ordinary Chinese. Arguably, the site also provides publicity for the Chinese contemporary art scene and the artists-in-residence will come into contact with international peers. This is the impoverished underfunded segment of the art world forming a temporary development alliance with the wealthy elite. This ambitious project flies in the face of the traditionally conservative system of art patronage in China, where the new rich middle class embellish their homes with traditional forms such as calligraphy, but seldom countenance experimental art. Moreover, state funds are rarely directed towards independent artists, although cities such as Beijing and Shanghai are keen to promote biennials to enhance their cosmopolitan status.

SPORT

Sport is regarded as a cultural industry in China and indeed one where creativity is now emerging as an input. Sport is linked to broadcasting and advertising and this assumes greater importance as the Beijing Olympics moves closer. The importance of sport as a creative industry can be illustrated by the case of cyber-gaming and the government supported China E-Sports. China E-Sports Games, or CEG has been officially listed as the 99th competitive sport in China. The first China E-Sports games was sponsored by the All-China Sports Federation, China Interactive Sports Development Co. and China Interactive Sports Communications Technology Co. in 2004. The event was a commercial enterprise: that is, competitors pay to play. In addition, the competitions are broadcast on cable television channels. CEG includes competitions for four popular real-time PC games: FIFA Football; Half-Life: Counter Strike; Warcraft III: The Frozen Throne; and StarCraft: Brood War. Prior to official endorsement by the All-China Sports Federation, several important international e-sport events had already been introduced into China. These included World Cyber Game (WCG) from South Korea, Electronic Sports World Cup (ESWC) from France and Cyberathlete Professional League (CPL) from the USA.

The emergence of sports marketing and sponsorship is now emerging as a mainstream industry in the lead up to the Beijing Olympics. Foreign investment in Chinese sport via sports marketing companies like IMG has helped sports to develop a brand profile. Investors including Nike, Coca-Cola, Motorola, Siemens, Heineken and Philip Morris have invested in high profile sports such as football, basketball and formula one motor racing. In recent years the Chinese corporations Legend Computers and Li Ning Sports Goods have entered into the marketplace (Ashton 2002).

Change in business models

Markets for new cultural products are rapidly emerging, aided by the fact that China has on tap one of the most valuable resources for product development:

large demographics of discriminating consumers willing to test new products and services. The domestic market for commercial creative industries is characterized by large numbers of persons engaged in cultural activities, both formally and informally. As Richard Kraus (2004) has noted in his recent publication *The Party and the Arty*, the arts-entertainment complex in China embraces a diversity of cultural workers and artists, who receive commissions, sponsorships and salaries from a range of state-owned enterprises – and more recently private business. Kraus writes that 'Arts angels have mixed motives, ranging from a generous desire to support culture to vulgar self-promotion' (213). In typifying this transitional funding cultural environment Kraus draws attention to new kinds of commercial patrons (220):

> One Chengde wine company sponsored a local spoken drama troupe when it made a television play glorifying the history of its wine. An engineering-supplies company in Zhejiang provided travel expenses to enable an amateur playwright to accept a prize, then publicized its philanthropy. The Yangzi River Power Company funds tours by the Beijing Opera Company of Hubei, which considered changing its name to the China Yangzi River Power Company Beijing Opera Troupe.

This funding is evidence of the changing landscape. Branding is an idea that is beginning to take root within China's media and investment, sponsorship and philanthropy are gradually increasing as the state moves further away from supporting the cultural sector. Within the formal sector (state funded troupes and institutions), a large percentage of funding goes to salaries and retirement pensions. Despite much rhetoric about cultural development and innovation from the central government, investment in cultural industries has never been a state priority. In fact, while yearly investment by central and local governments increased by an average of 19.08 per cent and 9.48 per cent, respectively, from 1998 to 2002, funding as a percentage of taxation income during the same period has declined rapidly. Investment nationwide as a percentage of income gained from the cultural sector has dropped from 10.6 per cent to 0.2 per cent (Wang and Song 2004). Much of this can be attributed to more efficient collection of revenue, and itself is testimony to the growing contribution of culture to GDP.

In attempting to offset this decline in government investment, there have been recommendations emanating from the Chinese Academy of Social Sciences that draw upon a national competitiveness paradigm: arguing for guaranteed funding for essential public cultural services, funds for strengthening national culture and funds to support key projects and institutions. In addition there are recommendations to subsidize cultural institutions that are commercial, and to open up ways of rewarding non-government investment in such enterprises through preferential tax schemes, echoing international models. In short, the argument is a mix of national development and commercial reality (Wang and Song 2004).

Financing creative industries in Latin America

Introduction

As in other markets, independent creative production in Latin America faces serious financing constraints. The region's fragmentation (with the exception of large markets in Brazil, Mexico and possibly Argentina) provides incentives for entertainment *majors* in the region to focus on distribution of imported products rather than on artistic development. This, in conjunction with the globalization of media outlets and promotion vehicles, generates an increasing disconnection of the local audiences with Indigenous genres, a situation that is illustrated in some Latin American music industries.

In the Latin American economies described in this chapter there is an excessive concentration of investment in large companies. This fact alone works to marginalize local cultural entrepreneurs. In addition, the lack of scale of the capital markets (especially the equity markets) generates barriers to the entry of investment capital to support small and medium enterprises.

It is not altogether surprising that finance for creative production is highly concentrated in government agencies. These, and small seed capital sums provided by multi-task producers themselves (distributors, financiers, etc.), are invested in the production of cultural goods that generally do not reach massive distribution. Both instruments are scarce by nature, and do not generate appropriate industry development incentives; indeed they may create dependency.

The Latin American music industry

The Latin music industry enjoys an average of between 4 and 5 per cent of the music industry sales globally. During the last decade it has experienced an average yearly growth of 4 per cent. During this period the industry has experienced steady growth in units, despite the significant impact of piracy on unit sales and late 1990s currency devaluations on total revenue (CAB 2003b).

There is evidence of strong consumption of local product (Mexico and Venezuela), of regional product (Colombia) and Portuguese product (Brazil) (Figure 3.3). In Brazil, 75 per cent of total domestic music consumption is estimated to be local product; local Colombian consumption is estimated at 46 per cent; and Venezuelan domestic consumption is valued at 35 per cent. There is also high regional Latin American music consumption, with Colombia consuming 45 per cent regional music products, Venezuela 35 per cent and Chile 35 per cent. Considering the popularity of local and regional music throughout Latin America there is potential to strengthen regional consumption and markets for 'Latin music'.

Though some countries possess strong independent production activity, especially in folkloric genres, majors are active in all Latin American countries and account for the lion's share of each local market (Table 3.5).

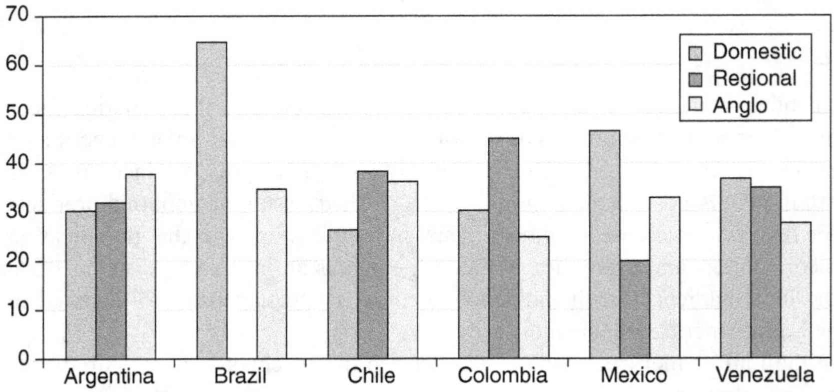

Figure 3.3 Consumption of domestic, regional and English products (source: Yudice, George (1998), 'La Industria de la música en el marco de las integración América Latina-Estados Unidos', seminario *Integracion Economica e Industrias Culturales en América Latina y el Caribe*, Buenos Aires).

Table 3.5 The 'majors' share of the Latin American music market

Market share	*BMG*	*EMI*	*Polygram*	*Sony*	*Warner*	*Indies*
Argentina	20	19	19	24	13	5
Brasil	13	16	20	17	15	19
Chile	18	20	18	24	17	3
Colombia	13	8	11	28	4	36
México	16	13	14	18	13	26
Venezuela	12	9	26	29	8	16
Average %	15	14	18	23	12	18

Source: CAB 2003b.

The film industry

Like the European film industry, the Latin American film sector has suffered from cultural barriers across countries, limited production capabilities, 'art focus' over 'commercial focus', as well as limited distribution and promotion skills and capabilities. The region is characterized not only by small to medium independent markets, but also by low per capita income and volatile economies. It is estimated that in Latin American countries through the 1990s, local film companies received approximately 0.5 per cent per capita public assistance in comparison with approximately 1.8 per cent for the European industry and 5.5 per cent for the US local industry (CAB 2003a).

Financing

The globalization of culture, led by American content and symbols, has had the effect of making cultural entities, practitioners and workers in developing countries more aware of the need for financing and management support. Support alternatives need to take into account the fact that the commercial output of creative production is at most levels uncertain and risks may only be mitigated by achieving critical mass and developing industry structures in which distribution channels 'connect' and help to facilitate supply and demand (Hearn *et al.* 2004). In addition, the distribution of investment between heritage and ongoing cultural industries development is typically biased towards the former, particularly in poorer regions.

As elsewhere the relationship between financing and industry development is unclear. First, to ensure the growth of competitive enterprises, there is a need to focus on getting the right mix between (purely) private support and grant funding. Second, there is the issue of how to execute strategies. From a quick review of the features below, it can be concluded that the solution is somewhere in the middle rather than on the ends.

Emergence of purely private investors Although it would be interesting to see venture capital funds targeting cultural start-ups, such entities act with the incentive to optimize profitability, and will only invest if the investment provides an 'exit path' towards value maximization (Hackett *et al.* 2000). There is also the issue of scale. Venture capitalists will not be attracted to initiatives that do not have a sizeable market potential, or that can transform from interesting niche cultural manifestations to reach larger markets.

Grant funding This is the traditional appeal to the public purse, usually on the basis of cultural worth and national identity. However, it leaves the cultural sector subject to the will of political turns and public capital availability. It also condemns the population to a diet of public culture and creates dependency within the cultural community, obstructing incentives for industry development and self-sustainability. There should be no diminution of public funding; however, it should be investment as much as grant-driven, treat its client base in the most business-like fashion possible, and strategically target key points of the value chain not only production inputs.

The fact that neither capital nor private investment have proved to be suitable funding for creative production makes clear the need and a role for new instruments that would be different in structure and could emerge from private-public partnerships. While public support can contribute to the new instruments' financial resources and a tolerance for investment tenors, private agents would contribute investment discipline, a link to a broader investment community and asset management know-how.

Sources of funding in the region

GRANT/STATE FUNDING

Due to scarce public investment capital available much of the state support has been provided as regulatory incentives and tax breaks. Extensive regulation to support cultural expressions and industries can be found in Latin American countries, particularly in the film and heritage sectors. No significant regulatory support was found in the case of the music industry.

In Chile, the Fondo de Artes y Cultura (FONDART) channels all government economic support to the sector. From its inception in 1992 the organization has financed almost 3,000 projects to the value of US$17 million. The fund is administered by the Ministry of Education and evaluates and selects projects based on quality, budget and viability.

In Colombia, the Ministry of Culture possesses limited resources for investment, most of which are dedicated to heritage preservation. Notwithstanding, an important amount of incentives and measures are targeted at culture and creativity, especially in the area of film. Film ticket pricing is exempt from VAT; Colombian income tax payable by foreigners will be calculated on the basis of 60 per cent of the generated income; no taxes on remittances of proceeds of movie exploitation. In order to encourage investment further, reinvested profits in any of the stages of movie production receive a 50 per cent exemption of income tax. All investments in the preservation of local movie material are 100 per cent deductible from income tax. The law provides various authorizations to the Minister of Culture to give further support to the cultural activity through regulatory changes.

Peru maintains similar film industry support schemes, including income tax exemption for revenue generated from motion picture commercialization (decree 42, 1995), and GST exemption for revenue generated from motion picture exploitation (decree 821, 1996).

In Venezuela 60 per cent of the yearly budget of CNAC (National Autonomous Cinema Centre) is dedicated to local movie production and 100 per cent of any investment in any stage or movie production is tax deductible.

In Argentina 10 per cent of all movie tickets, 10 per cent of all movie sales or rentals and 25 per cent of all income received by the National Radio Broadcasting aggregate funds the 'Motion Picture Fund' administered by the INCAA (National Cinema Institute for Audiovisual Arts). This fund finances production of local films and the functioning of drama and movie schools.

As of writing, no systematic commercial funding models – such as private equity funds and commercial credit lines – have been identified in the region. This type of financing typically does not suit small companies and creative enterprises. However, there are some instances of innovative strategies to build value from a low base.

Case study: distribution of 'Arepa 3000' by Latin World Records (contemporary popular)

Latin World Records (LWR) is a Venezuelan independent record label owned by Samuel Quiroz, a native Salvadorian and ex-investment banker. After more than 20 years in the finance world, Quiroz quit his job and with the support of his partners at Latin World Securities, founded Latin World Entertainment group. Since its inception the label has been characterized by an aggressive production schedule across a range of different genres including tropical, contemporary, pop and rock. The ability of LWR to sustain the scale of activity it has is largely the result of resources Quiroz has been able to marshal from his links and experience in the Venezuelan business and investment community.

After one year of Quiroz heading LWR, Luaka Bop, an American independent record label began looking for a distributor for the Venezuelan fusion band, Amigos Invisibles' (an increasingly popular national band with a unique sound) second album 'Arepa 3000'. One of the 'majors', EMI, had first option to contract though negotiations were not final. Learning of the proposed deal, Quiroz courted Luaka Bop and successfully obtained the distribution deal, although LWR at the time was primarily a small label focused on production and with limited distribution capacity. This was a major hurdle in obtaining the deal and only a firm commitment to purchasing a large number of CD units would convince Luaka's executives of granting LWR an exclusive distribution deal for this record.

Quiroz became acquainted with the forthcoming launch of a new prepaid mobile telephone product by Movilnet, one of the largest mobile operators in Venezuela. Realizing that this product targeted the same youth demographics as 'Arepa 3000', he conceived the idea of bundling the record with the prepaid mobile in a packaged deal. This would be the only way to get a legal copy of the record. Movilnet was fast to catch up on the idea and bought 80,000 units. This allowed Quiroz to secure the purchase of a number of copies quite in excess of Luaka's original sales estimates. A media campaign including TV and radio advertisements featuring the members of the band was launched.

This case illustrates a small indie label making a 'big hit' in their first participation in the distribution business through an innovative scheme. This scheme illustrated innovation: flexibility in the understanding of what the product was (from selling a CD to using it to support the sale of a mobile phone), understanding that 80,000 records at a wholesale price would not represent a major investment for a mobile telephony company, and understanding that rather than selling your product to the retail market you can bring an additional intermediary (the mobile company) to the value chain to strengthen your marketing situation and magnify the distribution impact of your production. Replicating the scheme elsewhere is a matter of identifying when large corporates can use music products (gifts, campaign launches, charity, image campaigns, etc.) in their product strategy.

Conceptually this case shows an alteration of the typical value chain where conventional distribution is bypassed in a form that does not generate retaliation from the channels. This allows for a wide distribution of a record, without losing value for the artist and the producer in the process. The record price is now embedded in the cost structure of the sponsoring company at a cost that only shows production cost (marketing and distribution have been 'camouflaged' in the campaign's cost), in effect eliminating the wide margins charged by distributors.

The value of this case is that regardless of the structure it was business sense and savvy that made it possible. No capital investment from the producer, or from the local record company, was required.

Case study: 'KANKANO Laboratorio Cultural' (contemporary popular)

The Colombian music market is characterized by the presence of all six majors and some independent local activity in the segment of tropical folkloric music. This supply structure has created important gaps in the offering of content and left an important number of artists in the margins of the market. Majors tend to produce artists that can be sold with the least local promotion and marketing effort. These are mainly international artists that reach the public eye through the ever growing effect of the international (mainly American) media which has been paid for by the holding companies of the majors.

To a group of local musicians it was clear that their options within this industry scheme were very limited and that, rather than trying to open a space for themselves in the current structure, the goal should be to define an alternative model in which production and promotion goals could be reached with the least amount of financial resources.

Various discussions and some opportunities (brought up by the landscape of the entertainment industry in Bogotá) helped create an idea that is on its way to consolidating a business model for musicians that require non-mainstream options for the production and distribution of their musical output, either in the form of CDs or live presentations.

'KANKANO Laboratorio Cultural' is one of the only venues in Bogotá dedicated exclusively to the presentation of live music, mainly fusions of folklore and other music genres like jazz, funk, reggae and rock. Rather than conceptualizing the idea as a pub, the owners, Gustavo Salcedo and Mayte Montero, use the place as the promotion and distribution site for high quality musical acts. In addition to having good acoustics (non-existent in other venues) the musicians are able to access recording and rehearsing space during the day.

Currently KANKANO operates in a 300 square metre site in the north of Bogotá, with capacity to host up to 400 people in one evening. Attendance has averaged 60 per cent to 70 per cent since the venue opened in January 2003.

As a business model KANKANO envisions the possibility of consolidating an independent record label that can be distributed 'in situ' or through mainstream distribution channels.[7] The natural next steps from its core production and promotion activities are artist development capabilities (i.e. tour support) and publishing. The fact that CD distribution will be stronger in Bogotá has made the owners think about the possibility of opening other venues in different parts of the country in the medium term. Opening similar venues (or franchising this concept) in other areas allows the possibility of tapping an important revenue source: tourism. An entertainment venue focused on high quality local acts could be an interesting tourist attraction in places like Cartagena or Santa Martha, two Colombian cities of major local and international tourist affluence.

This case study highlights that the project is the result of the initiative of artists who identified a trend towards an increasing relevance of the 'live act' in an environment where piracy allows cheap ownership of music products.

Indigenous Australian visual art

Introduction

The Indigenous Australian context is not a developing country context. However, the isolated, impoverished Third World environment in which Aboriginal and Torres Strait Islander art has been produced since the 1970s (Myers 2002; Altman *et al.* 2002) does strike many correlations with developing country contexts. Indeed, the lessons to be learned from the success of Indigenous Australian art exports have direct relevance to developing country contexts. Most importantly in the context of this study, despite the Third World conditions in which this art is produced, Indigenous Australian visual art has become an internationally renowned and economically significant Australian cultural export – arguably, one of Australia's most significant exports ever. This international success has largely occurred outside of public support and public subsidy frameworks; it has been driven by individual actors and it has drawn upon finance from private, philanthropic and foundational sources. In the seminal study *Painting Culture*, Myers (2002) illustrates that public subsidy and support mechanisms, whilst sustaining production in the 1970s, largely limited the commercial flow of Indigenous Australian art to 'uninterested ' domestic markets.

Over the space of three decades, Indigenous Australian art has become an industry reportedly worth between AU$100 million and 300 million (Altman *et al.* 2002: 3). It is estimated that there are 5,000 artists and painters working in the industry, making up between 25 and 50 per cent of total working Australian visual artists. This is a remarkable figure considering that the Indigenous population makes up approximately 2 per cent of the Australian population. In 1994 an Australia Council-funded study found that the income generated from *all* Indigenous Australian creative activities was estimated at $720 million. Visual artists surveyed in the Council report contributed $129 million to the economy – $66 million from their principal artistic occupation and a further $63 million from 'other arts work' (quoted in Langsam 1997). Putting these figures in perspective, the Indigenous Australian 'arts and crafts sector' total was about the same size as the bauxite ($774 million in 1992–1993, ABS) or copper ($875 million) industries and massively more important than uranium mining, valued at $193 million for 1993–1994 (Langsam 1997). However, it is important to note that collecting accurate figures for the value of Indigenous Australian art is difficult as much is produced in isolated communities and records are unreliable.

For Indigenous people in Australia, and elsewhere in developing countries, the raw material of content creation is culture and knowledge. Combined with the creative talent of the artist, the performer and the technician, this becomes a unique and distinctive intellectual property that finds its way into several markets (domestic – Indigenous and non-Indigenous, tourist and international) of which the most profitable is the elite international art or 'high art' market. The high end sale of Indigenous painting represents the meeting of Third World producer and First World art patron and connoisseur. Moreover, a major feature of indigenous visual arts is that the majority of the output is produced in remote parts of northern and central Australia. The production and sale of arts and crafts constitute the only private sector economic activity in some communities.

The circulation and delivery of Indigenous art characterize a value chain where cultural intermediaries play a key role, often drawing large profits from their activity (Table 3.6). Indigenous artists rarely negotiate directly with commercial galleries or retail outlets for the sale of their work. Their work is handled by Indigenous art centres or cooperatives. These organizations are staffed by art coordinators who operate as both commercial and cultural mediators between producers and mainly non-Indigenous procurers of Indigenous art. Commercial galleries and retail outlets also have a mediating role, but they rarely have direct contact with producers.

The Indigenous creative industries, despite their fragility, resemble mainstream creative industries, insofar as they are generally characterized by an over-

Table 3.6 Indigenous creative industries value chain

Content creation/origination	Intellectual property: the culture and knowledge of the Indigenous people of Australia and its expression in the form of oral history, craft, performance, writing, music and song design, etc.
Production and incubation	The process by which this intellectual property is transformed into products and services, including support mechanisms and resources, creative spaces, production infrastructure, manufacturing inputs, engineering, etc.
Circulation	The means by which products and services are promoted to retailers and advertised to the consuming public. This includes various media, the role of managers, agents, databases, mailing lists and web sites.
Delivery mechanisms	The point of sale or distribution of products and services
Current and potential markets	The market for Indigenous creative practice. This varies across practice. For example, the market (audience) for story tellers and ceremonial performance is limited whereas the market for broadcasting is consistent. The four principal markets are government services, international tourism, domestic, and the Indigenous market.

Source: Keane and Hartley, 2001.

supply of content providers (Caves 2000) and dependent satellite producers clustered around profitable links in the chain, notably distribution.

The following case study examines the international profile of Indigenous dot (acrylic) paintings and the relationship between its position within elite markets and finance. This account is not exhaustive and, although it makes historical references, is not an attempt at historical analysis of the developments leading to the establishment of an internationally successful export industry. It highlights the primary developments with an emphasis on drawing out the modes of finance involved in ensuring the success of this industry.

Box 3.1 Emerging indigenous creative enterprises

Indigenous creative industries are one of the least recognized but most vibrant and innovative sectors in Australia. In many instances, these creative enterprises thrive from minimal public funding and often community and local business support. The case of Indigenous 'high art' is just one example of the successful development of innovative, sustainable Indigenous Australian creative industries. Some examples include:

Cyber Dreaming: An innovative multimedia firm based in Brisbane. Web site: www.cyberdreaming.com/

Murri Radio: An Indigenous-operated country music community radio station based in Brisbane. It receives some public funding but receives 50 per cent of its funding from commercial sponsorship. It provides national niche programming (country music and Indigenous broadcasting) and has become the most successful community broadcaster in Australia. The station has ambitions to become self-funded in 3–5 years (Keane and Hartley 2001). Web site: 4aaa.org.au/

Goolarri Media Enterprises: Based in Broome, Goolarri is a cluster of integrated media enterprises – radio, television, film and television production services, recording facilities, events management and technical services – that links 16 Indigenous media groups throughout Northwest Australia and community organizations developing a range of media products for popular and mainstream markets. Goolarri can be characterized as an entrepreneurial management team utilizing local knowledge to create a commercializable media brand and generating local content that embraces respect for tradition. Web site: www.gme.com.au/

Bangarra Dance Theatre: Situated in New South Wales, Bangarra Dance Theatre is an internationally successful dance and performance company that combines Indigenous Australian tradition with popular contemporary dance styles. The company has now toured approximately 18 countries, undertaken extensive domestic tours and released a multimedia CD-Rom in collaboration with Australia's largest Telco. Web site: ww.bangarra.com.au/home.html

Case study: the internationalization of Indigenous Australian acrylic painting

THE BEGINNINGS

Until 40 years ago the Indigenous people known as the Pintupi lived in Australia's Western Desert without any involvement in the 'cash economy'. The Pintupi people, like many other Aboriginal groups, were brought in from the desert by the government during the 1950s and 1960s and settled on a government reserve at Papunya, north-west of Alice Springs (Allan 2001). It was here, as one commentator has noted, in the 'oppressive, desolate and poverty-stricken conditions … with one-sixth of residents dying of treatable disease between 1961–1966' (Allan 2001) that the Papunya Tula Art movement emerged during the1970s giving birth to contemporary Indigenous Australian acrylic 'high art',[8] part of an industry that is now Australia's most famous art export.

A school teacher posted at Papunya, Geoffrey Bardon, was an important figure in the early development of Aboriginal art. Before Bardon's arrival, Western Desert art was largely confined to Aboriginal ceremonial practices and some small-scale tourist sales (Allan 2001). Bardon was responsible for encouraging Indigenous Australians to express their traditional motifs and dreamtime stories through painting. In 1971 he submitted several acrylic works to the Alice Springs Caltex Art competition. The competition resulted in $1,300 in cash sales. Bardon later established an artist's cooperative at Papunya and in 1972 he helped establish the Papunya Tula Artists limited liability company. After this initial success, over 600 paintings and 300 smaller works were produced over the next 18 months (Allan 2001).

POLICY AND THE DEVELOPMENT OF A MARKET

From 1973–1975, Papunya Tula art production increased. The cash market, however, was still small scale and largely informal. Arts advisers visited painting communities periodically to pay artists for completed paintings and to commission new ones. There were small-scale exhibitions and modest sales to museums and art galleries in the Northern Territory, but the survival of the Papunya Tula art collective was largely the result of government action.

The principal backers of Aboriginal acrylic arts throughout the 1970s were two government bodies: the Aboriginal Arts Board and Aboriginal Arts and Crafts Pty Ltd. Whilst these two bodies had initial success in developing a market for Aboriginal art, according to Myers (2002: 134), 'there was a tremendous problem in maintaining a viable stream of circulation between artists desire to paint and scarce demand'.

A major policy problem that emerged was the purchasing procedure of Aboriginal Arts and Crafts. The company was developed to stabilize an income flow, foster production, increase employment and increase economic returns for artists. The company purchased paintings from artists, and acted as a wholesaler selling artworks to metropolitan retail outlets. The company paid for artwork at the point-of-sale, with the respective artist receiving payment immediately, not on consignment as was the procedure of most commercial galleries. The company failed to match sales with production rate, resulting in stock saturation, and the exhaustion of the company's funds. Consequently, no new paintings could be purchased, leading to prolonged delays between the sale of artworks and cash flow back into art collectives. Additionally, without start-up capital arts advisers – who are important intermediaries between artists and the market – were unable to buy collections for potential exhibitions.

In response, Aboriginal Arts and Crafts developed a 60-day system, where the art work would be held for 60 days, allowing time for artwork to be sold before a payment was made to the artist. However, this system also failed with artists wanting immediate payment in exchange for their work. Soon artists and advisers began selling artwork to sources outside of the company. Private collectors were later to become important buyers.

Grants from the Aboriginal Arts Board largely kept the Papunya Tula cooperative operational during the 1970s with its funds purchasing stockpiled paintings for museums and international 'cultural preservation' exhibitions (Myers 2002: 143).

The early stages of this market can be categorized as a *grants market.* Papunya Tula and other art collectives all competed for and became reliant upon limited funds from Aboriginal Arts and Crafts and the Aboriginal Arts Board. At the same time the government was attempting to develop the domestic 'uninterested market', namely, the broad population who had little interest in Aboriginal art. As Myers (2002) has argued, public support for the development of a market during this period can be characterized as a 'welfare' approach (135). Financial support was directed at the market without support directly going to producers in the form of fellowships or income support schemes, and was viewed as a 'culturally appropriate strategy for Aboriginal producers' (135).

During the early 1980s government policy shifted from a focus on cultural preservation to an emphasis on the development of an Aboriginal 'arts and crafts' industry: a broad term generally encompassing visual arts, souvenirs, crafts and performing arts. With this policy shift a more structured 'art world' emerged, generating increased journalistic attention, a growth in institutional recognition and acquisition and an expansion of retail galleries, collecting and curatorship (Myers 2002: 186). This policy rearticulation with a focus on 'economic enterprise' marked a concerted shift away from public subsidy (137). It was during this period of policy restructuring and industry development that the international success and development of international markets for Aboriginal 'high art' occurred, largely outside of public funding mechanisms.

THE 1988 DREAMINGS EXHIBITION IN NEW YORK

The 1988 Asia Society exhibition, *Dreamings: The Art of Aboriginal Australia*, held in New York from 6–31 October, was instrumental in the achievement of international critical acclaim and recognition and the initiation of export markets for Indigenous dot-art. The exhibition drew an attendance of 27,000 people, becoming the most successful event ever to be held at the Asia Society. It elevated Aboriginal art from being 'ethnographic art'(anthropological artefacts) to internationally renowned 'high art' sought after by elite up-scale galleries and collectors.

The *Dreamings* exhibition is important within the context of this study. First, the exhibition is an exemplary case of the successful production of cultural products for a *specific targeted audience*. The organizers of this exhibition carefully selected the venue. At the time the Asia Society galleries were important in the mediation of culture and commerce relations between the USA and Asia, the art was displayed in ways that were new according to 'high art' styles, and was displayed in renowned galleries rather than in museums as it had been in the past (Myers 2002). As Myers notes the organizers of the exhibition 'constructed an Aboriginal art that ... was always understood partly as being directed to an American audience' (244).

The financing of this event is indicative of the move towards new private partnerships. The financing is illustrative of the successful utilization of informal networks of people and institutions. The organizers of the event sought to raise finance through private sources drawn from the Asia Society's business network. The exploitation of the Asia Society's structure was important as it 'worked through its trustees and its other connections' including 'hired consultants who could make connections to corporations' (Myers 2002: 243). The organizers attempted to obtain finance through Australian corporations working in the USA and via influential and wealthy Australians with an interest in art living in the USA. The strategy was directed at informal people connections and elite networks (that is, the connections exhibition organizers had with various elites) and through the utilization of the Asia Society's private consultants.

While financial support for the event failed to eventuate from the major Australian and corporate funding sources, finance eventually did arrive from other sources. It could be argued that the exhibition discovered US financial interest in Aboriginal art. The exhibition received funding from the National Endowment for the Humanities,[9] and through associates of the Asia Society galleries network. In addition, the exhibition received funding from private/corporate sources such as the Andrew Mellon Foundation, the Starr Foundation and Westpac Banking Corporation.

THE NEW YORK MARKET, PRIVATE COLLECTORS AND PHILANTHROPY

While there is now a large number of public funding and grant schemes available for Aboriginal artists and arts enterprises through the Australia Council for the Arts,[10] international enthusiasm and most notably the New York market is largely driving demand, production and the development of the high end of the Aboriginal arts industry.

In July 2003 Sotheby's (an important auction house for the sale of Indigenous Australian art) in New York sold 560 Aboriginal art works at a total of AU$7.5

million (Cho 2004). Sotheby's percentage of international Indigenous Australian art sales has risen from 20 per cent in 1996 to 70 per cent in 2003 (Reid 2003). This market, and the international markets for Indigenous Australian art more generally, is characterized by a growing number of very serious collectors and a large number of occasional buyers (Reid 2003). The top end of the New York market is characterized by lower demand but higher returns for artists and the lower end is characterized by higher demand but lower value.

New York art galleries have become important purchasers of Indigenous Australian art. Since the *Dreamings* exhibition in 1988 there has been a dramatic rise in the number of up-market galleries specializing in Indigenous Australian art and general galleries that have substantial sections dedicated to Indigenous Australian art. There are now direct linkages between up-scale galleries and 'talented artists' and cooperatives. Galleries are reported to foster and encourage artists to produce works either specifically for their galleries or to be auctioned at Sotheby's, New York (Reid 2003).

Private collectors and philanthropy have become another significant mode of finance for the production of Indigenous Australian art. A primary example of this is through the consideration of the private collection of 89-year-old Florida billionaire, John W. Kluge. Kluge has amassed one of the largest collections of Indigenous Australian art outside of Australia, worth US$5 million in 1997 (and now estimated to be worth twice as much), containing 1,600 works from between the 1940s and 1990s. Kluge reportedly 'fell in love with Australian Aboriginal art' after seeing the *Dreamings* exhibition in New York in 1988 (Genocchio 2004). He bought his first pieces of Indigenous Australian art in 1988 – a total of 130 paintings for $500,000. The money from this sale was reportedly used by the 'impoverished reservation style community of some 700 people' to build an arts centre to contribute to the development of the region's art communities (Genocchio 2004). He also commissioned many pieces from individual artists and art collectives providing them with sources of income and investment. In 1996, arts agents hired by Kluge reportedly injected AU$500,000 into several Aboriginal arts communities in Northern and Western Australia over a period of two years.

It is important to note that whilst private and philanthropic streams of finance have potential for arts and creative industries development, more broadly they also create threats for individual producers. In the Indigenous Australian art context, private collectors, advisers and curators have been largely responsible for the exploitation of Aboriginal and Torres Strait Islander artists over the last three decades, with many artists not seeing any revenue from artworks worth thousands and in some cases hundreds of thousands of dollars. This also raises the issue of a need for appropriate copyright laws.

Conclusion

We have examined modes of financing creative industries in three different regions: China, Latin America and Indigenous Australia. While it is apparent that the term 'creative industries' has yet to be widely embraced, it is also evident that culture is increasingly used as a resource for development. In these countries, moreover, creative industries are still predominantly viewed as having a high association with traditional or national culture, a characteristic that has implications for future development in these locations. This conclusion is divided into three sections: emerging trends and issues, barriers and modes of finance, and lessons learnt from the case studies.

The ultimate question, however, is whether or not creative industries in developing countries can reach a level where they can compete in the global marketplace.

Emerging trends and issues

The role of culture in development is currently being reassessed. The issue we have canvassed here is not about access, but growing capacity and reforming financial mechanisms. Events such as the dot.com crash and financial crises in Latin America and Asia have reshaped expectations and reformed practices. Structural adjustments imposed by the IMF and the World Bank on developing countries may have had little direct influence on the cultural sector, but culture's increasing prominence as a contributor to GDP and national development means that flow-on effects have been registered: new management strategies and new business models have been taken up.

Creative industries are by nature risky business. Traditional industrial models cannot be imposed upon these industries. An interesting emerging trend is the development of safeguards and specific parameters as a feature of creative industries financing and risk management. Although these safeguards vary, they are designed to cater for the intangible nature of creative assets and outputs, to manage risk and to ensure the robustness of business models.

While it is important that national economic agendas recognize the intangible attributes and value of cultural assets, there is also a need to understand how traditional cultural segments are increasingly influenced by the marketplace. Culture has become a significant economic force in its own right and is beginning to target niche markets.

Developing the competitive advantage of creative industries is essential to the growth of export markets. Creative industries in developing countries may struggle to compete in international markets on a national level, but targeted development at a firm level may produce internationally competitive firms that in turn generate flow-on value for the broader economy. It is useful to think of competitive advantage in terms of a national innovation system. The competitiveness of creative industries can be optimized on a number of different levels: the level of the firm, the level of the sector, the regional level or a national level (see QUT *et al.* 2003). In this sense the growth of creative industries needs to be assessed from the point of view of innovation incentive structures. Such incentives can come from the state in the form of direct industry assistance, or in an enabling sense, by providing incentives to middle players in the value chain. To illustrate this need to fix the 'middle factors' to ensure development, the competitiveness of the Chinese film and music industries is hampered by the role of pirates who are not cultural intermediaries in the true sense and could be more gainfully employed in other areas of the economy.

Banking on Culture illustrates that while finance is essential for creative industries development, finance cannot be considered in isolation of other inherently connected issues. Once again this relates to the unique nature of the creative industries. As well as finance, creative enterprises require specialized business support, marketing, management development, attention to innovation, copyright protection and rights management.

The majority of finance is directed towards the content creation and production stages of the value chain. However, emphasis needs to be directed towards segments of the value chain that inhibit growth and information flows. This may – or may not – be the creation stage. As the majority of creative industries in developing countries emanate from deeply rooted cultural traditions, the impediments are not related so much to entry or production, but rather the packaging, marketing and distribution of creative products. For instance, financial assistance or incentive could be directed at the distribution platform so as to support local content, which in turn provides a showcase. It is also noted that in many sectors regulatory bottlenecks, as well as country-specific political and cultural barriers, act as primary barriers to development.

Financing is closely linked to a need for an awareness of *types* and *potential* markets for export. From an economic development perspective, cultural specificity works against the capacity for products from these regions to enter into mainstream global markets, with the exception being breakthrough cultural markets (world music, art-house cinema) and culturally proximate markets (e.g. Spanish- or Chinese-speaking markets). In terms of international export potential (in English- or French-speaking locations for instance), creative products from developing countries are often sought after by educated elites, who may pay higher prices but whose consumption is more symbolic than routine. In other instances there is potential for the development of 'regional' or Diaspora markets. In Latin America, for example, there is potential for the development and strengthening of markets throughout 'culturally proximate' neighbouring countries.

Barriers and modes of finance

A number of primary finance trends emerge from this study. First, there is no one specific creative industries finance model being used across the regions examined, but rather a multitude of different modes of finance being used and adapted according to the unique social, cultural, political and economic contexts in which respective creative enterprises operate. Second, institutional and informal people networks are extremely important in levering financial support and developing connections to financial sources. Third, while most modes of finance are aimed at the creation and production stages of the value chain, private partnerships (e.g. small local enterprises that form alliances with larger and sometimes international companies) rather than direct capital investment are becoming an important means in overcoming distribution and other market barriers. Strategic alliances with service providers, with high profile 'branded' media companies and with distributors are becoming a way forward for smaller innovative businesses. In this sense investment is counted not purely in monetary terms but in the value of untraded interdependencies such as skills, know-how, branding, etc. Further, there is recognition that cultural workers are often linked into peer networks that circulate information. Cultural workers increasingly are inheriting a role as service providers in the new economy. Business seeks out their skills to infuse creative inputs into non-creative fields, such as government, education and business promotion.

Alarmingly, but not unsurprisingly, large-scale capital investment is low. Because of the flexibility of the micro-finance model, the type of finance it delivers and the inherent safeguard features it contains, micro-finance offers a viable model to kick-start ideas and develop micro-enterprises to a level where they can obtain funding from other public or commercial sources. However, this mode of finance is only suitable for limited creative sectors. Larger commercial sectors require greater levels of capital investment and venture capital.

While new modes of finance are emerging, in certain sectors public subsidy still remains the primary form of finance. Public support mechanisms may still have a role to play in the future, however, they will need to re-focus on specific segments of the value chain where barriers stifle development. New technologies, and in particular partnerships with technology firms (ISPs, telco's, etc.), also provide a new avenue to enter global markets and to overcome distribution barriers. In this context countries that have networked information infrastructures in place have a considerable advantage.

Case studies

China

China illustrates the shift from a state-centred financing regime to a mixed financing model with the rise of new private partnerships and innovative financing arrangements. This mixed financing model draws upon a number of modes of finance including public tax concessions at one end (remnants of a state-centred model) and private direct investment, technological enabled private online partnerships, collaboration between art and real-estate, and philanthropic investment. China also illustrates the role of informal mechanisms in getting product into the marketplace. Irregular modes of production and distribution both inhibit and enable the flow of finance with creative industries.

Latin America

The Latin American case study illustrates some similar themes. Here reliance on foreign finance has led to weaknesses in the value chain. Most investment incentive schemes are directed towards foreign entities. However, innovative private partnerships (more the exception than the rule) are enabling new modes of distribution and creating synergy. Once again informal people networks play an important role in development, such as where a creator/producer is able to draw upon the institutional networks of another agent/intermediary.

Indigenous Australia

This case study exemplifies that a high-growth, high-economic value, export-orientated industry *can* emerge from an impoverished, isolated and initially undeveloped context. Several key issues emerge from this case study with direct relevance to the development of niche international markets and the raising of new private financial sources. Individual actors can successfully target and adapt 'traditional elite' cultural forms (without losing cultural uniqueness of integrity) to appeal to the tastes of a specific international audience and market. The mobilization and utilization of informal people networks can be a successful method of establishing an international network with linkages to important financial sources. The leverage of institutional networks with formal (business partnerships and international offices) or informal international networks (specialist consultants or informal people networks) can be an important means of obtaining finance and establishing financial streams. Philanthropic, foundational and private investment can be important financial sources for the production and distribution of 'traditional elite' art. Finally, these modes of finance are also potentially important in establishing international finance streams and international markets.

Notes

1 The authors are members of the Creative Industries Research and Applications Centre (CIRAC) Queensland University of Technology.

2 The Grameen Bank is the most renowned micro-finance bank in the world. It was established in Bangladesh 25 years ago and has now invested $1 billion primarily in the form of small denomination loans of about $30. The primary mode of finance is through peer group systems that lead to high repayment rates.

3 Banco Sol is a micro-finance institution, established in 1992 and operating in Latin America and the Caribbean. BancoSol provide several modes of micro-finance 'based on group guarantees, sequential lending, a close relationship with the client, simple and speedy procedures'. Available: www.mixmarket.org.

4 PlaNET Finance is an international NGO that fosters and acts as an umbrella organization for an international network of micro-finance institutions.

5 'Credit Delivery System' [Online]. Available: www.grameen-info.org/bank/cds.html [accessed 08/03/2004].

6 'General Institutional and Legal Data'. Available: www.mixmarket.org. [Accessed: 08/03/2004].

7 The fact that the distribution in the Colombian market is not integrated with production (not that it is prohibited) and is 100 per cent national brings interesting opportunities for independent producers.

8 Papunya Tula art is most famously known for the portrayal of traditional motifs in the form of acrylic 'dot' paintings.

9 NEH is an independent grant-making agency of the US government dedicated to supporting research, education, preservation and public programmes in the humanities.
10 See www.ozco.gov.au/boards/atsia/ [accessed 23/03/2004].

References

Allan, Susan (2001) *Papunya Tula: The birthplace of contemporary Australian Aboriginal Art*, World Socialist Web Site, published by International Committee of the Fourth International.

Altman, J.C., Hunter, B.H., Ward, S. and Wright, F. (2002) *Some competition and consumer issues in the indigenous visual arts industry*, no. 235, Discussion paper, Centre for Aboriginal Economic Policy Research.

Ashton, Chris (2002) *China: Opportunities in the Business of Sport*, London: SportBusiness Group Ltd.

Bergman, David (2004) 'From creativity to productivity', EDANZ Conference, Wellington, March 15–16.

Convenio Andres Bello (CAB) (2003a) *Impacto del Sector Cinematográfico sobre la economía colombiana: situación actual y perspectivas*, Bogota: CAB.

Convenio Andres Bello (CAB) (2003b) *Impacto del Sector Fonográfico en sobre la economía colombiana*, Bogota: CAB.

Caves, R. (2000) *Creative Industries: contracts between art and commerce*, Cambridge, Mass: Harvard University Press.

Chin, Saik Yoon, *Digital Review of Asia-Pacific (2003/4)*, Asia Pacific Development Programme, United Nations Development Programme, Penang: Southbound.

Cho, Ines (2004) 'Aboriginal Art: a modern primitivism', *Joins.com*, Dow Jones & Reuters, 29 January.

Chu, Yingchi (2002) 'The consumption of cinema in contemporary China', in S.H. Donald, M. Keane and Yin Hong (eds), *Media in China: Consumption, Content, and Crisis*, London: RoutledgeCurzon.

Collier, Andrew (2003) 'Hongkong Land to convert ageing factory into arts venue' *South China Morning Post*, 24 September.

Cunningham, S. and Sinclair, J. (2001) *Floating Lives: The Media and Asian Diasporas* Lanham: Rowman & Littlefield.

Curran, James, and Park, Myung-Jin (2000) *De-Westernizing Media Studies*, London: Routledge.

Cutler & Company. (2002) *Producing Digital Content: A consultancy to examine and advance the understanding of the production of digital content*, Department of Communications, Information Technology and the Arts: Canberra.

de Kloet, Jeroen (2002) 'Rock in a hard place: Commercial fantasies in China's music industry', in S.H. Donald, M. Keane and Yin Hong (eds), *Media in China: Consumption, Content & Crisis*, London: RoutledgeCurzon.

Fong, Mei (2003) 'Home turf advantage', *Far Eastern Economic Review*, 6 November.

Genocchio, Benjamin (2004) 'An artist bounty from the Australian wilderness', *The New York Times*, 7 March.

Gauthier, Maria Ochoa and Yudice, George (2002) 'The Latin American Music Industry in an Era of Crisis', November, Paper prepared for *The Global Alliance for Cultural Diversity*, Paris: UNESCO.

Hackett, Keith, Ramsden, Peter, Sattar, Danyal and Guene, Christophe (2000) *Banking on Culture: New Financial Instruments for expanding the cultural sector in Europe:*

Final Report, European Commission, Banking on Culture Partners, The Arts Council of England and the Gulbenkian Foundation.

Hearn, Greg, Cunningham, Stuart and Ordonez, Diego (2004) 'Commercialisation of knowledge in universities: the case of the creative industries', *Prometheus*, 22, 2: 189–200.

Hillman-Chartrand, H. and McCaughey, C. (1989) 'The arm's length principle and the arts: an international perspective – past, present and future', in Who's to Pay for the Arts? The International Search for Models of Support, M. Cummings and J.M.D. Schuster (eds), American Council for the Arts Books.

Jopson, Debra (2003) 'Two worlds, one mission', *The Sydney Morning Herald*, 2 August.

Keane, Michael (2002) 'Facing off on the final frontier: the WTO and the re-branding of China's national champions', *Media International Australia*, 105: 130–147.

Keane, Michael (2004) 'Brave new world: China's creative vision', *International Journal of Cultural Policy*, 10, 3: 265–279.

Keane, Michael and Donald, Stephanie H. (2002) 'Responses to crisis: convergence, content industries, and media governance', in S.H. Donald, M. Keane and Yin Hong (eds), *Media in China: Consumption, Content & Crisis*, London: RoutledgeCurzon.

Keane, Michael and Hartley, John (2001) *From ceremony to CD Rom: Indigenous Creative Industries in Brisbane*, Brisbane: CIRAC.

Keane, Michael, Moran, Albert and Ryan, Mark (2003) *Audiovisual works, TV formats and multiple markets*, Australian UNESCO Orbicom Working papers in Communications, No. 1, Brisbane: Griffith University.

Kim, Mi Hui (2002) 'Korean Netizens invest in local pix – homegrown product nabs more than 40% of B.O.', *Variety*, 2 Jan.

Kraus, Richard (1995) 'China's artists between plan and market', in D. Davis, R. Kraus, B. Naughton and E.J. Perry (eds), *Urban Spaces in Contemporary China: the Potential for Autonomy and Community in Post-Mao China*, Cambridge, Mass: Woodrow Wilson Center Press.

Kraus, Richard (2004) *The Party and the Arty in China: the New Politics of Culture*, Lanham: Rowman & Littlefield.

Langsam, David (1997) 'Aboriginal art – Australia's $100 million hidden industry'. Available: ourworld.compuserve.com/homepages/dingonet/aborigin.htm [accessed: 12/03/2004].

Luo Liyuan and Zhao Mulan (2003) 'Knowledge industries in Beijing', in Bhajan Grewal, Lan Xue, Peter Sheehan and Fiona Sun (eds), *China's Future in the Knowledge Economy*, Victoria University and Tsinghua University Press, pp. 326–333.

McGuire, Paul B. and Conroy, John D. (2000) *The Microfinance Phenomenon*, Brisbane: The Foundation for Development Cooperation.

Ministry of Culture (2003) 'Enterprise, Innovation Forum International'. Available: www.eifi.com.cn/gaofengzixun/wenhacy/whcy.htm [accessed: 24/03/2004].

Myers, Fred R. (2002) *Painting Culture: The Making of an Aboriginal High Art*, Durham: Duke University Press.

Nationwide News Pty Limited (2003) 'Struck by the beauty of Aboriginal Art', *Dow Jones & Reuters*, 3 December.

Nazirwan, Mohamad (2003) *The Way Forward: Future Direction and Strategies for Building a Sustainable Microfinance*, Canberra: The Commonwealth of Australia (AusAID).

O'Regan, Tom (2001) *Cultural Policy: Rejuvenate or Wither?* Griffith University, Professorial Lecture, Brisbane: Australian Key Centre for Cultural and Media Policy.

Porter, Michael (2000) 'Attitudes, values, beliefs, and the micro-economics of prosperity', in L. Harrison and S. Huntingdon (eds), *Culture Matters: How Values Shape Human Progress*, New York: Basic Books.

Preston, Paschal (2001) *Reshaping Communications: Technology, Information and Social Change*, London: Sage Publications.

Queensland University of Technology (QUT), Creative Industries Research and Applications Centre (CIRAC) and Cutler & Company (2003) *Research and Innovation Systems in the Production of Digital Content: Report for the National Office for the Information Economy*, Canberra: National Office for the Information Economy, Canberra.

Reid, Michael (2003) 'Aboriginal artworks set the standard', *The Australian*, 13 August.

Ryan, Bill (1992) *Making Capital From Culture: the Corporate Form of Capitalist Cultural Production*, Berlin: Walter de Gruyter.

Sachs, Jeffrey (2000) Notes on a New Sociology of Economic development', in L. Harrison and S. Huntingdon (eds), *Culture Matters: How Values Shape Human Progress*, New York: Basic Books.

Storper, Michael (1997) *The Regional World: Territorial Development in a Global Economy*, New York: Guilford University Press.

Throsby, David (2001) *Economics and Culture*, Cambridge University Press, Cambridge.

Throsby, David (2002) 'The Music Industry in the New Millenium: Global and Local Perspectives', October, Paper prepared for *The Global Alliance for Cultural Diversity*, Paris: UNESCO.

UNCTAD (2003) *Trade and Development Report 2003: Overview*, Geneva: UNCTAD.

UNCTAD (2004) *Creative Industries and Development: UNCTAD XI High-Level Panel on Creative Industries and Development*, February, UNCTAD, Geneva.

Wang, Jiaxin and Song, Wenyu (2004) *The Blue Book of China's Culture: The Development Report of China's Cultural Industry*, Beijing: Social Sciences Documentation Publishing house.

Yi, Jixiong (2000) *Innovation Theory (Chuangxin lun)*, Hefei:Anhui: Arts Publishing Company.

Yoon, Sun-kyung (2001) 'Swept up on a wave', *Far Eastern Economic Review*, 18 October.

Yudice, George (1998) 'La Industria de la música en el marco de la integración América Latina-Estados Unidos', seminario *Integracion Economica e Industrias Culturales en América Latina y el Caribe*, Buenos Aires.

Yudice, George (2003) *The Expediency of Culture: Uses of Culture in the Global Era*, Durham: Duke University Press.

Yusuf, Shahid and Nabeshima, Kaoru (2004) 'Urban development needs creativity: how creative industries can affect urban areas', World Bank. Available: www1.worldbank.org/devoutreach/article.asp?id=221 [accessed: 12/03/2004].

4 Film culture and industry in Burkina Faso

Teresa Hoefert de Turégano

At the Cannes International Film Festival 2005, Pierre Yameogo's latest film *Delwendé* was selected for the prestigious "Un certain regard" section. Yameogo is one of Burkina Faso's top film directors, and this is not the first time a film by a Burkinabè has been programmed at Cannes. Idrissa Ouedraogo brought global attention to Burkina Faso when his film *Yaaba* was selected for official competition and won the *Prix de la Critique* in 1989 and then again in 1990 when his film *Tilaï* won the prestigious *Grand Prix du Jury*. In 1997 *Buud-Yam* by Gaston Kaboré was programmed at Cannes. Kaboré is one of the most important film directors from Burkina Faso and a predominant personality of African cinema. In 2002 the festival selected three films made by African directors, *Abouna, notre père* by Mahamat Saleh Haroun (Chad), *Heremakono* by Abderrahmane Sissako (Mauritania/Mali) and *Kabala* by Assane Kouyaté (Mali). In 2004 *Moolaadé* by Ousmane Sembene (Senegal) won the prize in "Un certain regard," and new, younger generation directors are also emerging and gaining international recognition. In fact, almost every year since 1966 when *La noire de ...* by Ousmane Sembene was shown African films have been in the official festival programme. In spite of this impressive history it is still problematic to speak of a film industry per se in Burkina Faso or even of a regional film industry in French-speaking sub-Saharan Africa.

For many people, Burkina Faso and its neighbours like Mali, Chad and Senegal are only known as being least developed countries (LDC) and any of their more positive attributes are overlooked. The films made in Burkina Faso and its French-speaking neighbours compete with the world's top directors in international film festivals. This production is partially a result of certain aid mechanisms in Europe accessible by filmmakers from developing countries. It is clear that there is real potential for growth in the film and audiovisual sector. One of the most obvious reasons attesting to this potential is the existing production, so often achieved in spite of persistent precariousness, but which is already an indicator of what is possible. There is no shortage of stories to tell and there is an expertise of storytelling in various media; there is an enormous necessity for new African images to be circulated internationally and the desire thereof locally; there are talents in acting, in music, in costume-making, in directing and so forth. And it is only through doing more productions that new talent and skills will emerge.

The idea of helping develop the film and audiovisual sectors in developing countries is not a new phenomenon, certainly not in sub-Saharan Africa. European countries, most notably France, have been implementing policies to help develop the film sector for over 40 years. Some aspects of these policies have worked and others have not, because after all this time there is still no viable film industry in the sub-Saharan French-speaking region. In contrast, in neighbouring Nigeria where the historical process of the country evolved differently, there is a profitable video film industry today. This Nigerian industry as such is perhaps better seen as having some inspirational reference as opposed to the model to follow, for its development is also problematic, with profit-seeking as the apotheosis and video having the value of a disposable razor. I will return to this issue below. It is also worth pointing out some of the new global interest given to developing the film and audiovisual sectors in various regions of the world. An example of how the sector is being taken very seriously for its economic growth potential is the recent loan of $20 million granted by the International Finance Corporation (World Bank Group) for a private Cinema Park in Russia.

The notion of the potential of a film and audiovisual sector in Burkina Faso and sub-Saharan Africa as a veritable mechanism of economic growth inevitably resituates the role of culture onto the complex realm of culture as a resource or as it is so often referred to now, as "content." As "culture" is reconfigured in this perspective it is crucial to remain attentive to how it is instrumentalised in accordance with multiple economic and political imperatives. This reconfiguration of culture also occasions new modifications in the respective relationship it has to the consumer, but more critically in its relationship to the citizen.[1] On a more positive note, the value of cultural agency remains indubitable but in itself it is not necessarily sufficient to generate change. By linking it so obviously to economic growth and based on an understanding of the global industry and of the varied agendas of all the actors involved, cultural agency may be positioned in a more powerful manner.

This chapter looks at the film industry in Burkina Faso, taking an historical perspective, to ascertain the existing basis of the industry and efforts made to expand it, touching on some of the problems and challenges it faces. The first section sets out some of the main aspects linked to international intervention in the development of the film industry in Burkina Faso, based on its close relationship with Europe, and the second section looks more closely at the infrastructure already in place in Burkina.

The focus here is on Burkina Faso because it is representative of its French-speaking, sub-Saharan neighbours and at the same time it also stands out among them. It is representative because these countries have a shared political and economic history, in addition to various cultural commonalities. In contrast, Burkina stands out because it has the most structured film sector in the region with film legislation in place and it has a fairly consistent level of feature film production. The country has been able to combine and build on three central components, namely, actively engaged filmmakers, a history of government policy in favour of the sector and its role as a host of the largest film event on the continent, the biannual *Festival Panafricain du Cinéma et de la Télévision de Ouagadougou* (FESPACO). This combination has been crucial to the vitality of the film sector in the country. While Burkina has this comparative advantage, many of the difficulties it faces are the same as those of its neighbours, notably a lack of finance and of a fully operating infrastructure, various dependencies and a configuration of domination within the international film and audiovisual sector, among others. What is certain however is that the growth of a dynamic film and audiovisual industry will most likely evolve from regional solidarity and collaboration in combination with local projects and plans, as well as international support initiatives and investment.

Given that Burkina Faso is a relatively little known country a cursory overview may be useful. It is ranked as an LDC, has a gross domestic product (GDP) of US$4.2 billion (World Bank Group, 2003), a per capita income of US$360 similar to Mali and slightly above Chad or Niger,[2] and a purchasing power parity of US$1,200. For the period 2000–2002 it had an annual average per capita real GDP growth rate of 2.5 per cent.[3] The majority of the population exists on subsistence-level agriculture and export earnings come largely from cotton. France is one of its main trade partners, as is the Ivory Coast and China.[4] The services sector accounted for an estimated 44 per cent of the GDP in 2003, but it is largely due to the transport sector.[5] Burkina has a population of almost 14 million and a literacy rate of 27 per cent. There are numerous ethnic groups with a Mossi majority of about 40 per cent and the religious configuration is around 50 per cent Muslim, 40 per cent Animist and 10 per cent Catholic. Much of the male labour force migrates annually to the Ivory Coast for seasonal employment. As for the political situation, Blaise Compaoré became president in 1987 through a military coup ousting the revolutionary Thomas Sankara. Compaoré has made some democratic gestures in recent years, including calling an election and enacting a constitution, but he maintains total power backed through the military, permitting no effective opposition.

Finding viable statistics for Burkina Faso is extremely difficult even for basic information published by official sources such as the World Bank, Organization for Economic Cooperation and Development (OECD), the International Monetary Fund (IMF), the United Nations Conference on Trade and Development (UNCTAD), the United Nations Educational, Scientific and Cultural Organization (UNESCO) and the *Agence de la Francophonie* (AIF), which are often and generally disparate. Only UNESCO and the AIF tend to publish on the cultural sectors. There is some information circulating about media and telecommunications, but less on the film sector. World Bank data (2003) estimates per 1,000 people there are 23.9 fixed and mobile telephone lines, 2.1 personal computers and 3.9 Internet users.[6] The *CIA Factbook 2005* notes 131,240 televisions[7] (2002 stat.), 394,020 radios, and one Internet service provider.[8] There are about five daily newspapers and many more weekly and monthly papers.[9] Apparently there are about 2,500 subscriptions to satellite television in the country. According to the AIF the audiovisual sector in Burkina employs

700–1,000 people plus another 800 who are involved in projecting films on video in a workforce totalling 5.8 million.[10]

Within the cinematographic realm it is even more complicated. For example, general box office statistics for film in Burkina Faso are not really available, although it was possible to obtain some statistics from the *Société Nationale d'Exploitation et de Distribution Cinématographique du Burkina* (SONACIB), the national distribution company (liquidated in 2003), but only for the cinemas that it owned. Box office figures may be found on an individual basis for certain films, but they are not standardised. Discussions of having a fully functional national box office have long existed, but there always seems to be some obstacle. And in Burkina there is more information available than in neighbouring countries because SONACIB did have a monopoly and thus had information on the majority of the cinemas in the country. Even collecting information on the number of cinema theatres in the country is not necessarily easy (Table 4.1). While the total number of existing film theatres may provide one response, the total number of functioning theatres another. Distinctions also need to be made between the classifications of theatres: covered, air-conditioned, open-air and so forth, because the ticket prices vary, generally from €0.5–2.5. In addition, there are now approximately 2,000 other locations in Burkina where video copies are projected.[11]

A more critical question is really what type of film industry can prosper in Burkina Faso? Burkina's film history has largely consisted of making two or three professional 35 mm films per year that compete in international markets, but that are almost entirely dependent on international funding (Table 4.2). What is necessary is a locally/regionally sustainable industry that could in turn also contribute to the making of more expensive or more artistic or experimental productions. Both of these cinematic and visual spaces can nourish each other. The more high-cost productions are likely to still depend on international and European co-production financing, but this is the case in many countries today and not just the so-called developing countries. The main priority is developing a viable, independent local industry, and local energies are clearly working in that direction, as we will see below. In this respect the use of digital technology is making a difference.

Table 4.1 Cinema theatres in Burkina Faso[12]

1969	6
1985	55
1994	50
2001	50 (4 covered, 15 semi-covered, 36 open-air)
2002	34
2004	19 functional out of 60[a]

Source: various local sources.

Note

a Information received from Ismael Ouedraogo, Direction de la Cinematographie Nationale (DCN), Ougadougou, Burkina Faso, April 2005.

Table 4.2 Feature film production in Burkina Faso (for theatrical distribution)[14]

1971	1	1990	2	2000	2
1973	1	1991	1	2001	1
1982	2	1992	4	2002	2
1987	1	1993	2	2003	3
1988	3	1994	1	2004	4
1989	1	1995	2		
		1996	nc		
		1997	2 nc		
		1998	1 nc		
		1999	1		

Sources: Various, primarily the DIPROCI and the DCN for 2000–2004.

Note
nc – not confirmed.

International intervention and the history of the film sector in Burkina Faso

In order to understand the film sector in Burkina Faso as it is currently in place it is important to view the international input into the filmmaking sector in the country. In this respect the role of European intervention has been critical to its development bringing with it both positive and negative consequences. There are three major partners with an essential role in the French-speaking sub-Saharan region. The French government was the first to become involved in 1963, the *Agence de la Francophonie* (AIF) followed in 1988, and since 1992 the European Union has been involved in funding film in Africa, the Caribbean and Pacific region, with an official programme launched in 2000.[12]

France was profoundly interested in developing a film sector in sub-Saharan Africa and its efforts began during the colonial period. The motivational factors for France include cultural, political and economic matters. On the cultural level France sees the African members of the Francophony as having certain common cultural references that they would like to nurture. France's relationship with African countries does give it additional political clout in the international forum. On the economic level there is of course a trade relationship between France and the African countries, including the film and audiovisual sector, but the economic interests also lie in the fact that much of the sub-Saharan film-making was completed in France using French infrastructures. Nonetheless, the French cinematographic tradition and the policies that the French government applied in sub-Saharan Africa have contributed to a richness of the film culture in the region. The notion of *cinéma d'auteur* is still important to understanding the existing situation and the fact that sub-Saharan African film directors make films that compete in the top film festivals.

For many years the French Ministry of Cooperation and Development was the most important producer of African films.[13] On average they helped produce ten films every two years. From 1991 onward their overall budget for supporting cinema (mainly production, but also distribution, training, festival support and numerous other projects), in developing countries was approximately FF20 million per year (€3.5 million).[14] Since 2000 the Ministry of Cooperation has been incorporated into the French Ministry of Foreign Affairs, but funding support for African filmmaking has continued. The Ministry has a number of programmes to support filmmaking in Africa, in addition to the *Fond Sud*, a pillar of its policy, open to directors from developing countries and which has an annual budget of about €2.4 million.

French, and for the most part European, intervention has been and still is largely directed toward the production phases of filmmaking. One of the consequences of this policy has been the creation of an elite category of filmmakers, but a lack of material and infrastructural development in the countries themselves. For example, little effort was made to develop local distribution structures and the French maintained predominant control of these, even distributing American films. Laboratory work was largely done in France and very often materials and expertise were flown in for productions. There are of course always conditions to obtain aid and, for example, post-production work still has to be completed in Europe, meaning that the money is spent there. Additionally, awards were granted on the condition that there was a European producer involved and this has also had some detrimental effects. So on the one hand certain dependencies on European infrastructures have been perpetuated, while on the other hand there has been a veritable development of a film culture in the region. The French government has made considerable efforts in recent years to address these problematic issues and adapt their policies accordingly, particularly encouraging audiovisual productions and small local production companies working with digital technology.

The AIF supports African filmmaking in a number of ways, primarily by giving financial assistance for the production of films from francophone regions of the South. Among its other programmes the AIF film and audiovisual fund and its distribution prize total about €1 million per year. Its other activities include programming the films on TV5,[15] helping finance film festivals that show African films, supporting various television programmes related to the Francophony, as well as organising training programmes. In 1992 they restructured their production funding to include training and distribution aid, and not solely the post-production aid that had always been prioritised. Since 1994 the ACCT has given 80 per cent of its aid budget for the production of programmes destined for TV5 Africa. The AIF is particularly focused on audiovisual funding, convinced that it is the future of film production in the South, even to the neglect of direct aid to film production.

The European Union also allocates important amounts of funding to sub-Saharan African filmmaking. Within the framework of its cooperation and development policies with the African, Caribbean and Pacific region (ACP) a cultural chapter enables funding for filmmaking.[16] Through the funding provided by the EU Development Directorate an ACP filmmaker can receive financing, in particular for production and distribution. In addition the Development Directorate also supports numerous other projects related to film, such as festivals like FESPACO (supported since 1987), distribution initiatives like *Africa Cinemas* or organisations like the *Fedération Panafricain des cinéastes* (FEPACI). Between 2000 and 2004 the EU provided €14,243,717 for filmmaking and related activites in the ACP regions.[17] Among the differences between the EU aid and that of the other major partners is that the allocation of funds for a film is not dependent on the use of a European producer. The individual amounts disbursed by the EU have been comparatively higher than the other organisations and can reach up to 40 per cent of the total budget.

In sum, the EU, the French government, the AIF, as well as various other smaller organisations in a number of European countries and elsewhere continue to play a critical role in supporting and stimulating local African initiatives in the cinematographic and audiovisual realm. As is often the case with development assistance, funding is rarely given gratuitously and dependence can have insidious consequences. It is not surprising that there have been both negative and positive costs to this support.[18] However, international support remains useful on at least two levels, first, to encourage the development of a local industry and, second, to enable productions that are not uniquely seeking commercial viability. In any case there is always some form of negotiation among the partners, on the gains and losses of receiving support.

The film and audiovisual sector in Burkina Faso

Since its independence in 1960 Burkina Faso has implemented numerous initiatives to develop and ameliorate its film and audiovisual sector. Burkina nationalised its film theatres and countered foreign domination of film distribution, it created a Cinema Fund, it has enacted a Cinema Law and other legislation in favour of cinema. Perhaps more than its neighbouring countries the initiatives taken in Burkina have instilled a type of national pride in the film sector that in turn has contributed to its growth, but there is still a long way to go. This section examines the general organisation of the film and audiovisual sector in Burkina, in terms of production, television, distribution and exhibition, as well as a number of other initiatives. An historical perspective is woven through the analysis in order to understand the basis of the current situation.

Production

In 1961 a Cinema Service was created by the new government and attached to the Ministry of Information. The Service made newsreels and low cost, didactic short films, contributing to the development of the country. It was minimally equipped for 16 mm filming with a small editing and sound studio, although laboratory work had to be completed in Paris. Very rapidly the continuing role of France in the film sector caused dissatisfaction. In response to the foreign control of film distribution and exhibition in the country the Burkinabè government nationalised its cinema theatres in 1970. Film policy started with a bang in

Burkina Faso and at no less a level than the Presidency. On 5 January 1970 the government nationalised the film theatres and by presidential decree the *Société Nationale Voltaïque du Cinéma* (SONAVOCI) was created to replace the French companies that held a monopoly in the country.[19] In another monumental step a Cinema Fund was created in 1970. The *Fonds de Promotion et d'Extension de l'activité cinématographique* (No. 70/028/PRES/MFC 20 July 1970) was to finance national film production by collecting a small tax on all film theatre tickets sold.

The Cinema Service was handicapped with a tiny budget and very little money going into the Cinema Fund: a recurring theme in Burkinabè film history. In 1977 the government gave cinema an autonomous jurisdiction and created the *Direction du Centre Cinématographique* headed by Gaston Kaboré, one of Burkina Faso's best-known film directors today. Kaboré pointed out Burkina's intention to organise its cinematographic production in a manner resembling the French *Centre National de la Cinématographie* (CNC).[20] The Cinema Fund was to be used for producing films, but also for the maintenance and acquisition of equipment, and for FESPACO. Accordingly, the first feature length fiction film made in Upper Volta, *Le Sang de Parias* (1971) by Djim Kola, was made with the help of the Fund. By 1979 the Fund had contributed to two full-length fiction films as well as numerous educational films. But the situation declined and the Cinema Fund seemed to have fewer and fewer resources, in part due to ticketing fraud. In 1991, the new cinema code updated the status of the Cinema Fund (Zatu No. An VIII 0029 Bis/FP/PRES) increasing the tax. In theory, the Fund was to guarantee a continual level of production in the country, although in practice this was not the case. Financial difficulties, aggravated by debt and mismanagement, caused the Fund money to be used in emergencies for miscellaneous tasks so that there was nothing left for production.

Later it was the *Direction de la Production Cinématographique* (DIPROCI) that produced films in Burkina Faso and became a central hub for filmmaking in the entire region by renting its equipment and technicians. The *Centre National de la Cinématographie du Burkina* (CNCB) was created in May 1991[21] and supposed to be the central administrative body regulating all cinematographic activities in the country, bringing cohesion between the existing entities such as DIPROCI and SONACIB (formerly the SONAVOCI).[22] But the CNCB lacked financing with nothing coming in from the Cinema Fund and state grants that only covered operating costs. In addition, because the organisation of production in the country was dispersed, the DIPROCI had found itself occupied with certain administrative responsibilities for cinema and it continued to do so making an organisational shift difficult. In February 1997 the CNCB was amalgamated into the DIPROCI and the whole organisation was renamed the *Direction de la Cinématographie Nationale* (DCN)[23] and is a central hub of the filmmaking scene in the country. Perhaps the new cinema law[24] adopted in November 2004 will contribute to the revival of the Fund through a reorganisation of the national box office and to further structural clarification of the sector.

The State currently contributes to the film and audiovisual sector in a number of different ways. It provides direct support to various public structures in the film and audiovisual sector, such as the DCN, FESPACO and the Cinematheque. The government was contributing to the annual budget of the *Télévision Nationale du Burkina* (TNB), although it now seems to have ceased to do so. The Cinema Fund, when it is again functional, should benefit from a 15 per cent contribution from the distribution and exhibition sector. Once the new national box office is in place this should again be the case. Various government ministries and companies also finance documentaries or educational programmes linked to their activities. In the past the President has also been know exceptionally to intervene in some film projects in order to ensure their completion.

The first private initiative in film production was in 1981 by Martial Ouedraogo, who created the *Société Africaine de Cinéma* (CINAFRIC). It was equipped for all aspects of film production with the exception of laboratory work, which still had to be completed elsewhere.[25] CINAFRIC co-produced a few films, however it did not survive for long. Its rental rates were so close to European prices that it was not competitive. Filmmakers worked with the DIPROCI at cheaper rates or they continued to pay the costs of transporting material from Europe.

Today in Ougadougou, the capital, there is a quietly thriving production business. Beginning in the early 1990s a number of private production companies were created when Burkinabè directors established their own production companies to create a legal context for their films. But now the metier of producer is taking hold and more companies have been created. In 1990, Gaston Kaboré created CINECOM (*Cinéma et Communication*), Dany Kouyaté, another well-known director, co-founded *Sahelis* in 1992, which makes small-scale productions for the TNB such as the series *A nous la vie* and rents out its services and equipment.[26] Pierre Yameogo created *Dunia Production* and Idrissa Ouedraogo initially created *Films de l'Avenir* in order to be able to co-produce his earlier films, but then started anew with *NDK* and has been producing television series and sitcoms, such as *Kadi Jolie*. Regina Fanta Nacro has also created her own production company *Les films du défi* and there are many other local companies such as *Jovial Productions*, *Afrique Production* and *Media 2000*. *Clap'Afrik* together with another producer from Benin, co-produced a television series called *Taxi brousse*, which was not only successful with local audiences but has been programmed in a number of festivals internationally.

This evolution is largely due to the possibilities of digital filming which have developed considerably since 2000. In 2002 there were over 30 small production companies in the country mainly producing films and series for television. Directors like Idrissa Ouedraogo and Pierre Yameogo are using digital technology to produce television series and feature films as well as for their own work. Transfers between formats are still expensive, but less so than only using 35 mm film. This is clearly a dynamic and growing sector with much potential. There are still many challenges that the sector has to face. For example, there is hardly any private investment in the film sector, either local or international, and few banks, if any, are willing to provide loans for film production. A new bank guarantee scheme (*Fonds de garantie pour le financement bancaire pour les industries culturelles* – FGIC) has recently been created by the AIF, so that private companies working in the cultural sector can apply for loans; it functions through the *Banque d'investissement et de développement de la CEDEAO* (BIDC). Trained technical personnel are still needed and film materials are always necessary, as is the upkeep of that material, little of which can be done locally. In addition the government is more keen on decreasing its spending in the sector than on investing in it.

Television

In Europe and North America, television is indispensable to feature film production either through direct investment in pre-purchases or purchases, or indirectly through taxation and other financial agreements. In francophone sub-Saharan Africa the national television companies cannot really support film production in the same manner because they do not have the finances. Europeans often donate programming to African countries, as is the case of France through *Canal France International* (CFI). In other cases bartering is common practice, for example, a private company might purchase programmes for the television (this is often the case for the Latin American telenovelas) in exchange for having their publicity aired. Other programming (such as American television series) can sometimes be purchased at very low rates because they have already been amortized in other markets.

The TNB was created on 5 August 1963 by order of the President Maurice Yameogo. In 1988 it was given a small budget for the acquisition of television rights and improved its programming. The television in Burkina Faso has traditionally been concerned with making educational and documentary programmes. Cooperation between the filmmakers and the TNB is increasing, even if it does not participate in film production in the same way as European television companies. French policy has played an important role in helping develop the production of African television series and reflects a shift in policy that began to provide more funding for television production. For example, the series mentioned above, *Kadi jolie* and *A nous la vie* are produced with private money and European support. With the help of European funding the TNB had seven programmes by 1989 and "was the biggest exporter of African programs to the West."[27] According to the AIF, local, private production companies in Burkina produced 150 hours of fiction programmes between 1997 and 2002.[28] About 50 per cent of TNB programming is actually produced locally and the new series mentioned above have much to do with this. The TNB is now likely to face difficult times again as the government has withdrawn its support that covered the annual budget of television.

Distribution and exhibition

Just as in most other countries in the world, foreign films dominate Burkinabè screens and foreign distributors control commercial distribution. According to the AIF, distribution in Burkina Faso is dominated 97–98 per cent by foreign companies, compared with 99 per cent in Senegal and 90 per cent in Morocco.[29] This control began during the colonial period with two French companies, the *Société d'Exploitation Cinématographique Africaine* (SECMA) created in 1948 and the *Compagnie Africaine Cinématographique Industrielle et Commerciale* (COMACICO) created in 1959, who held exclusive rights for the import, distribution and exhibition of films. In Upper Volta (renamed Burkina Faso), SECMA-COMACICO owned all six cinemas and held a monopoly on distribution until 1970. The market was divided amicably between the two companies: the large American groups (Paramount, MGM, Rank and Warner Brothers) supplied SECMA, while the French, Indian and Egyptian distributors supplied COMACICO. They basically bought low quality films in block bookings, already amortized in other markets so the prices were low. The films were rented at fixed rates for a determined time period, regardless of the profits made by a film.[30] The French company *Union Générale Cinématographique* (UGC) purchased the two companies in 1973 and its filial the *Société de Participation Cinématographique Africaine* (SOPACIA), took over the market in francophone sub-Saharan Africa. In 1981 SOPACIA became the *Union Africaine de Cinématographie* (UAC) but in spite of the name changes the market continued to be dominated by foreigners.

In 1972, the heads of state of the members of the *Organisation Commune Africaine et Mauricienne* (OCAM) gathered in Lomé to address the problem of film distribution and the need for African screens to be controlled by Africans and not foreign distributors who did not show local productions. This was not the first time the issue arose. At the *Premier Festival Mondial des Arts Nègres* held in Dakar in 1966 African filmmakers agreed to create a regional organisation that would regulate all aspects of the cinema and this objective was reiterated on numerous other occasions. Indeed, there is a long history of decisions and declaration on African cultural policies in general and film policy in particular.[31]

Nevertheless, in 1974 ten OCAM states signed an agreement creating the *Consortium Interafricain de Distribution Cinématographique* (CIDC) and the *Centre Interafricain de Production de Films* (CIPROFILM). The headquarters was in Ouagadougou and Inoussa Ousseini, a filmmaker from Niger, was named Director-General. In 1979 a budget was finally allocated and they became operational in 1980. CIDC was to be the sole distributor of films in sub-Saharan Africa and thus able to negotiate the price and quality of the films to the advantage of the national distribution companies which it would help create. Above all, the organisation wanted to promote the distribution of African films and contribute to film production through CIPROFILM.[32]

However, CIDC closed in 1984, amid court cases, rumours of embezzlement, unpaid salaries and angered States.[33] If the circumstances left CIDC at a disadvantage from the outset, through a difficult contract with the French companies, it would appear that lack of cooperation among the states and management difficulties contributed to its demise. Member states had not reformed their tax structures even though a homogenised tax regime was essential to success. The absence of national ticket controls in most of the states prevented controlling the career of a film. Annual fees remained unpaid and promised loans were not forthcoming. The company was constrained to buy films from the same suppliers and was left without money to buy new films. The circuit basically remained under French control but supplied American films.

The Americans took advantage of the situation and entered the francophone market with SOCOFILM, which became the principal supplier in the region.[34] SOCOFILM was sold to the *Compagnie Franco-Africaine de l'Audiovisuel* (CFAA) in 1989, a holding company of the *Crédit Lyonnais* and the *Caisse Populaire*.[35] The CFAA was a principal supplier of films in Burkina Faso[36] and continues to do so today. The interests at stake in the distribution sector are high and no one wants to relinquish their power. In spite of this first unsuccessful attempt, it seems clear that the success of distributing African films will depend on a very solid regional entity.

In 1968, a breakdown of the nationality and type of films shown in popular cinemas was approximately 60 per cent American (Westerns), 15 per cent French (detective, war), 20 per cent Indian, Egyptian and Arab, and 5 per cent Italian, English and German.[37] The few African films that existed at the time were of no interest to the companies and the prices they offered to buy new African films were impossibly low. By 1995, 80 per cent of the programming in Burkina Faso consisted of American action films, Chinese (karate) and romantic musical films (Hindu).[38] Little has changed in this configuration and American films make the largest box office.[39]

Burkina Faso shows a comparatively high number of African films in its theatres. The distribution company SONACIB was majority owned by the State and had a monopoly. It was the only such national institution still functioning in the region after the dissolution of CIDC and CIPROFILM.[40] SONACIB owned about 17 cinemas in the country and the others were provincial or private cinemas. It supplied the country's cinemas with films on monthly contracts and maintained the equipment and trained personnel in the cinemas that it owned. SONACIB had the advantage of FESPACO and benefited from the access to African filmmakers and their films present at the festival. By 1993 SONACIB's portfolio included 50 African films including each *Etalon de Yennenga*, the grand prize of FESPACO.[41] Before 1992 the company would buy a copy of the film and divide the film receipts (40 per cent SONACIB, 60 per cent director), then it began renting the copy on six-month renewable contract and dividing the receipts (50–50). Some directors refused such terms and negotiated directly with private cinemas.[42] Many African film directors have had to organise their own film distribution, literally carrying the film to the theatre and hiring the ticket agents in order to have control over the film receipts.

In 1992 a provisory administration was named at SONACIB. The company had a huge debt and money was not being paid into the Cinema Fund. Problems of management and accounting, as well as a lack of proper controls of ticketing in the cinemas, contributed to the crisis. Approximately 20–25 per cent of the total receipts were being lost and fraud had increased. Each district was to use the municipal taxes for the upkeep of the cinemas and equipment, but no improvements were made. The 50 per cent devaluation of the FCFA in January 1994 aggravated the situation, doubling the price of film imports and causing an increase in electricity, water and so forth. In spite of the attempts by the general director to create more direct accountancy, reduce expenses and debt, and improve national ticket controls, SONACIB did not survive and was liquidated in 2003.

Instead of privatising the cinemas as neighbouring countries have done with disastrous results, a two-year transition period was declared. The *Association des Auteurs, Réalisateurs et Producteurs Africains* (ARPA), which is headed by the foremost film personality and filmmaker in Burkina Faso, Idrissa Ouedraogo, is now responsible for redressing film distribution in the country. Under these conditions the revivification of the distribution and exhibition sector can only be improved.

In addition, another distribution initiative has been initiated at the regional level. *Africa Cinemas* was created in July 2003 in order to improve the distribution and programming of African films in Africa. It is the kind of regional project that is necessary to ameliorate the distribution and exhibition sector, but it is off to a shaky start. It is jointly funded by the three major European partners (EU, France, AIF), but according to the *Association pour la Diffusion du Cinéma Africain* (ACID), which was created in order to resolve the problems that have surfaced with *Africa Cinemas* and that represent about 90 per cent of African distributors, the current structure of *Africa Cinemas* does not realistically take into account local needs.[43] Apart from the weaknesses of the programme, it is clear to the members of ACID that one of the big problems of distribution and exhibition in Africa is that there are not enough African films produced to respond to the demand. Nonetheless, the African film professionals all agree that a structure such as *Africa Cinemas* needs to exist.[44]

It is certain that the difficulties of distributing African films in Africa are numerous and while the numbers of producers have increased, this has been less so for distribution, not surprisingly, as it is generally dominated by major companies. Here again, the African filmmakers have had to be extremely multivalent and have also taken on this challenge. Piracy is also a challenging issue in Burkina Faso as there are so many informal projection sites. Given the weak per capita income in the country it is hardly surprising to see such a phenomenon. Nonetheless, the Burkinabè government created legislation in 2000 to counter the activity[45] and the Burkinabè copyright office (BBDA) works in this domain. In addition, the possibilities now offered by the Internet in terms of distribution (and marketing for that matter) and direct downloads of films could eventually prove to be an advantageous avenue for African filmmaking and its distribution.

Training

Among some of the other important local initiatives is the reopening of a film school in Ouagadougou. Since the *Institut Africain d'Education Cinématographique de Ouagadougou* (INAFEC)[46] closed in 1987, there have been only sporadic film courses and training programmes organised by a variety of organisations. The new *Institut Regional de l'Image et du Son* (IRIS) is the result of international collaboration through the *Programme de Relance de la Formation aux Métiers de l'Image et du Son* (PROFIS). The DCN in Burkina Faso, together with the French, Belgians and Canadians, are at the heart of the initiative. It is certain that for the film and audiovisual industry to develop in Burkina Faso and in Africa, new generations of local film directors, producers, technicians, and so forth, are crucial.

FESPACO

It is impossible to look at the film industry in Burkina Faso without taking into account the vital role of the FESPACO, which is the most important international African film festival. It is a cornerstone of Burkina's position as a cinematographic centre. In 1969 the first "Week of African cinema" was organised in Ouagadougou, which then became FESPACO in 1972, alternating yearly with the Carthage International Film Festival in Tunisia.

The festival is not only a crucial element for the film sector in the country and for the Burkinabè economy as a whole. FESPACO is the foremost ambassador of Burkina Faso. It brings the world to Burkina Faso and African films to Burkinabè screens. It has the patronage of the President and the support of the mass population, who battle crowds to attend the films, in addition to the international audience. The presence of international media at the festival is a rare opportunity to project African filmmaking, Burkina Faso and Africa, into an international forum in a positive light[47] and from an economic perspective the event also benefits Burkina Faso.[48]

In 1969 the film festival registered 10,000 spectators for all the films shown, while in 2005, Baba Hama, the festival director, noted that FESPACO counted about 450,000 spectators in terms of overall seats filled.[49] In 1983 the *Marché International du Cinéma et de la Télévision* (MICA) was created at the festival in order encourage the buying and selling of African film and audiovisual productions. In addition, the cultural and economic life in Ouagadougou booms during the event and includes all kinds of attractions like a huge market where merchants come from all over the region to sell artisanal products.

Conclusion

The Burkinabè government takes cinema very seriously and makes continual efforts to improve legislation in the film and audiovisual domain and to improve the overall organisation of the sector. Among numerous other laws Burkina Faso has also signed co-production treaties with France (1992) as well as with Togo, Ghana, Ethiopia, Mali and South Africa. At FESPACO 1991 President Compaoré announced a new measure consisting of customs exemptions and the elimination of taxes on African films distributed in Burkina Faso and in November 2004 the new Cinema Law was adopted. Burkina Faso has also enacted legislation on copyright, and has signed various WIPO treaties.[50] Creating the appropriate legislation is an essential step for developing the film sector and will have to be taken by all the countries in the region.

In the history of film in Burkina Faso and of French-speaking sub-Saharan Africa numerous initiatives and declarations have been made and organisations and associations created. Even in Burkina Faso, an African country at the forefront of film policy and production, things have not always moved forward smoothly. One of the challenges of developing the film sector in this region will be to channel all the different initiatives into a consolidated regional effort and this is entirely dependent on what happens at the local levels. Decrees made at regional levels will not miraculously enable the development of an industry, but at the same time the future of the film industry in Burkina Faso is dependent on what happens in the entire region.

It is certain that as public money for the social and cultural sectors is continually diminishing, private funding become increasingly necessary. There is an impending shift in the film and audiovisual sector where private sources will be necessary to the development of an industry and it will be up to African countries to remain vigilant as to how that shift occurs. In terms of the development of an industry many consider the Nigerian video-film industry a model.[51] Inexpensive productions using video technology mean that hundreds of films are made weekly.[52] They are local productions with Africans represented on screens and African narratives being told and invented and with the profits from one production serving to make another. However, marketers who are there to make money and are not necessarily interested in cinema or video basically run the business. The quality of many productions is lamentable by any cinematographic standards, and the films are often consumed like any other disposable product, where "content" has little to do with creativity. In flagrant contrast with Burkina Faso there are no longer any film theatres equipped for 35 mm projection in Nigeria, while in Burkina Faso there are no film theatres currently equipped for digital projection. Somewhere in between these extremes lie some solutions.

If the drawbacks of Nollywood, as it is called, can be avoided, the use of less expensive technology and the Internet present enormous possibilities for Burkina Faso and its neighbours. It is clear that Nigeria, with a population of over 100 million, has the advantage of economies of scale, and this reinforces the importance of regional cooperation in the francophone realm. While Nigeria has a competitive edge with inexpensive, locally based productions, South Africa is moving ahead with large-scale, more expensive and higher value, film productions. The francophone sub-Saharan region has to find a competitive way to fit into this continental configuration, and it must be possible.

This brings us back to the question of what form the film industry in Burkina Faso will take. Burkina has a rich film culture, it has a budding local production scene, it is grappling with the problems of distribution and exhibition, it is not neglecting the importance of film education and training, it has the best African film festival in the world, and it has a government that is working to create a structured, legal context for the film and audiovisual sector, in sum, many factors working in its favour. Whether these advantages can be translated into economic success remains to be seen.

Notes

1 See for example, Nestor Garcia Canclini, *Hybrid Cultures*, Minnesota: University of Minnesota Press, 1995; George Yúdice, *The Expediency of Culture: Uses of Culture in the Global Era*, Durham: Duke University Press, 2003; Toby Miller and George Yúdice, *Cultural Policy*, London: Sage Publications, 2002.
2 World Development Indicators database, World Bank, July 2005. www.worldbank.org/data/databytopic/GNIPC.pdf
3 UNCTAD, The Least Developed Countries Report 2004, UN: New York, p. 321.
4 www.cia.gov/cia/publications/factbook/geos/uv.html
5 AfDB/OECD African Economic Outlook, *Burkina Faso*, 2004, p. 84.
6 www.worldbank.org
7 In 1965, there were 50 privately owned and 130 publicly owned televisions in the country and by 1978 there were 6,000 televisions in the country. In 1994 Burkina Faso had 80,000 televisions, 15,000 VCRs and 300 satellite dishes.
8 www.cia.gov/cia/publications/factbook/geos/uv.html
9 www.presse-francophone.org/publications/pubburkina.htm
10 Organisation Internationale de la Francophonie, "Les industries culturelles des pays du sud: enjeux du projet de Convention internationale sur la diversité culturelle," August 2004, p. 82.
11 Clement Tapsoba, "Burkina Faso" *Cahiers du Cinéma*, no. hors-série, avril 2005, p. 45.
12 In 2000 the EU launched the ACP cinema support programme.
13 Michel Brunet, Director of the Cinema Bureau, French Ministry of Cooperation and Development, interview by author, Paris, 11 January 1996. It assisted the production of over 300 long films and 550 short films, both fiction and documentary, by directors of sub-Saharan francophone and lusophone Africa, the Indian Ocean and the Caribbean, although France has most actively promoted cinema in the 14 francophone countries of sub-Saharan Africa.
14 Michel Brunet, interview by author, Paris, 11 January 1996.
15 TV5 is a television that promotes francophone culture. It was a cooperative project created in 1983 by French, Belgium and Switzerland's French-speaking public television, and joined by Canada in 1986.
16 "The European Union and African, Caribbean and Pacific Cinema" brochure, no date.
17 George Goldenstern, "Evaluation rétrospective de la politique européenne d'appui aux cinémas de la zone ACP (200–2004) – Rapport de synthèse," April 2005, p. 6.
18 See for example, Teresa Hoefert de Turégano, *African Cinema and Europe: Close-up on Burkina Faso*, Florence: European Press Academic Publishing, 2004.
19 *L'Afrique Littéraire et Artistique* no. 9, February 1970, p. 90–91.
20 Gaston Kaboré, communication with author, Paris, November 1996.
21 Article 2, Kiti No. An VIII-0300/FP/MF/MIC/SEC portant création d'un Centre National de la Cinématographie du Burkina. The objectives of the CNCB were to create and organise legislation regarding cinema, control ticketing, control the financ-

ing of films made with and without State funding, centralise all the funding for cinematographic activities from the various ministries, survey all government subsidies and advance funding for cinema, maintain the public register, participate in the distribution of film authorisations, ensure the distribution of documentaries, help develop the non-commercial film sector, organise professional training and ensure the promotion of Burkinabè film at home and abroad.

22 Paul Zoumbara, interview by author, Ouagadougou, March 1995.

23 Emmanuel Sama, "Cinéma et audiovisuel Burkinabè," *Burkinescope*, no. 7, 2000, p. 14.

24 Loi No. 047–2004-/AN portant loi d'orientation du cinéma et de l'audiovisuel (November 2004).

25 Bachy, *Haute Volta* (1983), p. 66.

26 www.sahelis.com/fr/index.html

27 Hennebelle, ed., *Les télévisions du Monde – CinémAction*, Paris: Corlet, 1995, p. 319.

28 AIF 2004, p. 28.

29 Organisation Internationale de la Francophonie, "Les industries culturelles des pays du sud: enjeux du projet de Convention internationale sur la diversité culturelle," August 2004, p. 79.

30 Jean René Debrix, "Le Cinéma Africain," *Afrique Contemporaine*, no. 40, 1970. See pages 2–4 for details on the conditions of buying and supplying films by SECMA-COMACICO.

31 Among others see: UNESCO, "Meeting of Experts on Problems of Cultural Policies in Africa" (Dakar, 6–10 October, 1969) Final Report. SHC/CONF.40/3; Organisation of African Unity and UNESCO, "Cultural Industries for Development in Africa: Dakar Plan of Action," June 1992; Organisation of African Unity, "Symposium on Politics, Strategies and Experiences in the Financing of Culture in Africa," 5–9 June 2000, Abidjan, Ivory Coast, RAP/F:C:/006.Rev.1.

32 Inoussa Ousseini, Ignacio Ramonet and Paulin Soumanou Vieyra, "Un bilan africain," *Le Monde Diplomatique*, March 1979, p. 25.

33 Emmanuel Sama, "Le film africain étranger sur son propre territoire," *Ecrans d'Afrique*, no. 4, 1993, p. 59.

34 Boughedir, "Economie et thématique," (1986), p. 124.

35 Sama, "Le film africain," (1993), p. 61.

36 CFAA and SOCOFILM, which are both owned by SOFRACOM, rented most of the films seen in Burkina Faso until 1993 (SONACIB document, n.d., n.a.).

37 Debrix, "Le Cinéma Africain," no. 40 (1970), p. 4.

38 Tahita Sanata (SONACIB), interview by author, Ouagadougou, March 1995.

39 *Cahiers du Cinéma*, no. hors-série, avril 2005.

40 "Entretien: Justin Kagambèga – L'écoute est la clef de la réussite," *Regard*, no. 0120, 23–29 January 1995, p. 4.

41 In 1991, 18 full-length African fiction films were shown in Burkinabè cinemas accumulating a total of 465,667 entries. In 1992, 27 full-length African fiction films were shown for a total of 542,983 entries. In 1993, 31 full-length African fiction films were shown with over 550,000 entries. Justin Kagambèga, "Distribution et Exploitation – Cinéma Africain," (1994), p. 5.

42 Tahita Sanata (SONACIB), correspondence with author, 26 February 1996.

43 Rapport Final de la Réunion de concertation avec les benéficaires du programme Africa Cinemas, Bamako, 13–14 Octobre 2004.

44 "Conférence de presse Africa Cinemas/ACID (Afrique Cinéma Diffusion) lundi 28 février 2005 Fespaco," Notes by Aurore Engelen Loosen.

45 Décret no. 2000-1-6/PRFS/PM/MCA portant réglementation des projections publiques de vidéocassettes et autres supports assimilés et de l'exercice de la profession d'exploitant de vidéoprojection (2000).

46 Launched by UNESCO and the FEPACI in Burkina Faso in 1977.

47 Radio, television, news agencies and newspapers come from all over the world, i.e. Great Britain, France, Switzerland, China, South Africa, Algeria, etc. In 1993, 421 different media representatives were present at FESPACO (FESPACO documents). Each year more and more media representatives come from all over the world. In the last few years there has been a notable increase in American participation in the event, as well as from English-speaking Africa, notably Nigeria and South Africa.

48 Anne Vinsensini, "Cinéma Africain – un outil au service du développement – le cas du Burkina Faso," DEA thesis, Paris, 1990. See chapter two on Burkina's economic benefits from the festival. Also, according to the FEPACI and a study completed on the economic benefits of FESPACO for Burkina Faso, an estimated 700 million FCFA were generated for the country due to FESPACO 1989 (FESPACO documents).

49 Baba Hama, "Grand entretien Baba Hama, Délégué general du FESPAO," *L'opinion*, no. 385, 16–22 February, 2005.

50 www.wipo.int/about-ip/en/ipworldwide/pdf/bf.pdf, see also www.culture.gov.bf/Site_Ministere/textes/reglementation/reglementation.htm#droit

51 Jonathan Haynes, "'Nollywood': What's in a Name?" 8 July, 2005. african-cinema-conference@xc.org

52 Olivier Barlet, "Nigéria" *Cahiers du Cinéma*, no. hors-série, April 2005, p. 81.

Bibliography

"Conférence de presse Africa Cinemas/ACID (Afrique Cinéma Diffusion) lundi 28 février 2005, FESPACO" (notes compiled by Aurore Engelen Loosen).

Africa Cinemas, "Rapport Final de la Réunion de Concertation avec les benéficiaries du programme Africa Cinemas," Bamako, 13–14 October, 2004.

Bachy, Victor. *La Haute-Volta et le cinéma*. Brussels: OCIC/L'Harmattan, 1983.

Barlet, Olivier. "Nigeria" *Cahiers du Cinéma*, no. hors-série, April 2005.

Boughedir, Ferid. "Economie et thémathique des cinémas Africains 1960–1985." PhD diss. (Doctorat d'Etat), University of Paris VII, 1986.

Cahiers du Cinéma, Atlas du cinema/World Cinema Atlas, hors-serie, April 2005.

Debrix, Jean René. "Le Cinéma Africain," *Afrique Contemporaine*, no. 40, 1970.

Direction de la Cinématographie Nationale, Ministère des Arts et de la Culture, Burkina Faso. "Programme d'Appui à la diffusion du Cinéma et de l'Audiovisuel (PADICIA)," janvier 2001.

Eklou, Kokovi. "Financement des études audiovisuelles et cinématographiques en Afrique: une table-rond," *Le Point*, 15 February 2005. www.lepointauquotidien.info/-article-php?id_article=2248

"Entretien: Justin Kagambèga – L'écoute est la clef de la réussite," *Regard*, No. 0120, 23–29 January 1995.

"The European Union and African, Caribbean and Pacific Cinema," brochure, no date.

Goldenstern, George. "Evaluation rétrospective de la politique européenne d'appui aux cinéma de la zone ACP (200–2004) – Rapport de synthèse," April 2005.

Hama, Baba. "Grand entretien Baba Hama, Délégué général du FESPACO," *L'opinion*, no. 385, 16–22 February, 2005.

Haynes, Jonathan. "'Nollywood': What's in a Name?" 8 July, 2005. african-cinema-conference@xc.org

Hennebelle Guy (ed.). *Les Télévisions du Monde – CinémAction*, Paris: Corlet, 1995.

Hien, Gervais. "Burkina: la Sonacib privatisée," *Fespaco News*, no. 23, mai–juin 2004. www.fespaco.bf/fespaconews23.pdf

Hoefert de Turégano, Teresa. *African Cinema and Europe: Close-up on Burkina Faso*, Florence, Italy: European Press Academic Publishing, 2004.

Frédéric Lefebvre-Naré, Olivier Barlet, Lucie Pothin, Paulin Yameogo, "Soutenir le cinéma des pays du sud: évaluation rétrospective de la coopération française dans la Zone de Solidarité Prioritaire (1991–2001)," Avril 2003.

Ouattara, Abou. "Circulation de l'image au sein de l'UEMOA: Télévisions nationals et producteurs se concertent à Ouagadougou," *L'hebdomadaire du Burkina*, no. 156, 15–21 March, 2002.

Organisation Internationale de la Francophonie. "Les industries culturelles des pays du sud: enjeux du projet de Convention internationale sur la diversité culturelle," August 2004 (written by Francisco d'Almeida and Marie Lise Allemen in collaboration with Bernard Miège and Dominique Wallon).

Ousseini, Inoussa, Ignacio Ramonet and Paulin Soumanou Vieyra, "Un bilan africain," *Le Monde Diplomatique*, March 1979, p. 25.

Réponses au questionnaire sur l'Institut Régional de l'Image et du Son (IRIS), www.burkinabedumonde.org/saba.html

Sama, Emmanuel. "Cinéma et audiovisuel Burkinabè," *Burkinescope*, no. 7, 2000.

Sama, Emmanuel. "Le film africain étranger sur son propre territoire." *Ecrans d'Afrique*, no. 4, 1993, pp. 54–67.

Tapsoba, Clement. "Burkina Faso" *Cahiers du Cinéma*, no. hors-série, April 2005.

Union Economique et Monétaire Ouest Africaine, "Programme d'Actions communes pour la production, la circulation et la conservation de l'image au sein des états membre de l'UEMOA" (Document amendé suite à la réunion sectorielle des Experts et des Ministres de la Culture et de la Communication, Bamako, 1–5 juin 2004), Ouagadougou, juin 2004, pp. 87 (www.uemoa.int/actes/2004/CM/annexe_DEC_6_04_CM.pdf)

United Nations Conference on Trade and Development, *The Least Developed Countries Report 2004*, UNCTAD Secretariat, United Nations: New York, 2004.

United Nations Conference on Trade and Development, Creative Industries and Development TD(XI)/BP/13, 4 June 2004.

United Nations Educational, Scientific and Cultural Organization, "Meeting of experts on audiovisual services: improving the participation of developing countries," (Organised by UNCTAD with the cooperation of UNESCO) Geneva, 13–15 November 2002 (working document prepared by the UNESCO secretariat), Paris October 2002.

United Nations Educational, Scientific and Cultural Organization, "Meeting of experts on problems of cultural policies in Africa – Dakar, 6–10 October 1969 – Final Report," SHC/CONF. 40/3 Paris, 24 November 1969.

United Nations Educational, Scientific and Cultural Organization, "Work shop on culture and development in NEPAD's programme of action," Abidjan, Ivory Coast, 2–5 Septbember 2003. Final Draft Report (new partnership for African's development NEPAD).

5 The music industry and its potential role in local economic development

The case of Senegal

Andy C. Pratt

Introduction

This chapter takes the case of Senegal, a country that at first sight appears to be a fine example of successful creative industries development, based on learning and innovation, bolstered by an increasing international reputation. The success of musicians such as Youssou N'Dour has created a visibility and an appreciation for West African music in general, in addition to highlighting the music of Senegal. On the basis of this, one might assume that music had become an industry, and that it was delivering significant benefits to both artists and the nation. However this potential has not yet been achieved, and until critical obstacles and weaknesses in the Senegalese music economy are resolved, it is unlikely to be.

The structure of this chapter is as follows. The first section sets out the conceptual framework, arguing that one needs to understand the economic and social process of the production of music, rather than just focusing on its output, or its static structure. The task is made more difficult by the lack of data that exists – in Senegal as in most countries of the world. The second section describes the underlying contexts of the policy environment, and the cultural and social development of music in Senegal. The third section analyses the music production and consumption economy, and assesses the challenges and opportunities that exist for Senegal. The fourth section evaluates the policy steps that are needed and this is followed by a conclusion.

The conceptual framework – understanding the production of music

The intention here is to understand the process of production of music, to appreciate the local conditions, and the nature of the processes, actors and regulatory contexts. This aim differs from a traditional analysis of 'the music industry' as it focuses on the dynamic processes rather than the static structures; additionally, it seeks to understand the trans-local nature of production (that it, its extension over time and space). First, we examine the whole production process, from concept to consumed product, in order to pick up the dynamic iterations between processes that give rise to innovation, adaptation and learning. In so doing I am seeking to avoid the trap of narrow conceptions of either production or consumption. Second, I want to stress the situatedness of all of these processes. With the stretching across legal boundaries these contexts can be quite different at various stages of production. Furthermore, transnational patterns of production and distribution can shape music production, and the economic benefits gained from it. This approach has similarities with that of Peterson (1976) in music; also see Pratt (2004a; 2004b) for an elaboration on such an approach more generally across the cultural industries.

The conceptualisation of cultural production as a linked chain, or perhaps as a network, has proven useful in spreading the concern of researchers and policymakers away from the high profile winners and the multinationals, to the whole 'system' of production. This perspective is, however, limited by the lack of reliable and relevant data.

In recent years, a number of governments have attempted to 'map' or measure the size of the creative industries sector. A major hurdle, even in the most developed nations, is that such data does not exist because census taxonomies do not distinguish modern creative activities; furthermore, a proportion of these activities are not-for-profit, part of the third sector, or the informal sector of economies, and so are not measured. Moreover, creative activities are commonly engaged in on a part-time, or multiple job-holding, basis. Census data usually refer to the 'primary activity' of people.

Such limitations mean that secondary data, even in the most developed countries, provide a less than perfect basis for auditing the creative industries. Even in the best cases data tend to be confined to grossed up categories. As for primary data, there are still at a very early stage in all countries. In part this is because they are expensive, and require the justification of secondary data collection: a 'Catch 22'. However, detailed analyses of what are now regarded by many as significant economic activities in the world economy, and that are rooted in particular locales, are overdue. Moreover, it is clear that policies directed towards the cultural industries require a robust evidential base. In large part this is because the cultural industries do seem to demonstrate some differences from the mainstream economy; this has led to many questions being raised about the effectiveness of generic industrial policies being directed to the cultural sector. This chapter on the music industry in Senegal therefore contributes timely information to our understanding of the form and impact of this economic activity in a developing country context. The chapter uses both secondary sources, where available, and primary sources. Primary data were collected through interview survey, as part of a project commissioned by UNCTAD.

Contexts

The context of local musical development in Senegal

Post-Colonial Senegal has had a tough economic struggle with development. Although some recent growth has been achieved, unemployment is about 48 per cent, of which 40 per cent involves urban youth. Despite these economic problems Senegal has sustained a reputation within West Africa for its pioneering efforts to promote creative activities and to develop cultural policies. This is helped by the Franco-cosmopolitan atmosphere of Dakar. For example, the 1966 World Festival of Negro Arts held in Dakar highlighted President Senghor's policy of negritude (Cathcart 1989). It is against this background that new forms of popular music have emerged and been registered by an international market. However, while the developed world's interest in West African music (especially Senegal, Mali and Côte d'Ivoire) is recent, music has a long tradition in Senegal; one that has benefited from the innovative encounter with other musical traditions.

Musical performance and form in Senegal has four important strands. First, it is strongly rooted in folk traditions and ways of life. Hand-crafted instruments and local languages are the medium of expression. Performers were known as 'griots', who held inherited positions and performed ceremonial roles to communicate news, history and traditions. A sub-group of performers, troubadours, carried on a more popular role of performer and acrobat, creating general entertainment. The position of a musician was a respected one that was generally passed down through the patriarchal line.

Second, French colonial forms and preferences of musical performance were imported. These traditions were modified through the early post-colonial period via the popularity of Latin American styles, sung in Spanish, as well as the emergent North American soul and rhythm and blues. Slowly, traditional Senegalese instruments were re-introduced and local languages, notably Wolof, used. A central figure in this early modernisation phase was Ibra Kasse, who attracted a number of imitators and emulators.

In the late 1970s and 1980s a third shift can be noted, that of the infusion of electrical instruments with traditional forms. The ready availability of cassettes that made possible both the recording and listening of music with a greater ease and portability that either reel-to-reel tapes or vinyl discs had a great impact on the diffusion of musical styles. There was also a growing self-confidence in musicians to develop their own styles; initially with jazz forms, and later with a unique Senegalese sound, notably Mbalax. This period marked the first wave of European successes. The second wave, in the 1990s, coinciding with the emergence of 'world music' and epitomised by artists such as N'Dour, is of artists who have developed an international reputation, but retained strong links, and residence, in Senegal.

Fourth, at present there are a new wave of bands, such as PBS, Daara-J and Pee-Froiss, performing a local form of rap and hip hop music that has made

Dakar a world node (after New York and Paris) of this art form. The latest shift in the music business in Senegal has been the rise of women performers such as Viviane N'Dour, Coumba Gawlo, Ajah Sa and My Sane. Gawlo has had significant success in France (signed to the label BMG), being awarded a platinum disc for the sales of her 1998 album 'Yo Malé'.

The recent course of music development can be summarised in five steps. First, an existing folk tradition that is overlain with a colonial form. Second, a post-colonial pattern of hybridisation, an interweaving of Western pop, jazz and Latin traditions with Senegalese instruments and forms. Third, a reassertion of folk forms, with modern instruments, and a re-embroidering of hybrid forms with traditional instruments and language. Fourth, in an early phase, the physical re-location to Europe to tour and record music; Paris is commonly the base (Stapleton 1989). Fifth, European and international touring linked to world music festival circuits and Western world music performers, but artists remaining based in Senegal and recording music locally.

Policy context

Whilst there is general cultural policy in Senegal, and various incentives for musical production and promotion, there is no explicit coordinated policy for music in Senegal. In part this is because, unlike most art forms, contemporary music exists almost exclusively in the private sector. The tradition of public policy-making in Senegal, as in most major nations, has been a grant-giving culture; a music policy, if it existed, would have to have more of an industrial character. This section discusses the Senegalese collecting society for royalties, le Bureau Sénégalais du Droit d'Auteur (BSDA) the tax and copyright system, the public support of music and training issues.

The legal status of the *protection of copyright* in Senegal is clear. Senegal has signed up to the Berne convention which allows rights holders to assert their moral rights regarding properties; however, it has not signed up to the Rome convention which concerns secondary rights associated with radio play and performances of music in public places. In practice, legal agreements are one thing, implementation is quite another. Here the collecting society plays a central role. Even with this partial legal structure, as many other developing and developed counties find, day-to-day regulation is another challenge. Here, the front-line battle is fought by the collecting society.

Collecting societies are vital for the functioning of a private music industry. Musicians may gain income either from live performance, or through the collection of money associated with the rights to use their music in the form of the music and words, radio play or of a tax on the cassette (a private right to replay). The BSDA was created in 1972 to oversee the collection of royalties and regulation of copyright issues. It is run by a board comprising authors, composers and the Ministry of Culture. It collects taxes at the rate of 35 per cent for mechanical reproduction rights, 7 per cent for radio replay rights and 35 per cent for public places.

Finally, there is the issue of *taxation proper*. I mention at several places in this chapter the level of taxation on imported goods: sound carriers and musical equipment and instruments. Potentially, this is a disincentive to import these goods, but in most cases there is no local substitute; thus, it is a potential barrier to creative development. Beyond the level of taxes associated with copyright are local taxes on the hiring of musical venues and on ticket sales, as well as on drink sales within clubs.

Regarding *public support of musical projects*, there has emerged a national and a West African regional support structure for film production in Senegal, but not a similar one in the field of music, nor the arts generally. Senegal has set up a House of Culture, whose remit is delimited by a national consultative committee for the promotion of culture, which has as its objectives the promotion of performance, exhibition of film, concerts and symposia. It receives an annual grant of 20 million CFA; support is also made for a network of (national) regional arts centres. The National Festival of Arts and Culture (FESNAC) circulates bi-annually around the regional capitals and it's a stimulus to local initiatives. This event has been a productive place for the promotion of regional musicians; musicians may receive grants for musical instrument purchase and practice rooms.

In 1982 Senegal created a National Orchestra, its mission was to represent Senegalese patrimony, research Senegalese music and to accompany national and international visitors. The Orchestra has four areas of specialism: jazz, classical, variety and traditional. The Orchestra also performs a training function. The RTS, the national broadcasting organisation established in 1972, has also played a role through its broadcast of music. Its studios provided a valuable early base for bands to make simple recordings. In addition there are a number of cultural events that serve as showcases for music, the Lights of Goree, the Saint Louis Jazz festival, and the annual midsummer 'National fête de la musique', which provides multiple platforms for musical performance.

Other significant institutional support is available through the Communications Development Assistance Program (PADEC) that was set up in 2000, with an initial three-year programme, with support of the Canadian government the endowment is 600 million CFA. Radio France International (RFI) runs a competition 'Discovered in Africa'/World music award which plays an important role in promoting young musicians; the prize includes an international concert funded by the cultural and technical cooperation agency (ACCT) through the intergovernmental agency of the French-speaking world (AIF), CIRTEF (Conseil International des Radios-Télévisions d'Expression Française) and the Alliance Française. Whilst such initiatives provide publicity and access to an audience, there is a concern that they also have an unintended consequence of exporting musicians to France, rather than retaining them in Senegal.

The cultural initiatives support programme (Programme de Soutien aux Initiatives Culturelles: PSIC) is financed by the European Union, though managed by the Ministry of Culture. PSIC finances cultural projects in deprived and remote communities; its range of art forms covered includes music. Currently there are 14 projects supported, which corresponds to 65 per cent of the funds available; of this almost one-third (22 million CFA) is used in musical projects, mainly to aid the production and recording of tapes.

Music production in Senegal

The aim of this section is to provide an analysis of the production of music in Senegal. The Music Production System (MPS) is a version of the cultural industries production system, or production chain, that underpins the UNESCO (1988) concept of the cultural industries. In essence the model is simple, it follows six notional steps from the initial idea, through writing (called content origination), to making a recording (production), reproduction (distribution), consumption (retail or live performance), and includes archiving and education and training. These last two elements provide visibility for the cross-cutting and feedback elements that characterise the model.

Content origination

This step concerns the initial idea of a piece of music, and it also concerns the position of the artist; necessarily it implies training and education as well. This task requires time and resources. In the Senegalese case there has been a tradition, after the notion of the griot, of a singer-songwriter-composer. This combined with erratic interpretation and application of IPR rules has created tensions between those who specialise in just one of these tasks (see below). There has been a struggle, for example, to get recognition for the role of songwriters; this is often manifest in the decision to print the writer/composer's name on the cassette sleeve.[1] The situation of musicians is also problematic. A very small proportion are employed by the state in the National Orchestra, for the vast majority they are self-employed, engaged in multiple job holding, or engaged on contract for bands, or bars, restaurants and hotels. This erratic nature of employment is the norm the world over; it is a major stumbling block if music is envisaged to be a tool of economic regeneration.

The AMS is a local organisation formed to pursue the rights of musicians; however, as yet there is no collective agreement on contracts or wages (as in other countries which have Musicians' Unions). The remuneration of musicians still remains low. Clearly, if a band has a regular engagement in a club or restaurant then a note of stability may be introduced to their employment; however, a higher risk strategy involves touring internationally. This requires investment, and the possibility of erratic rewards. Likewise the same system can apply to recording, musicians commonly being paid on a one-off basis rather than contracting for a proportion of royalties.

Other bands adopt different systems, notably just being employed for the touring period. Some artists, or their management, adopt a strategy of being paid for a concert tour. With headline acts, common practice is for the 'star' to have a preferable deal, as well as being in sole receipt of any copyright income. The precarious nature of employment has prompted AMS to campaign for a form of social insurance for musicians.

There is very little infrastructure required for content origination aside from access to basic materials, and possibly a quite place to practise. These facilities can be found relatively easily.

Production

This stage involves making a master tape of the song that will later be reproduced; it includes recording and mixing the music. The main issue here is access to a recording studio. It is significant that recording studios have been constructed in Senegal (Dakar) in recent years. Prior to this there was no option but to travel abroad. In the late 1970s the recording hub of West Africa was Abidjan, Ivory Coast (Eyre 2000); otherwise it was Europe: usually Paris or London, but sometimes Brussels (Stapleton 1989). A few early recordings did take place in nightclubs using rudimentary mixing desks. The first local studios appeared in the late 1970s, however the norm was either the use of broadcasting studios or nightclubs. There are two international-quality studios in Dakar. Both establishments have a variety of studio sizes and digital recording and mixing facilities (48-track desks). In addition new technologies allow small-scale home studios. As in Europe and elsewhere it is possible to make reasonable recordings this way, but they are not a serious alternative to a full studio and its mixing facilities. It is not known how many 'home studios' exist.

The role of the producer is to be the impresario or organiser, sometimes also the engineer. Producers seldom have this as their only employment; commonly they will act as producer for one or two cassettes. An Association of Producers has recently been formed. Producers are usually the ones to advance money for the studio time so that musicians can make a recording and mass produce their tapes. Usually musicians receive a flat, once and for all fee, with no participaton in royalties.

The other key element is the recording engineer's expertise; there were local basic technicians, but there was a critical lack of recording engineers. This led to foreign engineers being brought to Senegal or recording taking place abroad. Alternatively, a basic recording may be done in Senegal and other elements added, and mixed, abroad. There appears to be no market in 'singles' and only albums are produced. In practice, this means that local recordings aimed at cassette distribution have 6–8 tracks. An international norm would be 12 tracks or more.

Reproduction (distribution)

The stage of reproduction is threefold. The first concerns the mass production of songs from a master tape and their transformation into cassettes, records or CDs (the sound carrier). The second involves the technical equipment and musical instruments, the machinery to make the sound carriers and production technology, as well as the domestic playback machines. The third comprises the channels of distribution (radio, TV and the Internet, as well as physical goods). We take these three issues in turn.

Mass production

Practically all Senegal's domestic recordings are currently distributed on cassette. There have never been any domestic vinyl pressing plants and, as yet, there are no facilities for commercial production of CDs. We identified three cassette duplication 'factories'; two associated with the two studios noted above, and a third, instigated in 2002, Keur Serigne Been (KSF). These facilities are able to produce 10,000 cassettes a day. Separate, but related, is the production of the artwork and packaging for the cassettes. The unit cost of these is between 15 and 30 CFA; promotional posters are also produced, often from the same artwork, at a common unit cost of 350 CFA.

There is a small import market for CDs and there is an unknown scale of trade in non-domestic cassettes. CDs and cassettes attract an import duty of 140 per cent of the price. The volume of the cassette trade is difficult to estimate as it overlaps with pirated recordings. Various estimates of the degree of piracy range between 60 and 90 per cent before the introduction of hologram marking in 2002; this may have been halved since that time. The Association of Producers suspects that much pirated material emanates from outside of Senegal: informants alleged that Guinea, Tanzania, Togo, Sierra Leone and Nigeria were most likely to blame.[2] However, informants also suggested that some small-scale duplication (up to 200 a day) originates within Senegal.

Equipment

Traditional instruments are manufactured in Senegal; there are no data on this industry or its output. However, we estimate it to be at the level of craft production. When one is considering the contemporary music business the concern is with modern electrical instruments, recording and playback equipment. It is clear that all of this equipment is imported; musical instruments, a category which includes recording equipment, attracts an import taxation of 70 per cent. Some data are available on the value of imports by various categories, although there are not especially useful for our task. However, an approximate total of such goods was 600 million CFA in 2002 (having doubled, in physical volume – the only measure available – in the previous six years).

Distribution/dissemination

Once duplicated, cassettes are distributed wholesale to retailers; this is normally carried out on a 'deposit' account. The wholesale price for cassettes per unit ranges between 700 and 900 CFA depending upon popularity of the artist. It is estimated that as much as 50 per cent of the national market is accounted for by one distributor (although products sometimes appear under a different label).

Modern music is but one part of the music market, something approaching 30 per cent of sales is of religious music, as well as a proportion of traditional or folk music.

Consumption

It is notable that there is very little consumption of non-Senegalese, non-Western music. On one hand the import taxation would dissuade buyers, but on the other one might have expected distributors or producers to license foreign music. There was little knowledge or interest in the products of musicians from other West African states; knowledge of Western pop forms comes from radio play. There are three routes to market: broadcast, retail and live performance.

Radio and TV

Radio stations seemed not to be interested in playing music from the region. This fact seems strange to those viewing the picture from a European perspective where world music is often marketed on a regional basis (West Africa), and interest is in the music of West African states, notably Mali and Senegal. There seems to be both a missed opportunity for external marketing, and one of the development of the musical form through cross-fertilisation. Some Senegalese distributors do export cassettes; representative figures were 10 per cent to Gambia and 15 per cent to Europe (of which half went to France). It is estimated that 1.5 million cassettes are legally produced per annum in Senegal.

An important area of promotion of artists and music is via radio and TV. Music videos have become very important in this respect. There are few data on output or use of this means of promotion. It seems clear that this part of the industry is at an early stage of development. Music videos are important as TV stations are prepared to play them, and as such provide another outlet for music. In a more traditional mode there are a number of radio stations broadcasting in Senegal. But, as Senegal is not a signatory of the Rome convention, the payment of royalties is idiosyncratic. Contributions are not made in direct reference to radio play, but negotiated through one-off settlements. Once again, the radio programmes have a limited range and either play Western or Senegalese music. Surprisingly, there is little programming of showcasing music from other West African countries or Africa more generally.

Whilst this deals with access to audiences within Senegal it is notable that a major means by which Senegalese music has found North American and European markets is through radio play. Specialist programmes and awards with mainly public broadcasters have led the way (BBC in the UK, RFI in France and NPR in North America). Likewise small independent, European-based, music distributors have also played a significant role in audience development (for example, World Circuit and Sterns in London).

Retail

This stage of the MPS concerns how cassettes and music eventually find their audience. Commonly, this is via a retail outlet or a live performance. It was from 1990 onwards that the cassette made its presence felt in the Senegalese marketplace and dynamised the music industry. The retail environment is based upon market sales; there is only one dedicated 'record shop' in Dakar. The vast majority of sales take place formally and informally in the Sandaga market. The retail price point is between 1,000 and 1,500 CFA per cassette. Sales are from market stalls and itinerant sellers. There is little if any market information aside from the recommendation of the merchant and the cassette cover.

It is notable that with such a hazy grasp of music sales in total, there is very little concrete information on sales by artist or album. There are some problems with the quality of data collection by BSDA, and with their redistribution of royalties to composers. The result is that there is no feedback between popularity and sales. The mechanism of the collation of charts that signal weekly sales, and in the West act as a means of sales promotion and concentration of demand, does not exist in Senegal. Until there are more data collected on retail sales, or on royalties paid, this cannot happen.

Live performance

Another means of access to market is via live performance. As has already been noted, Senegalese music has grown out of a nightclub culture; nightclubs have played a role in employing musicians, especially where there is a 'house band' of prospective stars. The nightclub is a vital space in that it offers musicians instant feedback on their performance. The level of national taxation on live performance can be as high as 40 per cent.

The majority of venues for live performance are located in Dakar, although some are to be found in the regional capitals. There is no audit (official or unofficial) of the number of nightclubs or their capacities, or the ranges of music that they promote. At its pinnacle is the Theatre Daniel Sorano, which has a capacity of 1,200. A larger venue, though only occasionally used for the purpose, is the Demba Diop Stadium, which has a capacity of 15,000. There are an estimated 30 clubs, plus a number of piano bars and hotel lobbies that act as performance spaces for bands or individual singers. There are four or five larger clubs with a capacity of between 500 and 700.

The other means of organising live performance is for bands to tour the country. Many nightclubs have their own basic sound systems and bands are able to tour from club to club. However, it is common for bands in other countries to take their sound system with them to guarantee the quality of sound and appropriate availability. There is a severe lack of basic infrastructure and expertise to 'tour' bands: there were only three sound systems in Senegal, and only one capable of being used at the stadium. One of the obstacles noted was the poor quality of local infrastructure to support large and heavy vehicles, the other was management.

Outside of Senegal the role of concert and festival promoters in bringing artists to Europe to gain initial exposure is the essential step to gaining a recording contract. Musicians tend to be 'discovered' by Europeans already involved in the music industry. This 'discovery' usually takes the form of arranging for the band to appear at a European festival or tour in Europe. Touring builds up a market for the band's music, and then an album is recorded in Europe, for a European/American label. The recording, commonly in Paris, uses local West African musicians and the 'star' of the band. The album, pressed as a CD, is then distributed via the record company (few find their way back to Senegal as a CD – as noted previously they attract a significant import tax). The band, or their star performer, may or may not return to Senegal. The 'Catch 22' is that bands have to leave Senegal to reach the economically significant stage of their careers. Many never return.

Education and training: a critique

The high school curriculum does not include compulsory music education, as far as we could observe there is little extra-curricula teaching of musical appreciation or performance. The Blaise Senghor cultural centre does hold a number of outreach workshops for children in the field of the arts generally. As noted above, the National Orchestra has a wide remit of specialist musical forms. The Music Conservatoire serves as a training school for members of the Orchestra. In turn this provides a vital, though small, trained cardre of musicians, some of whom play the role of musical arrangers for popular musicians when they record.

There is local recognition amongst those representing musicians that there is a deficit in knowledge both of consumers and producers about intellectual property rights, their regulation and control; notably how producers should assert their rights. Moreover, the AMS point to the issue of the low level of professionalism amongst its current and potential members. It is increasingly recognised that the skills of the management of bands, recording and touring, and the negotiation of rights amongst band members, and within a recording deal, are important issues and are in serious deficit. I have already noted that recording studios commented upon the lack of trained recording engineers and producers. This is a particular problem that encourages bands to record in Europe rather than Senegal. However, the problem extends to the management of bands too.

Archive and copyright issues

The BSDA is charged with the protection of intellectual property rights, although it has been argued that its remit is not as precise as it might be in how this task is pursued. Several commentators argued that the BSDA had until the recent past not been as effective an agency as it might ideally have been (Seck 2004). With its new director, significant changes have been made, notably by the introduction of a hologram system of stickers on cassettes to reduce piracy. Official holographic stickers are applied to legal cassettes and consumers are encouraged to choose legal over illegal ones. The system would seem to have been successful with registered sales data increasing by 50 per cent overnight. However, for a hard-pressed agency like the BSDA this is a mixed blessing, it has posed a major administrative burden on them.

The production of holograms is now an indicator of sales. The hologram itself has to be purchased by the wholesaler at 30 CFA. For each cassette the BSDA takes 8 per cent (average 80 CFA); 65 per cent of this sum goes to authors: 50 per cent to the composer of the lyrics, 50 per cent the music. Data from the BSDA indicate a healthy expansion of music sales. Something in the region of 110 new albums are released each year, sales have run from 467,000 in 1997 to 622,000 in 2000 and the value of receipts in 1997 was 291 million CFA (equating to sales of ten times this amount).

The BSDA has had a difficult time. Some commentators suggest poor management. Seck (2004) claims that the present incumbent entered the post to find only 50,000 CFA in the account. However, new management and the introduction of the hologram system have boosted royalty receipts significantly, and inevitably added to the administrative burden of BSDA. It is difficult to generalise, as with all music industry distribution the majority of cassettes are doomed to failure; some only last 1 month in the marketplace, others six months or more. A popular cassette may register sales of 50–80,000 units. The short life of a cassette, 3–4 months, compares with 12–18 months in North America. This simply means that Senegalese musicians are exploiting themselves.

A final issue concerns the vast reserve of indigenous and folk music in Senegal. These are not under copyright and locals and visitors can easily appropriate them. A system of protection and archiving might perform the function of protection and preservation of a rich heritage.

Evaluation

In the previous section I outlined the existing music production system in Senegal. I have shown that this system is characterised by a number of factors. The most striking is the isolation of the internal from the external system. This dualism functions effectively to reduce the impact of piracy for the international system. It also has the effect of stunting any potential growth that may develop the local music industry. Under these conditions there is little economic incentive to control piracy internally. First, if piracy were removed tomorrow, there is still only a limited income to be had from internal market sales. Second, the whole internal music system has effectively sidelined piracy as musicians get paid a one-off fee for recording and earn most income through live performance. As such – under the current conditions – piracy is not a central issue locally. However, this state of affairs leads to other barriers: first, the limited number of night clubs restricts the overall number of bands that can survive within such a system; second, musicians constantly have to produce new music and hence 'waste' their talent.

The musicians and the music industry in Senegal are constrained to a small market and minimal turnover, based upon a system that has little respect for copyright. Beyond this there are considerable risks that Senegal's musical heritage could be 'plundered' by external agencies and copyrighted by them. The possibility, for a few, of touring in Europe and collaboration with European and US musicians offers a real potential of breakthrough into international export markets. However, as much of the higher value and skill inputs through recording and distribution are currently external to the Senegalese economy there is little re-investment and economic development. Despite this fact, some musicians who have had success in the international market have, for personal reasons, invested in studio facilities in Senegal. However, it is revealing that skilled technicians and management come from outside; thus, once again the possibility of the transmission of such skills more widely is reduced.

The challenge for Senegal, and other countries in a similar position, is to 'upgrade' their skills and infrastructure (Gereffi *et al.* 2001; Bair and Gereffi 2003). This process is far from simple. The private initiatives pursued by various individuals in Dakar have developed a sound base of physical infrastructure for recording. Other public- funded initiatives have begun to address issues of management.

There is still a serious gap in relation to skilled producers and recording technicians that has yet to be addressed. The possibilities of touring within West Africa are, as yet, not being developed to any significant extent. In part this is dependent on basic infrastructure such as roads and electricity, on tour management and on market development. In the latter case, broadcast radio and television have a role to play in developing a regional music culture.

However, underpinning all of these initiatives is a key issue: copyright and intellectual property rights. What is clear is that an instant shift from one regime to another would fail. The transition, if it is to occur, has to be a slow one that involves fundamental changes in all of the agents and institutions involved in the music production system internally. Beyond this Senegal must face a further problem of how to retain as much of this local production infrastructure (soft and hard) as possible, as well as having a significant stake in distribution.

The fundamental changes that would be required concern a basic respect for ownership of music produced, and a recognition of the rights of songwriters and lyricists, as well as that of musicians and management. Moreover, the respect of audiences for these rights has to be instilled at school age. This change presents some challenges to the traditions of the griots, which is an issue that has to be resolved locally. Only if such changes are made can there be a flow of income that can sustain musicians and writers *as* musicians and writers. As professionals, they will then be in a position (economically and socially) to develop, train and hone their skills. Furthermore, once a regularisation of intellectual property rights is achieved, then Senegal can become more integrated into the regional and world economy (for music). Moreover, the introduction of property rights associated with traditional music (a sort of national 'commons') would protect that heritage and when exploited the revenue could return to the state.

Concurrently, Senegal would need to develop a music distribution infrastructure and local and regional markets for its output. It is clear that this is difficult in a world dominated by powerful multinationals. However, local talent agents, recording and management, and deals for distribution may achieve some autonomy. These issues, although vital, are beyond the bounds of this chapter.

Conclusion

The aim of this chapter has been to explore the role of music in local economic development. I have shown that in Senegal, as in many similar small nations, music has the potential to contribute to local economic development. However, the current nature of music production – and its supporting institutions – is currently insufficient for such a task. I used the concept of the music production system to highlight the integrated nature of music production and the multiple points of stress within it. It is such an evidence base – one that is locally specific – that is required to address these issues and build effective policy.

Overall, it is quite remarkable that Senegal's musicians have achieved so much. The inadequacies, or incompatibilities, of the local music system compared with international ones have led to two problems: first, the export of talent and higher value activities; second, little pressure to reform notions, and practical understanding of, intellectual property rights. As noted above a 'big bang' reform is not likely to work to change this system – potentially it would destroy it. A range of subtle changes would need to be made based upon a clear understanding of where the music industry currently stands in terms of production processes and where it is desired that it be in the future.

In terms of policy, community music has traditionally fallen into the realm of cultural policy: usually with the objectives of promotion of national identity to the world. As identity promotion is not generally seen as an economic objective activities associated with it are seldom evaluated as such. This chapter has suggested that music might also be viewed as an economic activity. However, this is not to suggest that it is only a commercial activity. By stressing the whole production process we can see that some aspects of music production are not 'economic'; in any situation a *balance* has to be struck between the for-profit and the not-for-profit: it should not be an 'either/or' decision. Thus, the promotion of a musical heritage at an economic loss in a narrow sense could be seen as the sustenance of a valuable musical heritage, a resource or a training facility for musicians and for audiences. Many musicians shift between commercial and non-commercial activities within their career, or even within a season. The withdrawal of one or the other opportunity can be mutually corrosive. Hence, an appreciation of a *hybrid* music production system requires policy-makers to explore innovative areas of mixed economy policy-making. Potentially, state or third-sector agencies could play a role in real strategic support planning of the development of this important industry.

As has been noted above, this vision, that is of an appreciation of the full music production system, requires insightful and meaningful information to provide a robust evidence base for policy-making. Here both secondary data collected by census and other existing survey tools may need to be refined. Inevitably, such information collection will need to be supplemented by focused primary data. An appreciation and the development of critical thinking about policy-making that acknowledges the subtle interface between for-profit and not-for-profit activities is also important. It is only with these notions in place that it will be possible for countries such as Senegal to reap the benefits of its musical expertise in a sustainable manner that will feed back into economic development locally.

Acknowledgements

I would like to thank Zeljka Kozul-Wright and UNCTAD, for initiating the mission on the music industry of Senegal and supporting the methodological approach and commenting on drafts (with the cooperation of ILO and UNESCO). This paper draws upon the report written by me for that project (Pratt 2004c). I would like to thank Biram N'Deck Ndiaye for help with interviews, interpreting and background research. The chapter is dedicated to the current and future musicians of Senegal.

Notes

1 In this case writers are unable to assert their moral right to their work, and to protect their IPRs.

2 We did not receive any concrete evidence to establish this. Interestingly, Eyre (2000) discusses the issue of piracy in Mali. He claims that a major source was Sierra Leone. Initially the pirates had been based in Liberia (importing cassettes from Asia). Elsewhere Eyre discusses how artists are in constant battle with the pirates, even resorting to releasing their albums in the rainy season when pirates will be held up by poor transport.

Bibliography

Bair, J. and G. Gereffi. 2003. Upgrading, uneven development, and jobs in the North American apparel industry. *Global Networks – a Journal of Transnational Affairs* 3 (2): 143–169.

Burnett, R. 1995. *The Global Jukebox*. London: Routledge.

Cathcart, J. 1989. The music of West Africa: a period of transition. In *Rhythms of the World*, edited by F. Hanly and T. May. London: BBC Books.

Eyre, B. 2000. *In Griot Time*. London: Serpents Tail.

Feld, S. 1994. Notes on world beat. In *Music Grooves*, edited by C. Keil and S. Feld. Chicago: University of Chicago Press.

Frith, S. and A. Goodwin, eds. 1990. *On Record: Rock, Pop and the Written Word*. London: Routledge.

Gereffi, G., J. Humphrey, R. Kaplinsky and T.J. Sturgeon. 2001. Introduction: Globalisation, value chains and development. *Ids Bulletin – Institute of Development Studies* 32 (3): 1–8.

Goodwin, A. and J. Gore. 1990. World beat and the cultural imperialism debate. *Socialist Review* 20 (3):63–80.

Gronow, P. 1998. *An International History of the Recording Industry*. London: Cassell.

Hesmondhalgh, D. 1996. Flexibility, post-Fordism and the music industries. *Media Culture & Society* 18 (3): 469–488.

Hesmondhalgh, D. 2002. *The Cultural Industries*. London: SAGE.
Negus, K. 1993. Global harmonies and local discords; transitional policies and practices in the European record industry. *European Journal of Communication* 8 (3): 293–316.
Negus, K. 1999. *Music Genres and Corporate Subcultures*. London: Routledge.
Peterson, R.A. ed. 1976. *The Production of Culture*. London: Sage.
Pratt, A.C. 1997. The cultural industries production system: a case study of employment change in Britain, 1984–91. *Environment and Planning A* 29 (11): 1953–1974.
Pratt, A.C. 2004a. Creative Clusters: Towards the governance of the creative industries production system? *Media International Australia* 112: 50–66.
Pratt, A.C. 2004b. The cultural economy: a call for spatialized 'production of culture' perspectives. *International Journal of Cultural Studies* 7 (1): 117–128.
Pratt, A.C. 2004c. The music industry in Senegal: the potential for economic development. A report prepared for UNCTAD.
Pratt, A. C. 2005. Cultural industries and public policy: An oxymoron? *International Journal of Cultural Policy* 11 (1): 31–44.
Seck, T. 2004. *Radio interview, Wal Fadjri*, 8 March.
Stapleton, C. 1989. Paris, Africa. In *Rhythms of the World*, edited by F. Hanly and T. May. London: BBC Books.
Taylor, T. 1997. *Global Pop: World Music, World Markets*. London: Routledge.
Throsby, D. 2001. *Economics and Culture*. Cambridge: Cambridge University Press.
Wallis, R. and K. Malm. 1984. *Big Sounds from Small Peoples: the Music Industry in Small Countries*. London: Constable.

6 The sounds of Brazil

The popular music and the music industry

José E. Cassiolato, Marcelo Matos and Helena Lastres

Introduction

The concepts of creative and cultural industries have been recently introduced into the development agenda. According to a UNESCO document they:

> add value to contents and generate value for individuals and societies. They are knowledge and labor intensive, create employment and wealth, nurture creativity – the "raw material" they are made from – and foster innovation in production and commercialization processes. At the same time, cultural industries are central in promoting and maintaining cultural diversity and ensuring democratic access to culture.
>
> (UNESCO, 2000)

The increased importance of international trade in cultural goods and services may partially explain the new interest in such an industry. It grew an average 8.1 percent per year from 1980 (amounting US$95.3 billion) to 1998 (when it reached US$387.9 billion) (UNESCO, 2000).[1] However, international trade in cultural goods and services has been extremely concentrated in the developed world.

Among the creative industries, the music industry stands up as an important element of a development strategy. The music industry is already recognized by international agencies (such as UNCTAD and ILO) and national governments as one of the fastest growing export service sectors (Anderson *et al.*, 2000). Labeled by some as "a complex animal" (Malm and Wallis, 1992: 5), it encompasses a variety of actors. Since music is easily personalized and transmitted, it also permeates many other services across cultural borders, like advertising and publishing, TV and radio, cinema and other performing arts. An important component of the industry is its concentration, which is also increasing. Four mega-enterprises control over 90 percent of US sales and between 70 and 80 percent of world sales of music records (Burnett, 1995: 18). Brazil is not an exception. These same enterprises control more then 80 percent of the market (Barbosa, 2003).

The domination by these companies of all and correlated aspects of the market (software and hardware, film and video, etc.) has ignited an important debate about the control of media and cultural industries and how harmful it can be for local indigenous cultures. However, there has also been a line of reasoning that suggests that developments in information and communication technologies are continually opening up new forms of musical production and distribution, and increasingly permitting small local producers to penetrate local and global markets. In fact, developments in information technology are affecting copyright – the foundation of the industry since the 1970s. Therefore, the global and local structures of the music industry are going through some fundamental changes. Also, by bringing production costs down and by accelerating the diffusion of novelties, new technologies are challenging the traditional structure of the music industry. One can argue that there is, nowadays, a double movement with concentration of music production and rights by the majors and the fragmentation of forms of production that challenges the structure of the industry.

The production process of music is essentially a creative, innovating act characterized by various degrees of novelty and originality. Hence the localized nature of musical activities, which is an important complementarity to the globalization trend. Current changes in the industry and its crisis have to be understood within this framework of overarching transformation.

These transformations are actually bringing threats and opportunities to developing countries in general and to Brazil in particular. The Brazilian case is interesting for the development debate for several reasons. Its large size and regional differences mean that extreme diversity is found in cultural and music traditions. At the same time common language and strong national identity mean that such diversity is accompanied by national appeal. Several different music festivals (of which the Rio Carnival is the most widely known) occur in various parts of the country all over the year and they have national repercussion and participation. There is an abundance of skilled local talent and live music scenes and performances characterize the country's cultural landscape.

Another important characteristic of Brazilian music which is common to other developing countries is its high level of informality. It is also common to find all over the country playing musicians that do not ask for any payment in return for their performance. Informal working relations also abound in the Brazilian music industry, making it difficult to be measured.

There are other features worth mentioning regarding the formal industry in Brazil. One is that most music records sold are local music. This makes Brazil the only country, apart from the USA and Japan, where locally generated products are responsible for at least 80 percent of the internal market. The second is the size of the formal market: in the mid-1990s, with sales of US$1.4 billion, Brazil was the sixth largest market in the world. Subsequent crisis in the Brazilian economy meant that sales dropped to US$724.7 million in 2000 and US$540 million in 2001 when Brazil became the twelfth largest market (IFPI 2005).

This chapter aims at analyzing the Brazilian music industry. The second section will briefly present the evolution of music in Brazil. The third section will show the Brazilian music industry, while the fourth will discuss public policies. The chapter finishes with a brief discussion of possibilities of a diversified music manifestation vis-à-vis a mass consumption market and points to the main policy implications.

Evolution of popular music in Brazil

The Brazilian popular music has been coined by Antonio Cândido, one of our most distinguished intellectuals, as "the daily bread of national culture" (Diniz 2006). The evolution of Brazilian music reflects the singular formation process of Brazilian society, marked by its multiethnic and multicultural features. It has been strongly influenced by a series of economic and political events.

Brazilian popular music is the direct and inseparable result of the mingling of races and their cultures. As the poet and composer Ricardo Cravo Albim (1998: 278) pointed out: "Brazilian popular music began when, in the slave quarter of a mansion somewhere, the Indians started to imitate the slaves as they clapped their hands and the white colonizers abandoned themselves to the magical, mellifluous singing of the slave."

In fact, there are two key moments in Brazilian history that could be singled out as those which had the most significant impact in the music scene. The first came with the abolishment of slavery and the subsequent urbanization process that gained momentum in the last decade of the nineteenth century and the first decade of the twentieth century. The second resulted from the industrialization process that has transformed the Brazilian economic landscape since the 1950s, the expansion of the internal market and the inclusion of social segments that were marginalized before.

The first of these moments made it possible, albeit slowly, for music creation to benefit from the contact between different cultural roots. For three centuries of colonization, the songs for the ritual dances of the Indians and the African songs of the slaves, both based on percussion instruments, were mostly separated from the ballads of the Europeans colonizers that had their origins in the medieval towns of the twelfth to fourteenth centuries. All this started to change when slavery was abolished, at the end of the nineteenth century, and urbanization developed at the beginning of the twentieth century. These processes provided means for different types of music to integrate. From the convergence of the different cultural manifestations, unified by the Portuguese language, emerged the popular Brazilian music (Vasconselos, 1991).

The growth of the cities led to a diversified urban population, where different cultures and ethnic groups started to interact. In this context, the first styles of Brazilian popular music appeared: the *lundu* and *modinha*. The combination, that "sensually and slowly matured over four centuries" (Albim, 2005), gave rise to the *choro*, the *maxixe*, the *frevo* and the *samba*.[2] The mixed population began to organize into recreational groups, initially called *cordões carnavalescos* (carnival circles) and later *blocos carnavalescos* (carnival troupes). In 1893 the first *ranchos* (carnival clubs) were created in Rio de Janeiro; small groups that began to take part in the carnivals producing a type of orchestral music that would give rise to one of the most endearing musical forms of Brazilian music: the *marchas-ranchos* (marches-parades) (Albim, 2005).

Technical change also had a significant impact. These initial music styles had their expression amplified by the introduction of the phonograph recording activity at the beginning of the twentieth century. Foreign records were imported, igniting a process of mixture between local and foreign music (Zan, 2001). A market of recorded music evolved in the country with the foundation, in Rio de Janeiro in 1900, of Edison House, a locally owned firm that commercialized cylinders, discs, phonographs and gramophones and which set up the first Brazilian recording studio, stimulating the production of local music.[3]

In 1913, Edison House associated with a foreign company to set up the first recording industry in Brazil. At the end of the 1920s Victor, Odeon, Columbia, Parlophon and Brunswick had set up subsidiaries in Brazil. All of this had a significant impact on the music landscape. Since the duration of the songs were limited by the recording techniques to about four minutes, musicians began to create music with more concise letters and melodies of simple memorization, setting the scene for the beginning and consolidation of a mass music market (Silva, 2001).

From the 1930s to the early 1950s, under the Vargas dictatorship, Brazilian music evolved under a discourse marked by nationalism and the search for cultural identity. The introduction of the electrical recording system led to better sound quality and the artists started to develop a more melodic singing style. The 1930s were also marked by the expansion of the radio, which became the main music diffusion medium with live musical programs for large audiences (Tinhorão, 1998). Along the diffusion of the radio the music market expanded and three large companies – Odeon, RCA Victor and Columbia – dominated the market. A very important mark of this period is the breaking of social barriers in the creation and consumption of music, epitomized by the partnership of Noel Rosa, a young upper-class university student, with leading poor samba composers such as Ismael Silva. This partnership produced the most beautiful sambas of the period and in fact meant the popularization of samba, losing its original ethnic identity to become a symbol of national culture (Zan, 2001).

It was in the 1950s that the second of the above-mentioned key moments in the evolution of Brazilian music happened. Industrialization meant increasing of the home market for different products, including music products. Television was introduced in the 1950s. Together with radio it helped to promote regional music styles in the whole country.[4]

Live programs on radio continued to be important till the late 1960s. However, from the mid-1950s to the end of the 1960s television played a key role. First, the beginning of television transmissions offered an alternative access to music for the conservative segments of the upper classes, those that could afford the high price of TV sets. This antagonism between "higher" and popular culture led to a deeper segmentation of the music market. Television and the conservative middle class promoted an invasion of foreign rhythms, in particular boleros and rumbas, along with the youth-oriented styles, such as the cha-cha-cha, rock and twist.

The reaction produced three interconnected movements. Initially the upsurge of *Bossa Nova* in the more intellectualized segments of the middle class in Rio de Janeiro revolutionized Brazilian music and created the conditions for the first and everlasting incursion of local music into the international scene. *Bossa nova*, which incorporated into samba elements of jazz and classical music, was born as a response to a period of stagnation in Brazilian popular music and the above-mentioned invasion of foreign music. It was also a by-product of the optimism generated by import substitution industrialization. During the late 1950s and early 1960s several new artistic movements emerged in Brazil along with *Bossa Nova*: in cinema with the *Cinema Novo* (New Cinema movement), in poetry with *Concretismo* (Concretism) and even in classical music with the *Dodecafonistas* (followers of Schoenberg's harmonic idiom) (Albim, 2005).

The second movement was a reaction to the 1964 military regime. There was a polarization between intellectualized and conservative positions. On the one hand, music was significantly influenced by the politicized speech of the left-oriented youth and their valuation of popular cultural roots (Napolitano, 2002). MPB (popular Brazilian music) was marked by politically engaged lyrics protesting against the dictatorial regime. Estimates suggest that during the military regime more than a thousand songs with ideological content were censored (Zan, 2001). On the conservative side, the iê-iê-iê came to the front stage. It was performed by a group of musicians called the *Jovem Guarda* (Young Guard) and consisted of an adaptation of rock-and-roll with unpretentious lyrics and without any ideological content.

In such a landscape of ideological polarization, the third musical movement was developed in the State of Bahia. The *Tropicalismo* attempted to overcome this dichotomy, incorporating varied national and foreign music elements. *Tropicalismo* was recently summarized by one of its founders, Gilberto Gil, one of our most famous musicians and Minister of Culture in the 2003–2006 period, in the following way:

> Here, in this tropical land, almost thirty years ago, we were young people from different parts of the country who understood: we belong to the world and the world belongs to us. We are part of everything and we are in every part. That consciousness pushed us to create a new music that was at the same time the oldest music. We uncovered tradition, we paid tribute to our old masters, we celebrated the new revelation of bossa nova and allowed ourselves to be shaken by the whirlwind of rock 'n' roll. We believed that the future was to live in the present.
>
> (Gil, 1993)

The industrialization process also ignited an important institutionalization process in the music industry. It is true that music associations were already set up in the 1930s, but it was in 1965 that the main recording companies created the Brazilian Association of Discs Producers (ABPD). In 1973, the Central Office of Collection and Distribution (ECAD) was set up. ECAD assumed the role of collecting and distributing the copyrights related to musical execution. An important achievement of ABPD was the setting up by government of a law allowing for tax breaks in 1967 and which fomented the production of national recordings. Another incentive for local music production came with the multiplication of musical programs on the television, especially the "Song Festivals" in the late 1960s that became an important place for the revelation of new talents.

But, perhaps the most significant result of the industrialization process of the 1950s to the 1970s was the consolidation of a national phonographic market. It was not only the import substitution process that was extended to the production of records that was important (Pessoti, 2001). Even more relevant was that the market was enlarged with the inclusion of lower income segments and that these segments wanted more national content than the foreign-influenced elite. As a result, for the first time most records sold began to be of local origin: in 1959, 70 percent of records sold in Brazil were foreign, while at the end of the 1960s the national titles represented the majority (Eugênio, 1999). Multinational companies simply directed efforts to promote and to produce records of national musicians. The Brazilian market became more segmented, with new musical styles figuring among the best sellers (Machado and Zan, 2002).

From the 1980s onwards periods of bust and boom occurred as economic and social crises unfolded. This was also a period when intense reconfiguration of the phonographic industry was observed worldwide as globalization proceeded. This will be discussed in the next section where the music industry will be analyzed. From the musical point of view, however, there has been an explosion of several regional feasts, which became the backbone of an important music entertainment industry in Brazil.

There are many musical manifestations across the vast national territory, each with characteristics specific to the different regions and most dating back to eighteenth and nineteenth centuries. They are folk festivities and annual events in specific regions, which conform a significant number of local productive systems based on musical activities. Some examples are: the already mentioned carnival of Rio de Janeiro and Salvador; the *Festas Juninas* (the June feasts of Saint John) of Campina Grande and Caruarú in the northeast; the party of the *Bumba-Meu-Boi* in Parintins in the Amazon region (a monumental spectacle in the Amazon rainforest); the Cavalhadas of Poirenópolis in the center-west (a three-day music festival which culminates with a representation of the Christian and Moor conflict ending in a party); and several off-season and winter carnivals, which take place in virtually every northeastern state.

These mass festivals/spectacles have been consolidated over the last 20 years. It was estimated that, in the year 2000, the Brazilian entertainment industry received US$5 billion of investment (Albim, 2005). It is important to mention that in the last 20 years Brazil has developed a significant operational and technical capacity to support large and complex musical projects. One of the first large events was the musical festival Rock in Rio in 1985. The third edition of this event, in 2001, consolidated the Brazilian spectacle industry position on the international scene. The festival had an audience of about 1.5 million people and more than 50 million people watched on television. This four-day event brought nearly US$213 million to the local economy of Rio de Janeiro. The administrative organizer of the event directly supervised 42 activities and 363 sub-activities necessary for the project to succeed; it signed about 150 contracts with more than 100 companies for the construction of the City of Rock (Medina, 2002). The trademark of Rock in Rio has already been exported: since 2003 there has been a Rock in Rio in Lisbon. It is argued that Brazil became an attractive host for these international events, not only because of the organizational expertise it developed, but also because of a unique characteristic of the Brazilian audience: its enthusiastic participation and interaction with the artists during musical spectacles.

It is also worth mentioning districts in larger cities and localities that have their entire economy based on music. Just in the state of Rio de Janeiro there are two examples: Lapa, the old bohemian district in the city of Rio de Janeiro, that since 1999 has become an important stage for new talents of the MPB and Conservatory, an interesting case of preservation of cultural traditions (see box 1).

Box 6.1 The local music system of Conservatory

Conservatory is a small village in the Northeast of the state of Rio de Janeiro. This village has around 5,000 inhabitants and for more than 50 years has preserved traditional music manifestations. The musical activity is strongly rooted and is practiced by a local group inspired by the ideal of preserving that tradition and without economic interests.

Since the early 1990s Conservatory's music activities became known to a large public and an entire tourist infrastructure developed around this main attraction. Cultural tourism became the district's main economic activity. The musical style of *seresta* and the performance of *serenata* (serenades) are the main attractions and the economic activities related to tourism and leisure constitute the major sources of income. In addition, the proliferation of hotels, bars and restaurants also offers a stage for professional musicians. All these elements led to a virtuous experience of local development and the district presents a high average level of income and no unemployment (Lemos *et al.*, 2005).

All these events represent music "clusters" throughout the Brazilian territory (Lemos *et al.*, 2005). They are very important for local social and economic mobilization and for the reinforcement of diversity and specific cultural identity. But they also exert a significant impact on the whole production chain associated to music and on other related activities such as tourism (lodging, transport, feeding, etc.).

The music industry

The diverse activities related to music constitute an important industry that has significant impact on job and income generation. This is in fact a complex system that encompasses economic activities such as the production of master recordings and their reproduction, marketing and distribution, massive diffusion through the media, commercialization, live performance, administration of intellectual property rights and production and commercialization of music reproduction devices and musical instruments.

In other words, beyond the artists and performers themselves – singers, musicians, songwriters and so forth – cultural industries also demand technical support personnel, equipment, music studios, graphic designers, recording engineers, lighting technicians, producers and managers. We can add entertainment attorneys, promoters, publishers, publicists and many more. Also as ICTs are becoming central to the development of these activities, ever more complex hardware and software are needed. Figure 6.1 is an attempt to capture the complexity of the music industry and production chain.

The economic importance of the Brazilian music industry

One of the main difficulties for assessing the economic impact of the music industry is to compile data, given the inappropriateness of the traditional sector classification and the high degree of informality of the industry. Also it is difficult to determine the share of firms and workers who directly deal with music in the above-mentioned activities.

Table 6.1 presents official statistics for 2004 regarding sectors of activity directly related to music, which can be identified in the Brazilian National Classification of Economic Activities. In 2004, these sectors accounted for more than 6,000 firms that employed about 73,000 people. The sectors with the highest level of employment are radio (31,000 people) and manufacture of sound devices (16,000 people). Multiplying the annual average wages in each sector by the respective number of employees, we get total wages of about US$278 million for these sectors. The selected sectors represent around 0.25 percent of the sum of all economic activities both in terms of overall employment and total wages in 2004.

These data do not include the musicians themselves (composers, performers, etc). However, it is estimated that Brazil had approximately 87,000 professional musicians and composers in 2001 (Lemos *et al.*, 2005). Adding this number to the previous data, we obtain a contingent of about 160,000 people working directly with formal music activities. The modest character of this estimate is evident. However, one has to remember the difficulty of data gathering for some important activities (such as live performance, and popular feasts that exploded in the 1990s) and the informality of the sector. Most Brazilian musicians are amateurs and have other occupations besides music. The large majority of these amateur musicians perform in nightclubs and

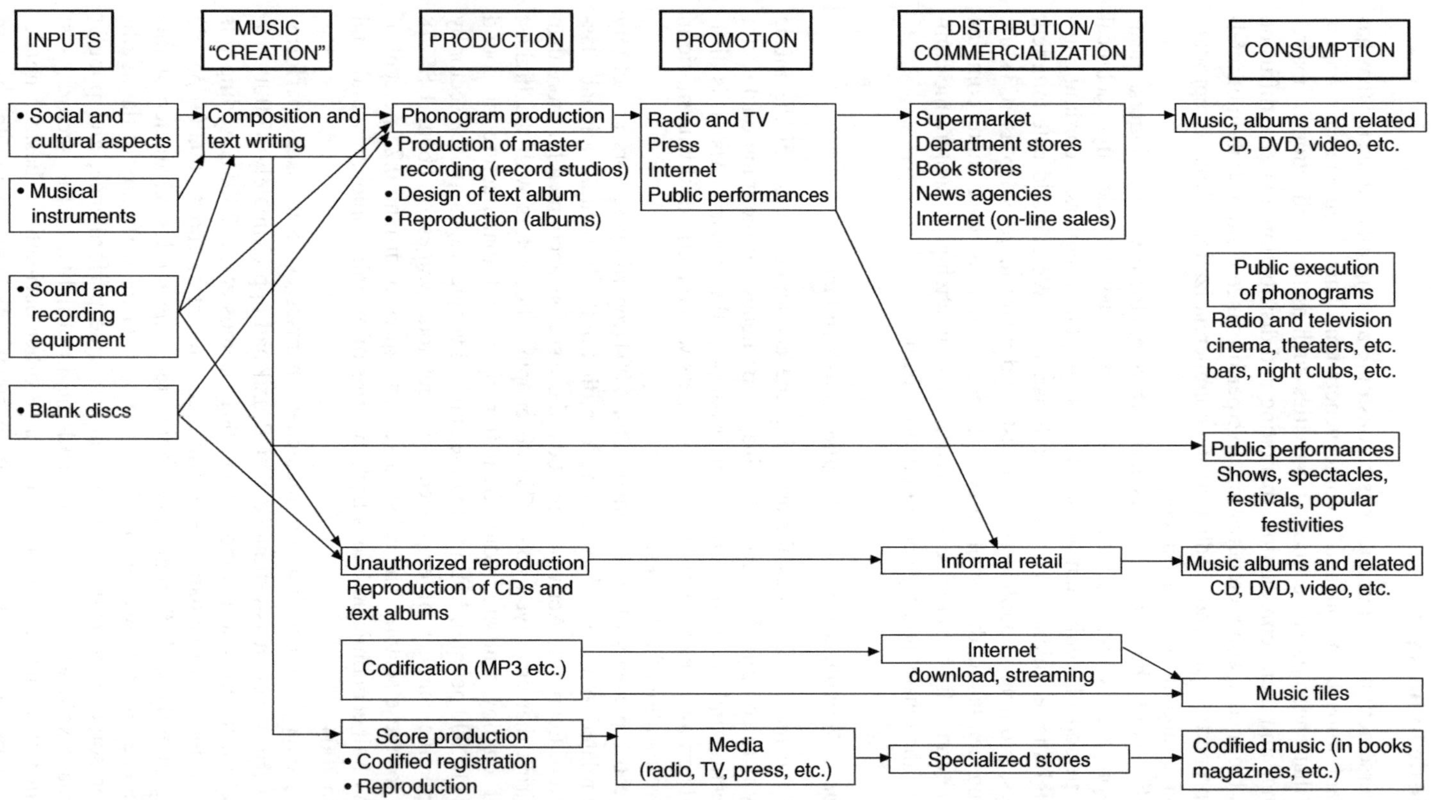

Figure 6.1 A stylized scheme of the music industry.

Table 6.1 Number of firms, employees and wages in sectors related to music, 2004

	Firms	*Employees*	*Annual average wages (R$)*	*Total annual wages (R$)*
All sectors	6,387	73,182	3,796	277,799,468
Edition of discs, tapes and other recordings	173	1,146	5,876	6,734,228
Reproduction of discs and tapes	74	2,873	6,199	17,809,267
Blank discs and tapes production	15	251	3,336	837,423
Production of radio and TV receivers and of sound reproduction devices	240	15,864	5,092	80,784,389
Production of musical instruments	114	2,272	3,174	7,211,951
Radio activities	2,549	31,206	3,306	103,157,243
Activities related to theater, music and other artistic and literature activities	1,863	11,757	3,742	43,993,040
Administration of show houses	196	1,614	3,036	4,900,125
Other activities related to live performance	1,178	6,199	1,996	12,371,801

Source: Annual Report of Social Information (RAIS), 2004.

establishments without contracts, which makes precise statistics for this activity almost impossible.

The example of the Rio de Janeiro Carnival illustrates this point. Estimates suggest that the event generates about US$430 million every year (Medina, 2002), creating about 60,000 jobs directly related to the parade of the samba schools and 180,000 indirect jobs (Araújo, 2002).

One important part of the music industry is the production of musical instruments. This occurs in many different regions of the country, but is heavily concentrated in the state of São Paulo where, in 2002, 65 percent of formal firms (114) and 83 percent of formal employees (2,272) were located. The value of production in this sector was about US$28.9 million in 2003. Brazil is a net importer of musical instruments, as can be seen from Table 6.2. Exports grew from US$1.2 million in 1989 to US$4.1 million in 2003, while imports grew from US$11.3 million in 1989 to US$19 million in 2003. Although imports are higher than exports, they represented only about 34 percent of apparent consumption in 2003, estimated to be US$43.9 million by the Brazilian Institute of Geography and Statistics. It is important to note that both exports and imports of musical instruments have fluctuated significantly during the last 15 years as a result of macroeconomic policies. Imports reached a peak of US$69 million in 1996 as import controls were virtually abandoned immediately after the stabilization program of 1994. As it proved necessary to re-establish some control of imports and as the Real devalued in the last part of the 1990s, imports rapidly decreased and exports grew significantly from US$2.1 million in 1996 to a peak of US$6.5 million in 2000, when the appreciation of the Real impacted nega-

Table 6.2 Brazilian trade of musical instruments (million US$)[a]

Year	*Exports*	*Imports*	*Trade balance*	*Brazilian share in world market (%)*
2003	4.1	19.0	–14.9	0.09
2002	3.3	27.1	–23.8	0.08
2001	4.7	31.3	–26.7	0.12
2000	6.5	38.6	–32.1	0.16
1999	4.0	31.3	–27.3	0.10
1998	2.1	52.7	–50.6	0.06
1997	2.9	66.6	–63.7	0.07
1996	2.1	69.4	–67.4	0.06
1995	2.4	59.8	–57.4	0.06
1994	3.0	38.1	–35.2	0.09
1993	2.2	23.3	–21.1	0.07
1992	0.9	12.8	–11.9	0.03
1991	1.0	16.3	–15.3	0.03
1990	1.2	13.5	–12.3	0.04
1989	1.2	11.3	–10.2	0.04

Source: Comtrade/UNSTATS.

*Note

a Products of the classification site rev 3: Musical instruments (8981, 8982 and 8989).

tively on the level of exports. Macroeconomic instability has affected the music industry as a whole in the last decade as is going to be analyzed in the next section.

The consumption of recorded music in Brazil: recent developments and the role of macroeconomic changes

As already mentioned an important feature of the Brazilian music industry is the significant proportion of national music in the total music consumed in recorded form. Apart from the USA and Japan, Brazil is the only country with a high share of national music in the total market. In the case of the USA more than 90 percent of music consumed is local, while in Japan and Brazil this percentage reaches about 80 percent.

This impressive characteristic of the local market started to show in the late 1960s, as already mentioned. Up to then foreign music dominated the national market. Several reasons explain such change. Most important was the combination of import substitution industrialization, technical change and the upsurge of new consumers that together helped to widen the internal market. These new consumers (middle and lower classes) were much more influenced by local content than the foreign biased elite that could afford to buy records before. However, locally generated music was responsible for around 60 percent of the total market from the late 1960s to the early 1990s. It was in the 1990s that the definitive consolidation of Brazilian music was established, as can be seen in Figure 6.2. In 1991, 60.6 percent of music consumed was of national origin, 38.3 percent was international music and 0.9 percent corresponded to classical music. The proportion of national music grew throughout the decade reaching 75.9 percent in 2000 and 79.8 percent in 2003.

The importance of national content becomes more evident when considering data for the albums that received a "golden disc"[5] in 2004: 72 percent of prized albums were national music. The four large multinationals released 76 percent

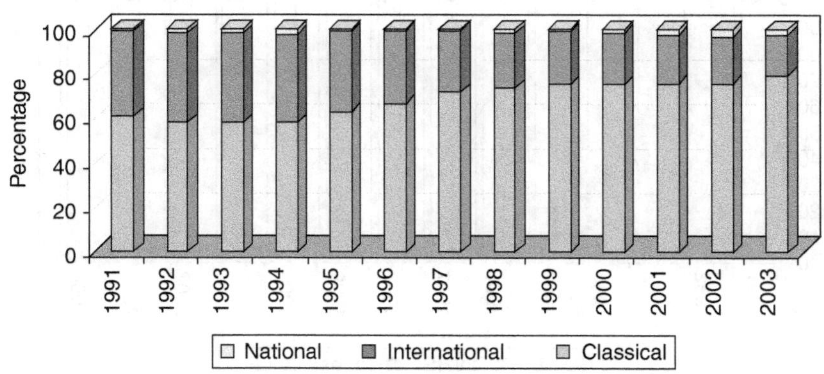

Figure 6.2 Share of national repertoire in the Brazilian music market (source: ABPD (2003)).

of these best sellers and the Brazilian company Som Livre another 10 percent[6]. Among the majors the percentage of best sellers with national content remains very high, accounting for 67 percent of their golden disc albums. Considering the few albums that achieved more then 125,000 copies sold, 36 (or 78 percent) were of national content and only ten (or 22 percent) were of international music (ABPD, 2005).

The proportion of national music in both total sales and best sellers is close to 80 percent. In the case of most European countries the specialization on foreign content would leave the majors with a still considerable market share, around 50 percent. In the Brazilian case, if the majors did not focus their efforts on national music they would dominate only 20 percent of the Brazilian market. The high level of national music consumption can be regarded as a "natural protection" for the Brazilian music industry and musicians, since it imposes limits to the majors' tendency to focus on the production of international repertoire as a defensive strategy in periods of crisis.

The increase in the share of national music in total consumption is associated with a significant increase in total consumption of music in the 1990s after stagnation in the 1980s. One important determinant of the increased consumption was the delayed introduction of the CD player in Brazil. Although it was introduced in the 1980s, it only became dominant in the 1990s (Figure 6.3). In this period it stimulated the substitution of CDs for record collections. As pointed out by Pessoti (2001) this was one of the main factors explaining the high growth rates of the market in the period. In recent years, formats that include both audio and video are gaining an increased share. Music DVDs and VHSs represented only 1.5 percent of sales in 2000 and accounted for 34.2 percent of the market in 2004.

Similar to what happened in the 1960s, the increase in consumption in the 1990s was affected positively by some structural changes in the Brazilian economy. First, one should stress the role of the macroeconomic stabilization

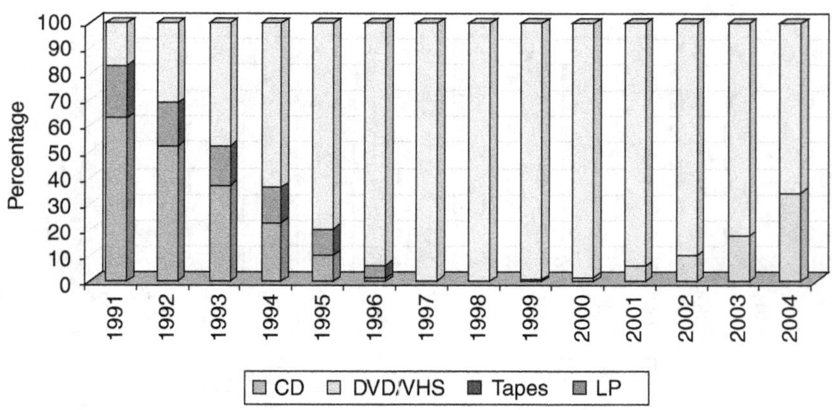

Figure 6.3 Transition of physical supports for music in the Brazilian market (source: ABPD (2003)).

plan (the Plano Real) in 1994. In the short run, control of inflation and a relative increase in the purchasing power of most people had a significant positive impact on rising music consumption in general and in local content in particular.

Two factors related to the economic stabilization plan led to a significant expansion of music consumption.[7] With the end of high inflation there was a once and for all increment in the purchasing power of the population and an explosion in consumption. After sales had oscillated around 40 million units from 1991 to 1993, the market jumped to 63 million units in 1994, 75 million in the following year and reached a peak of 108 million units in 1997, with total sales totaling around US$1.28 billion. The amount of music sold and the revenues (in national currency) remained at the 1997 level until 2000 (Table 6.3).

Increase in music consumption during the first years of the Real Plan was also supported by the overvaluation of the national currency. After 1994 there was also an explosion of music imports. According to data of the United Nations Statistics Division, Brazilian imports of recorded media averaged US$7.9 million per year in 1989–1993, jumped to around US$30 million per year in 1994–1998 and fell to an annual average of US$18.4 million from 1999 to 2004, as shown in Table 6.4.

Additionally the data show a continuous growth trajectory of Brazilian recorded music exports. Brazil has a constant, but decreasing, commercial deficit in the recorded music industry. Although Brazil has only a marginal share of the international music market, its exports are growing faster than world total imports since the early 1990s. Brazilian exports grew from US$1.8 million in 1989 to about US$15 million in 2004 (an annual growth rate of 15.2 percent)

Table 6.3 Recorded music sales in Brazil[a]

Year	*Units (millions)*	*Million R$*	*Million US$*[b]
1991	44	–	400.4
1992	32	–	284.9
1993	43	–	444.4
1994	63	511.3	802.0
1995	74	915.9	1,000.0
1996	100	1,324.6	1,319.1
1997	108	1,377.1	1,269.5
1998	105	1,360.4	1,176.0
1999	97	1,213.0	664.4
2000	104	1,326.2	713.9
2001	78	998.4	448.6
2002	79	1,034.1	388.9
2003	56	601.0	195.3
2004	66	706.0	241.4

Notes

a Source: own elaboration based on data published by ABPD.

b Sale value for 2003 and 2004 are available only in national currency. Value in US$ is based on the conversion by the respective annual average exchange rates (commercial exchange rate for US$ purchase – Source: IPEADATA).

Table 6.4 World imports and Brazilian trade of recorded music[a]

Year	*World imports*		*Brazilian exports*		*Brazilian imports*		*Brazilian exports/ world imports (%)*
	Million US$	*Index*	*Million US$*	*Index*	*Million US$*	*Index*	
1989	5,666.99	100	1.79	100	5.33	100	0.03
1990	7,309.55	129	1.24	69	6.28	118	0.02
1991	8,607.24	152	1.51	84	10.55	198	0.02
1992	10,476.09	185	4.65	260	5.26	99	0.04
1993	10,986.54	194	9.38	525	12.00	225	0.09
1994	12,923.27	228	6.54	366	31.77	596	0.05
1995	15,324.39	270	8.60	481	34.82	653	0.06
1996	16,411.06	290	10.11	565	33.54	629	0.06
1997	16,402.89	289	11.13	622	33.91	636	0.07
1998	17,244.15	304	13.72	767	21.04	395	0.08
1999	19,096.14	337	19.47	1,088	16.16	303	0.10
2000	19,543.26	345	16.74	936	18.86	354	0.09
2001	19,181.58	338	10.57	591	19.48	365	0.06
2002	19,483.50	344	10.60	592	19.26	361	0.05
2003	21,966.36	388	14.35	802	19.08	358	0.07
2004	23,937.90	422	14.95	836	17.45	327	0.06

Source: COMTRADE/UNSTATS.

Note

a Items 8,987 (records and other recorded media – excluding magnetic tapes) and 8,986 (magnetic tapes, recorded) of the product classification SITC rev 3.

and the world imports grew from US$5.6 billions to US$24 billions (an annual growth of 10 percent).

However, the boom lasted only a few years as the gains brought by the Real Plan eroded for most of the population after 2000. The market decreased to 78 million units and total sales of US$448 million, in 2001, and only 66 million units and sales of US$241 million in 2004 as seen in Table 6.3. The Brazilian music market, which was in the 14th position in the world ranking until the end of the 1980s, reached the 6th position at the end of the 1990s. Due to the crisis at the beginning of the century, the Brazilian market has fallen again to the 12th position in 2001 (Pessoti, 2001).

The crisis of the national music market has as its main determinants the weak performance of the economy and the fall of purchasing power of the average citizen. Surprisingly, the music industry did not decrease the very high prices of records as a response to the crisis. This, together with the diffusion of new technologies that make the costs associated with the copy of a CD almost negligible, are considered as the main causes of piracy.

The reaction of the Brazilian music industry to the crisis was, instead, the reduction of new national titles released. The growth of the domestic market until 2000 was characterized by an increasing number of new titles, by an increasing share of national titles and by a decrease of the foreign titles released by the industry. In 2000, national titles accounted for 59.3 percent of the 2,568 new titles released. Since 2001, the number of national releases is decreasing while that of foreign releases is growing steadily. In order to cut costs large multinationals decided to follow a defensive strategy, since the release of national titles involves greater costs (with authors, artists, studios, graphical production, etc.), while in the case of foreign products, as these costs were already written off, it involves only costs of licensing and reproduction. Consequently, in 2003, national titles accounted for only 33.2 percent of the total 3,251 releases (ABPD, 2003).

This strategy has not influenced the trend of increasing consumption of national music, which continues to grow. Two trends are noticeable, however. First, the reduction of national releases was accompanied by an effort by the majors to concentrate on a reduced number of national, superstar artists. Second, there was an explosion of small, local, independent firms in the recorded music industry.

The recorded music industry: the majors and the independents

As mentioned above, one specific characteristic of the Brazilian recorded music industry is its domination by a few large multinational companies since it was set up 100 ago. An industry characterized by significant economies of scale and high barriers to entry favored the continuous concentration and domination of the market by these established multinationals.

As presented in the Table 6.5, in 2002, Universal (with 21.8 percent of the market) was the leader of the market followed by Sony Music (with 16.3

Table 6.5 Market share and CD sales of the main recording companies in Brazil, 2002

	Recording company	*Market share (%)*	*Revenues (US$ million)*
1	Universal	21.8	1.65
2	Sony Music	16.3	1.24
3	Warner	14.8	1.12
4	BMG	14.8	1.12
5	Som Livre	14.6	1.11
6	EMI	12.1	0.92
7	Abril Music	4.7	0.36

Source: Barbosa (2003).

percent), Warner (14.8 percent), BMG (14.8 percent) and EMI (12.1 percent). As Sony and the BMG merged at the beginning of 2005, they are now the leader dominating about 30 percent of the market.

Historically, the few cases of local firms that were able to enter into this closed club are those belonging to large local media groups. Radio and television have been crucial elements for the development of the music industry in general and the recorded music industry in particular during the last decades. These media contribute to taste formation and, most importantly, they are decisive for the success of a released album on the market.

Since the 1930s the radio became one of the main music diffusion tools. At the end of the 1990s, radio was present in more than 90 percent of Brazilian households (Gomes Júnior, 2000). Although it was surpassed by the penetration of the television in Brazilian homes, it is still the media consumed with most frequency. Despite the declining share of advertisement revenue in radio, the segmentation of the radio channels by age and social groups enables the maintenance of a faithful audience. In particular, modular frequency stations and those directed toward the young public are crucial for the diffusion of music. Up to now, the relation between the recorded music industry and the radio has been marked by the payment of the "jabá" (the Brazilian name for payola) for the diffusion of new songs and albums.[8] "Jabá" is crucial since the frequency the single is played on the radio determines the success of the album that contains that music.

The communitarian radio stations play an important role, since they have direct communication with members of specific groups. In particular, communitarian radios offer a more democratic space for artists who do not have any access to the large recording firms (Peruzzo, 1998).

TV and cinema production are other important media for music diffusion. Films, series and *novelas* (Brazilian soap opera) have a large impact on music consumption, airing specific songs, which leads to the commercialization of the respective sound tracks. Other media are live programs and specialized music stations, like the Brazilian MTV, where singles are aired through video clips. TV activities also create specific music for diverse functions: sound tracks, vignettes, inserted in advertisements, etc.

The most important example is that of the largest Brazilian television network, Rede Globo. As part of the powerful media group Globo,[9] it is able to gain from using the organization's different communication channels, particularly its TV network. It commands more than 50 percent of the total audience, particularly through its *novelas*. In the 1970s it created one subsidiary to compete in the music market: a recording company, *Som Livre*, that produces sound tracks. Through agreements with other recording companies, it releases compilations of singles from different artists as soundtracks of the *novelas* and other programs. Because of the high audience of television programs, the respective soundtrack albums often achieve considerable sales. For the other recording companies it is lucrative to license singles to Som Livre, since the massive exposition in the media also foments the sales of the artists' albums that contain those songs.[10]

It was for this reason that Som Livre was able to gain an important share of the market. In 2002, Som Livre accounted for 14.6 percent of CDs sold in the country. There was also another company that belonged to another Brazilian media group with significant participation in the national market, Abril Music (4.7 percent of the market in 2002). However, it was closed in 2003 as part of the crisis. Although the Abril media group is very important in the printed media it has no part in the television market, which may also explain its failure.

Despite the oligopolistic structure of the music industry, the 1990s witnessed an increase of independent companies. The advances in recording technologies and the gradual insertion of technologies based on microcomputer, with great impact on the reduction of production costs, enabled an increasing participation of independent national enterprises such as Biscoito Fino, Eldorado, Velas and Trama (Silva, 2001). In November 2005, there were about 100 independent companies affiliated to the Brazilian Association of Independent Music (ABMI), which was created in 2001.

In a country as large and diversified as Brazil, the independents are exploiting niches left aside by an industry that is concentrated in the two largest cities: Rio de Janeiro and São Paulo. Independent companies are present in the whole Brazilian territory catering for regional markets and presenting opportunities for the large number of artists that do not have access to the majors. As already mentioned, one of the main criticisms about the majors is that, as part of their strategy to cope with the crisis, they are not very interested in launching new titles of local content by local musicians, preferring to concentrate on commercializing superstars (both local and foreign). For example, in the first semester of 2004 the four majors launched only 48 new CDs of local artists. During the same period, just Biscoito Fino, one of the most successful of the independents set up in the late 1990s, launched 50 new titles. The other 20 launched approximately 150 new titles (Torres 2004).

There is also a significant number of local, highly successful and famous artists who are breaking with the majors to set up independent firms, individually or collectively. However, the growth potential of these firms is limited, since the distribution channels – which offer bigger profitability and present significant barriers to entry and which effectively put the music on the media and the market – are still restricted to the majors.

The majors are following a strategy of outsourcing the productive stages to some independents, keeping control of the distribution activities. Through this type of "division of labor", the majors have attained a reduction of production costs and risks associated with the formation of artists while maintaining their ability to act in diversified markets (Vicente, 2000). Majors concentrate on exploiting related property rights from a large catalog of artists.

The current organization of the music industry presents significant challenges for the independents to compete with the large multinationals. Forced to a complementary position, besides exploring market niches of little interest to the majors, they associate with the majors, carrying on stages of the production chain that do not interest them.

In a sense, their modus operandi suits the oligopolistic activities of the majors. By the very nature of their operation, they develop music outside the mainstream, attracting new audiences. However, once this starts to show significant success, and becomes a potential threat to market dominance, independents are simply bought out or absorbed by the majors.

To overcome the problems related to access to the media, the diffusion of independent work could be promoted on local radio and television channels by the respective local governments. The diffusion on public radio and television channels has only a limited impact in Brazil, because of their small audience. Representatives of the independents are fighting for another way to overcome this barrier by eliminating some of the majors' advantages. A legal case is being elaborated to turn the practice of the "jabá" into a crime. They argue that the radio channels dedicate very little time to advertisements because they are paid to play specific singles continuously. This media could be economically sustainable without the "jabá" by dedicating more time to advertisements and playing a more diversified repertoire.

Intellectual property rights and piracy

The music industry worldwide has been marked by moments of rupture and reorganization, as a consequence of technological change (Huygens, 2001). The diffusion of digital technologies represents one of these rupture moments, reducing the costs of production, reproduction and distribution of music. These developments have created a very uncertain economic environment for traditional players in the music industry. They allow musicians to offer their music directly to their "customers", and create opportunities for new intermediaries to enter the market offering a mix of new and old services. They also permit people to buy music in an easier, cheaper and quicker way, either in digital or physical form. Among other things, such developments pose a threat to the industrial structure worldwide that has been based, in the last 30 years, primarily on the control of property rights.

In Brazil, the music industry put the blame for the crisis, at least partially, on the increase in the number of illegal copies. According to ABPD, in 2004, 52 percent of the CDs sold in the country were illegal copies (ABPD, 2005).

The "piracy threat" to the industry in Brazil has been constantly mentioned as a major problem to be tackled by both government and industry. But although the institution of copyright in the industry is assumed by the large multinationals as a backbone, without which the whole system would collapse, some analyses are arguing that the whole system is not sustainable, particularly because most of the revenues from IPRs are appropriated by the recording companies and music publishing companies and only a small part goes to the musicians (Andersen *et al.*, 2000; Dolfsma, 2000).

Towse (1999) indicates that, in the case of the United Kingdom, for example, the artists receive 20 percent and the musicians who take part in the recording of the master tape receive 12.5 percent. The remaining 67.5 percent belongs to the recording and distribution companies. In Brazil the same unfair division of the IPR revenues is verified. Thus, these revenues do not represent the stimulus for music creation as argued by representatives of the music industry.

Another problem with the industry's view about copyrights and piracy, which is pertinent to the Brazilian case, is that statistics of the recording industry have consistently misrepresented "pirated" products as "lost sales". As Dolfsma (2000) pointed out, this is problematic in countries (particularly developing ones) where there is no affluent middle class with spending power. As we can assume that in Brazil the users of "pirated goods" are people without enough rent to afford the high monopolistic prices charged by the majors, it is very unlikely that they would buy at the full price.

Some authors argue that it is the institution of copyright itself that is not adequate for the reality of the music market, leading to little benefit for the creative agents (Dolfsma, 2000; Kretschmer, 2001). The strategy of the majors seems to be an attempt to control the on-line music market, as a way to guarantee the copyrights exploitation.

Up to 2005, the use of the Internet in Brazil has had only a negligible impact on the music industry, both in relation to illegal music exchange and to formal sales of music.[11] Market research ordered by the ABPD reveals that Internet was responsible for only 5 percent of DVD sales and 2 percent of CD sales in 2004. Music downloads are still so limited that they have not been contemplated in the research.[12] Data of the United Nations reveal a total of 14.3 million Internet users in Brazil. The number of users with a fast connection is only 1.1 million, according to data of the Federal Service of Data Processing (SERPRO).

The problem of piracy in Brazil seems to be intimately related to the contraction of purchasing power by the middle and lower classes and to the oligopolistic structure and the price strategy of the music industry. Despite the historical income inequality of the country, the lower social classes (C, D and E) have the larger share of the Brazilian formal market (51 percent according to information of ABPD – Brazilian Association of Phonogram Producers). The growth of the size of the national market seems to be more associated with the perspective of economic development and reduction of distributive inequality.

Public policies

Formal policies targeting the cultural industry in a comprehensive way are a recent endeavor in Brazil. However, support for culture and music has a long tradition in the country, even if most of this support was limited to fiscal incentives given to private enterprises financing cultural projects. Most of the criticism of this kind of support is that it always targets types of cultural and musical activities which are consumed only by the highest elites in big urban centers, such as opera and theater. Therefore, cultural policy in Brazil had the biased characteristic of using tax to subsidize cultural consumption of the upper classes, leaving in a marginal state popular culture activities and actors.

The experience of applying tax incentives to the music industry gained momentum in the 1960s, within the broader industrial policy aim of promoting imports substitution. It is also worth noting the Law of Fiscal Incentives of 1967, which allows for the application of the Tax on the Circulation of Merchandises (ICM) incident on the commercialization of international recordings to the production of national recordings. International albums that are reproduced in Brazil also benefit from this incentive, as "national" is understood as "produced in Brazil" and not as "national music" (Silva, 2001). This incentive still remains today, but now it applies to the commercialization of any recorded music. Initially up to 70 percent of the tax could be deducted, but in 2005 this was reduced to 40 percent.

The Rouanet Law of 1991 (8,313/91) represented an improvement since it allows the reduction of the value of the income tax of firms or individuals that sponsor cultural projects. The sponsor can deduct from its income tax up to 100 percent of the project value, limited to 4 percent of the total due tax (Natale and Olivieri, 2004). Together with this law, the National Program of Support to Culture (Pronac) was created with the aim of collecting and directing resources to cultural projects.[13] State and municipality governments also implement laws to promote culture based on tax discounts. In the case of the State of Rio de Janeiro, the State Law of Culture (Law 1,954/92) grants fiscal incentives (2 percent of the State Tax on Circulation of Goods and Services).

Cultural policies are gradually attempting to broaden their targets from activities that are consumed by the elites to those more related to popular culture. At the federal level, the emphasis on promoting a more systemic and democratic support to cultural production and consumption was made explicit by the present Ministry of Culture, after its inauguration in 2003. This perhaps reflects the fact that the Minister of Culture, in the period 2003/2007, is the popular composer and singer Gilberto Gil. In the pursuit of a broader democratization of cultural expression, the central aims of cultural policies have become the mobilization of local popular cultural richness and the promotion of an effective cultural diversity in the country. Additionally, the Ministry stresses the need to consider simultaneously the symbolic dimension of culture, its importance for citizenship and its economic dimension. One example, given to illustrate these policies, is the Program of Living Culture (Cultura Viva), created in 2004. It has as a main focus the promotion of culture as an element for social inclusion, citizenship and local development. The main targets of the program are the low-income population and people in situations of social vulnerability, as well as Native American communities, agricultural communities and the remaining *quilombos*.[14] The main action is the creation of "Points of Culture" to foster artistic and cultural activities in the most varied urban and agricultural localities of Brazil (Brasil, 2004).

The program aims at encouraging local protagonists and the cultural agents are supposed to have autonomy to decide how to structure the activities of the Points of Culture, based on the specific features of each cultural manifestation. The creation of digital recording studios is encouraged, enabling the production of CDs in small quantities and the diffusion of music through the Internet. Other incentives relate to the training of technicians for these studios and general music classes. Each Point of Culture receives a grant up to R$185,000 for a two and a half year period. This project marks a pioneering public initiative in the direction of a more democratic production. In fact, many Points of Culture act like small independent recording enterprises, promoting new talents. Up to 2005 more than 300 Points of Culture were nominated by the Ministry of Culture, several of them specialized in music activities (Brasil, 2004).

One of these cases is Conservatory, the above-mentioned village in northeast Rio de Janeiro, where weekly music festivals (serenades) – rooted in the locality and sustained by local protagonists – induce most of its economic activities. It now counts on the support of the program Cultura Viva and a Point of Culture is being installed in the local House of Culture. A digital recording studio is being installed and professional training for sound technicians is going to be offered. Local cultural entrepreneurs are assuming the coordination of the Point of Culture and aim to direct its activities to the specific needs and potential of Conservatory (Lemos *et al.*, 2005).

Another initiative is the Pro-music project, formalized at the end of 2005. According to the Ministry of Culture its main objective is to promote the diffusion and export of Brazilian music to the world. The project is carried out by the Ministry of Culture, the Export Promotion Agency (Apex), the Brazilian Small Enterprises Support Agency (Sebrae) and representatives of the music sector. The main action of the program is the National Plan for Brazilian Music Exportation and the creation of the mark "Music of Brazil". It follows three main guidelines: diffusion of Brazilian music abroad, the creation of new business relations and the stimulation of demand for Brazilian music. Accordingly, the following actions are foreseen: creation of the Music of Brazil web site; music promotion on radio and TV; seminars and courses for improving the qualifications of entrepreneurs; information about the international market and its requirements; support for participation in international music fairs; diffusion of Brazilian music abroad; promotion of international tours of Brazilian artists; attraction of specialized foreign journalists; and creation of a Brazilian music catalog directed at export activities.

Conclusions

Music is a fundamental part of the Brazilian cultural identity and national music accounts for more then 80 percent of the total music consumed in the country, both in terms of CD sales and radio execution. It also achieves a significant recognition around the world. This recognition derives from the quality of the composers, musicians, compositions and from the variety of rhythms and styles. More specifically, different musical styles represent a constituent of the identity of specific groups and are associated with specific cultures, races, genders, religions and localities. Because of this diversity, Tinhorão (1998: 9) characterizes the "many forms of Brazilian music" as the "meeting of many cultures corresponding to the reality and the degree of information of each part of society".

Since it is a society formed by the convergence of many cultures, the constant assimilation and incorporation of these contributions is a specific trace of the Brazilian culture and one of its virtues. This process was called by Oswald de Andrade (1928) "anthropophagi" – a process of cultural resistance, not through the acceptance of external esthetic and cultural standards, but through the assimilation and transformation of these into something genuinely Brazilian. As also stressed by Ricardo Cravo Albim: "The extraordinary Brazilian capacity to incorporate, swallow, ruminate the most diverse cultures – in my opinion the most original contribution of Brazil for the history of civilizations in this millennium – finds exactly in our musician, its more vehement, provoking and stimulant mirror" (2005: 1).

Musical manifestations are in fact innumerable in Brazil and considered as a source of inspiration and renewal of the area. However, a number of analysts have pointed to the threats of the trend of cultural production becoming dominated completely by a market logic – in which only products of ample consumption are promoted – and have warned that this may impose serious limits on the manifestation of cultural diversity (Adorno and Horkheimer, 1996). It has also been noted that artists and musicians are not always aware that they exert a function of cultural resistance, and that this could threaten the continuity of these cultural manifestations in the long run (Dias, 1999).

There are important policy implications of this discussion. Considering that cultural activities exceed a purely economic logic and constitute the basis of the Brazilian identity, it is not only important to provide means for popular diverse manifestations to have a space in the market, but also to guarantee their survival and reproduction. These issues can not be ignored by public policies, even if their main policy objective is to increase the contribution of the music industry to the economy and to the creation of employment and income.

In this line, most policy conclusions of this chapter go in the same direction as the policies presently adopted in the country. In the first place is the importance of reconciling economic, cultural, social and political angles and objectives for achieving long-term development of the area. The exclusive emphasis on promoting the economic side could impose serious threats to popular musical expression, and, therefore, faces the threat of not being sustainable. Additionally, policies should seek to overcome the recurrent critique that the actions, mainly those in the form of tax incentives, reach only a relatively small part of the population, and especially those with high income level.

The creation and promotion of "Points of Culture" seems an interesting attempt to harmonize not only these angles, but also federal government actions with local public and private initiatives, giving means and voice to local actors who are vital to their definition and implementation. The coordination of local, municipal state and federal governments is also a crucial policy step, particularly in the case of a country with the institutional and territorial dimensions of Brazil.

This chapter concludes by stressing three points. First, the high-risk nature of music-related activities, their volatility and invisibility, as well as their socio-political and economic role, call for unconventional ways of looking into their long-term development and financing. Second, and as argued in other works,[15] the systemic focus on all the related activities and actors involved in this *creative industry*, coupled with the development of instruments capable of mobilizing them collectively are expected to provide wider and more sustainable results. Finally, experimenting with and evaluating different initiatives are expected to provide relevant knowledge about what is really required (and works) in terms of policies aiming to deepen the roots and enlarge the various sounds of Brazil.

Notes

1 The study on the international flow of cultural goods (UNESCO, 2000) includes products from the following "cultural industries": printed matter and literature, music, visual arts, cinema and photography, television and radio, and games and sporting goods.

2 The *lundu* is a music style of black origin characterized by cadenced rhythm and lyrics that usually comment on daily street life. The *modinha* is basically of white origin, characterized by a European song-form, with highfalutin lyrics about love that was invariably unattainable. The *Choro*, played with guitar, piano, flute, cavaquinho and *bandolin*, consists of complex modulations and melodies, demanding a high level of competency and talent by performers. The *Maxixe* is an adaptation of the polka, the musical comedy style of European origin. Popular musicians, *chorões*, perform it with the flute and guitar (Albim, 2005).

3 For details see Zan (2001) and Piccino (n.d.).

4 The most important regional styles are Guarânia (of Paraguayan origin), Sertaneja music (Brazilian country music of the middle east and southeast), *Baião* (developed in the countryside of the northeast region of the country at the end of the nineteenth century) and *Carnival Marchinhas*, simple melodies with strong popular appeal, and ironic, sensual and funny lyrics (Albim, 2005).

5 A "golden disc" is an award to an album that sells at least 50,000 copies.

6 It's worth mentioning the increasing importance of gospel (religious) music. Eight albums sold more then 50,000 copies in 2004, seven of which were released by MK Publicitá, a recording company belonging to an evangelic church (ABPD, 2005).

7 The high consumption of music was also stimulated by declining cost of sound reproducing and recording devices and their diffusion into Brazilian households. The boom in the consumption of these devices happened in the first years after the stabilization plan of 1994. According to the National Electro-electronics Producer Association (ELETROS), the historical high was achieved in 1996 with nearly 5.5 million units sold (841,000 radios, 3.8 million sound systems and 832,000 compact disc players).

A main determinant for the declining prices was the increasing competition of imported products. After the initial boom in consumption, an excess of supply has also contributed to the declining prices of these products since 1997.

8 "Jabá" is a payment to radio stations and/or program presenters to guarantee a record is in the play lists of radios for a determined period. According to André Midani, an ex-executive of one of the majors in Brazil, the big recording companies spend between US$25 million and 33 million on "Jabá" every year. Folha de São Paulo, 21 May 2003.

9 The main Brazilian communication group, present in the printed media, radio, open and paid television and as a content provider for the Internet.

10 It is worth mentioning the recent growing presence of media groups related to Protestant churches. These religious institutions experienced a stunning growth throughout the last decade, both in terms of adepts and of assets. Some of these churches turned faith into a real business, acquiring television and radio stations and even creating their own recording companies. This phenomenon of religious music has a specific public and the artists are promoted through the media owned by the churches. This virtuous process in music production and promotion can be compared with the experience of Rede Globo, but with bigger growth potential, since religious music has a continually growing and faithful audience.

11 There are only a few legal music download services in Brazil. It's worth mentioning the pioneering experience of iMúsica, which distributes and manages digital media. Its catalog, initially supplied by independent recording companies, was expanded with the entrance of BMG and EMI Music into the business. Currently, it manages music sales for web sites as Saraiva.com.br, Americanas.com.br, SomLivre.com, etc. (Leal, 2005).

12 "Music on-line blows up in the world, but is still starting in Brazil", by Luiz Fernando Vianna and Thiago Ney. Folha de São Paulo. Folha Online, 4 October 2005.

13 According to the Ministry of Culture, since 1996, US$1.2 billion was channeled to cultural projects and US$223 million was directed specifically to musical projects. The amount for musical projects in 2004 was US$29.7 million.

14 *Quilombos* are communities comprising African slaves who escaped captivity. They developed territories for housing, resistance to white domination and social organization. Estimates suggest that there are 1,098 *Quilombos* communities located in almost every state in Brazil.

15 Lastres *et al.* (2003), Lastres and Cassiolato (2005).

Bibliography

ABPD – Associação Nacional dos Produtores de Disco (2003). *Relatório anual mercado fonográfico.* [Online]. Available from: www.abpd.org.br [cited 18 January 2004].

ABPD – Associação Nacional dos Produtores de Disco (2005). *Estatísticas e dados de mercado.* [Online]. Available from: www.abpd.org.br/estatisticas_mercado_brasil.asp [cited 9 January 2006].

Adorno, T. W. and Horkheimer, M. (1996). A indústria cultural: o esclarecimento como mistificação das massas. In *Dialética do esclarecimento.* Rio de Janeiro, RJ: Zahar.

Albim, R. C. (1998). Música popular. In F. Weffort and M. Souza (eds) *Um olhar sobre a cultura brasileira.* Rio de Janeiro, RJ: Associação dos Amigos da FUNARTE.

Albim, R. C. (2005). *Dicionário Cravo Albin da música popular brasileira.* [Online]. Available from: www.dicionariompb.com.br [cited 1 December 2005].

Andersen, B., Kozul-Wright, Z. and Kozul-Wright, R. (2000). *Copyrights, competition and development: the case of the music industry.* UNCTAD, Discussion Papers, No. 145, January.

Andrade, O. de (1928). Piratininga ano 374 da deglutição do bispo sardinha. *Revista de Antropofagia*, Vol. 1, No. 1, May.

Araújo, P. Q. (2002). Escolas de samba e relações de trabalho: entre a passarela e o barracão. In F. S. Earp (ed.) *Pão e circo: fronteiras e perspectivas da economia do entretenimento.* Rio de Janeiro, RJ: Palavra e Imagem, pp. 165–207.

Barbosa, M. A. (2003). *Mercado fonográfico brasileiro na encruzilhada.* [Online]. Available from: www.webinsider.com.br/venoticia.php?id=1604 [cited 22 November 2004].

Brasil, Federal Government (1998). Law no 9.610, from 19 February 1998. [Online]. Available from: www.planalto.gov.br/ccivil/leis [cited 19 August 2004].

Brasil, Ministery of Culture, (2004). *Cultura viva: programa nacional de cultura, educação e cidadania.* [Online]. Available from: www.cultura.gov.br/sys/skins/cultura_viva_capa/img/cartilha_cultura_viva_pt-br.pdf [cited 23 November 2005].

Brazil–U.S. Business Council (2004). *Counterfeiting and piracy in Brazil: the economic impact.* Washington, DC. [Online]. Available from: www.brazilcouncil.org/usermedia/MediaLibrary/Counterfeiting_and_Piracy_in_Brazil.pdf [cited 17 November 2005].

Burnett, R. (1995). *The global jukebox: the international music industry.* London: Routledge.

Cassiolato, J. E., Lastres, H. M. M. and Maciel, M. L. (2003). *Systems of innovation and development: evidence from Brazil.* Cheltenham: Elgar.

Dias, M. (1999). Um massacre cultural sem precedentes. *Jornal O Estado de São Paulo, Caderno 2*, 7 June.

Diniz, A. (2006). *Almanaque do Samba: a história do samba, o que ouvir, o que ler, onde curtir.* Rio de Janeiro, RJ: Zahar.

Dolfsma, W. (2000). How will the music industry weather the globalization storm. *First Monday*, 5 (5). [Online] Available from: www.firstmonday.dk/issues/issue5–5/dolfsma/ [cited 17 November 2004].

Earp, F. S. ed. (2002). *Pão e circo: fronteiras e perspectivas da economia do entretenimento.* Rio de Janeiro, RJ: Palavra e Imagem.

Eugênio, M. N. (1999). A indústria fonográfica no Brasil e a MPB (1960/1980). Paper presented at *Conferência Internacional de História das Empresas*, Curitiba, UFPA.

Faperj and Coppe/UFRJ (2002). *Economia da cultura: a força da indústria cultural no Rio de Janeiro.* Rio de Janeiro, RJ: E-papers.

Freire Filho, J. and Herschmann, M. (2003). Rethinking hierarchical distinctions in Brazilian music. *Journal of Latin American Cultural Studies*, 12 (3), pp. 34–358.

Gil, G. (1993) *The music of the world is bigger than world music.* [Online] Available from: www.gilbertogil.com.br/sec_textos_list.php?page=3&id_type=3 [cited 28 December 2005]

Gomes Júnior, J. (2000). A publicidade no Rádio: origem e evolução. Paper presented at *XXIII Congresso Brasileiro de Ciências da Comunicação.* Campo Grande, MS, September. Available from: intercom.org.br/papers/xxiii-ci/gt05/gt05b4.pdf [cited 25 November 2005].

Huygens, M. W. (2001). Coevolution of firm capabilities and industry competition: investigating the music industry 1877–1997. *Organization Studies*, 22 (1), pp. 971–1011.

IFPI – International Federation of the Phonographic Industry (2005). *The Recording Industry: World Sales 2005.* Available from: www.ifpi.org/content/library/worldsales2004.pdf [cited 19 January 2006].

Janotti, J. S. (2005). Música popular ou música pop? Trajetórias e caminhos da música na cultura mediática. *Encontro Latino de Economia Política da Informação, Comunicação e Cultura*. Salvador, BA, Faculdade Social da Bahia, 9–11 November 2005.

Katz, J. (2003). The Jamaican economy at a cross-roads: technology, education and growth. Unpublished manuscript, IDB, Washington, DC.

Kozul-Wright, Z. and Stanbury, L. (1998). *Becoming a globally competitive player: the case of the music industry in Jamaica.* UNCTAD, Discussion Papers, No. 138, October.

Kretschmer, M. (2001). *Music in electronic markets: an empirical study.* [Online] Available from: nms.sagepub.com/cgi/reprint/3/4/417 [cited 6 December 2004].

Lastres, H. M. M. and Cassiolato, J. E. (2005). Innovation systems and local productive arrangements: new strategies to promote the generation, acquisition and diffusion of knowledge. *Innovation: management, policy & practice*, 7 (2–3), pp. 172–187.

Lastres, H. M. M., Cassiolato, J. E. and Maciel, M. L. (2003). Systems of innovation for development in the knowledge era: an introduction. In J. E Cassiolato, H. M. M. Lastres and M. L. Maciel (eds) *Systems of innovation and development: evidence from Brazil.* Cheltenham: Elgar.

Leal, R. S. (2005). Erros de marketing no mercado fonográfico: o caso da queda na vendagem de cd's. *Diálogos & Ciência*, 3 (5).

Lemos, C., Matos, M. P., Schatz, P., Pereira, M., Cassiolato, J. E. and Lastres, H. M. M. (2005). *Cultura e desenvolvimento: o APL de música de Conservatória/RJ.* RedeSist/IE/UFRJ. Available from: www.sinal.redesist.ie.ufrj.br [cited 1 December 2005].

Machado, M. and Zan, J. R. (2002). Segmentação no mercado fonográfico brasileiro: 1968–1975. Paper presented at *X Congresso interno de iniciação científica da UNICAMP*, September.

Malm, K. and Wallis, R. (1992). *Media policy and music activity*. London: Routledge.

Medina, R. (2002). A indústria de espetáculos. In *Economia da cultura: a força da indústria cultural no Rio de Janeiro.* Faperj and Coppe/UFRJ. Rio de Janeiro, RJ: E-papers.

Napolitano, M. (2002). A música popular brasileira (MPB) dos anos 70: resistência política e consumo cultural. Paper presented at *IV Congreso Latinoamericano de la Asociación Internacional para el Estudio de la Música Popular*, Mexico City.

Nassif, L. (no date). *A indústria da Música Brasileira.* [Online]. Available from: www.culturaemercado.com.br [cited 30 August 2004].

Natale, E. and Olivieri, C. (2004). *Guia de produção cultural Brasileiro 2004.* São Paulo, SP: Editora Zé do Livro.

Núcleo de Estudos de Economia da Cultura (no date). *Cultura em números: a produção cultural na economia brasileira*, Vol. 2. Rio de Janeiro, RJ: Print Comunicação Empresarial.

Peruzzo, C. K. (1998). Participação nas rádios comunitárias no Brasil. Paper presented at *XXI Congresso Brasileiro de Ciências da Comunicação.* Recife, PE, September.

Pessoti, G. C. (2001). A indústria fonográfica no Brasil e na Bahia. *Bahia análise & dados*, 11 (2), pp. 131–141.

Piccino, E. (no date). Um breve histórico dos suportes sonoros analógicos: surgimento, evolução e os principais elementos de impacto tecnológico. *Sonora*, 2. Available from: hosting.iar.unicamp.br/artigos_pdf/02SuportesAnalogicos.pdf [cited 29 November 2005].

Sá, M. T. (2002). Cadeia: bens eletrônicos de consumo. In *Estudo da competitividade de Cadeias Integradas no Brasil: impactos das zonas de livre comércio.* MDIC/MCT-IE/UNICAMP.

Schulze, R. (1994). Hit record trends on the German market for popular music. Paper presented at *First International Conference on Cultural Economics*, ACEI conference. Witten, August.

Silva, E. D. (2001). Origem e desenvolvimento da indústria fonográfica brasileira. Paper presented at *XXIV Congresso Brasileiro de Ciências da Comunicação*. Campo Grande, MS, September.

Silva, E. D. and Jesus, R. C. (1999). A revalorização do rádio no plano de mídia. Paper presented at *XXII Congresso Brasileiro de Ciências da Comunicação*. Rio de Janeiro, RJ, September. Available from: www.intercom.org.br/papers/xxii-ci/gt06/06j23.PDF [cited 25 November 2005].

Tinhorão, J. R. (1998). *História social da música popular brasileira.* São Paulo, SP: Editora 34.

Torres, S. (2004). Multis usam jabá para censurar a produção musical brasileira. *Hora do Povo*, 16 July.

Towse, R. (1999). Copyright and economic incentives: an application to performers' rights in the music industry. *Kyklos*, 52 (3), pp. 369–390.

UNESCO (2000). *Study on international flows of cultural goods, 1980–98*. Paris. Available from: www.uis.unesco.org/template/pdf/cscl/IntlFlows.pdf [cited 1 December 2005].

UNESCO (2005). *25 questions and answers to explore key concepts and ideas related to culture and trade in the context of development.* [Online] Available from: portal.unesco.org/culture/en/ev.php-URL_ID=2461&URL_DO=DO_TOPIC&URL_SECTION=-512.html [cited 19 November 2005].

Vasconselos, A. (1991). *Raízes da música popular brasileira.* Rio de Janeiro, RJ: Rio Fundo.

Vicente, E. (2000). A indústria do disco no Brasil: um breve relato. Paper presented at *XXIII Congresso Brasileiro de Ciências da Comunicação*. Manaus, AM, September. Available from: intercom.org.br/papers/xxiii-ci/gt22/gt22a3.pdf [cited 22 November 2005].

Zan, J. R. (2001). Música popular brasileira, indústria cultural e identidade. *EccoS*, 1 (3), pp. 105–122.

Data sources

Brazilian Independent Music Association (ABMI) – www.abmi.com.br

Brazilian Disc Producer Association (ABPD) – www.abpd.org.br

National Agency of Telecommunication (ANATEL) –www.anatel.gov.br/indicadores/default.asp

Central Collecting and Distributing Bureau (ECAD) – www.ecad.org.br

Economic database of the Applied Economic Research Institute (IPEADATA) – www.ipeadata.gov.br

Annual Report of Social Information (RAIS) from the Ministry of Labor and Employment –www.mte.gov.br/EstudiososPesquisadores/PDET/Acesso/RaisOnLine.asp

Federal Service for Data Processing (SERPRO) – www.serpro.gov.br

United Nations Statistics Division (UNSTATS) – unstats.un.org

7 The audio-visual sector in India

Arpita Mukherjee[1]

Introduction

India has a thriving audio-visual sector. It is one of the oldest sectors of the economy: the Indian film industry is more than 75 years old, and the music industry is more than a century old. With around 800 dialects and 15 officially recognised languages, several religions, various styles of art, architecture, music and dance and several lifestyles from urban to rural to tribal, India is often referred to as a melting point of cultural diversity. Indian audio-visual industry has helped to preserve the country's rich and varied cultural heritage, shape public opinion and safeguard the democratic system. This creative industry has also contributed significantly to employment.

Audio-visual services are one of the fastest growing sectors of the Indian economy. With liberalisation and globalisation, India's trade in audio-visual services has increased. Indian music and films have always been appreciated in countries with large non-resident Indian (NRI) and South Asian populations. However, in the past decade these exports have increased rapidly. Since the mid-1990s, India started exporting television content and many domestic broadcasters ventured into international markets. More recently, audio-visual producers from countries such as the USA are outsourcing certain production and post-production services to developing countries such as India, China and Taiwan which have comparative advantage in labour and can offer quality services at lower cost. India has created a niche for itself as a content-producing country and an outsourcing hub for services such as animation, graphics, post-production and special effects. Many Indian companies are entering into collaborative ventures with renowned international players to improve the quality standards of their products and enhance global reach.

This chapter presents a snapshot of the Indian audio-visual sector, highlighting the recent trends and developments and government policy with respect to this sector. The first section provides an overview of the size and structure of the sector. The second section lists the economic, social and other factors promoting the growth of the Indian audio-visual sector. Since government plays an important role in promoting audio-visual services, The third section discusses the measures taken by the government to stimulate the growth of this sector. India has been successful in maintaining cultural diversity while keeping the trade links open. The fourth section highlights how the Indian government has been successful in balancing the dual objectives of promoting and preserving cultural diversity and increasing trade in audio-visual services. The last section draws the main conclusions.

Size and structure of the audio-visual industry

A large part of the Indian audio-visual industry is in the private sector. Within the private sector, certain segments such as cable television and films are largely dominated by the informal sector. There is no official estimate of the size of the industry and most segments do not have a centralised agency for tracking data. Moreover, many companies are not willing to share financial information or do not have a transparent accounting practice. Of late, some industry associations along with consultancy organisations have tried to estimate the size of the industry and its future growth potential. Although these estimates vary, they nevertheless give an indication of the size of the sector. The two most recent estimates are the CII (Confederation of Indian Industry)-KPMG estimate and the FICCI (Federation of Indian Chambers of Commerce and Industry)-PwC (PricewaterhouseCoopers) estimate. Both these reports were published in March 2005. The CII-KMPG study covered five segments – television, film, music radio and others (live entertainment, interactive games, etc.). The FICCI-PwC also covered five segments – television, films, live entertainment, music and radio, but did not cover animation and gaming, which is a growing sub-sector. Segment-wise composition of the audio-visual industry as estimated by CII-KPMG study is shown in Table 7.1. This study estimates that the industry will grow from around US$4.9 billion in the year 2004 to US$13 billion in 2010. The FICCI-PwC study shows that the size of the Indian entertainment industry was US$4.5 billion in 2004 and estimates it will reach US$10 billion by 2009. Both the studies estimate that the industry will grow at the rate of 18 per cent per annum. As a proviso to these forecasts, it should also be remembered that although the audio-visual industry is growing at a fast pace, it is still small compared with other service sectors such as software. The size of the Indian IT (information technology) and software services was estimated at US$12.8 billion at the end of 2003–4, which was a 29.6 per cent growth over the previous year.[2]

Television

Television is the largest segment of the audio-visual sector, contributing to about 60 per cent of the total revenue. In 2005, for example, it was worth 164 billion Indian Rupees, compared with 69 billion for film. This sector comprises two major segments – Doordarshan, the public service broadcaster, and private players (including broadcasters, production companies and cable operators). The modes of operation and funding structure of these two segments are widely

Table 7.1 Segment-wise composition of the entertainment industry

Segment-wise breakdown (INR billion)	*2003*	*2004*	*2005E*	*2006E*	*2007E*	*2008E*	*2009E*	*2010E*
Television	122	139	164	189	228	266	325	371
Film	52	59	69	83	99	114	129	143
Music	10	10	10	11	11	11	12	13
Radio	2	2	3	4	5	6	7	8
Others (live entertainment, interactive games, etc.)	9	11	16	23	30	39	48	60
Gross unadjusted revenues	195	222	261	309	373	436	521	595
Less: overlap (sale of film broadcast and music rights) netted off	7	6	7	8	11	13	16	18
Add: overseas' distributors' margin from sale of Indian films	8	8	8	7	8	9	10	11
Entertainment revenues at retail value (INR billion)	196	222	262	309	371	432	515	588
US$ billion (conversion rate – $1 = Rs 45)	4.36	4.93	5.82	6.87	8.24	9.6	11.44	13.07

Source: CII-KPMG, Indian Entertainment Industry Focus 2010: Dreams to Reality, March 2005.

Notes

a The summation of the figures may not match due to rounding off.

b Conversion to US$ is done by the author.

different. Doordarshan has a social responsibility and its operation and delivery is not related to profits alone. It is partly funded through budgetary grants. Private broadcasters do not receive any direct financial support from the government and they operate on a commercial basis.

Doordarshan, with around 23 channels, covering 78 per cent of the land area and around 90 per cent of the population, is one of the largest terrestrial broadcasting networks in the world. To maintain cultural diversity, Doordarshan has a three-tier programming service: national, regional and local. The national channel caters to the information, education and entertainment needs of the people through its various stations located across the country. The regional and sub-regional channels located in various states disseminate regionally relevant programmes, while the local stations set up in district headquarters are area specific and provide entertainment and information to local communities.

With the liberalisation of the economy in the 1990s, private broadcasters were allowed to operate, initially through the cable network and in recent years new delivery platforms such as DTH (direct-to-home) and IP TV (Internet protocol-based television) have emerged. During their initial years of operation, most satellite channels were in an analogue format and free-to-air, and were financed by advertisement revenues and subscriptions. As channels multiplied, there has been a stiff competition among them to increase their share of advertisement revenue. This has propelled them to explore alternative revenue sources and, more recently, many of them have become pay channels. Competition among channels and fragmentation of audiences has also led to mergers and acquisitions. In line with global developments, broadcasters are gradually shifting to digital technologies.

Cable television is the fastest growing segment within the television industry. However, the cable industry is highly fragmented and is characterised by the presence of a few multi-system operators and a large number of unorganised small cable operators catering to specific localities. Since the unorganised cable operators do not have a transparent accounting practices, the subscription revenue is often underquoted, making it difficult to estimate the size of the sector.

Film

Film is the most popular form of entertainment in India. India is the largest film-producing country in the world, producing an average of 900–1,000 films annually (in the year 2004, 934 films were certified for release). Since its beginning in 1931 more than 67,000 films, short-films, documentaries, and so on, have been produced in over 30 different languages and dialects. Films contribute to around 27 per cent of the total revenue of this sector.

Unlike the global film industry which has an oligopolistic structure, the Indian film industry is informal, highly fragmented and characterised by investment forms of proprietorship and partnership. The development of the industry is localised with some states such as Maharashtra, West Bengal, Andhra

Pradesh, Karnataka and Tamil Nadu, focusing on film production while others, such as Gujarat, focusing on the development of film infrastructure (theatres, multiplexes, etc.). The industry is labour intensive and employs over six million people – around five million directly and more than a million indirectly.

In India, the number of people visiting cinemas is large. In 2004 (Figure 7.1), box office admission reached a record of 3,100 million – the highest in the world. However, due to the unorganised nature of the industry and the fragmented distribution chain, box office receipts are not often recorded properly. Ticket prices are also low and Indian film industry's revenue is only around 1 per cent of the total global film industry revenue. Due to low average admission price and under-declaration of box office receipts, the box office spending is much lower in India compared with countries such as the USA. Unlike the USA, which earns only 35 per cent of its film sector revenue from cinema viewership, in India 70 per cent of the revenue is from domestic and overseas cinema viewership. It is only recently that new modes of delivery such as home videos are increasing.

Investment in Indian films is also much lower compared with other international productions. In 2000, the average expenditure per film was US$13.6 million in the USA, US$9.4 million in the UK and only US$0.6 million in India.[3] This is mainly because, compared with India, other major film-producing countries invest substantially in special effects, post-production and film marketing; although India's relatively low labour costs are also of course a contributing factor.

Outsourcing

India is fast developing as an outsourcing hub for post-production services, animation, graphics, special effects, and so on, and the size of the industry was estimated at US$250 million in 2004.[4] This sector has largely grown under private initiatives and many software companies are now entering into animation, graphics and special effects. NASSCOM estimated that over 27,000 people were employed in this sector in 2001. Not only are animation, graphics and special

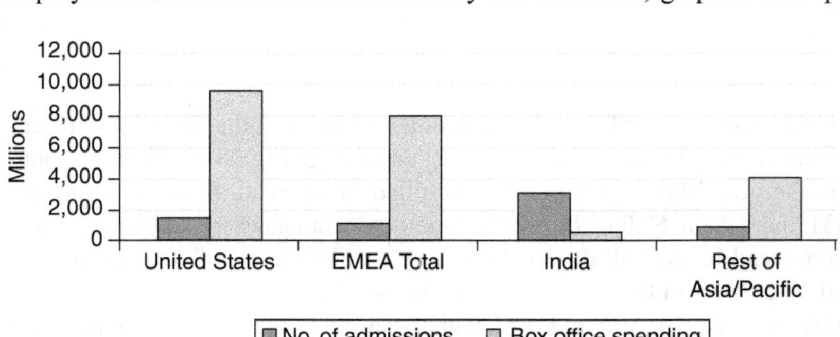

Figure 7.1 Admission numbers and box office receipts (source: PwC Global Entertainment and Media Outlook).

effects for films and television outsourced to India, there is a growing demand for outsourcing animation for advertisements and computer games. Overseas entertainment giants such as Walt Disney, IMAX and Sony are increasingly outsourcing cartoon characters and special effects to Indian companies. In the past few years, Hyderabad-based Ramoji Rao Studios provided equipment, crew sets and post-production facilities to more than seven Hollywood films including Oscar-winning *Gladiator*.

India has several advantages in this sector. With a large pool of highly qualified manpower, India is in a position to offer post-production services at a much lower cost than developed countries. The cost of producing a half-an-hour animated programme in the USA is around US$250,000–400,000, in Korea and Taiwan it is around US$110,000–120,000, while in India it costs approximately US$60,000.[5]

Indian companies are in the process of investing in hi-tech studios and implementing strict quality standards to provide leverage for their manpower advantage. Companies such as Maya Entertainment Limited, Crest Animation Studio Limited, Prasad Studios, Jadooworks and Toonz Animation have set up state-of-the-art studios that are capable of offering end-to-end services of desired quality. Cities such as Mumbai, Chennai, Bangalore and Trivandrum have emerged as the country's animation hub.

Since these services are labour intensive it has increased employment in this sector, and one of the major challenges before the companies is to find employees with the right skill levels. To overcome this hurdle, companies such as Maya Entertainment Limited have set up in-house training facilities for skills such as CGI animators and graphic designers. Some Indian companies such as UTV Software Communication Limited and Toons Animation India Private Limited have set up offices in the USA to tap the business potential. The use of animation, graphics and special effects in domestic production has also increased, improving the quality of production. Indian companies are now creating their own animated films based on Indian folklore and mythology and are marketing them internationally. Some of these are made in collaboration with foreign companies, whereby Indian companies gain access to the international technical know-how and skills. Since computer-based animation films can be produced at 30–40 per cent lower cost than traditional animation films, most animation studios are investing in setting up infrastructure for computer-based animation.

Music

Like the global music industry, which is facing an economic recession, the size of the Indian music industry has shrunk from INR13.5 billion (US$300 million) in 2000 to INR10 billion (US$222 million) in 2004.[6] Prior to the 1990s, there were a few large players in music production and the segment was dominated by film and devotional music. Post-1990s with the advent of satellite channels, non-film music, remixes and Indi-pop (Indian pop) music has gained popularity and all major international music companies have entered the Indian market. However, unlike most countries, the Indian music industry is heavily dependent on film music, whose share is around 65 per cent of the revenue. The process of technological development is slow and physical formats to date account for around 92 per cent of the revenue.

Radio

Radio in India is dominated by the public sector broadcaster – All India Radio (AIR), whose transmission covers over 91 per cent of the land area and 99 per cent of the population. Apart from AIR, 21 private-owned FM (frequency modulation) channels have established operations in 12 major cities since privatisation in the year 2000. To date, the growth of radio has been modest. The AIR has not been successful in increasing its advertising share, which is its sole source of revenue. Advertising constitutes 2 per cent of the revenue in India compared with 13 per cent in the USA and 21 per cent in Sri Lanka. Private players have recently started their operations and are facing several problems such as high licence fees. The government is in the process of streamlining its regulations to support private participation.

Summary

As the Indian audio-visual industry is maturing, there has been a shift from informal to formal formats. The industry has realised that for technological development it is important to attain scale economies. Consolidation and vertical integration among content producers, distributors, exhibitors, broadcasters and music companies has been a common feature in the industry. Many Indian companies are also entering into collaborative ventures with renowned global players.

With technological development and increased specialisation, the skill levels in audio-visual industry are rapidly changing. In the past, the bulk of the sector was unorganised, small and fragmented and employed low-skilled workers. With increasing use of technology, employment has shifted to specialised skills and professionals. As the sector is becoming organised, job security has increased. The demand for high-skilled workers is forcing companies to invest in training and in-house skill development. Specialised training institutes under the private sector are coming up.

Determinants of growth

Various factors have supported the growth of the audio-visual sector. India is one of the fastest growing economies in the world, with an average GDP (gross domestic product) growth of around 6 per cent per annum over the past decade. This GDP growth has resulted in growth of per capita income and purchasing power which in turn has led to increased consumption of audio-visual services.

An annual consumer survey conducted by NCAER (National Council of Applied Economic Research) since 1985–6 shows that the growth of the high-income class since 1995–6 has been around 19 per cent. The middle-income class is also increasing at a fast pace, especially in rural India, and the low-income class is shrinking. As economic growth is expected to be at a minimum rate of 6–7 per cent in the next five years, it is predicted that the high- and middle-income classes will continue to expand while poverty will continue to decline, creating a sustained demand for audio-visual products.

Rising domestic demand

The growth of knowledge-based sectors such as software and BPO (business process outsourcing) have created new job opportunities and raised the income levels, especially of the younger generation. The educated, young, high-income population is allocating a larger part of its budget to consumer goods and entertainment. Demand from this segment is prompting the audio-visual suppliers to invest in innovative content providers (multiplex movies), new technologies (digital technologies) and different platforms for content delivery (webcasting, DTH, video-on-demand). With the average Indian becoming younger, it is likely that spending on entertainment will continue to rise in the future.

The large population base and unsaturated market provide huge potential for growth. For instance, with over 119 million households with television, India is one of the largest television markets in the world. However, in 2004 cable television only reached 42 per cent of the total television households and about 25 per cent of the total households. Broadcasters (both domestic and international) and production houses have pointed out that although purchasing power in India is lower than developed countries and hence prices of audio-visual products are lower, the large population base and huge untapped market provides significant scope for high volume consumption. Given that per capital income is rising, prices of television sets are falling and the market is not saturated, it is expected that the television industry will continue to grow at a rate of over 15 per cent in the next five years.

International markets

An important factor which supports the growth of the audio-visual industry is the demand for India-specific products both domestically and from Indian and other South Asian populations abroad. The niche audience base has given the Indian entertainment industry a natural protection from foreign competition. India is one of the few markets where inspite of no major restriction on import of foreign films, quotas or local content requirement, the share of foreign films is only 6–7 per cent. Due to the strong demand for local content, even foreign television channels operating in India have to telecast local productions which, in turn, led to the growth of content-producing companies. The presence of over 20 million NRIs (non-resident Indians) and their strong affiliation for the

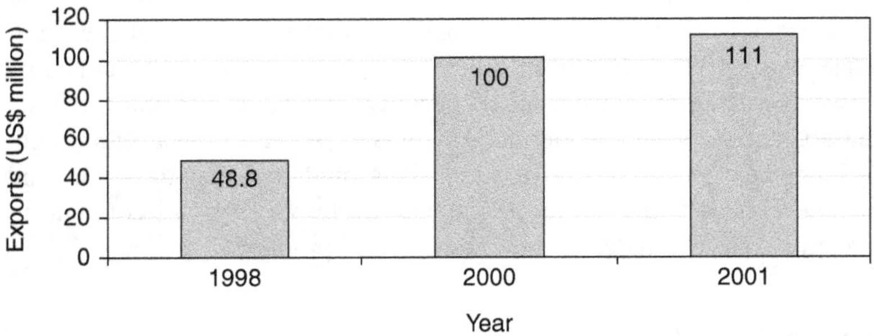

Figure 7.2 Film exports from India (source: Federation of Indian Chambers of Commerce and Industry).

indigenous culture have made Indian products internationally acceptable. There is no official estimate of India's total export of audio-visual products and services, but information provided by organisations such as Film Federation of India shows that Indian films are exported to over 95 countries worldwide. The exports of films have grown over the years as shown in Figure 7.2. Almost 30 per cent of the total number of films produced is released overseas generating 65–70 per cent of the total revenue of the film.

Global comparative advantages

Another factor promoting the growth of audio-visual services in India is the availability of high-skilled, low-cost manpower. With a large pool of qualified manpower at competitive prices, India is in a position to offer post-production services at a much lower cost than developed countries, and countries such as the USA and UK are increasingly outsourcing part of their production, animation, graphic, special effect and other services to India. One of the major advantages of India over other developing countries such as China is that animation requires familiarity with the English language and Indians have a high degree of English proficiency and are able to understand Western humour. The quality standards of Indian audio-visual products are also perceived to be higher than those of China.[7] It is expected that this will be one of the fastest growing segment, growing at a rate of around 30 per cent in the next five years. NASSCOM estimates that by 2008, the digital content development, engineering and design industry alone will employ around 300,000 people.[8]

Government initiatives

Different measures have been taken by the Indian government to support the growth of audio-visual services.

Support and promotion

Unlike many European countries, there are very few direct subsidies in India. Moreover, direct subsidies have reduced over the years due to the financial crunch. Around 90 per cent of the subsidies allocated to this sector are given to the public broadcasters – Doordarshan and All India Radio. Doordarshan has a social service obligation and is partly funded through an annual grant voted by the Parliament to meet this obligation. The government has also tried to ensure a wide audience base for Doordarshan through various regulatory measures, such as the "must carry rule" for cable operators and monopoly of Prasar Bharati over terrestrial broadcasting – the largest broadcasting network in India.

Private broadcasters do not receive any direct subsidies. However, various indirect incentives are given through the annual budget in the form of tax concessions/exemptions, such as reduction in custom duties on studio equipment, removal of excise duties on recorded tapes for television content and broadcast, and so on. Various incentives are offered to promote exports, develop India as a post-production hub and support the growth of the animation industry. For instance, revenue earned from exports of film software is exempted from income tax.

In the film industry, which is largely private, various incentives are offered by the government. India has government-funded training institutes which provide training in the art and technique of film making and television production. The government also has a small budget to support upcoming directors, low budget films and non-commercial films. For this purpose the government has set up the National Film Development Corporation (NFDC), which produces films with socially relevant themes. It has a scheme for giving commercial loans of up to US$0.07 million for cinema construction. Of late, the NFDC is suffering from financial constraints and it is becoming extremely difficult for this organisation to finance film production and cinema construction. In fact in the past 5–6 years, the NFDC has not disbursed any loans for construction. In addition, every year the government organises film festivals to provide a platform for Indian film makers to interact with their global counterparts and showcase their creations.

Both central and state governments offer incentives for the development of infrastructure. For instance, the Union Budget (2002–3) announced an exemption of 50 per cent profits from tax under Section 801B of the Income Tax Act for the construction of large convention centres and multiplex cinemas in non-metropolitan areas for a period of five years. At the state level, the Gujarat government has provided a seven-year tax holiday for construction of multiplexes. Some states, such as Andhra Pradesh and Maharashtra, provide concessional land for studio construction, development of film cities, and so on. Many state governments have set up a State Film Development Corporation to support production of films in local language. The Karnataka and Gujarat governments offer subsidies for producing films in regional languages and also provide various tax exemptions for locally produced films. The state of West Bengal imposes a higher entertainment tax[9] on non-Bengali and foreign films. All these measures have been taken to promote local productions.

The government also provides different incentives to promote and encourage film exports. The revenue earned from exports of film software is exempted from income tax. The duty paid towards the import of raw stocks is refunded back to the exporters by the way of duty drawback. On average, an exporter receives approximately US$25 to 30 as duty drawback per print.

On the regulatory front, various initiatives were taken to support the growth of this sector and to encourage private participation. For instance, in order to enable the film industry to corporatise and to access institutional finance, the government conferred formal industry status to this sector in the year 2000. As a follow up, the Reserve Bank of India and the Industrial Development Bank of India formulated guidelines for banks and financial institutes to finance the film sector. In January 2004, TRAI (Telecom Regulatory Authority of India) was given the authority to regulate the cable and broadcasting services. TRAI has come up with several recommendations, some of which have already been implemented. The government has also initiated the Communication Convergence Bill, 2001, to promote the development of the entire communication sector in a scenario of increasing convergence of technologies in IT, telecommunication and audio-visual services. Similarly, copyright protection is essential for the growth of the creative industries. Several amendments were made to the Copyright Law to bring it up to international standards. The amendment in the year 1999 made the Copyright Act fully compatible with the TRIPS (Trade Related Aspects of Intellectual Property Rights).[10] In 2000, when the government first started allowing private players in FM broadcasting, private players suffered heavy losses because the licence fee and operational costs were too high. To encourage private participation, the government reformulated its policy and the Phase II policy was announced on July 2005. The revised policy allowed FM radio players, new as well as existing ones, to switch over to a revenue-sharing regime from the current licence fee structure.

Liberalisation

Prior to the 1990s, India was a closed economy. Since the 1990s, government started implementing a series of reforms and liberalisation and the audio-visual sector is also a part of it. Reforms in the audio-visual sector were initiated to improve productivity, efficiency and global competitiveness and to enhance the choice available to Indian consumers.

In the television sector, the most important development was to end the monopoly of Doordarshan, the public service broadcaster, in the early 1990s and allow private/foreign broadcasters to telecast their programmes through the cable network. A series of reforms have been initiated since then. In 2001, to enable the distribution of content through alternative platforms, the government removed the ban on reception and distribution of television signals on Ku-band and allowed the operation of DTH services. Subsequently, the government dissolved the monopoly of the public service provider VSNL (Videsh Sanchar Nigam Limited) in uplinking, which was forcing most foreign channels to uplink from countries in South-East Asia. The new policy allowed any television channel that is aimed at Indian viewership, irrespective of its ownership, equity structure and management control, to uplink from India. It also allowed the Indian news agencies to have their own uplinking facilities for the purpose of newsgathering and its further distribution to other news agencies/broadcasters. In radio, the public broadcaster, All India Radio, had a monopoly till the year 2000, when private FM channels were allowed to operate. The government has also liberalised the FDI (foreign direct investment) regulations. The current regulations are given in Table 7.2.

From its inception, a large part of the film industry was under the private sector. The government, however, had imposed several restrictions on import of foreign films and foreign investment in the film sector. These were gradually removed. Prior to the 1990s, the National Film Development Corporation (NFDC), under the Ministry of Information and Broadcasting, had the sole authority to import films. Foreign film-producing companies and trade associations had to enter into an agreement with NFDC for import and distribution of their products in India. This restriction was removed in 1992. In the same year, government removed the quantitative restriction on the import of films[11] and the prohibition on dubbing of foreign films in Indian languages. However, certain qualitative checks on foreign films continued till the year 2002 (for example, the requirement that the film had won an award in an International Film Festival recognised by the Ministry of Information and Broadcasting). A new policy was initiated in that year which allowed the import of films without a licence. The only restriction present is that any film exhibited in India has to be certified by the Central Board of Film Certification. Arguing that an inflow of technical know-how, finance and skill would improve the quality of film production, distribution and exhibition the government removed the foreign equity restrictions in this sector. From March 2002 onwards, 100 per cent foreign direct investment is allowed in film financing, production, distribution, exhibition, marketing and

Table 7.2 FDI regulations in television and radio

Segment	*FDI limit*
TV software production	100 per cent FDI allowed subject to certain conditions
Setting up hardware facilities	49 per cent FDI allowed
Cable network	49 per cent FDI allowed subject to certain conditions
DTH	20 per cent FDI allowed within the overall limit of 49 per cent of foreign equity
Up-linking of news and current affairs TV channel	26 per cent foreign equity allowed
FM broadcasting	20 per cent foreign investment is allowed

Source: Extracted from CII-KPMG Report, Indian Entertainment Industry Focus 2010: Dreams to Reality.

associated services through the automatic route (i.e. prior approval of the Central Bank, Reserve Bank of India, was no longer required). Since advertising is a major source of revenue for the creative industry, 100 per cent foreign investment was allowed in March 2002 through the automatic route.

The policy to liberalise the audio-visual sector in a phased manner and to implement complementary reforms has led to a significant growth of this sector, increased India's export of audio-visual services and widened the range of choice available to consumers. The entry of domestic and foreign satellite channels increased demand for television content leading to the growth of programme-producing companies. From a few production houses catering for the public broadcaster, the software-producing industry is now characterised by large corporations catering to both domestic and international markets. Earlier, India was an importer of television content. Now the country has emerged as a hub for animation, graphics, sound recording and other post-production services. Competition from foreign players and access to international technical know-how and best practices has not only improved the domestic production quality but has also encouraged the Indian producers to explore international markets. Indian exports of films and television programmes have increased significantly in the post-liberalised era. The Electronic and Computer Software Export Promotion Council estimated the export of television content at US$74 million in 2001, which accounted for 20 per cent of the total revenue of the content-producing sector.

Exports of films have also increased in the post-liberalisation period. Many Indian producers are using international distributors present in India, such as Columbia Tristar Films of India Limited, to distribute their productions in international markets. Access to international technical know-how is improving the production quality. Many Indian directors, artists, musicians, technicians and actors have received international recognition and are now working with renowned global banners. In the past, Indian films largely catered to NRIs and other South Asian populations, but in recent years films such as *Monsoon Wedding* have been globally accepted. The Indian industry is now exploring new markets such as Japan and China. In the past, it was difficult for film producers to access institutional finance and they largely depended on private financers who charged high rates of interest leading to high costs of production. After the sector was given industry status, film financing from organised sources has increased. In 2004, around 100 films received institutional finance.[12]

Associated sectors have also gained from the liberalisation. For example, a large number of Indian software companies are now providing animation, graphic and other post-production services to both Indian and foreign companies. The advertising industry is booming. The entertainment industry is integrating with development of other sectors such as organised retailing. Employment in the sector, especially in areas such as animation, graphics and special effects, is also increasing.

Public–private partnerships

The development of India's audio-visual industry is a classic example of public–private partnership. India's government has played the role of a facilitator rather than a protector – removing barriers faced by the sector and implementing complementary regulations to support its growth. The government policy in India has focused on maintaining the cultural diversity and increasing the productivity and global competitiveness of this sector. The Indian experience is, however, not unique, and similarly the audio-visual sector in China has witnessed rapid development since liberalisation.[13] The Chinese government, too, plays the role of a facilitator supporting the growth of this sector. Various incentives are offered in China to encourage private participation in audio-visual services. For instance, to accelerate the development of the animation industry, Zhejiang Province listed this sector as one of its leading industries. It offered a monetary incentive of a 1 million yuan annual bonus for the development of its own animation brands. The State Administration of Radio, Film and Television promised privately owned animation companies that they would be given equal treatment as state-backed firms. Due to these incentives, the city of Hangzhou is fast developing as a major animation hub.

Local identity versus globalisation

The Indian government strongly believes that a culture's survival is not ensured in its insularity but in its ability to absorb the best of other cultures. In a globalised world it is not possible for the audio-visual industry to grow and prosper in isolation. Creation of audio-visual products is expensive and companies are now focusing on the delivery of content through multiple formats in different markets to reap the production cost. In an age of digitalisation and technological development it is increasingly difficult for government to restrict the entry of foreign content. Due to limited customer base, lack of financial resources and technical know-how, the creative industries of many developing countries (especially where there is limited funding for this sector) find it difficult to reap economies of scale. Inflow of funds, technical know-how and best management practices would enable the sector to become more organised and to gain scale economies. Competition from foreign products would force the domestic industry to improve productivity and upgrade quality standards. It will widen the choice available to Indian consumers. However, there is a fear among some segments of the society that intense competition from global multinationals can weaken the ability of domestic players to grow and prosper. To enable the sector to grow in a globalised environment, the main objective of the Indian audio-visual policy is to strike a balance between preservation of the rich cultural heritage of the nation and increase efficiency and global competitiveness of the sector through privatisation and foreign investment.

India is a nation of rich cultural heritage. Since independence various measures have been taken by the government to preserve and to promote its cultural diversity. The quasi-federal nature of governance has made it easier for different cultures and language forms of art to thrive and prosper. The different ministries/departments of the Central Government such as the Department of Culture and Ministry of Information and Broadcasting are responsible for drawing up the overall policy relating to the audio-visual and cultural sector. India is divided into 29 states and six union territories. Different state governments have their respective ministries/departments to promote indigenous culture within their state and market it both domestically and abroad. Both the central and state governments have worked together to ensure that content is produced in different languages taking into account the different lifestyles, religions and customs of different sections of the society. For instance, in India, films are produced in more than 30 different languages and dialects. In the year 2004, out of 934 films produced, only 245 were in Hindi and the rest were in other languages such as Tamil, Telegu and Bengali. Good-quality regional cinema is showcased to Indian and global audiences through government-sponsored film festivals.

Television and radio are important media to promote the indigenous culture. Through the Public Broadcasters – Doordarshan and All India Radio – the government ensures that a proper mix of programmes in national and regional languages is telecasted. To enable the public broadcaster to reach a wider audience, the government funds the services through annual budgetary grants and has made significant investment in infrastructure. The public broadcasters have a wide coverage and are available free-to-air. To have an appropriate programming mix, Doordarshan and All India Radio have a three-tier programming service: national, regional and local, which addresses the cultural concerns of various communities at different levels. The government has also imposed a "must carry" rule making it mandatory for all cable operators to retransmit three Doordarshan terrestrial channels on prime band, two national and one regional. Since Doordarshan and All India Radio have a public service obligation and receive public finance, their programme mix is different from that of the private channels.

To enhance investment in this sector, encourage inflow of advanced technology and enable domestic industries to become competitive in export markets, the government has gradually liberalised this sector carefully, monitoring the impact of liberalisation at each stage. As discussed in the previous section, the industry has responded positively to the liberalisation drive and India has emerged as one of the important global players in the audio-visual sector. The uniqueness of Indian policy is that the government has not taken any measure to restrict the entry of foreign content. On the other hand, measures were taken to upgrade the production quality and promote exports.

In certain segments, such as television broadcasting, the entry of foreign players has led to intense competition, adversely affecting the commercial revenue of the public broadcaster. For instance, Doordarshan's share in the total advertisement revenue accruing to television fell from 100 per cent in 1988, to 76 per cent in 1995, to 26 per cent in 1999.[14] To survive in the competitive environment, Doordarshan is in the process of upgrading its technology, developing a strong marketing strategy and improving programming quality. It is also exploring alternative sources of revenues, such as selling television programmes to channels aboard, renting studios and programming facilities, and so on. The television sector as a whole has gained. The entry of private players led to the rapid growth of the television industry, making it the largest segment of the Indian entertainment industry. Liberalisation has also widened the choice of programmes available to Indian viewers. From less than five channels available in the late 1980s, a household connected to cable television now has access to around 100 channels – both domestic and international. Many private players have started telecasting programmes in regional languages, which has enhanced the demand for regional language programmes.

Since there is a strong demand for Indian content in India and internationally (from NRIs and South Asian populations), the entry of foreign players did not affect the market share of Indian production. On the other hand, international producers operating in India have to reorient their products to cater specifically to Indian culture and tradition. Hence, the production of Indian content increased.

The government realised India's competitive advantage and is promoting India as a hub for post-production, animation, special effects and graphics. Similar steps are being taken by other developing countries such as China and the Philippines. The Chinese government offers incentives to the animation industry in its Special Economic Zones, while the Philippine government has designated animation as one of its top priority industries. India, China and the Philippines are examples of developing countries which have leveraged their core competence in supply of skilled manpower to enhance their share of trade in audio-visual services.

India's government has taken a proactive stand in its international engagements. To showcase India's creative industry globally and enhance cultural cooperation, the government has signed bilateral cultural agreements with around 115 countries.[15] Under these agreements, cultural exchange programmes have been signed with 83 countries. These include exchange of performing artists, cultural exhibitions, and so on. The government has also entered into film co-production agreements with several countries such as Canada and the UK. These agreements encourage film producers of the relevant countries to produce films jointly that reflect, enhance and convey the diversity of culture and heritage in both countries.

India does not support the idea of excluding cultural goods and services from future trade negotiations. The country is in the process of signing various bilateral/regional agreements, and various measures are being initiated to promote India's cultural industries under these agreements. For instance, in the Indo-Singapore Comprehensive Economic Cooperation Agreement, which was signed in 2005, India and Singapore proposed to cooperate in the field of media such as print, film and broadcasting through co-production of television content and films, sharing of information, marketing and exhibition of each other's content, and so on.

India is a member of the WTO and is actively participating in the ongoing Doha round of GATS (General Agreement on Trade in Services) negotiations. There are wide differences of opinion among WTO member countries as to the treatment of audio-visual services under the GATS. While the European Union (EU) and others have pointed out that audio-visual services are linked to preservation of culture and should not be treated like other services, countries such as the USA have pointed out that audio-visual services can be traded as any other services. India's stand is somewhere in between. Although India acknowledges the need for cultural diversity and has made a conscious effort to preserve it, it does not agree with the view of excluding cultural goods and services from future trade negotiations, given the growing commercialisation of this sector, and India's role in it. In fact, India is one of the few countries which made commitments in the audio-visual sector during the Uruguay round of negotiations. In the current Round, India made requests to many of its trading partners such as Australia, Brazil, the EU, Indonesia, Malaysia, the UAE and USA in audio-visual services. The requests focused on full commitments under market access and national treatment in Modes 1 and 4.[16] More specifically, India has requested its trading partners to remove barriers to cross-border delivery of services through electronic means such as Internet and to allow the temporary movement of persons across borders. India has also indicated that it is willing to liberalise its commitments in this sector in return for increased market access in areas/modes of export interest.

Conclusions

The audio-visual industry is one of the fastest growing sectors of the Indian economy. Its rich cultural heritage together with other factors such as high GDP growth, reduction in poverty, increased spending on entertainment, lower age group of the population, demand for India-specific products and the availability of low-cost skilled manpower have encouraged the growth of this sector. With liberalisation, globalisation and technological developments, the sector is witnessing rapid expansion. The entry of domestic private sector and foreign players has increased the availability of content and enhanced the choice available to Indian consumers. India's exports of audio-visual products have also increased. From an exporter of films and music, India has now created a niche for itself as an exporter of post-production services and is developing as an outsourcing hub for animation, graphics, special effects, and so on. Technological developments and increased specialisation have led to consolidation and vertical integration. Competition from foreign players has encouraged the domestic industry to upgrade technology to global standards and improve the quality of productions. Producers are now delivering their content through multiple platforms and are exploring new markets. The skill level in the sector has also changed since certain activities, such as animation where India is developing competence, require specialised skills.

India's audio-visual sector has largely grown under private initiatives, with the government playing the role of a facilitator – initiating appropriate regulatory and fiscal reforms to support the growth of the sector and enhance exports and investment. Government policies have focused not on protecting the domestic industry from foreign competition but to make it globally competitive. Appropriate policy initiatives have been taken by the government to promote the indigenous culture and ensure cultural diversity. The Indian government does not agree with the view that liberalisation will make its audio-visual industry susceptible to international competition leading to cultural degeneration. It is of the view that a culture's survival is not ensured by its insularity but by its ability to absorb the best of other cultures. In some circumstances, liberalisation can adversely affect the audio-visual industry, if it crowds out the domestic players; but this has not happened in India. India is one of the few countries which have been successful in preserving and promoting the indigenous culture and at the same time enhance trade links. This is due to various reasons. The most important is the high level of consumer demand for India-specific content – both in the large domestic population in India, and also internationally. Such large consumer markets give the Indian industry a natural protection. Second, post-liberalisation, access to international technical know-how and finance has improved the quality of production and made the content more appealing to a wider global audience. Like other developing countries such as China and the Philippines, India has successfully leveraged its core competence in the supply of skilled manpower to develop animation, special effects, and post-production industries.

Notes

1 Senior Fellow, Indian Council for Research on International Economic Relations, New Delhi, India. I would like to thank Prerna Ahuja for her excellent research assistance.
2 NASSCOM Strategic Review 2005, The IT Industry in India.
3 Mukherjee (2003).
4 NASSCOM: A Report on the Animation Industry 2005.
5 FICCI-PwC Report (March 2005), The Indian entertainment industry, an unfolding opportunity.
6 CII-KPMG (March 2005), Indian entertainment industry Focus 2010: Dreams to reality.
7 www.rediff.com/money/2005/mar/16spec1.htm
8 www.atimes.com/atimes/South_Asia/GD21Df05.html
9 Entertainment tax is the tax levied at the exhibition stage on cinemas, theatres, cable operators, etc.
10 However, there are certain problems with the implementation of the Act which the government is trying to resolve.
11 Previously only 100 titles were allowed to be imported.
12 Although this number is small compared with the number of films produced in India, it shows that the industry is slowly moving towards corporatisation.
13 Much of the liberalisation in China has been due to its WTO commitments.
14 Mukherjee (2003).
15 Department of Culture, Government of India, Annual Report, 2004–5.
16 GATS classifies services trade under four different modes: Mode 1 (cross-border

trade), Mode 2 (consumption abroad), Mode 3 (commercial presence) and Mode 4 (movement of natural persons).

Bibliography

Annual Report of Department of Culture, Government of India (2004–5).

Annual Report of the Ministry of Information and Broadcasting, various issues.

Asia Times, India animated by special effects outsourcing, 21 April, 2005. Web site: www.atimes.com/atimes/South_Asia/GD21Df05.html

CII-KPMG, Indian entertainment industry Focus 2010: Dreams to reality, March 2005. Web site: www.in.kpmg.com/pdf/Focus_Dreams_to_Reality.pdf

FICCI-PwC Report, The Indian entertainment industry, an unfolding opportunity, March 2005.

Mukherjee, A. (2002), India's trade potential in audio-visual services and the GATS, Working Paper 81, ICRIER, New Delhi.

Mukherjee, A. (2003), Audio-visual policies and international trade: the case of India, Report 227, Hamburg Institute of International Economics.

Mukherjee, A. (2004), "Cultural diversity and trade liberalization: the case of India", in *Trade and Culture*: Issues in 2004, Conference Paper of Centre for Trade Policy and Law, Chicago, www.carleton.ca/ctpl/pdf/conferences/tradeandcultureposting4.pdf

NASSCOM, A Report on the Animation Industry 2005.

Rediff.com, If it's animation, its must be India! 16 March, 2005. Web site: www.rediff.com/money/2005/mar/16spec1.htm

TRAI, Recommendations on issues relating to broadcasting and distribution of TV channels, 1 October, 2004.

8 Copyright-based industries in Arab countries

Najib Harabi[1]

Introduction

In Arab countries there is a widespread impression that there has been a decline in creative and artistic activities which, in turn, has led to a decline in the output of copyright-based industries in those countries. Since there has been no systematic collection of data/statistics for verifying this impression, a systematic empirical study was needed, in order to provide scholars, business leaders and policy-makers with sound advice and assist them in making informed policy decisions concerning this important issue. It could have been, however, quite costly and time consuming to conduct such an analysis for all copyright-based industries and for all Arab countries. Therefore, a selective approach was required. This consisted of choosing four key copyright-based industries in five selected Arab countries (Morocco, Tunisia, Egypt, Jordan and Lebanon) and thus conducting five national case studies (the final reports of these case studies are listed in the Bibliography).[2]

The present chapter synthesizes the results of the national case studies and thereby gives a comparative account of the performance of the four copyright-based industries in the five selected Arab countries. The rest of the chapter proceeds as follows: after a description of the objectives of the study; the next section outlines the methodology and is followed by the major results. The last section concludes with recommendations for public policy.

The overall purpose of the project was to help estimate the economic importance of the copyright and related or neighboring rights industries in five Arab countries, as well as to identify the main problems that those industries are currently facing. It should therefore be seen as an important step towards fulfilling the following objectives:

1 To describe the economic performance of key copyright-based industries in Egypt, Jordan, Lebanon, Morocco and Tunisia, including the contribution of each category of industries to GDP, employment and foreign trade.
2 To understand the economic performance of those industries, the focus here being on qualitatively analyzing the major determinants (positive and negative factors) affecting the growth process of those industries; the

determinants include cultural, economic, legal (notably IPR), social, technological and political factors.

3 To provide policy-makers and business leaders in the Arab region and international development institutions with theoretically sound, evidence-based advice on the issues analyzed in the project.

Methodology of the study

In order to achieve the objectives of the study, we have followed a standard approach used in applied economics. Inspired by the state of the art in this field, we first developed a common theoretical understanding of the questions at hand and then tried to find empirical evidence for those questions. Both steps are discussed in more detail below.

Theoretical background

In order to illustrate the economic importance of copyright-based industries (first objective of the study), economists have so far used the following three indicators:

- Gross Added Value of all copyright-based industries as a percentage of total Gross Domestic Product (GDP).
- Share of employment in all copyright-based industries as a percentage of total national employment.
- Share of foreign trade in all copyright-based industries as a percentage of total national foreign trade.

However, the actual computation of the three economic indicators as applied to copyright-based industries – see, for instance, Miller and Strooberger (1993) and Siwek and Mosteller (1999) – came up against both methodological difficulties and the crucial problem of a lack of appropriate data (for a good discussion of these issues, see WIPO 2003).

The first methodological difficulty is that of defining exactly what industry should be considered a copyright-based industry. Second, what are the (upstream and downstream) boundaries of the copyright-based industries? In other words, what parts of the value-chain of the copyright-based industry should be included in the analysis? In publishing, for example, around the central activity of writing and organizing the production of publications there is the manufacture of paper and the retailing of books and periodicals. Should those peripheral activities also be included in the calculation of the economic importance of the publishing industry or not?

An empirical answer to these questions has been given in a study by the International Intellectual Property Alliance (IIPA). It distinguishes between "core" and "total" copyright-based industries. The "core" industries are those that create copyright works as their primary product. They include the motion picture industry (television, cinema and home video), the recording industry (records, tapes and CDs), the music publishing industry, the book, magazine and newspaper publishing industry, the computer software industry (including data processing, business applications and interactive entertainment on all platforms), legitimate theater, advertising and the radio, television and cable broadcasting industries. The "total" copyright-based industries encompass both the "core" industries and portions of many other industries that create, distribute or depend on copyright works. Examples are the retail trade (a portion of which involves the sale of video and audio material and books, for example), the doll and toy industry and computer manufacture (see, for instance, the 2002 IIPA Report compiled and edited by Siwek 2002).

A third methodological problem is that the number of copyright-based industries varies over time. The computer software industry, for example, has been an important component of all recent studies, but was mentioned only as a secondary feature in some earlier studies. Comparisons of the economic importance of copyright-based industries at different times and between different countries are therefore difficult to make.

Last but not least, the problem of availability of reliable data, especially in developing countries such as the Arab countries, has to be emphasized (for more country-specific and industry-specific data problems the interested reader is advised to look at the national case studies).

A few empirical studies on the economic importance of copyright-based industries have been conducted in a number of countries on the basis of the methods briefly discussed above. They all had to find a solution to the difficulties and problems mentioned (for a survey of some of the studies, see Silberston 1998 and Alikhan 2001). For the USA, for example, the IIPA has been regularly publishing studies on the economic importance of copyright-based industries. For the MERCOSUR countries (Argentina, Brazil, Paraguay and Uruguay) and Chile, WIPO and the State University of Campinas (Argentina) have for the first time conducted a joint study on the economic importance of copyright-based industries. Some results of that study are used for comparative purposes (see introduction).

With regard to the second objective of the study – understanding the factors that affect the economic performance of copyright-based industries in five Arab countries – we have chosen a theoretical background based on a model (the Diamond Paradigm) developed and used by Michael E. Porter of Harvard University (see Porter 1990), which is itself derived from the structure–conduct–performance (SCP) paradigm in economics (Bain 1956). According to this model, the economic performance (or competitive advantage) of any industry is affected by the following four major forces:

- production factor conditions
- demand conditions
- related and supporting industries
- corporate strategy, structure and rivalry.

Production factors include basic inputs such as land, labor, capital, infrastructure, natural resources and scientific knowledge. In addition to these general-purpose factors Porter emphasized the need for specialized inputs that include highly specialized pools of skills, applied technology, infrastructure and even sources of capital that are tailored to the actual needs of particular industries. These specialized factors are not natural endowments; firms and governments create them. Their presence or absence in an industry is critical to its economic performance.

The second determinant of competitiveness is demand conditions. They include the contribution of both the size and the character of the home-market demand to the industry's product or service. National and international success grows out of having local customers who are among the most sophisticated and demanding in the world for products and services. Size, while important, is nevertheless less crucial than character. Sophisticated, demanding local buyers provide a window on advanced customers' needs; they prevail on local firms to meet high standards in terms of product quality, features and service. By meeting such demands local companies often gain a competitive advantage in foreign markets.

The presence or absence of suppliers and related industries that are internationally competitive is the third point of the Porter Diamond. A firm may not need local suppliers for all of its inputs, but it clearly benefits from having a critical mass of competitive suppliers of specialized components, machinery and services nearby. Far more significant for competitive advantage than mere access, says Porter, is the advantage that home-based suppliers provide in terms of innovation and upgrading based on proximity and close working relationships.

Suppliers and end-users located close to each other can take advantage of quick and constant information flow, joint work on improvements and mutual motivation to progress. In addition to supplier industries, home-based competitors in related industries, or industries with similar skills, technologies or customers provide similar benefits: information flow, technology interchange and opportunities for sharing, which in turn increase the rate of innovation and upgrading.

The fourth determinant of performance and competitive advantage and the fourth point of the Porter Diamond is corporate strategy, structure and rivalry. These determinants encompass the conditions in a country that govern how companies are created, organized and managed, as well as the nature of domestic rivalry. According to Porter, intense local rivalry is one of the most significant pressures on companies to innovate and upgrade.

The four determinants of the diamond – production factor conditions; demand conditions; related and supporting industries; corporate strategy, structure and rivalry – shape the environment for competing in particular industries. The determinants themselves are subject to the influence of two other variables: (1) government and (2) chance. It would be tempting, as Porter has argued, to regard government as a fifth determinant, especially because its role is so prominent in most discussions on competitiveness. Yet this would be wrong: government is best seen not as an independent determinant of competitiveness but as an agent that makes its presence felt through the four determinants of the diamond. The other outside influence on the diamond is chance. Such events as major technological discontinuities and significant shifts in key factor costs such as energy, not to mention wars and other massive economic and political dislocations, alter conditions in the diamond and can cancel out the advantages of entrenched competitors. While chance events may make for shifts in competitive advantage in an industry, the attributes of local environment determine what nation, state or city exploits them. The locality with the most favorable diamond will be the most likely to convert chance events into competitive advantage.

Another point Porter emphasizes a great deal is that the four determinants of competitiveness constitute a dynamic system that is as important as its parts – or perhaps more so. The effect of one part of the diamond on competitive advantage depends on the state of the others. Serious weakness in any one determinant will hamper an industry's potential for advancement. The four determinants are thus self-reinforcing. In sum, the system (diamond) can work both as a virtuous and as a vicious circle of mutually supporting forces at industry level.

The last point in the Porter model that should be mentioned here is the relationship between the diamond and the building of clusters. On the basis of numerous industry case studies, Porter observes that a firm's ability to perform and upgrade continuously is strongly influenced by its proximity to advantages in the diamond. Having capable rivals, suppliers, sophisticated customers and providers of specialized factors nearby ensures more rapid information flow, more fluid working relationships and greater pressure to perform. Such dynamics lead to the formation of clusters of nationally or internationally competitive industries (including at a regional level involving two or more countries). Clusters of industries that compete nationally and internationally are the driving force behind economic development in a nation or region; their mutually reinforcing character energizes performance, fosters upgrading, spawns new firms and new industries and stimulates demand for local industries.

Empirical approach

With regard to the first objective of the study – estimating the economic importance of copyright-based industries – we have relied basically on facts and figures published by national and international institutions. Unfortunately, data on copyright-based industries from those sources are either not available or insufficient in the Arab countries under consideration. This is due to a number of factors. First, relevant economic data, if available, are highly aggregated (national accounts data), and cannot therefore be used for assessing the economic importance of copyright-based industries. Second, since the existing Standard Industrial Classification (SIC) used by national statistical agencies for collecting data at corporate and industry levels are also highly aggregated (mostly at the three-digit level), they are not suitable for adequately analyzing the value-chain of copyright-based industries. Third, additional statistical sources (such as corporate and household surveys data) are not available in all five countries, and even if they are they use heterogeneous definitions, concepts, sampling methods, and so on.

This last remark is unfortunately also true for the national research teams working within the present WIPO study. They have not, for instance, always used the same definitions, sampling methods, and so on, for their country studies. For example, while the Egyptian study considers the film industry exclusively in terms of the production of films, the Lebanese study looks also at the production of advertisements and video-clips, firms involved in the retail distribution of films and also schools and training institutions. There is a more complex problem in the Jordanian statistics: official statistics do not make a clear distinction between the audiovisual sector and music or other sound recording, either at the production level or regarding international trade. For a comparison of the similarities and differences between the industry studies in the five Arab countries, see Tables 8.1 and 8.2.

The consequences of these problems are, first, that we can say very little in quantitative terms about the economic importance of copyright-based industries in the selected Arab countries and, second, that even if data are available at the national level, comparisons between the countries are very difficult to make, as we shall see below. Finally, since the present study analyzes a selected group of only four core industries, the results can only partly reflect the importance of the entire copyright-based sector in the economy, apart from which it is not appropriate to make international comparisons.

As for the second objective of the study – understanding the factors affecting the economic performance of copyright-based industries in five Arab countries – the research teams collected original qualitative and quantitative data themselves. For that purpose we developed a comprehensive questionnaire (88 items) based on the Porter model briefly described above. It covered all major aspects of the model and thus contained general questions on the firm (10), on the economic performance of firms (2), on supply conditions (13), on demand conditions (9), on related and supporting industries (13), on market structure and firm strategy (20), on government policies (13) and, lastly, concluding questions on the future expectations of firms in copyright-based industries (8). The questionnaire – its detailed structure can be found in the Appendix – was designed as a guide for face-to-face interviews for a basically exploratory analysis of the four copyright-based industries in the selected Arab countries.

Owing to the limited financial resources available, it was agreed that the survey would not cover a "representative" sample – in statistical terms – of all firms and experts in the five countries, but rather a limited number of "important" firms and experts in all four industries located in the five Arab countries. The national research teams were thus able to conduct 242 interviews not only with representatives of firms, but also with industry and government experts. Of those interviews, 15 percent were conducted in Morocco, 14 percent in Tunisia, 15 percent in Egypt, 25 percent in Jordan and 31 percent in Lebanon. In terms of

Table 8.1 Industries covered by the study[a]

	Morocco	*Tunisia*	*Egypt*	*Jordan*[b]	*Lebanon*
Motion picture industry					
• Television	X	O	O	X	O
• Theatrical and	O	O	O	X	O
• Home video	X	O	O	X	O
Recording industry					
• Records,	X	X	X	X	X
• Tapes and	X	X	X	X	X
• CDs	X	X	X	X	X
Music publishing industry	X	O	X	X	X
Publishing industry					
• Book,	X	X	X	X	X
• Journal and	O	O	O	O	X
• Newspaper	O	O	O	O	X
Computer software industry, including					
• Data processing,	X	X	X	X	X
• Business applications	X	X	X	X	X
• Interactive entertainment on all platforms	X	O	O	X	O
Legitimate Theater	O	O	O	O	O
Advertising	O	O	O	X	X
Broadcasting industries:					
• Radio	O	O	O	X	O
• Television and	O	O	O	X	X
• Cable	O	O	O	X	X
Other industries (specify)					
• Film production		X	X		Printing,
• Film distribution		X	X		Live shows, Concerts, Festivals Schools and Training Institutions

Notes

a X = covered by the national case study; O = not covered by the national case study.

b For Jordan: since there is no film industry in this country, the Jordanian research team examined the audiovisual sector instead. In addition, owing to overlaps and minute size, advertising has been combined with radio, TV and cable broadcasting.

industry coverage, 32 percent of the interviews were done in the book publishing industry, 17 percent in the music recording industry, 22 percent in the film industry and 29 percent in the software industry (for more detail see Table 8.2). The survey was conducted in the five countries in 2002 and 2003.

In addition to the quantitative limitations on the number of firms and experts interviewed, the national case studies – with the exception of Lebanon – do not focus much (if at all) on the opinions of creators, artists, actors, directors, musicians, and so on, but almost exclusively on those of firms involved either in the

Table 8.2 Number of interviews for the four copyright industries of Arab countries

	Morocco	*Tunisia*	*Egypt*	*Jordan*[a]	*Lebanon*	*Total*	
Book							
Firms	16	09	07	09	12	53	
Experts	00	01	02	06	16	25	
Total	16	10	09	15	28	78	32%
Music							
Firms	04	04	03	05	03	19	
Experts	05	01	01	07	09	23	
Total	09	05	04	12	12	42	17%
Film[a]							
Firms	05	09	10	10	04	38	
Experts	01	00	02	02	10	15	
Total	06	09	12	12	14	53	22%
Software							
Firms	04	08	10	15	08	45	
Experts	02	01	02	06	13	24	
Total	06	09	12	21	21	69	29%
Total	37	33	37	60	75	242	100%
	15%	14%	15%	25%	31%	100%	

Note

a For Jordan: since there is no film industry in this country, the Jordanian research team examined the audiovisual sector instead.

production or in the distribution of copyright-based goods and services, and seldom on firms operating in the whole value-chain. The focus has largely been on the "core" industries and thus has not included (in most cases) distributors, retailers, and so on (parts of the "total" industries). In other words, important parts of the value-chain in the four copyright-based industries are under-represented in the survey and analysis.

Last but not least, one important point should be kept in mind while reading and interpreting the results of those interviews given below: all the survey data used in this study were the product of subjective judgments based on imperfect information.[3] In sum, from a methodological perspective the present study is an exploratory, primarily qualitative analysis of four copyright-based industries in five Arab countries.

Major results

The purpose of this section is to present the main results concerning the two major objectives of the study: (1) estimating the economic importance of copyright-based industries and (2) understanding the factors affecting that performance. The emphasis will be more on the comparison of those results among the five Arab countries. The reader interested in the details of the individual countries is referred to the national country studies presented separately.[4]

Overall view

The economic importance of copyright-based industries is measured, as mentioned above, by three indicators: (1) Gross Added Value in relation to GDP; (2) share of national employment and (3) share of foreign trade (export and import). In the case of the five selected Arab countries Table 8.3 summarizes the major quantitative results.

With regard to the first indicator, Lebanon seems to have – in relative terms – the highest contributions from copyright-based industries to its GDP, followed by Jordan, Tunisia, Morocco and Egypt.

As for the second and third indicators, data are unfortunately not available for

Table 8.3 Economic importance of the four copyright industries in selected Arab countries

	Morocco (1999)	*Tunisia (2000)*		*Egypt (2000/ 2001)*	*Jordan (2000)*[h]		*Lebanon (1999)*	
Share in GDP (in %)								
Book	0.299	0.37		0.02[f]	0.2		0.843	
Music	0.161	0.02		0.02[f]	<<0.1		0.216	
Film	0.045	0.09		0.02[f]	<0.1		0.108	
Software	0.030	0.16		0.05[g]	0.4		0.451	
Total	0.534	0.64		<0.1	0.7		1.618	
Share in employment (in %)								
Book	n.a.	n.a.		n.a.	0.1		0.79	
Music	n.a.	n.a.		n.a.	<<0.1		0.19	
Film	n.a.	0.2[a]		n.a.	<0.1		0.12	
Software	n.a.	1.2[b]		n.a.	0.2		0.13	
Total	n.a.	n.a.		n.a.	<0.5		1.22	
Share in exports and imports (in %)								
Book	n.a.	0.04[c]	0.5[c]	n.a.	0.6	0.2	3.36	0.39
Music	n.a.	0.06[d]	0.03	n.a.	0.1	0.1	n.a.	
Film	n.a.	n.a.	n.a.	n.a.	0.4	0.2	n.a.	
Software	n.a.	0.3[e]	n.a.	n.a.	1.4	0.9	n.a.	
Total	n.a.	n.a.	n.a.	n.a.	2.4	1.2	n.a.	

Notes

For Tunisia:

a Average of new jobs created over the period 1996–2001.

b Average of new jobs created over the period 1998–2001.

c Printed material (year 2000).

d Recorded tapes (year 2000).

e Software only (year 2000).

For Egypt:

f Of GNP (not GDP) in 2000.

g For 2001.

For Jordan:

h Since there is no film industry in this country, the Jordanian research team examined the audiovisual sector instead.

most of the countries in the study. For Lebanon and Jordan only, rough estimates suggest that 1.2 percent of the overall labor force is employed by the four copyright-based industries in the former and less than 0.5 percent in the latter. As for the estimated contribution of the four copyright-based industries to foreign trade, data are available for Jordan only: 2.4 percent of all exports and 1.2 percent of all imports come from the copyright-based industries of this country.

Of all copyright-based industries, book publishing seems to be the most important in most Arab countries with the exception of Jordan and Egypt. Its contribution to GDP seems highest in Lebanon, followed by Tunisia, Morocco, Jordan and Egypt.

The contribution of the music recording industry to GDP varies from country to country. Its contribution to GDP seems highest in Lebanon, followed by Morocco, Jordan, Tunisia and Egypt.

In most of the countries under consideration the film industry contributes less than 0.1 percent to GDP. The highest contribution is in Lebanon, followed by Jordan, Morocco, Tunisia and Egypt.

Of all the copyright-based industries, software is either the most important – in Egypt and Jordan – or the second most important – in Lebanon and Tunisia. Only in Morocco is it the least important.

Book industry

The overall economic performance of book publishing varies from country to country. It has been seen as positive in Lebanon and Jordan, as negative in Tunisia and as very negative in Morocco (see Table 8.4).

The good economic performance of book publishing in Lebanon and Jordan can be explained basically by a combination of positive production factor conditions (labor in Jordan and capital in Lebanon), positive demand conditions (domestic in Jordan and foreign in Lebanon) and favorable interaction with the upstream and downstream industries. In contrast, the perceived adverse position of the book publishing industry in Morocco and Tunisia is due to poor production factor conditions (mainly lack of capital), weak support from peripheral industries (especially downstream firms) and insufficient government support (lack of demand stimulation).

The position of the Egyptian book publishing industry is mixed. On one hand the industry enjoys positive production factor and demand conditions, positive support from downstream industries and healthy domestic competition, but on the other hand it faces serious obstacles to its further development. There is for instance a lack of support from upstream industries, such as paper manufacturing or book and publishing equipment (printers, ink cartridges, etc.). These important ingredients are not produced locally, and must therefore be imported on terms that are not always beneficial (high tariffs and taxes). This situation indicates that the critical requisites for a local cluster of firms to operate in the Egyptian book publishing industry are missing.

Table 8.4 Synthesis of results for the book industry

Indicators	*Countries*				
	Morocco	*Tunisia*	*Egypt*	*Jordan*	*Lebanon*
Overall performance	– –	–	(?)	+	+
Role of supply					
Labor	+	0	+	+	–
Capital	– –	–	+	0	+
Role of demand					
Domestic demand	– –	0	+	+	–
Export market	– –	0	+	0	+
Role of related industries					
Upstream	–	+	–	+	+
Downstream	–	–	+	+	+
Other firms	–	–	0	0	0
Role of market structure					
Domestic competition and strategies	0	+	+	–	–
Foreign competition	0	0	0	0	–
Role of public policy					
Development of human resources and technology	+	+	–	–	– –
Infrastructure and investment	+	+	–	–	– –
Stimulation of demand	–	0	0	0	– –
Enforcement of IPRs	– –	0	–	0	–
Firms' expectations	+	+	0	0	0

Note
0 = None; – = Poor; – – = Very poor; + = Good; + + = Very good; (?) = Cannot be determined.

In all countries the enforcement of IPRs in the book publishing industry is weak. Copyright protection is not widely used as a positive means of enhancing the economic performance of this industry.

Music industry

The overall economic performance of the music recording industry also differs from country to country. It is considered positive in Egypt and Lebanon, negative in Morocco, very negative in Tunisia and unchanged (neutral) in Jordan (see Table 8.5).

The encouraging performance of this industry in Egypt and Lebanon can be understood as a result of a favorable combination of good production factor conditions (especially labor and human capital), demand conditions (especially the possibility of exporting to other countries), adequate support from upstream and downstream industries and lively domestic competition. In both countries the performance of the music industry is due to private sector effort and not to government support. On the contrary, public policy is seen (especially in Egypt) as having an adverse effect on the music industry.

Table 8.5 Synthesis of results for the music industry

Indicators	*Countries*				
	Morocco	*Tunisia*	*Egypt*	*Jordan*	*Lebanon*
Overall performance	–	– –	+	0	+
Role of supply					
Labor	–	+	+ +	+	–
Capital	–	– –	+	0	+
Role of demand					
Domestic demand	–	– –	+	–	–
Export market	–	–	+	0	+
Role of related industries					
Upstream	+	–	+	0	+
Downstream	–	0	+	0	+
Other firms	0	0	0	0	0
Role of market structure					
Domestic competition and strategies	0	–	+	–	+
Foreign competition	–	0	0	0	+
Role of public policy					
Development of human resources and technology	–	+	–	–	+
Infrastructure and investment	–	0	–	–	–
Stimulation of demand	0	0	–	–	+ +
Enforcement of IPRs	– –	– –	–	– –	– –
Firms' expectations	– –	–	+	0	+

Note
0 = None; – = Poor; – – = Very poor; + = Good; + + = Very good.

The poor economic performance of this industry in Morocco and Tunisia is attributed to unfavorable production factor conditions (lack of capital), adverse demand conditions (both domestic and foreign) and insufficient support from downstream industries (in Morocco) and upstream industries (in Tunisia). In neither country is public policy perceived as helping to mitigate those serious problems.

In all countries under consideration the enforcement of IPRs in the music recording industry is very weak. This seems to be seriously detrimental to the economic performance of that industry.

Film industry

The overall economic performance of the film industry is considered positive in Lebanon, negative in Morocco and Tunisia and mixed in Egypt (see Table 8.6).[5]

In Egypt experts have identified both positive and negative factors affecting the development of this industry. The positive include favorable production factor conditions, good demand conditions (especially the opportunities for export, particularly to other Arab countries), adequate support from upstream

Table 8.6 Synthesis of results for the film industry

Indicators	*Countries*				
	Morocco	*Tunisia*	*Egypt*	*Jordan*	*Lebanon*
Overall performance	–	–	(?)	+	+
Role of supply					
Labor	+	+	+ +	0	–
Capital	– –	–	+ +	0	–
Role of demand					
Domestic demand	– –	–	+	–	–
Export market	– –	0	+ +	+	–
Role of related industries					
Upstream	0	+	+ +	+	+
Downstream	– –	0	+	+	+
Other firms	0	–	–	+	0
Role of market structure					
Domestic competition and strategies	0	0	–	0	+
Foreign competition	– –	–	–	0	– –
Role of public policy					
Development of human resources and technology	+	+	+	–	– –
Infrastructure and investment	+	–	–	–	– –
Stimulation of demand	0	–	–	0	– –
Enforcement of IPRs	–	0	–	–	– –
Firms' expectations	+	–	0	+	–

Note

0 = None; – = Poor; – – = Very poor; + = Good; + + = Very good; (?) = Cannot be determined.

a For Jordan: since there is no film industry in this country, the Jordanian research team examined the audiovisual sector instead.

and downstream industries and supportive public development of human resources and technology. On the other hand, competition (both domestic and foreign) and the role of public policy (especially with respect to infrastructure building, stimulation of demand and lack of IPR enforcement) are regarded as having an adverse effect on the development of this prestigious industry in Egypt.

In Morocco and Tunisia lack of capital, weak demand (both domestic and international), inadequate support from downstream firms, limited distribution channels, fierce foreign competition and insufficient public policy (especially the deficient infrastructure in Tunisia) are the major negative factors explaining the poor economic performance of this industry. That low performance has been recorded in spite of the availability of adequate labor and government efforts to develop human resources and technology.

In Lebanon there is hardly any film industry, and current output is very small (one or two films a year). This is due to a vicious circle of poor production factors (lack of finance and competent professionals), unfavorable demand conditions (lack of interest in locally produced films both inside and outside

Lebanon) and strong foreign competition. Consequently there are practically no local supporting and related industries. Government support is weak. Corporate and expert expectations are understandably bleak for this industry.

In most of the countries in the study the enforcement of IPRs in the film industry is seen as weak. The impact of copyright-based protection on the economic development of the industry is perceived as negative.

Software industry

Of all the copyright-based industries studied here, only the software industry has been unanimously seen as performing well or very well in all five Arab countries. Almost all factors of the Porter Diamond register positively. This optimistic view is not only true of the recent past development of the industry: it also holds for its future. Corporate expectations are good in all countries (see Table 8.7).

So, what explains this special case? It is basically the combined beneficial effect of major components of the Porter Diamond, such as good production factors (availability of finance and credit), sufficient demand (from both the private and public sectors), adequate support from upstream and downstream

Table 8.7 Synthesis of results for the software industry

Indicators	*Countries*				
	Morocco	*Tunisia*	*Egypt*	*Jordan*	*Lebanon*
Overall performance	–	+	+ +	+ +	+
Role of supply					
Labor	–	+ +	+ +	+	+
Capital	+ +	–	+	+	+
Role of demand					
Domestic demand	+	+	+	–	–
Export market	+	+	+	+	+
Role of related industries					
Upstream	0	+ +	+	+	+
Downstream	+	0	+	+	+
Other firms	+ +	+	+	+	0
Role of market structure					
Domestic competition and strategies	+	+	+	–	+
Foreign competition	–	+	–	0	+
Role of public policy					
Development of human resources and technology	–	+	+ +	+	+
Infrastructure and investment	+	+	+ +	+ +	+
Stimulation of demand	0	+	+ +	+	–
Enforcement of IPRs	– –	+	–	+	– –
Firms' expectations	+ +	+	+	+	+

Note
0 = None; – = Poor; – – = Very poor; + = Good; + + = Very good.

industries (ICT industry and others), strong domestic competition and deep involvement of public policy, coupled with international aid, both private and public (see for instance the case of Jordan).

The only dark area in this picture is the persistence of piracy and the illegal use of software in Arab countries, especially Lebanon and Morocco.[6] As in other copyright-based industries, the enforcement of IPRs in the software industry remains weak.

Recommendations

The third objective of the present study, as already mentioned above, is to provide Arab policy-makers, business leaders in the Arab region and international development institutions with theoretically sound, evidence-based advice on the issues of the copyright-based industry. On the basis of the evidence submitted in the Arab national case studies and on evidence from other countries we will be able to draw up some general recommendations. For industry and country-specific recommendations, the reader is referred to the national case studies presented separately.

In the light of the evidence that copyright-based industries in the Arab countries selected for this study have not yet achieved the level of development (in either absolute or relative terms) of both other developing and developed countries, we can conclude that there is great potential, which should be systematically mobilized. This can only be achieved by a well-designed and implemented process of upgrading and innovation in companies, industries and clusters. Public policy can play an important part in this process; indeed it should play four fundamental parts in the process of development of the economy in general and of copyright-based industries in particular.

The first such part is that of improving the quality and availability of the generalized inputs that companies draw upon, such as educated human resources, physical and technological infrastructure and capital.

Second, government should encourage upgrading and innovation with the aid of rules, regulations and incentives. Through regulations, tax policies, the enforcement of IPR and antitrust laws and many other measures, governments influence the climate in which companies compete. That influence should be used to encourage investment and other determinants of economic performance.

Third, government should leverage its investment in skills, research capabilities and infrastructure to facilitate the process by which all local clusters form and develop. Such investment feeds whole groups of firms and industries. Thinking in terms of clusters rather than industries also encourages firms to work closely with suppliers and customers.

Fourth, and most subtly, government leaders should challenge local companies and people in their regions to raise their sights and strive for greater competitiveness. The ability of government to signal the future fosters economic upgrading.

Looking at these four government roles more closely, we can see that they are consistent with a modern view of the role of the State in the economy. They advocate neither a laissez-faire nor a strongly interventionist industrial policy. They operate in tandem with the Porter Diamond presented earlier (see Porter 1990). With reference to this model let us see what kinds of action policy-makers in Arab countries should take in order to influence positively the different components (the dynamics) of the diamond as applied to their copyright-based industries.

1 Policies affecting production factor conditions:
   - Invest in human resources by building a strong basic education system for all citizens, thus eradicating illiteracy, by setting high educational standards, by supporting institutions that develop specialized skills and, last but not least, by creating incentives for company investment in training.
   - Support science and technology by creating incentives for private R&D, backing research and technological infrastructure for cross-cutting technologies and industries and promoting wide dissemination of basic scientific knowledge.
   - Invest in physical infrastructure; the special needs of copyright-based industries should also be taken into consideration.

2 Policies affecting demand conditions:
   - Stimulate early demand.
   - Act as a sophisticated buyer in purchasing.
   - Use regulation to foster upgrading and innovation.

3 Policies affecting related and supporting industries:
   - Facilitate cluster development.
   - Base regional policy on clusters.

4 Policies affecting strategy, structure and rivalry:
   - Introduce a capital allocation system that encourages investment.
   - Promote local competition by deregulating the structure of industry and strictly enforcing antitrust policy and IPRs.
   - Expand interregional and international trade and investment by opening markets, promoting exports and attracting appropriate foreign investment.

Appendix: structure of the questionnaire

Section I. General questions on the firm

- Corporate name.
- Field (s) of corporate activity (music, software, book publishing, audio-visual, etc.).
- Position in the value-chain of the industry (supply of inputs – author of book, software etc. – production, distribution, etc.).
- Position in the firm of person interviewed.

- Date of foundation.
- Number of employees in 2000/2001.
- Capital in 2000/2001.
- Volume of physical output 2000/2001.
- Volume of sales 2000/2001 (in national currency).
- Past evolution (growth rate) of sales over the past five years.

Section II. Questions on the performance of firms

- Growth of sales in the last two years.
- Growth of market share in the last two years.
- Growth of number of employees in the last two years.
- Growth of profits (after taxes) in the last two years.
- Growth of cash flow in the last two years.
- Growth of other indicators (specify) in the last two years.
- Overall performance in the last two years.

Section III. Questions on supply conditions

- Number, skills, training, etc. of employees in the firm.
- Availability, structure and sources of financing.
- Price/quality ratio of other inputs (electricity, postal services, telephone, domestic transport, port services, airport services, shipment).

Section IV. Questions on demand conditions

- Size and determinants of domestic demand.
- Consumers targeted.
- Character of domestic demand (demanding, anticipating foreign demand, etc.).
- Foreign demand (exports).

Section V. Questions on related and supporting industries

- Number of and cooperation with local suppliers.
- Availability of specialized inputs.
- Horizontal cooperation with other firms.
- Contribution of supporting industries (insurance, legal services, banking, marketing, etc.).
- Contribution of public institutions (universities, R&D organizations, etc.)

Section VI. Questions on market structure and corporate strategy

- Market structure (number of firms, etc.).
- Intensity of domestic competition.

- Market access and other market entry barriers.
- Entry barriers for foreign competitors (foreign competition).
- Existence of an explicit business strategy (number of people involved, goals, strengths and weaknesses of the firm, etc.).
- Image of the firm (held by customers, competitors, etc.).
- Existence of an explicit IPR strategy.

Section VII. Questions on government policies

- Government policies in human resource development (education, health, training, etc.).
- Government policies in science and technology.
- Government policies in physical infrastructure (transport, shipment, utilities, etc.).
- Government as a buyer of cultural goods (demand stimulation).
- Government policies in industry-specific investment, building clusters, protecting IPRs, protecting competition, setting price controls, attracting foreign investments, etc.

Notes

1 Professor of Economics, University of Applied Sciences, Northwestern Switzerland.

2 In January 2001 the World Intellectual Property Organization (WIPO) launched such a research project. Under the overall supervision of WIPO the author of this paper served as the international project coordinator. He coordinated the whole project, organized interaction among the participants, monitored the progress of the country studies and supervised the production and delivery of the various national reports. The author is grateful for WIPO for its authorization to reproduce my contribution to the final WIPO report. Thanks are also offered to this institution for very useful comments.

3 See Bertrand and Mullainathan (2001) for a general discussion about problems related to subjective survey data.

4 A word of warning: when reading and interpreting the figures given in this section, one should keep in mind all the methodological and statistical difficulties mentioned above.

5 In Jordan the research team reported on the audiovisual sector in general, as this country does not have a film industry.

6 In Egypt, according to Ahmed Ghoneim, team leader of the Egyptian national study, “software development does not suffer from IPR problems.” However, software in general, which is normally imported from abroad, is still facing the problem of piracy (mainly due to its high price), although this problem has been lately “narrowed and scaled down” (e-mail dated July 14, 2003).

Bibliography

WIPO national case studies

al Khouri, R. (2004), *Performance of Copyright Industries in Jordan*; paper prepared for the WIPO Project on "Performance of Copyright Industries in Selected Arab Countries." Geneva: WIPO.

Ghoneim, A.F. (2004), *Performance of Copyright Industries in Egypt*; paper prepared for the WIPO Project on "Performance of Copyright Industries in Selected Arab Countries." Geneva: WIPO.

Lahouel, M.L (2004), *Performance of Copyright Industries in Tunisia*; paper prepared for the WIPO Project on "Performance of Copyright Industries in Selected Arab Countries." Geneva: WIPO.

Melki, R. (2004), *Performance of Copyright Industries in Lebanon*; paper prepared for the WIPO Project on "Performance of Copyright Industries in Selected Arab Countries. Geneva: WIPO.

Sekkat, K. and Achy, L. (2004), *Performance of Copyright Industries in Morocco*; paper prepared for the WIPO Project on "Performance of Copyright Industries in Selected Arab Countries." Geneva: WIPO.

Other references

Alikhan, S. (2001), "The Copyright Industries and Their Contribution to Economic Growth," paper presented at the *WIPO/ISESCO Conference on Intellectual Property* organized by WIPO and ISESCO, Baku, May 21–23.

Bain, T. (1956), *Barriers to New Competition.* Cambridge MA: Harvard University Press.

Bertrand, M. and Mullainathan, S. (2001), "Do People Mean What They Say? Implications for Subjective Survey Data," *American Economic Review: Papers and Proceedings* 91(2): 67–72.

Besanko, D., Dranove, D., Shanley, M. and Schaefer, S. (1996), *Economics of Strategy*, John Wiley & Sons.

Caves, E. R. (2000), *Creative Industries: Contracts Between Art and Commerce.* Cambridge MA: Harvard University Press.

Frey, B. S. (2000), *Arts and Economics: Analysis and Cultural Policy.* Berlin: Springer.

Kaplinsky, R. and Morris, M. (2003), *A Handbook for Value Chain Research.* Ottawa: International Development Research Center (IDRC).

Miller, J. and Stroobergen, A. (1993), *Employment in Copyright Based Industries.* Council of New Zealand Inc/BERL, Willengton, March.

Porter, M. E. (1990), *The Competitive Advantage of Nations.* New York: Free Press.

Silberston, A. (1998), "The Economic Importance of Copyright," in *Creativity & Intellectual Property Rights: Evolving Scenarios and Perspectives.* Proceedings of an International Conference, Vienna, Austria, July 12–14.

Siwek, S. E. (2002), *Copyright Industries in the U.S. Economy: The 2002 Report*, prepared for the International Intellectual Property Alliance, Economists incorporated.

Siwek, S. E. and Mosteller, G. (1999), *Copyright Industries in the U.S. Economy: The 1998 Report*, prepared for the International Intellectual Property Alliance.

Towse, R. (2001), *Creativity, Incentive and Reward: An Economic Analysis of Copyright and Culture in the Information Age.* Cheltenham: Elgar.

World Intellectual Property Organization (WIPO) and State University of Campinas

(2002), *Study on The Economic Importance of Industries and Activities Protected by Copyright and Related Rights in the MERCOSUR Countries and Chile: Highlights.* Geneva: WIPO.

World Intellectual Property Organization (WIPO) (2003), *Guide on Surveying the Economic Contribution of the Copyright-Based Industries.* Geneva: WIPO

9 The IPRs and the music industry in the Caribbean

Vanus James

Introduction

This chapter identifies the expanding economic opportunities in the audio-visual sector/music industry for countries in the Caribbean region; with the general aim of informing developing countries on new trends and their relevance to policy making and future international negotiations on related issues.

The area covered in this chapter includes the Bahamas, Cuba and the mainland countries of South America, such as Venezuela, Guyana and Suriname. The arguments also apply to the main centers of unofficial Caribbean integration beyond, for example, Brooklyn, Miami, London and Toronto. A disproportionately large part of the data relates to the English-speaking countries of Trinidad and Tobago and Jamaica, only because limitations of time and space have not allowed exploration of materials from other territories.

The next section opens by introducing the Caribbean audio-visual sector in general, and the chapter then focuses in particular on the music industry and its structure and dynamics. It is then shown how creative supply and demand, associated net economic rents and transformation of the audio-visual sector are generated by pricing decisions and the patterns of accumulation of productive capital and capacity of various kinds, as well as of knowledge and technology, already mentioned. It is this transformation and rent creation process that makes the emerging copyright regimes especially relevant. This relevance is clarified in the next section. The argument here, and of the chapter as a whole, is that, despite their current limitations, the copyright regimes being established in the Caribbean are increasingly ensuring that creators can reap fair amounts of the rewards from the products they help to create, even in the context of continuous technological change. Thus, copyrights help to ensure that the process of dynamic transformation of the audio-visual sector is regenerated repeatedly on a continuously expanding and sustainable scale. In turn, this sector contributes to the long-term development of the Caribbean economy. The limitations of the copyright regimes relate to their lack of supporting enforcement arrangements, including arrangements for public education, and their likely irrelevance without a strong program of public education. The final section summarizes the findings of the chapter and identifies the associated policy implications. Policy recommendations relate to the strengthening of the local copyright regime, networking and the establishment of related arrangements that would support the underlying economic and social dynamics of creative activity.

The audio-visual sector of the Caribbean

The audio-visual sector is an important component of the services sector in the Caribbean. It comprises film, video, radio, television and emerging digital media. In Trinidad and Tobago, there are 15 operating radio stations, with none having foreign interests. Government has significant share holdings in four of these stations. In Jamaica, there are ten radio stations, of which only one has any public ownership. There are three local television stations in Trinidad and Tobago, two of which are owned by government. The other is mainly locally owned, with no more than 25 percent of shares held by foreign interests, and with complete local decision-making. There are also five cable operators, none of which are publicly owned. Jamaica also has three television stations, in one of which government has significant shares. Policy in Jamaica requires majority holdings by Jamaican or CARICOM interests.

The music industry lies at the core of this sector, and has as its main products live performances and sound recordings (Guidberg, 1994: 5). In the Caribbean, this core has a dynamic and indigenous component with a number of related dance and festival activities. New products in the industry are identified as property through copyright. Copyright defines and protects the performing and reproduction rights of the musicians and performers to their property.[1] They also protect the users of the outputs of musicians and performers, such as broadcasters and record labels. In each case, they assure the relevant owner of intention to protect sale of the property and access to the incomes and related rights embodied in the created property. The ownership provided by copyright is "a bundle of decision-making rights: right of control over the use of the owned object, right to determine allocation of the income attributed to the object, and right to dispose of the owned object" (Neuberger, 1994: 25; Sterling, 1999: 23, 27). Copyright, however claimed or enforced, is the social foundations of the industry.

Consumption

In 1975, the main items included in audio-visual consumption in Jamaica were television, radio, records, cinema and horseracing (Statistical Institute of Jamaica, 1975). In 1989, the items classified as audio-visual are television, tape recorders, radios, stereo-hi-fi, records, cinemas and plays. It is important to note that plays did not feature in the important commodities of 1975, but did so in 1989. This indicates that there was a change in the importance of this mostly local supply to audio-visual activity in the Jamaican economy over the 14-year time span.

For 1998, cinemas and plays remained, while tape recorders and radios were replaced by radio-cassette players and stereo-hi-fi by component sets, both signaling some degree of technological change in the communications industry. The impact of the developing IT was felt mainly in the introduction of entirely new items such as computers, cable television and videocassette recorders in the set of important consumption items.

The ratio of the weights for the audio-visual sector items to the sum of the weights for all items, gives a picture of the relative importance of these items in domestic consumption. In 1975, the audio-visual sector of Jamaica accounted for about 2.06 percent of consumption. By 1989, this share had risen to 2.5 percent. The share increased only slightly to 2.6 percent in 1998.

Supply

Sound numerical estimates of the share of domestic audio-visual consumption that is met by domestic supply are not readily available, but this share is known to be significant in a few areas, such as radio and music. Film and television programming in the Caribbean are dominated (some say more than 95 percent) by the American and European supplies of culture, broadcast mainly through satellite and cable, with an important supply through video stores and pirates. Even the talk shows describing traffic in New York on a Monday morning are broadcast live by Caribbean television. The domestic share of local television and video production is tiny, with only the basic offerings of local news and live coverage, some local talk shows, music videos and one fledgling effort at regional programming by the Caribbean Broadcasting Union that is still surviving today. There are also some occasional local television productions, but local "film" that addresses the art of cinematography is almost nonexistent in the Caribbean. Except for occasional accommodations of local topicality, all cinemas sell only foreign fare about foreign issues. A growing component of the local airplay is going to video production done locally and in the ethnic communities of the USA and the UK (Henry and Nurse, 1996: 19).

Radio too continues to maintain a tradition of a mainly foreign offering of song and other programming. However, radio does appear to be doing significantly better than television, film cinemas and the new digital media, with a fairly large pool of local talk shows taking up large portions of the programming day, complemented by deejays offering local fare in music and coverage of live entertainment events.

With respect to music, current reports from COTT indicate that, presently, about 75 percent of the total copyrighted material played on air in Trinidad and Tobago is foreign. This seems to have been an improvement from approximately 79 percent in 1997. In Jamaica, foreign music accounts for only 47 percent of total radio airplay year round. During the Carnival season, the percentage for Trinidad and Tobago falls dramatically to 49 percent. Read with the data for Jamaica, this gives some indication that there is significant untapped potential for use of local music year round in the Caribbean.

The emerging digital media, in particular computers and related software, are all imported and facilitate a continuation of the dominance of foreign music and film, mostly downloaded from the Internet nowadays. Except for local access, the bulk of Internet services are imported. However, the technology also opens up other options for domestic creativity through creation of web sites and interactive manipulation of copy.

Entrepreneurs in radio, television and cinema have been establishing significant "intangible investments" in knowledge, goodwill, contacts, and so on, in the Caribbean audiovisual sector. All the major stations have adopted a conscious strategy of seeking and monitoring market share, and many, especially the private media, have established cooperative links with foreign conglomerates to ensure viability.

In general, the traditional audio-visual sector of the Caribbean is essentially a sector of high import content. Its firms, especially those in television and digital communications, are not inherently creative. Apart from the links to local music and dance, they also do not operate in a strong supporting local network of linked activities and institutions, through which to foster creativity and supply adjustment to ensure flexible market response and gain market access or market share (whether local or foreign).[2] For these reasons, the sector does not currently facilitate a high rate of accumulation of assets on the account of many domestic households it employs.

However, the available data suggest important prospects for progress, almost all of which are bound up in the direct demand, and the linkages and institutions, generated by the dynamic core of the indigenous music industry. This industry uses creative inputs and generates creative outputs through a set of mutually reinforcing activities. Vital aspects of its creativity under domestic control rely on domestic know-how and demand creation, and generate growing domestic technology and thus growing (domestic and international) markets, all as a dynamical system. Moreover, over the years, this subsector has invented relevant and vibrant social institutions,[3] and has relied on strategic collaboration with government for development impetus.[4]

According to the theorems of Best (1968), Best and Levitt (1969) and James and Celestin (1999a, 1999b), such a process constitutes a strategic development dynamic and raises the prospects that development of this core could transform the entire audio-visual sector. It could raise the domestic rate of profit, the rate of accumulation of assets held by participating households and thus the rate of growth of consumption per capita. However, while the subsector is highly organized for strategy, strategic collaboration with other sectors is not adequately orchestrated through effective decentralization of many social institutions, and the business units in the subsector are highly informal. It is likely that substantial progress may require further improvements in internal organization and copyrighting, along with improved access to policy-making powers that can augment the capital and profit realization capacity of the entrepreneurs (Best, 1970–, 1977–; James and Celestin, 1999b). These are the issues addressed in the rest of the chapter.

The live music and related performances (festivals) industry

Born as normal forms of self-assertion and organization, music to foster religious celebration, music for fertility dancing or as the call and response of storytelling, social/political critique and attack, this nexus of activities has developed in reaction to the violence and repression of Caribbean history. To ensure the survival and sustenance of the African and Asian spirit, and to heal the psychological scars of slavery, strict indenture and colonialism, much of which was inflicted by the relentless attacks and bannings inspired by the European Church, song and dance in the Caribbean had to be both routinely creative and subversive of European society and its social norms. Thus, they have tended to function simultaneously as the people's religious and ceremonial media, their coded popular newspaper ("tabloid and scandal sheet rolled into one") and media for language retention and development, which "went with and enhanced the spirit of rebellion" (Rohlehr, 1990: 1, 4, 8–15, 17–25, 57–86; Watson, 1995: 17; Chang and Chen, 1998; Mason, 1998: 9, 12, 20; Gibbons, 1999: 1; Patasar, 1997; Ramlogan, 1996; Ramnarine, 1997; White, 1998: 8).[5]

Given its multicultural and Mediterranean structure, Caribbean society has spawned several genres of music and related dance (festivals). With respect to music, these genres include calypso, primarily of Southern Caribbean origins, which itself has given rise to other forms such as soca, rapso, and jam and wine. There are also versions of traditional music of East Indian origin which, together with calypso, have given rise to chutney-soca. The most popular international forms, reggae and dancehall, are primarily of Jamaican origin. From farther north come the salsa, samba, rumba, meringue and zouk of Puerto Rico, Cuba, the Dominican Republic and Haiti. The Caribbean also lays claim to its own hybrids of parang, gospel, rhythm and blues, pop and the like (Rohlehr, 1990; Persad, 1997; Sankerali, 1997; Chang and Chen, 1998; White, 1998). The cutting edge of the dance activities is the carnival with its emphasis on masquerade (mas). Mas, like film, is a visual form, manufactured and displayed artistically for the entertainment of viewers. It is carnival's replacement for film, complete with new annual productions, lead characters, and so on, and is legitimately placed within the Caribbean audio-visual sector. Moreover, it is an interactive form.

Functioning as the heart and soul of the audio-visual sector, Caribbean music has exploded creatively in various rounds over the years, spawning associated manufacturing activities (COTT, 1998: 2). Today, the creativity continues unabated, driven by changing circumstances and featuring a "rowdiness and violence" and raw sexuality that are still much misunderstood, even feared (Rohlehr, 1990; Mason, 1998; Gibbons, 1999, see introduction by Louis Regis; Baek and Hedegard, 1999).[6] The industry is generating supply for the audio-visual sector, and demand from it, in forms such as Carnivals, "Calypso Shows" and "Reggae Shows," "Soca Fetes," "Beach Limes," "Dancehall," "Sessions and *Bashment* Sessions," and religious "Bashment Concerts."

The music industry in the Caribbean – structure and dynamics

Firms as suppliers

Throughout the region, the music industry simultaneously offers employment and other economic opportunity, especially to the disadvantaged, and serves as an intangible commodity that can be used as input or output to compete for income opportunity in domestic and international markets, and as revolutionary media of communication. The two main participants on the supply side of the music industry are the following: (1) the composers/performers who provide the primary output of song-writing, instrument playing and stage performance. They tend to operate as informal sole proprietors and "household-firms;" and (2) the recording companies, operating as registered corporations, that sign artists and producers to produce recordings or videos of songs or performances (Watson, 1995; Kozul-Wright and Stanbury, 1998:7).

Other major performers in the industry include the carnival bands, steelbands and "sound systems." The "sound systems" evolved in the hi-fi revolution of the 1960s, with a critical stimulus provided by radio, one of the high impact technologies of the day (Watson, 1995; White, 1998: 13). On the Jamaican scene, these have evolved into outdoor discos with "6–8 foot high loud speakers and a unique atmosphere" (Baek and Hedegard, 1999: 9, 10). Their creative application of imported technology is emphasized by White (1998: 13–15).[7]

Intermediate supply linkages

Input linkages with the domestic (indigenous) manufacturing sector are strong, especially because of the highly integrated nature of the music bands/performances and institutions. A significant number of the instruments used by the performers are manufactured locally, including African and Asian drums, shak-shak and the like.

A major component of innovative domestic supply into the music industry is the steelpan, which grew out of the tamboo-bamboo and African drums, and is manufactured out of oil drums. The instrument continues to evolve today. The mounts and racks that facilitate movement of the steelpan are all locally manufactured out of steel and the recycled parts of abandoned motor vehicles. Sound systems also rely heavily on domestic manufacture of the 6–8 foot high boxes and boxes of smaller sizes that are used in the performances. Naturally, the local construction industry provides a significant supply of construction services, establishing plant and installing equipment.

Perhaps more important than all of the above is the purchase by distributors from the recording business and studios which prepare digital audio tapes (DAT), cassettes tapes, press records, CD replicates and videos, and make dub-plates (Baek and Hedegard, 1999; Henry and Nurse, 1996: 18). In Trinidad, there are six studios that can be considered major in terms of viability in the local industry (Henry and Nurse, 1996: 18). In addition, there are seven other more marginal studios, which nevertheless continue to do reasonably well enough to survive, mainly through "the production of jingles for the local and regional advertising market" (ibid.: 19). Caribbean Sound Basin, one of the local majors, has established some of the best facilities in the Caribbean for preparation of DATs, CD masters, cassette duplication and small-scale CD replication, the typical outputs of the local industry. It has attracted significant demand from both the local and international distribution chain (ibid.: 18).

Within the last four months, a small CD manufacturing plant has been established in Jamaica, based on used equipment imported from Germany.[8] Its viability (normal profits) is premised on the ability to find demand for about 100,000 CDs per month in the local, regional or foreign market. Such viability is not guaranteed because the small size of the capacity established, and the lack of technological originality and creativity of the manufacturer and the local manufacturing environment will tend to leave the investor in a constant need to catch up with the majors in the international industry. This problem is compounded by two other factors: (1) the problems of worker management associated with the capitalist format of such manufacturing; and (2) the small size and non-interactive (non-creative) character of the domestic demand, and lack of independent access to the foreign market. The problem is not new; it has plagued the manufacturing of vinyl records since the inception of the Caribbean recording industry (Henry and Nurse, 1996: 20) and, more generally, the import substitution manufacturing of the region.[9]

Other forms of intermediate input linkages to manufacturing appear as demands for original dubplates and records by the sound systems, discos and nightclubs. The flow of dubplates as intermediates is moderate and once again creative, because "they are produced for sound systems and radio play, or as promotional releases to record companies." Further, "being one-off means they are unique and can be highly valuable" (Baek and Hedegard, 1999: 55; White, 1998: 16, 17). The emergence of this creative product is a direct example of how competition influences creativity. White (1998: 16) notes that the spur to this creative use of the dubplates in the dancehall came from the need "for music to outdo rival systems and command loyal audiences from the mass public. 'Kill a sound bwoy and ram the dancehall'."

The primary music suppliers are linked structurally backwards (i.e. on the input side of the industry) to other intermediate service industries. For example, contracting skills to composers/performers and mediation in the relationship of the latter with the recording companies are procured from producers/agents who tend to operate as informal enterprises. The service of signing up the composer/performer and licensing of songs to recording companies is supplied by publishers; marketing of recordings and videos to programmers is supplied by promoters, who usually operate as informal sole proprietors. The skills of contract negotiation are supplied by attorneys, who typically operate as sole proprietors. The service of ensuring adequate accounting for royalties is supplied by accountants. Finally, the service of management is supplied by managers, themselves mostly informal sole proprietors and household firms, who engage and coordinate the services of support personnel and workers. Sometimes the composer/performer also functions as manager, but this phenomenon is disappearing rapidly (Watson, 1995; Kozul-Wright and Stanbury, 1998: 7, 16–27).[10]

Also looking backward to linkages on the side of inputs into music and recordings, radio, television and cinema continue a longstanding and growing tendency to broadcast and thus advertise local music and dance festivals, and thereby increase the flow. This effect is also complemented by the stimulus to crossover generated by the persistent play of local music, and of Latin American, African, Asian and especially European and American music, on the audio-visual media (White, 1998: 10–13). It is widely claimed that payment for these services typically comes in the form of deals made directly with deejays and other operators, "off the books" of the stations, though there is increasing formality in this area.

Intermediate demand linkages

The tourism sector is perhaps the greatest source of music-related demand from outside the audio-visual sector. Baek and Hedegard (1999: 17, 18) report that, with respect to Jamaica, "Sunsplash alone attracts 200,000 people year" a large percentage of whom are tourists, and that "25,000 Japanese tourists alone visit every year because of the festivals." The all-inclusive hotels, the fastest growing segment of the tourism industry with the highest local content of inputs, routinely supply reggae music shows of various vintages as part of the normal fare. The data on stopover visitors provide some clues as to the scale of related demand. Estimates from the Jamaica Tourist Board indicate that total stopover visitors were approximately 1,192,194 persons in 1997, and the number of annual visitors has been growing at approximately 2 percent per year since 1995.

The heavy reliance on the carnivals of the tourism industry of the Southern Caribbean is now the stuff of legend, as in the calypso "Miss Tourist" by the Lord Kitchener. For example, for a 19-day carnival period in 1997 and 1998, the number of visitors to Trinidad and Tobago increased from 24,947 to 32,071. Visitors spent approximately TT$64.5 million in 1997 and TT$88.7 million in 1998, signaling that there might be ongoing productivity increases. The decline in the share of the entertainment industry and the increase in relative spending on accommodation and meals point to the gains that can accrue to the tourism sector from changes in behavior when the music industry is growing.

Second, there is increasing use of music as an intermediate input by local radio, television and cinema. This is evident in the growth of local airplay and of royalties from these sources to the copyright agencies.

The intra-industry linkage of performers and sound systems to the festivals and dance subsector is understood to be high, justifying the claim that music and related performances are the soul of the audio-visual sector. Music performance is the single most important ingredient of the fetes and festivals, even for the carnivals that are normally heavily focused on masquerade and mask making.

The claim holds for the Jamaican reggae festivals to an even greater degree than it does for the carnivals of the region.

Social institutions

Music and related performances evolved, and could only have flourished, through the development of a significant number of institutions providing opportunity for collaboration and coordination to the participants in the industry. These make up substantially for market failure (Kozul-Wright and Stanbury, 1998: 4). Some provide active collective administration organizations and representation in the Caribbean directly and indirectly to songwriters, lyricists and music publishers, with special reference to management and licensing of the performing and reproductive rights in their copyright (Berry, 1999: 21; Watson, 1995: 18–20; COTT, 1999).[11] Others serve as institutions of representation in lobbying government and as leaders spearheading the internationalization of the industry (Watson, 1995: 18–20, 61).[12] The Steelband Association, later to become Pan Trinbago, was founded as early as 1949, and worked assiduously to "shape the steel pan movement" and help bands become "centers of musical excellence rather than just a focus for carnival time misbehavior" (Mason, 1998: 61). One political party, the PNM, used the steelbands and the calypsonians to attract the masses to its politics and, together with many businesses, provided critical systematic organizational, social, employment and other economic supports for carnival bands and other participants in these art-forms to end their violent tendencies (ibid.: 61).

Perhaps even more significant has been the collaboration of government with the aforementioned institutions to foster creative expression in the region. In Trinidad and Tobago, since 1957, various incarnations of the National Carnival Commission have been the means by which government provides funds and administrative support for the organization of competitions that stimulate the creative expression of the musician and composer (Mason, 1998: 31). For example, since 1992, government subventions in support of carnival have averaged more than TT11.2 million. In Jamaica, the Jamaica Cultural Development Commission (JCDC) collaborated with the private sector to provide the same type (but not necessarily the same scale) of service for the national festival song competition and other aspects of the industry (Watson, 1995: 19).

Increasingly today, the industry has access to young entrants who receive relevant musical and other artistic training and share applicable research carried out in the school system. While schools have not yet been brought to the music and performance bands in the way appropriately proposed by Best (1970–, 1977–) and by the Policy Research and Development Institute *et al.* (1998), some music has been brought to the schools. The steelpan is routinely taught as an optional instrument in many secondary schools in Trinidad and Tobago. Also, while formal training still emphasizes so-called "classical" pieces for illustration, there is an increasing tendency to turn to the carnival, steelpan, soca, chutney and reggae for these purposes.[13] Advanced training is now provided by centers such as the Edna Manley School of the Performing Arts in Jamaica and, more recently, the University of the West Indies, which has established a "Unit of Reggae Studies" at Mona, Jamaica, and a "Creative Arts Center" at St. Augustine, Trinidad.

Finally, in recent years, there have been increasing efforts through NGOs, government and local watchdog groups to provide for copyright protection of the creative outputs of the sector. The principal initiatives here are updating of the local copyright law set up in the light of WIPO's initiatives.

Use of primary factors: imports

A high proportion of the inputs used by the industry, including the physical capital, is imported, but exact estimates are not available. Except for the steelpan and related instruments, performers rely on imported instruments, such as pianos and guitars. In Trinidad, the vast majority of CD manufacturing services are also imported (Henry and Nurse, 1996: 20). The situation is much the same in Jamaica and, despite the entry of a CD duplicating plant, is likely to remain so. The reason is that the plant exists in a static manufacturing environment without the necessary network of interdependent manufacturing activities, research functions, social institutions, financing and other linkages that foster creativity in manufacturing and marketing.

As performers, sound systems import hi-fi equipment, such as CD players, DVDs, amplifiers and tuners. Their main local input is the box used to house the loud speakers, but it is important to be cognizant of the creativity of the technology of application of the imported inputs (White, 1998: 13, 14).[14]

Use of primary factors: labor

Firms in the music industry make significant use of paid labor. This is especially true of those enterprises that are involved in downstream manufacturing of music CDs and other sound recordings and videos, though the carnival bands, calypso tents and other firms use significant wage labor. The tendency seems to be that the more the capital outlay required, the greater the use of wage labor. Specific data are not readily available on the number of paid workers versus the number of own-account workers employed in the industry. However, it seems to be organized mainly around self-motivated own-account labor and entrepreneurial households – the household-firms using own-account labor supplied by kin (including friends) and associates – rather than a set of wage laborers and capitalists bound together primarily by legal strictures. This is especially true of many acts involved in performances, including the sound systems, steelbands, carnival costume manufacturers and the carnival band. Since the latter aspects of the industry emerged in communities which experience high rates of structural unemployment, there is a large number of persons willing to lend assistance at low rates of pay, or to function as entrepreneurs even when prospects of significant reward are slim in the first instance. More important perhaps, Caribbean history has bred a predominating disposition on the part of households to be involved in industry, wherever remotely possible, as self-reliant entrepreneurs (Best, 1968, 1975; James, 1997).

The labor constraint in the industry features a positive work ethic and high work effort, a condition that is highly untypical of Caribbean labor (Best, 1968; James and Celestin, 1999a). One reason for this seems to be the demonstration effect of the high proportion of own-account workers who spread the ethos of positive self-motivation and commitment to efficient and creative work (Mason, 1998).

Management by shared objectives and management for creativity

Even though managerial efficiency by participants might not be optimal in the Caribbean, it also seems clear that there is a supporting managerial style underlying the successes achieved. Mason (1998: 32, 80–82) observes that carnival bands and calypso tents in Trinidad brings together artists and dancers in an experimental theater-like and arty atmosphere, in which the ethic of fast and efficient work and an undeniable spirit of camaraderie always prevails. His observations suggest a management style based on shared broad objectives, with considerable room for the creative expression of the individual. Similarly, Ramoutar's (1996) interview with two of the main manufacturers for the mas camp, Viera and Velasquez, reveals their preoccupation with the need to be creative, and the need for "scope to be more creative."

A similar approach is evident throughout the industry all over the region. This is probably due to the heavy reliance on own-account contractors. However, there is no evidence of rigidity in the relationship between the managers and those who function as paid employees. Rigidity, when it appears, seems to be primarily for the purpose of ensuring discipline with respect to specific events, such as the practice sessions. Yet, at all times, considerable room is left for individual experimentation to achieve the excellence that is expected. There is significant hierarchical structure in any band, but with considerable flexibility with respect to who holds any leading position. The discriminating factor seems to be skill to perform the required function (Mason, 1998: 73).

In general, the survival and development of the Caribbean music industry seems to be based on a flexible process of management by shared objectives, the most important of which is creativity. This is made possible by a perception of shared ownership by individuals and communities, and a common view of their destiny (James, 1997; Mason, 1998: 57–77). It is also made possible by the characteristic of each organization, and ultimately the industry, as primarily a set of interdependent, but self-reliant entrepreneurs.

Access to finance and the dynamics of supply and demand

There seems to be an increasing tendency for entrepreneurs in the music industry to be able to rely on formal finance and amortization to do business.

However, the pace of change is slow. Watson observes, for example, that some individuals in the industry have managed to create meaningful relationships with the financial services community. However, the majority of operators still achieve little success in gaining access to bank-supplied finance and still face a severe credit constraint (Watson, 1995: 24, 25, 28). Among the promoters and record companies, "62 percent financed their business by either personal investment or by funds from family and friends," which, in the light of popular culture, points to a significant role for Rotating Savings and Credit Associations (ROSCAs). Similar observations have been made by Kozul-Wright and Stanbury (1998: 16, 18).

The observations of Baek and Hedegard (1999: 12) suggest a high degree of dependence on recurrent "revenues" to fund operations and seem to reinforce the need to rely on work efficiency and creativity of work to survive and expand. For example, because of "the simple lack of revenue at many sound systems, funds are not available to pay for top acts and live shows," so these have evolved as outdoor operations that make their facilities available to musicians and other performers who are looking for an opportunity to try out new acts.[15]

Dominance and concentration

Although there is no accurate count, a large number of artists participate in the Caribbean music industry. Mason (1998: 33) refers to "scores of calypsonians" in Trinidad, "whose songs never make it onto the radio or onto vinyl or CD." There are a few "big artistes" who are internationally popular, earn the most money and receive the widest coverage on the airwaves.[16] Nevertheless, the music composition and performance activities are clearly not dominated in any very meaningful sense by any set of musicians or entrepreneurs. The same is true of steelband activities in Trinidad and Tobago or night club performances, or even the associated studios and producers. In Jamaica, despite the relatively high share of market controlled by some studios, Kozul-Wright and Stanbury (1998: 17) observe that there are "at least 50 studios" of which as many as 20 "may be considered major." Their finding is corroborated by Baek and Hedegard (1999: 33). Similarly, Baek and Hedegard (1999: 10) quote a figure of 500 sound systems but note that "[n]o one knows the exact figure, as sound systems come and go."

However, significant concentration and centralization are beginning to appear, and may have long existed, in other areas of the music industry, and certainly in the linked audio-visual sector. Stone Love dwarfs the other sound systems of Jamaica, in terms of both equipment and the number of personnel (Baek and Hedegard, 1999: 12). Two reggae festivals, Reggae Sunsplash and Sumfest, dominate the Jamaican scene, even when account is taken of the emerging Jamaica carnival (ibid.: 17). The Jamaica carnival, for its part, is also organized and dominated by the owners of one of the large local studios. In the distribution and marketing aspect of the business, a few firms are clearly dominant, and are likely to become more so over time as they increasingly penetrate the overseas market (Baek and Hedegard, 1999: 43; Kozul-Wright and Stanbury, 1998: 17). In Trinidad and Tobago, only one significant studio exists. Mason (1998: 44) describes the recording industry in Trinidad as "small and ad hoc." Of the Jamaican scene, Watson (1995: 23) notes that "small producers face … stiff competition from major distributors … who have the finances and contracts at their disposal to exploit opportunities and increase revenues."

Pricing

To capture gains from the highly creative music process, the leading operators seem to practice strategic pricing. For example, it is well known that costumes and band places are supplied to order and the size of the band varies according to the demand taken up. Price discrimination does feature in the industry, but price variation within a market period is not a significant aspect of demand management and efforts to win rents. Instead, emphasis is on worker effort, quality and innovation in process and product, and creative marketing (James, 1997). Historically, calypso has been marketed partly through its association with rum (alcohol), an attraction that was hinted at in Lord Invador's calypso "Rum and Coca Cola" (Mason, 1998: 94). Reggae similarly has flourished on the marketing wings of marijuana, a link that is made clear in Tosh's "Legalize It" (Chang and Chen, 1998). In both cases, the links to popular, typically but not always radical, roots and culture are vital to successful marketing.

There are suggestions of an absence of emphasis on economies of scale as a pricing tool. Mason notes that "Although in theory the larger bands should be able to offer lower prices to their members through economies of scale, it is invariably the smaller outfits that offer the cheapest mas." Greater reliance is placed on price differentiation and marketing strategy. To deal with inadequate demand from the fixed-price and differentiation strategy in a location, firms move supply between markets (Mason, 1998: 82, 83; James, 1997). Among sound system competitors in Jamaica there is similar evidence that the emphasis is the same. Systems strive for access to one-off dubplates that are unique. And, "if a sound system has the best dubplates, it can play the wickedest tunes on the hottest riddims around," so, "whoever has the best dubplates is King" (Baek and Hedegard, 1999: 55). Similarly, it is the uniqueness of the offerings that fuels the growth of the number of studios in Jamaica (ibid.: 33).

The general principle is that, faced with variations in demand during a market period, the tendency of suppliers in the core of the audio-visual sector is primarily to adjust the level and quality of supply, not the level of price. Of course, over time, both price and supply vary with the dynamic adjustment of aggregate demand.

Copyrights, consumption and exports

Marketing, self-reliant market penetration capacity, and supporting arrangements for distribution and retailing represent important constraints on the development of Caribbean music (Henry and Nurse, 1996: 23).[17] There is significant agreement that five or six "major" international corporations use control of access, in combination with control of technology, to ensure market dominance today (Henry and Nurse, 1996: 7, 10; UNCTAD, 1999: 44). The creation of increased access through steady population movement into, and multiculturalization of, the mass markets of the USA and Europe, together with local area networking and strategic behavior in the music industry in the Caribbean, is helping to slacken this constraint.

However, Caribbean-based promoters and distributors, and their ethnic counterparts in the mass markets, generally remain tiny and weak competitors in comparison with the might of the international majors. Promoters and distributors in the Caribbean, and even in the corresponding Caribbean communities abroad, utilize relatively little of the available audio-visual and information technology, especially the mass media, trade fairs (such as MIDEM), to ensure direct and content-specific promotion of artists and products (Henry and Nurse, 1996: 23, 24). This is so, even given the extensive reliance on promotion of fetes and popular airplay by radio and television to achieve publicity (ibid.: 17). One reason seems to be the high cost of using existing audio-visual supply.

Role of the copyright regimes

Considerable gain in market performance in the Caribbean has also been made through the development of copyright regimes that define and enforce the rights of composers, lyricists and music publishers to be rewarded for the public use of their works, whether through live performances or recordings (COTT, 1999: 2). Up-to-date copyright laws have been passed in Jamaica (The Copyright Act of Jamaica, 1993 and the Copyright Amendment Act, September, 1999) and Trinidad and Tobago (the Copyright Act of Trinidad and Tobago, 1997). These laws have brought the countries' statutes into line with current international conventions.

In Trinidad and Tobago, a reasonably sophisticated supporting local collection facility has also been established through COTT, its affiliations with the Performing Right Society Ltd of the United Kingdom, and the affiliations of the latter with other rights societies throughout the world. The facility is reinforced through affiliations with the international Confederation of Authors Societies (CISAC) and the International Bureau of Societies Administering the Rights of Mechanical Recording and Reproduction (BIEM). It includes mandatory licensing and regular surveying of the market to identify and monitor users. In Jamaica, a Copyright Tribunal has been established to provide jurisdiction over licensing and royalty matters (Watson, 1995: 19), and moves are underway to establish the Jamaican Association of Composers, Authors and Publishers (UNCTAD, 1999: 54). There is still dependence on the Performing Rights Society of the United Kingdom, which historically has been preoccupied with ensuring the royalties of British operators (Watson, 1995: 19; UNCTAD, 1999: 54).

All Caribbean regimes are deficient on enforcement arrangements, with inadequate training of judges and other officers of the court, and with limited deterrence measures in the hands of rank and file police officers. Part of the difficulty is the expense of establishing these arrangements, training programs and supporting public education programs in any one country. Further, public and private education have not been focused on raising awareness of the value of IP and respect for IP rights among lawyers, accountants and the public at large (Henry and Nurse, 1996: 18–24). The regimes have a one-size-fits-all character, with no special arrangements to deal with local problems, such as those relating to the specific forms of uncertainty of access to income, frequently associated with considerable violence, in the relation between the lyricist/artist, the promoters, the producer and other entrepreneurs. Ultimately, the regimes will open the local audio-visual sector to foreign direct investment (FDI), especially by the international corporations, without necessarily boosting domestic networking or providing regional governments with the regime of measures needed to maintain control of domestic economic and fiscal policy. Local participants are unlikely to be able to compete "openly" with such investors. Thus, the associated FDI is likely to raise the costs of domestic economic management without any guarantee of adequate compensating access to new markets or technologies.

Despite these deficiencies, the collection facilities are securing increases in royalties and other payments due to local, regional and international participants, and therefore the gains to the region in terms of employment in user industries (manufacturing, broadcasting, electronic dissemination) and collecting societies. The boost that the copyright regimes give to the growing capabilities of the industry, combined with population movement, have resulted in significant and fairly dynamic sales of musical compositions and performances, sound systems, festivals and recordings. Indications are that in Jamaica, maximum sales of a disc are 30,000, but the typical range is between 5,000 and 20,000 (Watson, 1995: 22; Kozul-Wright and Stanbury, 1998: 27). The industry "can release up to 200 new singles weekly in Jamaica alone" (Baek and Hedegard, 1999: 3; also, Watson, 1995: 21). In 1994 Jamaicans wrote or performed more than 4.5 percent of the singles and 7 percent of the albums sold in the UK, which had a market of more than US$1,976 million in 1993 (Watson, 1995). Some estimates place the value of Jamaican music worldwide at US$1 billion (Kozul-Wright and Stanbury, 1998: 18). Similar data may reveal an equally spectacular export dynamic for the carnivals. It is also documented that the industry's fortunes are highly cyclical (Watson, 1995: 15–21; Kozul-Wright and Stanbury, 1998: 24).

Outcomes

Income and distribution

It has been reported that net of costs, "reggae acts are not making any money from the business," and that "concert and stage performances on the local scene rarely make profits" (Watson, 1995: 15, 26). Even so, artists are accused of charging "exorbitant … appearance fees" for events such as the reggae festival of Jamaica (Watson, 1995: 26). There is also the view that "only a very small portion" of the global income generated by Jamaican music "is earned by Jamaicans or finds its way into the domestic economy" and "[t]he greater share of the value added chain in the industry remains under control of the non-Jamaican industrial players." The total earnings of Jamaica from its music industry has been estimated crudely at US$450 million by Kozul-Wright and Stanbury (1998: 24). One explanation of the low rate of return is that much of the music comes from small producers, and "wholesale prices at which small producers have to sell their records to major distributors are too small" and can hardly cover "pressing and label costs, not to mention royalties" (Watson, 1995: 23). Another is that "the local acts are not selling" internationally as much as they might in the light of their creativity, primarily because of inadequate internal business organization (ibid.: 15).

Mason (1998: 26, 42) observes that in Trinidad

> [t]he classic calypsonian would lead a seat-of-the-pants existence for most of the year, perhaps earning big sums of money during the two months of hectic activity around carnival, then resorting to living off his wits for the remaining ten…, pushed back into the deadening poverty from which he probably came. Only a handful of performers were ever able to make a full-time living out of calypso. [Currently] [t]he number … making a full-time wage out of calypso is increasing, standing now at about a dozen or so out of a total of up to 200 nationwide.

Indications are that, although income growth is cyclical, productivity and income trends point upwards. Driven by the changing music, there are now more successful competitions in Trinidad that can attract the young, win priority attention from commercial radio stations and pay higher prizes than in the past (Mason, 1998: 51, 52). Opportunities abroad are better, and more full-time musicians, typically operating in self-contained "soca bands" or "posses" are able to survive on Caribbean music today than at any time in history (ibid.: 42, 51). During the 1990s, for example, the total collection by COTT grew at an average rate of 23.9 percent and local distribution 42.5 percent. Consistent with all this, COTT had reported that, even though foreign music continues to dominate the local scene and is valued higher than local music, 1999 was its best year ever. It "collected $5 million from people and radio stations who bought licenses to play music assigned to the organization, even though only 20 percent of this was for local members (Joseph, 1999: 23).

A DJ sound system and accompanying live performance on a big truck for a mas band in Trinidad can earn "anything from TT$10,000 to TT$60,000 for the two days." (Mason, 1998: 82). When this is distributed among the various claimants, net earnings per person are likely to be moderate at best. In the case of the steelpan, there is the "exceptionally gifted pannist," "a few lucky enough to be in the handful of professional touring bands that can travel the world with a repertoire of songs" and make significant income. However, earnings per person, per hour, have traditionally been small, even for the most successful local bands (ibid.: 68, 70).[18] Relative to revenue and even support from sponsors not exceeding $60,000, the typical band operates at a loss as "it can cost up to TT$140,000 to prepare the average steelband for the season." So, in general, "the loyal pannist receives a pat on the back, a few handshakes and the chance to come back next year." As for the carnival bands, "no one knows the true picture, for it is undoubtedly obscured by creative accounting. As a rule,... the big bands make big money and the smaller bands just get by" (ibid.: 82). What seems clear is that substantial leakage of income away from musicians and performers occurs because of inadequate copyright enforcement and downright piracy (ibid.: 44, 45).

With respect to the indirect income generated by music and related arts in the domestic economy, there is significant evidence of something of a bonanza. It has been suggested that "carnival generates an estimated TT$400 million in income through increased commercial activity such as food, drink and advertising." (Mason, 1998: 122). Some estimates are that more than US$200 million is spent by tourists visiting each carnival.[19] However, other estimates suggest that the figures might be higher. These indicate that "the typical visitor is between 35–44, female, single, well-educated and spends an average of TT$4,076 for seven to 14 days," giving a rough average in the region of $400 per day by the typical visitor.[20]

It is useful to assess the nature of the relationship between various forms of income in order to gauge how copyright regimes might enhance competitive capacity and employment. In particular, for the music industry, it is useful to assess the shape of the distribution between returns that households use to finance consumption and those that they use to finance investment in human capital, management, technological change, worker speed up and the development of, and participation in, social institutions. All the above indications relating to pricing and creativity suggest a positive relationship between all rates of return and associated factors. In particular, there would be a positive relationship between the level of human capital and labor and the rate of returns to such factors. Similarly, there would be a positive relationship between the level of social knowledge/technology, investment in physical and social capital and worker quality, and the rates of returns to these factors. Even though specific data on the relations are sparse, the hint is that energetic enforcement of the copyright laws will be highly rewarding for Caribbean society.

Some insight can be gained by considering how income is shared between participants. In this regard, it has been reported that in Jamaica "[c]urrently (and historically) most of the local musicians and recording artists do not receive adequate compensation for their creative efforts, either through royalties or shares of income from the sale of recorded music" (Kozul-Wright and Stanbury, 1998: 19, 20). Similar claims have been made by Watson (1995: 22). Some clues are also available about the relation between the returns to artists and those to producers/promoters and agents. On this, Watson (1995: 27) reports that "there is constant dispute as to the ownership of musical products," and therefore, presumably, the reward from them. With respect to the distribution of income among participants in Trinidad, there seems to be the expected significant inequality engineered by various entrepreneurs. Mason (1998: 32) observes that in the calypso tents "[e]ach calypsonian is paid a different rate according to status and bargaining power, which can lead to rows and walkouts. Tent managers are occasionally accused of exploitation and non-payment, and conflict between entrepreneurs and artists is commonplace." However, the data presented above suggest that, through the development of stronger copyright regimes in the region, all these relationships are being reshaped to favor the creators. If that is so, the factor–reward relationships would all tend to be positive and development oriented.

In principle, however, adequate weight cannot be given to these claims, especially as that relates to the going rate of return in the industry, until carefully designed empirical investigations are done. Alternative data are also not available on the level of consumption per capita of participating households. Further, there are no data on the relationship between their per capita consumption and their spending per capita on growth of plant capacity, innovation, participation in social institutions, human capital and the speed of work, or management. Moreover, identification of the transformational significance of the structure of earnings in the industry would require comparison with other industries that have relied on no Caribbean creativity at all.[21] Similarly, analysis of wages, rates of return and income distribution requires quite specific data, such as are not available anywhere in the region today. There is little reasonable empirical ground on which to assess claims about the returns to the labor and efforts of musicians, sound systems, carnival bands and the like, and the relationship of such rents (growth in value) to the rate of asset accumulation.

Growing opportunity and competitive strategy

The music industry is dynamic and strategic, and clearly is transforming the audio-visual sector. New music and related performances and festivals are emerging rapidly and providing grist for radio and deejays, making more profitable existing and new occasions that television might cover, and providing more materials that can inform film and television productions generally. Aging and obsolescence are correspondingly rapid. In this scenario, if copyright is not well defined, almost instantaneously available, and enforceable, then it becomes quickly irrelevant to the creator of the product. For this reason, the rent-creation methods of the industry, and their realization through copyright regimes, are looking increasingly attractive.

Audio-visual operators, seeing new opportunities in the new dynamic sector, are now pushing autonomous changes of their own. Local deejays and their reporters are being given more leeway to promote and cover occasions, and generate revenues from covering corporate events with the techniques and atmospheres popularized. Local television is increasingly gearing up to improve the quality of production and coverage of events. The ongoing attempt to use television and videocassettes to market the Caribbean music product is picking up speed. In addition to learning by doing, the new activities and processes to be covered by radio and television mean that new skills will have to be learned.

Just as changes in the music and performance industry are dictating changes in television and radio, so are the responses of the wider audio-visual sector dictating further changes in the music and performances industry. There is an increasing effective demand for improvement in financing, contracting and negotiations, mediation with record companies, signing up and licensing arrangements, marketing of recordings and videos, adequacy of collections and accounting, and management and internal organization. These skills ultimately have to be, and will be, learned partly with the help of private sector training programs, and partly with the help of public sector training initiatives. The principle of linkage effect is pervasive here, but finance and marketing deserve special mention.

Introduction of more sophisticated ways of doing things in the audio-visual sector, especially its dynamic core, has to be financed. The growing profitability of music and performance, like that of television and radio, brings with it increasing credit-worthiness. Therefore, financing will have to be forthcoming, and an increasing share of total costs in the craft sector will have to become amortized costs. This will augment the flexibility and adaptability of these enterprises, shifting them more and more into the modern capitalist mode of operation in which, increasingly, their fundamental constraint is demand. Financing is a highly skilled activity, accompanied as it is by the need to manage default risks and guarantee optimum returns on loan portfolios. Thus, specialists to deal with the entire audio-visual sector have to be trained.

Marketing and salesmanship also must change. With innovation and speed-up, the firm increases the amount of rent that it can realize from any investment, and thus raises the potential for gaining and holding competitive advantage. But to convert this potential into reality, it must attempt to penetrate all markets, local and foreign, with the most appropriate program of selling and sales supports. Advertisements have to be properly designed and pitched to the right audience. Across the system, this increases the need for marketing, advertising specialists, sales persons, public relations managers, and the like. As a result, training needs are growing, but training cannot be done without teachers and a range of supporting infrastructure and services, all of which will have to be provided in a timely and relevant manner (Kozul-Wright and Stanbury, 1998: 2). Thus, there are growing pressures for a general burst of activity in and around the audio-visual sector. Positive response to these pressures will merely boost the domestic circular flow of income and output, partly because success on these fronts will result in an educated consumer who will continue to pitch in by changing the level and type of demand for the services of the distributive sector and the products of the music and performance generally on the one hand, and radio and television, on the other.

In summary then, music is transforming the audio-visual sector through several avenues. They include: the introduction of new processes of production to do old things; the introduction of new or improved commodities; the opening up of new markets and creation of new tastes in the domestic and foreign market; the securing of new sources of supply; and the introduction of new methods of business organization. And, related to these, as the experience with carnival has shown, the innovations that cumulate serve as a means of systematically getting more work done within a given period of time. This effect on the speed of work is raising output rates and levels, raising productivity, cutting unit costs and facilitating accumulation over time. If these processes are sustained, the falling unit costs will help to stabilize prices, even as aggregate demand and well-rewarded employment is growing.

As this process advances, the social institutions, including government, are developing and coming under increasing pressure to supply supporting capital and legal regimes, regulate competition and cater for market failure. The new copyright regimes are examples of this process with respect to the vital market for IP. Similarly, however, there is no guarantee that the financing needs created by expansion, either on the side of supply of skill or supply of savings, will be met by the private sector. The private market may also fail to fill the void for relevant music and manufacturing skills in a timely manner. As the system develops, the social institutions are repeatedly being forced to step in, evaluate the gaps in the resource markets, the gains from filling the gap, and then act accordingly. In the long run, of course, some of this intervention will be paid for by revenue generated from the audio-visual sector itself.

Sustainability and changes in communications technology

At the level of the unit, the impact of changing technology has always been to change the options and opportunities of those involved in production and exchange. Change has always tended to favor those who can and will adapt, generally by raising the effectiveness of labor effort and the profitability of investment, and to make into relatively irrelevant classics those who will not.

The effect of such change was felt early in Trinidad in the 1960s, as steelbands were displaced by sound systems as the preferred accompaniment for carnival revelry and party. The reason was failure to amplify, miniaturize and increase their mobility rapidly enough (Mason, 1998: 64, 65, 74, 77). In contrast, other elements in the music industry benefited from being able and willing to adapt. Of reggae, Baek and Hedegard (1999: 2) write that "when the digital age started influencing other music forms in the mid 1980s, traditional reggae melodies were transformed into a type of 'dancehall' originally called 'DJ', this created an entirely new craze in fashion and dance," which is displacing the traditional reggae in the marketplace. Of calypso, Mason (1998: 45) writes that "in recent years, the 'traditional' commentary-style calypso … have lost significant ground to the more vacuous 'jam and wine' with its essentially meaningless lyrics and exhortations." Mason (1998: 47, 48) also observes that "the move to frivolity and slackness" is part of "a world wide trend to music as pure entertainment, as an aspirational activity dedicated more to the gods of sex, money and ego than any purely altruistic political or social message." Much of the trend has foundations in technological change and diffusion.[22]

This process of creation is being more radically modified by the emerging digital technology. Together with the Internet and communications satellites, this technology allows for easy access and retrieval, storage, manipulation, transmission and dissemination of author's works. The original works remain pivotal, but these techniques of digital representation and modification make many instruments (and creators and processes of creation) irrelevant after a work has been created. As noted above, these technologies facilitate a continuation of the dominance of the foreign supply of music and film, mostly downloaded from the Internet nowadays. However, this possibility would be realized only if the creative potential of the media is not perceived and time is not taken to explore it. As with the other versatile media, it brings the potential for favorable radical change of the terms of trade, based on creative domestic supply.

The representation of objects in digital form, database storage and electronic access techniques, coupled with the three main inherent properties of information, dramatically raise the prospects for creative application of data. Information is not consumable in the traditional sense that goods are consumed by being used; rather, information remains available no matter how much it is used. Similarly, information is non-transferable in the traditional sense of exchange, with loss to the seller (giver) and unretrievable transfer to the buyer (receiver), as is true of the transfer of goods between persons. The giver can retain possession of information even though the receiver also has possession (McLaughlin, 1988). Perhaps most important in this context, because it is not lost by use, but rather generates more in a dynamic social process, information accumulates (socially) the more it is used. A change in the terms of trade between the local and foreign audio-visual sectors, though evidently desirable, has not proven to be easy to achieve in the past. When the power of the digital medium of storage and retrieval, and the nature of information, are taken together, the desired change is more likely to become easier to achieve in the present circumstances, assuming the necessary investment in creative application.[23]

Since the opportunity for creative interaction is available to any user with access, it makes piracy a very attractive and lucrative business for those in an exchange relation who are appropriately inclined, even the concept of piracy could make sense in this context. In general, digital compression is driving a communications revolution and simultaneously is enhancing the capacity to pirate (Ryan, 1998: 161). In any private commercial transaction, it is property rights that are exchanged at a price. Thus copyrights are the basis on which the individual can identify the costs of production and exchange transactions and hence determine the profitability and feasibility of engaging in the transactions of the audio-visual sector as described above through all the linkages and other analyses provided above (Neuberger, 1994: 23). In general, if the relevant entrepreneurs are not assured of these copyrights by some means, they could not be assured of a fair price or cost for use. This is the issue brought to the fore again by the new technologies.

Summing up: the role of copyrights

In the context of all the discussions presented above, one can adequately evaluate the true economic importance of copyrights. The data above generally clarify why, in the context of the audio-visual sector, rights to creative works may not be adequately and clearly defined relative to the domain of (market) participation, as Libling (1978) has long pointed out, and if defined, may be unenforceable because of technology. Problems with such rights can have profound effects.

Musicians and performers, for example, could not reap fair amounts of royalties and other payments due from users. Record shops and broadcasters and collection societies, which employ these inputs in manufacturing, broadcasting, electronic dissemination and collection services, might face potentially unfair accusations and high-cost lawsuits. In either case, assignment of value or cost of sales of products and services and consequent benefits will tend to be ill-defined and contentious.

Further, insofar as one recognizes that "fair competition" laws exist which provide some right of access to all these creators and users, serious questions arise as to the interests which should predominate. How should the rights of musicians, for example, be balanced against those of studios or the television station, keeping in mind the problem of the public interest in access? (Sterling, 1999: 26) Yet, if they are not currently well-adjudicated by society, such adjudication might only be resolved in a time-consuming process, which ultimately makes the whole exercise irrelevant in the light of the speed of ongoing technological change. Thus, at some point in the process, those who stand to lose the most could generally be expected to desist from engaging in the activities discussed, and the entire industrial process will break down. This risk is real unless dealt with by adequate social policy. To the extent that those who abandon the process are the musicians and the performers, the sound systems and the entrepreneurs of the festivals, the entire development process described above is in jeopardy, because the rest of the audio-visual sector does not display a similar independent creative tendency or capability.

All of this still has to be placed in the additional new context of changing information technology, since the latter is rapidly changing the implications of market demand and exchange for the modern supplier of copyrighted products. These implications are not as simple today as they used to be, and seem to be urging a shift of focus from enforcement of rights through traditional deterrence to enforcement based on education. Musicians are always looking for a way out of the problem of the inadequate protection of property provided by the copyright regime. For example, to escape piracy of cassette tapes or CDs, "many calypsonians now concentrate on making videos of their carnival offerings in the hope that a Road March win will propel them onto the North American music channels and the wider international market" (Mason, 1998: 44). However, with the changing technology allowing ever clearer and cleaner copies, piracy of video is likely to be very significant abroad, and this might provide no way out in the long run.

As important as the problem of direct copy of videos and cassettes might be, such problems now pale in significance before those that are implied by the fast developing digital technology. Digital technology (especially MIDI) is facilitating an increasing degree of *interactivity* which is the "biggest communication revolution since telephony and radio" (Ryan, 1998: 171). The new IT (including MP3 and Bitmusic) is offering new business risks to loss and piracy as well as new business opportunities in marketing and speed of transactions. In the IT world where downloading, uploading, sending and diskette storing is a way of life, it is no longer clear when (if at all) copyright rights are infringed. The global market for pirated compact discs and tape cassettes, as piracy is defined in law, was worth more than US$5 billion in 1996.[24]

Indeed, the technology has developed to the stage where copyright law by itself is not readily protective of creative property in any exchange relationship between a creator and another person, such as a producer, because ease of manipulation makes it nearly impossible to achieve meaningful detection and enforcement with deterrents. The modern player in today's "cyber culture" sees information as free, views IP as an "oxymoron," and argues that the "copyright cartel" wants to "grab it all" and prevent the "revolution of the interactive, universally wired world" (Ryan, 1998: 170–171). This perspective is reflected in the writings of *Wired* magazine, dubbed the unofficial journal of the interactive community.

Policy development for the music industry

In this final section of the chapter, we set out the implications of the above discussions for the formulation of coherent policy as it relates to the development of the audio-visual sector in general and music and related performances in particular. The data and analysis presented above suggest that Caribbean economies operate in a rapidly globalizing world economy. In this environment, the emerging copyright regimes in the Caribbean are making a significant contribution to the development of the audio-visual sector generally, and its music industry in particular. They facilitate the continued development of music as a local network of consumption and capacity creation that fosters and promotes high levels of creativity, which in turn generate growing rates of quasi-rents and growing employment that sustain the transformation of the audio-visual sector.

Given the objective of increasing the rent earned in the music industry through the investment in capacity of all relevant forms, two major policy issues suggest themselves. The first is the critical significance of copyrights; secure property rights must be a premise of participation, and the method may have to be creative and moral in the light of changing technology and the dynamics of realistic competition. The second is that, even with copyrights in place and enforceable, the general laws of the economy are not to be ignored; a solution must also be found to the limitations which the extent and variations of the market put on the development of the music and related arts industry. A key aspect of that solution is the establishment of adequately democratized institutions of collaboration in economic policy-making. The policies that are implied by the dynamics of the industry also amount to an effective competition policy. The reason is that they also focus on the enhancement of competitive capacity to make such supply-side adjustments as are necessary to earn rising rents and rewards to labor in a growing and increasingly diversified domestic and international market.

Strategy, data and social capacity for policy-making

The key evidence relevant to policy-making in the light of the current copyright regime is that the participants in the music industry function in a strategic manner, responding to aggregate demand by supply-side adjustments of capacity and capacity utilization that are focused on creativity and worker effort. The pace of development of capacity and capacity utilization depends on the extent and variation of the market. The evidence above suggests that the extent and variation of the music market depend on the scale and interactive nature of consumption, net exports, government spending and, especially, investment, whether by domestic or foreign capital, as well as of spending for improvement of technology, and managerial and worker efficiency. The evidence also suggests dependence of the music market on the extent of development and democratization of relevant social institutions and the accompanying participatory spending initiatives. It is these conditions of market development, complete with copyright regimes, which underlie accumulation of capacity and increase in rents in the Caribbean music industry.

One vital role for the social institutions of this networking process is the management of demand to limit the negative effects on rents and employment of variations in demand. Adjustment to variable demand through variation of supply requires forecasting of the path of the sales of the participatory unit. In turn, this requires judgments about the path of aggregate demand in the local and regional economy, along with the capacity of the firm to win a share of that demand without spoiling the market through price adjustments.

However, the market in a Caribbean industrial economy tends to signal inappropriate forecasts of collective behavior.[25] Currently, the music market seems to be slow, but would pick up with growing domestic demand that can increase incomes in the hands of the local youth and women. Also, much of the ongoing technological change is exogenous and imported, so there is no telling what particular forms might work. Further, the new copyright laws are in place, but other elements of the regime are not, so the proceeds of investment might be lost to piracy. A similar rationale applies to capacity creation and use in traditional sectors. So the market signals are to hold on investment and wait until signs are clearer, just when the opposite is needed to stimulate more technological change and growing work effort. For adequate use of the newly installed capacity, including the copyright regime, it is necessary for aggregate demand to expand. However, the market and social processes signal the opposite behavior. The result is a cumulative decline and loss of opportunity for the music industry.

Adequate stimulus to the music market in this environment requires collaborative and democratized planning of spending initiatives by government at all levels, business and the other social institutions servicing music and other industries.

A key difficulty in this regard is the lack of adequate statistical data on the music industry. This problem typically stems from at least two factors. One is the mistrust between government and the participants in the industry, for reasons that range from a feeling of alienation among participants in a traditionally neglected industry to suspicion that taxation is the motivation for the data collection. The other is the geographical spread of participants and the associated limited flow of information to government and other highly centralized decision-making bodies. Progress on this front requires a sound program of policy-oriented (operational and financial) data collection for timely policy analysis and decision-making. Such data should supplement current Surveys of Establishments in the region, and in many cases could be collected through current Living Standards Measurement Surveys (Deaton, 1997). Together with a program of education of policy-makers about the findings of such studies, these data should provide a reasonable basis for identifying the competitive capacities and practices of the relevant firms and household-firms being studied and the form of strategy relevant to existing circumstances.

With this process at work, local and island governments should collaborate with representative social institutions to stimulate the development of local culture and foster differentiation in the industry. This would facilitate the steady development of aggregate demand and responsive supply. The democratization and development of social institutions implied by this process would tend to lower the going discount rate and interest rate, and raise access to vital social assets including schools, infrastructure, and so on, while providing a sound basis for targeting benefits.

Development of clusters and improvement of innovation policy

Consistent with the strategic intervention described above, sound policy must continue to monitor and promote collaboration to develop the linkages among the various specialized aspects in the industry. It must support the development of musical composition, performance, instrumentation, strategic financing, production, recording, publishing, legal services, retailing, marketing, copyright regime, and so on, in order to boost generation of quasi-rents. Moreover, it seems necessary that this must be done while promoting the options for individual entrepreneurship in preference to the expansion of wage-labor. Policy must also seek to widen the networks. To achieve this, at least two related productive clusters must be promoted. One should encompass the traditional audio-visual sector, with special reference to cinematography and the dance festivals. The other should encompass the domestic manufacturing components of the industry, incorporating steelband, sound recordings, videos, and the like. In each case, policy must ensure the development of relevant social institutions, strategic financing, scientific research, productive capital, interactive feedback from linked firms and consumers, marketing and IP regimes covering copyright and patents, among other matters.

In support of these efforts, some policy initiatives should focus directly on providing incentives for the development of differentiation through innovation. The current competitions which lie at the heart of the Caribbean music industry should be strengthened and broadened through significantly improved financing and the development of new types of competitions to reflect the trends of change in music and related performances. Other incentives target operators that actually introduce innovations, for example, by reimbursing some percentage of documented costs. Further, some incentives should focus on workers to enhance attitudes and speed. Such incentives might include training options to improve artistic and technical skills, and worker flexibility. Of considerable significance here would be programs that introduce schooling and formalized research into the creative institutions, including the church. It is likely that, in each country, significant gains can be made through the development of appropriately located institutions dedicated to formal research into, and related training about, new methods, products and marketing options. It would also be reasonable to train through apprenticeship schemes, attaching students to the great masters and teachers in a manner reminiscent of the development of the classical music genre in the North Atlantic (Towse, 1993).

With the increasing integration between tourism and entertainment in the Caribbean, and with the increasing internationalization of the tourism market in the Caribbean, significant synergies in training for these industries should be sought through training and apprenticeship in several languages and culture spheres. Because of the multilingual and Mediterranean character of the Caribbean culture sphere, if this program is simultaneously conducted in several appropriate countries, the unit cost of achieving its gains is likely to be low relative to the gains won. To achieve these gains in a coordinated way, training for the integrated local area networks should be brought under the manpower planning and implementation agendas of each Caribbean society, and full advantage taken of opportunities for distance learning, using the Internet and other facilities. Finally, corresponding to this, and taking into account the high rate of change of the information technology underlying the production of music and related performances, accelerated depreciation facilities for the various operators may prove useful as a stimulant to the investments needed to ensure innovation and speed-up.

Copyright law as policy

With respect to continuing improvement in the copyright regime, one vital policy need is to realign the competing rights in favor of the local creators as to foster the transformation of the audio-visual sector through their initiatives, and ultimately stimulate the transformation economy and society as a whole. There are two reasons for this to be the necessary alignment. The first is that in the Caribbean today, the overriding public interest is in fostering the engines of growth in order to stimulate sustainable development. The second is that, as a struggle for opportunity, competition requires emphasis on the capacity to compete, the methods of competition and the comparative strength of competitors. This struggle must be regulated to favor the creative elements that constitute the engine of growth in Caribbean society, in much the same way that property laws favor the risk-taking capitalist relative to paid labor.

In some ways, this principle is already implicit in all copyright law, since it is widely noted that, where labor is the essential ingredient of the property identified, the distinction is made between "creative" labor which is protected and "non-creative" labor which is not. It is also well established that the matter of "fair dealing" is perhaps the most important defense to an action for copyright infringement (Benson, 1995). It only remains for policy to ensure that the explicit formulation and enforcement of *both copyright and competition law* recognizes that, in Caribbean society, local creativity must be given priority, less because of individual's rights, and more because of the vital interests and opportunities of society as a whole.

Whatever the difficulties and hence methods involved, facilitation of the development of the community-based, national and Caribbean-wide institutional capacity to protect copyrights and realize related revenues is an essential aspect of appropriate policy for music and related arts. As the difficulty of enforcing copyright grows with changing technology and the dramatic shortening of the product cycle, the appropriate policy perspective seems increasingly to be that copyright law must be enforced through education about the advantages of using information in a creative but legal manner, when compared with piracy. This should be combined with two distinct initiatives as discussed below. One relates to the use of TRIPS as copyright policy and as a Trade-Related Investment Measure (TRIMS). The other relates to the supporting taxation, marketing and business financing policy.

TRIPS as copyright policy and as TRIMS

In conceiving of the role of TRIPS as copyright policy, it is important to note that this agreement emerged out of difficult negotiations between dominant countries, such as the USA and UK, and so-called developing countries that opposed the idea of including TRIPS under the GATT.[26] The primary beneficiaries of TRIPS, as well as of the WTO, are the international corporations that are able to locate operations strategically around the world without inordinate fear that technological know-how will be imitated and related rights infringed, leading to loss of associated monopoly, competitive advantage and related rents. This is particularly important in the light of the growing ease of copying cutting-edge technology and know-how, especially by some Asian countries (Rampersad, 1997: 237–239). Thus, the significance of the drive by the USA to harmonize intellectual property laws is that such harmonization protects the US-based international corporations from loss of revenue occasioned by insufficient protection of technology internationally.

In this light, one reason to support adequate (re)formulation of TRIPS as local policy is that it is really a form of TRIMS that can attract the international corporations and other foreign investors to invest in the Caribbean music industry. Foreign direct investment (FDI) continues to be important in the Caribbean and, keeping in mind the need to promote networking, can play a role in the development of film and other aspects of the traditional audio-visual sector, as well as the related manufacturing sector. As the WTO rules take effect, the international community is moving increasingly in the direction of dictating national policy, and the international corporations are calling the main shots away from enforcement of requirements such as employment of local labor, use of indigenous inputs, transfer of technology and facilitation of local equity investments (Rampersad, 1997: 230, 232). Also, the capacity to ignore and circumvent local fiscal and economic policy is one of the costs of large-scale FDI through international corporations (Rampersad, 1997: 231). By attracting international corporations and other forms of foreign financing, TRIPS might provide some room for the expansion of the Caribbean music industry through improved access to new markets and technology, while allowing indigenous investment to continue as the principal source of funds for its development. Because of the highly localized nature of the industry and much of its information system, such a move would draw the foreign investor into a local network and enhance the capacity of Caribbean people to dictate the path of progress.

However, the argument in support of TRIPS is more general. The Caribbean tends to benefit from the explosion of creativity at the level of lyrics creation, live performances, dance festivals and associated manufacturing. The proceeds of these initiatives can be readily lost to piracy and other forms of loss if all nations are not forced to implement and enforce copyright laws. Strong and harmonized international laws stimulate innovation through income protection. Within the ambit of a creative industry, the opposing view that global protection might raise the cost of access to necessary technology and markets is not very persuasive. The growing ease of access to relevant technologies is also making the associated worry about the effects of monopolistic restrictions on trade increasingly irrelevant.

What seems more relevant is that local copyright regimes should address some of the specific gross violations in the Caribbean. This principle refers to matters such as the web of uncertainty in the relation between the lyricist/artist, the promoters, the producer and other entrepreneurs in the local industry. It also includes the need for support from the beneficiary countries, such as the USA, to the Caribbean countries to meet the considerable cost of adequate administrative bureaucracy, training of officers of the court, enforcement and public education throughout the region.[27]

Other policy supports: marketing, finance, depreciation and taxation

One support needed is the development of marketing techniques that enable firms to price some products, such as shows and consumer hardware, in such a way as to cover the loss of market opportunity through music that can be pirated by copying CDs, and so on, or downloaded from the Internet. To the extent that copyright is embodied in a form, such as a CD, which is essentially an easily pirated joint product, the latter might be treated as a marketing tool. The musician or artist might tend to de-emphasize the importance of copyright, treat such forms as free commodities and emphasize the importance of other realizable value, such as from live shows. Similar tactics are becoming evident on the part of the international majors. The latter increasingly make available music through forms such as the MIDI technology and the newer MP3 and Bitmusic technologies that allow almost limitless interactive modification, duplication and free distribution while seeking to recoup gains from the pricing of the equipment used to play the music and effect the interactive change. The astute policy-maker may need to assist participants with the development of the capacity to market the product that runs the least risk of piracy. This would include the development of classic venues for the staging of shows and festivals, with adequate arrangements for market differentiation.

Another relevant support is a taxation regime that targets the users of consumer hardware in the music and entertainment industry and seeks to recoup some of the losses from piracy of IP. Policy design for the music industry should also evaluate and exploit the room that exists to use taxation of tourism, other services, the traditional audio-visual activities such as radio and television, and other beneficiary sectors. The taxes are only likely to generate a net benefit if revenue proceeds are earmarked for use in the development of the music industry, with special reference to the support of the process of innovation and the development of worker efficiency. For example, some of the proceeds might be used to improve prices and other incentives associated with competitions, training programs and apprenticeship schemes, and other institutional development initiatives. Such a policy would also amount to a program of protection of revenues potentially due from copyrights but actually lost to pirates. At the same time, it would tie the major producers of hardware for the use of IP, the international corporations, into the network that benefits creators of IP. Such an approach would result in an increased flow of revenues to the creators of IP, and foster further bursts of creativity. This seems to constitute a generic opportunity yet to be adequately exploited by policy.

In this context, the close association between the development of the music industry and marketing capacity should become a major focus of policy-making. To develop this market, it is necessary that each country in the Caribbean region adopt a package of initiatives, including research, training, apprenticeships and development of physical and social (institutional) infrastructure, to improve the reliance on local knowledge and culture in the marketing of products. Such initiatives would involve market differentiation mechanisms that increase the visibility of products and processes, and thus of artists and festival producers. At the same time, it is necessary to enhance the capacity of the local industry to market its products through the collaborative or commercial use of modern information technology for distribution, particularly marketing-oriented web sites, while increasing the use of available means to limit piracy. For example, it might be necessary for incentives to be given to the private sector or some institution of social capital to develop Internet malls for the music, entertainment and related industries. Such sites use an appropriate browser (with appropriate search engines) simultaneously to sell a cafeteria of services and products such as a wide variety of CDs, movies, music clips and other entertainment-related goods and services to both the consumer and the creator, and therefore bring the latter together for information and distribution purposes. They are widely used by all the major participants in the industry, and are typically not cost-effective for any single artist or operator to develop and use.

The flow of benefits from these initiatives would translate into new initiatives only if the operators in the industry can increasingly find funding for the larger investments in physical and human capital that are continually needed for effective participation. The increasing tendency to rely on finance and amortization, combined with the traditional tendency for the financial sector to discriminate against participants in the music industry, implies the need to improve the level and terms of access of operators to social finance. Across the region, significant initiatives are already underway in this regard, but these should be strengthened and broadened.

Notes

1 In general, performing right is "the right to perform works in public, broadcast works or communicate works to the public." Reproduction rights refer to acts such as "printing of sheet music or lyrics, recording of music either on a sound carrier (e.g a record, tape, CD) or in a film, video, television programme, or commercial advertisement" (COTT, 1999).

2 That is to say, they do not form a separate network or "industrial district" or "cluster" in the sense intended by Asheim (1994), M. Best (1990), Bellandi (1994) or Clancy and Twomey (1997).

3 For example, Pan Trinbago which services steelbands, and the National Carnival Bands Association of Trinidad and Tobago.

4 This was achieved through institutions such as the National Carnival Commission of Trinidad and Tobago (NCC) and the Jamaica Cultural Development Commission.

5 In Trinidad and the Southern Caribbean, faced with the official efforts to ban or stymie Afro-centric organization, the people turned to dance assembles, tamboo-bamboo calinda bands, Bongo groups and later the carnival bands, and perhaps most importantly, the Afro-centric religious assemblies, such as the Shango and the Spiritual Baptists, which encased all the music and dance forms and served as the most basic roots and links to Africa and its fertility dances or technical, political and social commentary with story and song. Reggae and the modern Jamaican Dance festivals emerged similarly. It has evolved into the popular "dancehall" today, but finds its real roots in the Afro-centric religions of Poccomania and later Rastafarianism (Baek and Hedegard, 1999; Watson, 1995: 17, 18).

6 Some of the misunderstanding is evident in Stolzoff (1998) in which the fact that dancehall expresses the "violence" of Jamaican society, and is a medium through which prospects of use of violence as a means of social control are signaled, is confused with the "violence" of the music itself. The same mistake was made repeatedly from the very inception of Caribbean music in slavery (Rohlehr, 1990).

7 As Baek and Hedegard (1999: 10) describe it: "Sound systems differ from discos due

to the mixture of recorded and live performances. Singers and deejays appear on stage, singing to instrumental B-sides of singles ... people called "selectors" choose the music.... Deejays then announce the music and help generate the special atmosphere whilst the selectors run the play list, aided by mixers who cue the singles ready for playing."

8 This information was gleaned during a visit to the plant with Dr Zeljka Kozul-Wright of UNCTAD. At least one operator in Jamaica and one in Trinidad replicates CDs, but these produce output on a small scale and of uncertain quality that cannot find a firm place in the world market and may be suitable only for demos (Henry and Nurse, 1996: 20).

9 Henry and Nurse (1996: 21, 22) provide some details of the expected net income from vinyl production in the current market in Trinidad and show that local manufacturing operations cannot compete on a price/cost basis with foreign operations in the USA and Canada.

10 Kozul-Wright and Stanbury (1998) provide considerable and important detail for the interested reader.

11 The major ones in the region in this regard are (1) The Performing Right Society Limited (PRS) of Jamaica; (2) the Copyright Organization of Trinidad and Tobago (COTT); and (3) the Barbados Agency for Musical Culture, Inc. (BAMCI). Other collective administrative organizations include: Jamaican Association of Composers, Authors and Publishers (JACAP); Barbados Association of Composers, Authors and Publishers (BACAP); Jamaican Copyright Licensing Agency Limited (JAMCOPY); Hewanorra Musical Society (HMS); Société Haïtienne de Gestion de Droit d'Auteur (SHAGDA); Jamaica Musical Rights Administration Society Limited (JMRAS); Copyright and Entertainment Services, Inc. (CES); Copyright Organisation of Grenada (COG); Neighbouring Rights Association of Trinidad and Tobago (NRATT) and The Society for the Administration of the Rights of Composers in Guyana.

12 For example, Pan Trinbago, Trinidad and Tobago Unified Calypsonians' Organization (TUCO), the Jamaica Federation of Musicians and Artistes, and the Sound Systems Association of Jamaica.

13 The trend to use of local music was boosted by the publication of local music books such as Prospect, G. A. (1978), *A Practical Tutor For Steel Pan Instrument Double-Second Pan*.

14 As White (1998: 13, 14) documents, "Once again, Jamaicans were creatively borrowing elements from outside and adopting them to suit their distinct needs. The purposes for which, and the manner in which, this technology came to be enlisted was, at the time, unique. Not even in the countries where the amplifiers, players and speakers were manufactured were such systems organized. Although Jamaicans did not manufacture the equipment, ground-breaking electronic enthusiasts existed who were capable not only of repairing the amplifiers but also of building them. The assemblage of mega-wattage amplifiers, banks of speakers and record 'libraries' in a unit that could move from place to place brought into being a 'peculiar' Jamaican [technology and] institution."

15 For this reason, "Sound systems also play a major role as talent spotter. Many new artists try their latest offerings on the sound system audience. If response is positive, the tune may be released as a single" (Baek and Hedegard, 1999: 12).

16 In Jamaica, these include Bob Marley in the early years, Ziggie Marley and the Melody makers, Beenie Man, Bounty Killa, Buju Banton, Sizzla and Luciano (Watson, 1995: 15–18; Kozul-Wright and Stanbury, 1998: 16, 17). In Trinidad, there are Sparrow and Kitchener in the early years, and David Rudder and Marshall Montano more recently. Arrow remains the most popular in the rest of the region.

17 Indeed, these authors state that they are the major constraints.

18 For example, as of 1998, the victorious band at the Panorama competition in Trinidad wins about TT$60,000. However, "with around 100 band members to pay out there is

relatively little financial reward" for the "intense effort" that amounts to about "180 hours over a six week period up to carnival practising nightly in the panyard" (Mason, 1998: 68, 70).

19 (Mason, 1998: 124 quoting *Trinidad Express*, 9 Feb. 1997).

20 Mason (1998: 125) summarizing reports from the Tourism and Industrial Development Company (TIDCO).

21 The historical experience of the Caribbean suggests that the leakage of added value and the associated stagnation fostered by the latter industries is high relative to the creative sector.

22 It is worth observing that a similar split is evident in mas. One of the older mas designers has openly declared, with obvious hyperbole, that "all those people parading naked, showing their crotches, are not playing mas; they are playing something else but not mas" (Ramoutar, 1996: 25).

23 This raises the need for many musicians and composers/arrangers to retool with the digital technology in order to become even more versatile and remain competitive.

24 International Federation of the Phonographic Industry (IFPI) statistics, used in Sterling (1999: 27).

25 This would be applicable even if forecasting capabilities are in place, and is even more applicable because in most cases the forecasting capabilities are generally not available.

26 In the end, the USA used its power to force the strongest opponents, Brazil and India, to abide by its Super 301 Trade Law, while giving concessions to weaker opponents in relation to textiles and agricultural exports (Rampersad, 1997: 237).

27 The policy should be seen in the light of the fact that nearly 80 percent of regional collections are sent abroad.

Bibliography

Alleyne, M. (1998) "Babylon Makes the Rules: The Politics of Reggae Crossover," *Social and Economic Studies*, Vol. 47, No.1, pp. 65–77.

Anderson, Birgitte and Jeremy Howells (1998) "Innovation Dynamics in Services: Intellectual Property Rights as Indicators and Shaping Systems in Innovation," *CRIC Discussion Paper* No. 8, February. University of Manchester.

——, and Ian Miles (1998) "Intellectual Property Rights, Innovation and Services," *Center for Research on Innovation and Competition*. Manchester: University of Manchester.

Asheim, B.T. (1994) "Industrial Districts, Inter-firm Cooperation and Endogenous Development: The Experience of Developed Countries," in UNCTAD (1994), *Technological Dynamism in Industrial Districts: An Alternative Approach to Industrialization in Developing Countries?* UNCTAD/ITD/TEC/11. New York: United Nations, pp. 91–142.

Baek, Henrik and Hans Hedegard (1999) *Dancehall Explosion*, Fredericksberg C: Samler Borsen.

Barro, Robert J. and Xavier Sala-i-Martin (1995) *Economic Growth*. New York: McGraw Hill.

Beckford, George (1972) *Persistent Poverty*. London: Zed

Beesley, M.E. (ed.)(1996) *Markets and the Media: Competition, Regulation and the Interests of Consumers*. Institute of Economic Affairs.

Bellandi, M. (1994) "Decentralized Industrial Creativity in Industrial Districts," in UNCTAD (1994) *Technological Dynamism in Industrial Districts: An Alternative Approach to Industrialization in Developing Countries?* UNCTAD/ITD/TEC/11. New York: United Nations,, pp. 73–84.

Benson, Christopher (1995) "Fair Dealing in the United Kingdom," *European Intellectual Property Review*, Vol. 6, pp. 304–306.

Berry, Paul M. (1999) "Feasibility Study Relating to Regional Collective Management of Copyright in the Caribbean," prepared for *WIPO Roundtable on Collective Management of Copyright and Related Rights for Caribbean Countries* (Montego Bay, Jamaica, June 7–9), WIPO in cooperation with the Ministry of Commerce and Technology of Jamaica.

Besen, S.M. (1987) *New Technologies And Intellectual Property: A Rand Note*. Santa Monica, CA: Rand.

—— and Leo J. Raskind (1991) "An Introduction to the Law and Economics of Intellectual Property," *Journal of Economic Perspectives*, Vol. 5, No. 1, pp. 3–27.

Best, Lloyd (1968) "A Model of Pure Plantation Economy," *Social and Economic Studies*, Vol. 17, No. 3.

—— (1970–) *Tapia*, Tunapuna: Tapia House.

—— (1975) "A Biography of Labor," in G. Beckford (ed.), *Caribbean Economy: Dependence and Backwardness*. Mona: ISER, pp. 147–158.

—— (1977–) *Trinidad and Tobago Review*, Tunapuna: Tapia House.

—— (1980) *International Co-operation in the Industrialization Process: The Case of Trinidad and Tobago*. Port of Spain: TTRIWI.

—— and Levitt (1969) *Externally Propelled Growth and Industrialization* (3 Vols. mimeograph). Montreal: McGill University.

Best, M.H. (1990) *The New Competition: Institution of Industrial Restructuring*. Cambridge: Harvard.

Bornstein, M. (ed.) (1994) *Comparative Economic Systems*. New York: Irwin.

Braunstein, Y.M. (1989) "Economics of Intellectual Property Rights in the International Arena," *Journal of the American Society for Information Science*, Vol. 40, No. 1, pp. 12–16.

Chang, Keven O'Brien and Wayne Chen (1998) *Reggae Routes: The Story of Jamaican Music*. Kingston: Ian Randle Publishers.

Cheung, Steven N.S. (1986) "Property Rights and Invention," *Research in Law and Economics: The Economics of Patents and Copyrights*, Vol. 8, pp. 5–18.

Clancy, P. and M. Twomey (1997) *Clusters in Ireland: The Irish Popular Music Industry: An Application of Porter's Cluster Analysis*. Research Series. Paper No. 2. National Economic and Social Council.

Cooper, C. (1998) Guest Editorial, *Social and Economic Studies*, Vol. 47, No. 1, pp. 1–4.

Copyright Organisation of Trinidad and Tobago (1999) *A Guide to COTT*.

—— (1998) *COTT: 1998 Year Book*.

Cornish, W.R. (1996) (3rd edn) *Intellectual Property: Patents, Copyright, Trade Marks and Allied Rights*. London: Sweet & Maxwell.

Deaton, A. (1997) *The Analysis of Household Surveys: A Microeconometric Approach to Development Policy*. Baltimore: Johns Hopkins.

Devonish, H. (1998) "Electronic Orature: The Deejay's Discovery," *Social and Economic Studies*, Vol. 47, No. 1, pp. 33–53.

Edwards, Nadi (1998) "States of Emergency: Reggae Representations of the Jamaican Nation State," *Social and Economic Studies*, Vol. 47, No. 1, pp. 21–32.

Forstner, H. and R. Balance (1990) *Competing in a Global Economy: An Empirical Study on Specialization and Trade in Manufactures*. Prepared for the United Nations Industrial Development Organization. London: Unwin Hyman.

Gibbons, Rawle (1999) *A Calypso Trilogy*. Kingston: Ian Randle.

Government of Jamaica (1993) *The Copyright Act, No. 4 of 1993.*

Guidberg, Hans Hoegh (1994) (2nd edn) *Copyright: An Economic Perspective.* Sydney: Australian Copyright Council.

Hall, Susan (1994) "Multimedia: Does Anacon Provide a Route to Future Protection?" *Entertainment Law Review*, Vol. 6, pp. 191–193.

Henry, Ralph and Keith Nurse (1996) "The Entertainment Sector of Trinidad and Tobago: Implementing an Export Strategy." Report prepared for the Industry and Trade Division, TIDCO.

Irish Music Industry Group (1998) "Raising the Volume: Policies to Expand the Irish Music Industry: A Submission to Government." (mimeo) Irish Business Employers Confederation.

James, V. (1997) "Lewis on Class Formation in the Caribbean," *Social and Economic Studies*, Vol. 45, No. 4.

—— and L. Celestin (1999a) "Production and Prices in a Caribbean Economy" (unpublished).

—— (1999b) "Democracy and the New Regionalism," unpublished.

JAMPRO (1996) "Marketing Plan for Music & Entertainment, 1996/1997." Jampro/Jamaica Film, Music & Entertainment Commission.

—— and Jamaica Film, Music & Entertainment Commission (1999) *Sounds Of Jamaica Music: An Industry Directory.*

Joseph, Terry (1999) "COTT Collects Best Revenues Ever," *Daily Express*, December 7, p. 23.

Jussawalla, Meheroo (1992) *The Economics of Intellectual Property in a World Without Frontiers: A Study of Computer Software.* New York: Greenwood Press.

—— Snow, M. and Y. Braunstein (1988) "Major Issues in Information Service Trade," *Pacific Focus*, Vol. 3, No. 1, pp. 71–89.

Kingma, Bruce (1996) *The Economics Of Access Versus Ownership: The Costs and Benefits of Access to Scholarly Articles via Interlibrary Loan and Journal Subscriptions.* New York: Haworth Press Inc.

Kirsch, Jonathan (1995) *Kirsch's Handbook Of Publishing Law.* Los Angeles: Acrobat Books.

Kozul-Wright, Zeljka and Lloyd Stanbury (1998) "Becoming a Globally Competitive Player: The Case of the Music Industry in Jamaica." UNCTAD/OSG/DP/138.

Lewis, Arthur (1954) "Economic Development with Unlimited Supplies of Labour," *Manchester School*, Vol. 22, pp. 139–191.

Libling, D.F. (1978) "The Concept of Property: Property in Intangibles," *The Law Quarterly Review*, Vol. 94, January, pp. 103–119.

Mason, P. (1998) *Bacchanal! The Carnival Culture of Trinidad.* Kingston: Ian Randle.

McLaughlin, J.D. (1988) *Land Information Management.* Oxford: Clarendon Press.

Miller, Jude and Adolf Stroombergen (1993) "Employment in Copyright Based Industries." Copyright Council of New Zealand, Inc.

Neuberger, E. (1994) "Comparing Economic Systems," in M. Bornstein (ed.), *Comparative Economic Systems*. New York: Irwin.

O'Gorman, C., E. O'Malley and J. Mooney (1997) *Clusters in Ireland: The Irish Indigenous Software Industry: An Application of Porter's Cluster Analysis.* Research Series. Paper No. 3. NESC.

Patasar, M. (1997) "The Development of Indian Music in Trinidad and Tobago," *Caribbean Dialogue*, Vol. 3, No. 4, pp. 67–71.

Persad, U. (1997) "Calypso and Chutney: Parallel Development and Integration," *Caribbean Dialogue*, Vol. 3, No. 4, pp. 77–80.

Phillips, Jennifer (1985) *The Economic Importance Of Copyright*. London: The Common Law Institute of Intellectual Property Limited.

Policy Research and Development Institute and Tobago Plan Team (1998) *The Tobago Development Plan,* Vol. 4. Scarborough, Tobago: Policy Research and Development Institute.

Ramlogan, Tej (1996) "Indian Music in Historical Perspective," *Natrang*, Vol. 1, No. 9.

Ramnarine, T.K. (1997) "Historiographical and Methodological Problems in Tracing the Origins of Contemporary Indian-Caribbean Music," *Natrang*, Vol. 1, No. 10.

Ramoutar, H. (1996) "An Interview with Mas Designers and Wire Benders in Trinidad during Carnival 1996," *Natrang*, Vol. 1, No. 9.

Rampersad, F. (1997) *Critical Issues in Caribbean Development. The New World Trade Order: Uruguay Round Agreements and Implications for CARICOM States*. Kingston: Ian Randle.

Republic of Trinidad and Tobago (1997) *The Copyright Act, No. 8 of 1997.*

Rohlehr, Gordon (1990) *Calypso and Society in Pre-Independence Trinidad*. Tunapuna, Trinidad: Gordon Rohlehr.

Ryan, M.P. (1998) *Knowledge Diplomacy: Global Competition and the Politics of Intellectual Property*. Washington, DC: Brookings Institute Press.

Sankerali, B. (1997) "Creole and Post-Creole: The Music of Carnival," *Caribbean Dialogue*, Vol. 3, No. 4, pp. 89–92.

Silberston, Aubrey (1998) "The Economic Importance of Copyright." *Proceedings – Creativity and Intellectual Property Rights: Evolving Scenarios and Perspectives International Conference* (Vienna, Austria, July 12–14). Brussels: Centro Internazionale Congressi.

Statistical Institute of Jamaica, *National Income and Product*: Preliminary Report, 1998, Reports, 1989, 1975.

Sterling, J.A.L. (1999) *World Copyright Law*. London: Sweet and Maxwell.

Stolzoff, N.C. (1998) "Murderation: The Question of Violence in the Sound System Dance," *Social and Economic Studies*, Vol. 47, No. 1, pp. 55–64.

Thurow, Lester C. (1996) *The Future Of Capitalism: How Today's Economic Forces Shape Tomorrow's World.* New York: Penguin.

Towse, Ruth (1993) *Singers In The Market Place: The Economics of the Singing Profession*. Oxford: Clarendon Press.

UNCTAD (1999) *The Science, Technology and Innovation Policy Review: Jamaica.* Geneva: United Nations.

—— (1994) *Technological Dynamism in Industrial Districts: An Alternative Approach to Industrialization in Developing Countries?* UNCTAD/ITD/TEC/11. New York: United Nations.

Watson, Pamela B. (1995) *The Situational Analysis of the Entertainment (Recorded Music) Industry*, Watson & Company Consulting Services, Inc. (prepared for the PIOJ on behalf of the Government of Jamaica and the UNDP).

White, G. (1998) "The Evolution of Jamaican Music, Part I: Proto-Ska to Ska," *Social and Economic Studies*, Vol. 47, No. 1, pp. 5–19.

WIPO (1997) *Agreement on Trade-Related Aspects of Intellectual Property Rights* (TRIPS). Geneva.

World Bank and OECD (1999) *A Framework for the Design and Implementation of Competition Law and Policy.* Washington, DC: The World Bank and The Organization for Economic Co-operation and Development (OECD).

Part III

Policy responses

10 Promoting creative industries

Public policies in support of film, music, and broadcasting

Verena Wiedemann

Introduction

This chapter examines policy options available to decision-makers in developing countries to promote and strengthen their domestic cultural industries. It focuses on three specific industries in the audiovisual sector – film, music and broadcasting, both television and radio.

The chapter considers policies that have been undertaken to promote these industries in both industrialised countries and in developing ones. It recognises that policies in developed countries, while providing useful insights, often cannot be seamlessly applied to the developing world, at least not in the early stages of development of the industries.

A major premise is that no single set of policies can be described as optimal for the developing world. Instead, effective policies must be customised on a country-by-country basis, taking into account the state of each country's creative sectors, its resources, and its other policy priorities.

The structure of the chapter is as follows. The first section sets out the minimum general conditions that are vital for the long-term prosperity of creative sectors in any country, namely freedom of expression, strong intellectual property protection, media pluralism, and concern for the social welfare of artists. Without these 'horizontal conditions', creative industries cannot even begin to flourish in a sustainable way. The remainder of the section describes sector-specific policies that are more directly related to creative industry production and trade. The second section examines the film industry, often regarded as the 'crown jewel' of the audiovisual sector. It explores illustrative policies such as subsidies, loans, tax incentives, and content quotas.

The third section examines the music industry. The key observation is that developing countries enjoy a position of great natural strength in this sector. With a rich and diverse heritage to draw from, music is one of the key creative sectors of developing countries with the potential of establishing a thriving industry sector with export possibilities. This section describes a host of measures that policy-makers can take, many of them derived from the film production context. It expresses optimism that local artists can find their voice, not least because the Internet is revolutionising music distribution in unparalleled ways.

The fourth section argues that broadcasting (television and radio) holds tremendous potential as a platform to promote cultural industries. A viable broadcasting system creates demand for domestic audiovisual content through programme commissions, co-productions between broadcasters and independent producers, and broadcasters' purchase of independent productions. Evidence suggests that a dual broadcasting system featuring public service broadcasters and commercial broadcasters with comparable market shares ensures a strong basis for a country's creative audiovisual industries. It concludes with a description of community broadcasting, a form of non-profit broadcasting based on citizens' initiative and a focus on local issues. This model, in particular, has experienced many successes in developing countries.

The fifth and final section examines the opportunities and challenges presented by the international framework in connection with efforts to nurture creative industries in developing economies. On the opportunity side, two strategies stand out. First, developing countries can adopt measures to promote cultural co-operation, as in the case of bilateral and plurilateral co-production agreements. Second, developing countries can target key international programmes that provide aid and know-how in the cultural field. This section also notes a number of challenges arising from international trade rules administered by the World Trade Organization (WTO). The section's key point is that developing countries must be cautious about the commitments they make to trade liberalisation because such commitments can later be invoked to prevent a country from supporting its creative sectors, even though the country never intended to relinquish its flexibility in this way.

'General framework' conditions required for a successful creative industries sector

Freedom of speech and information

Artistic creativity on a broader scale flourishes best if certain framework conditions are in place. One such 'horizontal' condition is freedom of speech and information. It allows artists and those aspiring to become creators to explore, to draw inspiration from different sources, to express publicly their personal tastes and preferences, and to experiment with avant-garde ideas and techniques irrespective of the rules of convention. Thus, societies that are open, both within and in relation to one another, are a key prerequisite to successful, creative industries. Artists and producers must be exposed not only to the richness of their own cultural heritage but also to that of foreign cultures and artistic trends that inspire their artistic creations. This exposure also helps ensure that artistic works will reach not only domestic audiences, but international ones as well.

Freedom of speech and freedom of information are the basis for such openness. Article 19 of the UN Universal Declaration of Human Rights guarantees the 'freedom to hold opinions without interference and to seek, receive and impart information and ideas through any media regardless of frontiers'. This fundamental human right encourages openness and democratic dialogue within countries, as well as dialogue between and among different societies and cultures.

Intellectual property rights protection

The prosperity of creative industries – indeed their very survival – presupposes legal protection of the unique act of artistic and intellectual creation. Thus, intellectual property (IP) rights and their effective enforcement are critical preconditions for the development of these sectors in all countries.

In order for rights holders effectively to pursue their rights to prohibit or to authorise the use of their rights, and, in the latter case, to collect the remuneration due to them, collecting societies have proven to be a helpful tool. Rights holders entrust the management of their rights to these entities, which in turn assert those rights on behalf of their members. In effect, by aggregating and centralising the enforcement function, collecting societies reduce the transaction costs that otherwise would be imposed on authors to enforce their rights.

IP regimes should not discriminate against the recognition of creative works in which developing societies have a comparative advantage. In recent years, there has been increasing alarm that the developed world has used intellectual property rights to the detriment of developing countries by making it difficult if not impossible for them to assert their interests in indigenous knowledge, folklore and culture, and genetic resources originating within their boundaries.

While such intangible heritage has traditionally been deemed to be within the public domain and thus not subject to legal protection, this notion has begun to change. For example, UNESCO, along with various other international institutions, has designed a model law for the protection and promotion of the cultural heritage of the Pacific Islands.[1] The model law, which recognises new rights, protects two categories of 'owners' of traditional knowledge and cultural expression, namely the group or clan that created it, and individuals recognised by the community as guardians of traditional knowledge. It grants protection to such cultural expressions as songs, oral recitals, manual arts, dances, theatre, ceremonies, rituals, drawings and architectural styles.

Safeguarding media pluralism

Media pluralism is another pre-condition for cultural diversity and a country's ability to reap the full benefits of its creative potential. Just as censorship by a government will curtail creativity, so does the control of media production and distribution facilities that are concentrated in just a few hands entail the risk of stifling diversity of opinion, and with it, cultural diversity.

Developing countries may be inclined to dismiss the need for rules on media pluralism, especially when their most pressing concern is attracting sufficient private investment to launch a media industry in the first place. However, structural safeguards, such as limiting the number of television and radio licences a single owner may hold, and restricting cross-media ownership of press undertakings and broadcasting organisations, need to be in place from the outset. Once a company has been allowed to secure a dominant position in a media market, experience suggests that governments are unlikely to be able to impose their political will for divestiture or a reduction of market share. By then, the undertaking may have such a grip on public opinion and hence the political process that it is simply too powerful to be subjected to any limitations of market share.

One of the cornerstones of any policy to foster media pluralism, as well as cultural diversity, is the creation of a dual broadcasting system. Such a system features a financially viable public service broadcaster with editorial independence and the obligation to produce and broadcast high quality domestic content across a wide range of programme genres. The presence of the public broadcaster provides a measure of structural balance against media concentration within the second pillar of the dual system – the commercial broadcasters.

Economic and social status of artists

Artists and creators are typically self-employed or operate small companies. Their revenues are often sporadic and unreliable. In these circumstances, they find it difficult financially to secure their retirement or ensure proper health protection. A comprehensive cultural policy to foster creative industries must address these destabilising factors.

Granting freelance creative industry workers access to a country's social security system under the same conditions that apply to other self-employed professionals is a good first step. For those with minimal incomes, who find it hard to make the required social security payments, a special fund supplementing the periodic mandatory contributions to the state pension system can be helpful. For example, India has established the Cine Artists Welfare Fund, a charitable trust administered by the government-funded National Film Development Corporation (NFDC). The trust is financed with proceeds of the film *Ghandi* and offers welfare support to elderly film artists through various funding schemes.[2]

Audiovisual content: feature films and television productions

Traditionally, feature films for cinema have been considered the most prestigious and desirable form of audiovisual production from the perspective of artistic achievement, audience appeal, and a country's international reputation and prestige. In designing audiovisual public policies, it is increasingly necessary to think in broader terms of audiovisual content production, not only for cinema, but for television and multimedia as well.

The starting point must be the realisation that today's electronic media landscape is a multiplatform environment in which the economic success of an audiovisual production depends on the exploitation of multiple and distinct audiovisual markets. In the case of feature film, successful marketing starts in the cinema, but then continues down the value chain to DVD and video sales and rentals, and on to pay-per-view, pay-per-channel and free-to-air television distribution. Also, in the near future, online distribution of feature films via cable networks, ADSL telephone lines, and the Internet will provide additional distribution channels.

Policy overview

Public measures to support audiovisual industries begin with the recognition that in most countries, audiovisual productions, standing alone, often are not commercially viable. This can be due to many factors, the most common being the small size of domestic markets; inadequate supply of creative talent with the necessary technical, legal and economic know-how; insufficient training for script writers, producers, directors, camera men, sound engineers and similar experts; underdeveloped or inaccessible distribution and exhibition facilities for domestic content; inadequate private capital; underdeveloped local audiences; paltry export opportunities; or, most likely of all, a combination of some or all of these factors.

National subsidy schemes aimed only at production are an imperfect and incomplete answer to such market deficiencies. Once a film is completed, its producers face the challenge of how to market and distribute it. The Indian government has taken note of the importance of marketing and distribution – in addition to production – a fact that no doubt helps explain the considerable success India has enjoyed in exporting its films, particularly to the Asian and Arabic countries. The government-funded National Film Development Corporation (NFDC) was established as early as 1975 and pursues policies in support of a wide range of activities, including film financing, production and distribution, cinema financing, film export and import, television marketing and technical projects.[3]

Developing countries often face much more fundamental challenges, particularly where no audiovisual industries exist and must, in effect, be created from scratch with little public funding. Such countries are likely to depend on co-operation with other countries, for example through bilateral and multilateral co-production agreements and special support schemes offered by more affluent countries, assistance from international organisations and public–private partnerships on the international level.

Subsidies for audiovisual content creation and distribution

The most successful audiovisual policies comprise a combination of all the elements in the audiovisual production process where weaknesses can be identified. There is no use funding the production of a feature film if the finished work has no distribution outlets. No step that is critical in the overall process should be omitted or overlooked.

Pre-production covers the preparation of the conceptual outline for a project and its initial plans for budgeting, script writing, searching for partners, financing, and marketing and distribution. Many audiovisual policies target this crucial development phase by allocating most or at least a substantial measure of funding to it.

If co-financed[4] projects go into production and achieve a return, the film makers/producers may keep the subsidy but are required to reinvest the amount of their original support in the development of one or more additional production projects.[5]

The Australian Film Commission, for example, offers funding for the development of feature films, documentaries, animation, interactive digital media and television projects.[6] Film foundations with limited resources may elect to concentrate their audiovisual funding support on a few well-defined areas, such as script development or the promotion of young untested talent.[7]

Typically, the conditions for the direct funding of productions are designed to ensure that the local creative industries benefit directly from the public funds. This can be done, for example, by tying the grant to the nationality of the filmmaker, residency or commercial presence in the country or region providing the funding. Alternatively, support may depend on the overall nationalities of the film creators, its cast and/or technical crew.[8]

The UK Film Council, while providing funding to film projects across many genres, also focuses on special sectors. For example, the *Premiere Fund* subsidises only popular genre feature films that are expected to be commercially viable and attract audiences around the world. Its aim is to strengthen the global capacity of the UK film industry and to promote export opportunities.

Support for *post-production* includes funding for subtitling or dubbing, festival presentations, promotional tours of the film director or actors and advertising. These are most often directed to producers. Measures to foster distribution and marketing are typically directed to distributors and exhibitors. They include subsidies for marketing measures as well as for film copies for theatre distribution.

Some audiovisual support schemes address the distribution and marketing of domestic productions across borders. For example, the European *MEDIA* programme provides funding for the screening of non-domestic European films across the EU Member States in order to encourage the exchange of films across European borders. This programme offers financing to sales agents, based on their market performance, in support of wider transnational distribution of European films and further investment in new European films.[9]

Switzerland has taken a step to further the idea of promoting the diversity of audiovisual productions on cinema screens. Diversity of content in cinemas is understood in a truly international sense and is not limited to the promotion of domestic or regional content. Under the Swiss law, distributors and exhibitors are required to co-operate with each other to ensure that in each Swiss region there is a diversity of offerings from a sufficient number of different countries. The films must be in diverse genres and styles, and are allocated based on the number of cinema screens in each region.[10] In the event that the industry fails to implement effective measures, the government may levy a so-called development tax on ticket sales of the movie theatres of a region that fails to achieve the required level of diversity, to help finance new cinemas with more diverse offerings in that region.

Funding for *professional training* must cover the entire range of the creative production process, from scriptwriting, to film direction, camera use, sound engineering, cutting and the use of new technologies. Producers must understand applicable legal requirements, copyright management, financing, marketing and distribution. They also need information on potential niche markets, for example for documentaries or television series, and on potential investors and international co-production partners.

Publicly available *directories and databases* identifying all players in the industry, including potential investors, films produced, holders of copyrights, public support mechanisms, relevant trade shows and festivals, and legal requirements and restrictions are a useful resource for the creative producers about to embark on a project. Increasingly, such databases are available online. A good example is the central Internet portal known as *KORDA*. This database is financed by the Council of Europe[11] and provides comprehensive information about public support mechanisms for audiovisual productions throughout Europe, including those made available by Europe to creators from third countries.

International *film festivals, trade shows and film awards* are a popular means of attracting public attention and large audiences nationally and internationally to domestic and foreign productions. They are also ideal for industry professionals to make valuable contacts with creative talent from other countries, to learn about state-of-the-art film-making techniques and marketing strategies, and to gain access to international distributors. This is why governments regularly make funding available to their filmmakers and industry executives for travel to such events. Festival awards will significantly raise the visibility of a film, its producers, director and actors, and thus boost the prospects of successful marketing.

Funding mechanisms and sources of funding

Film producers usually face a fundamental problem: they cannot offer guarantees to commercial banks in return for a loan, and most financial institutions, unfamiliar with the special requirements of the audiovisual industry, consider loans to production companies to be too risky. Under these circumstances, one of the few ways for filmmakers to raise capital is through public funding schemes designed to foster domestic audiovisual production.

Public loans may be repayable fully or in part depending on the commercial success of a film. They may also carry a requirement that the amount of the loan be matched by the same amount of private investment, or be co-funded in some other proportion with public funding up to 80 per cent or more of production costs. Typically, funding is also conditional on certain criteria involving the language of the film, the shooting location, the use of national technical resources, the payment of the majority of salaries to nationals, the editing and copying locations, the nationality or place of commercial presence of the producer, and the like.

A distinction must be made between project funding and automatic funding. The former is based on an assessment of each individual production project; the latter is an automatic subsidy based on the commercial success of a work, typically the number of theatre tickets sold. Such box office rebates are designed to help already commercially viable production companies grow even further, because the money received is to be invested in the next project.[12] Unlike project financing, artistic standards play no role in automatic funding; it is designed solely as an industrial policy to foster the competitiveness of the domestic audiovisual industry.

Tax incentive schemes are as varied as public loan programmes. Some countries, such as Canada and Australia, offer tax credits. In these cases, the country offers the producer a tax rebate on a percentage of the costs of production. Since this scheme comes into effect only after the money for the production is spent, it may not solve the upfront cash flow problems of the producers, unless they find a bank willing to grant them a credit based on the promise of later tax relief.[13]

Tax allowance systems provide that tax payers may write off the cost of production, or acquisition of a film, or even the taking of shares in a film production company, against their tax liability. These schemes typically attract private investors with large incomes, who have a particular interest in such immediate deductions given the high marginal tax rates they pay. In order for the investor to recoup his money, he is guaranteed licence payments from the distribution of the film over a certain period of time. Typically, such tax allowances are conditioned on nationality requirements of the cast and crew, as well as the location and content of the film.

Another way to raise money for audiovisual production is to *oblige broadcasters* by law to invest in domestic film and television industries. The European directive on *Television without Frontiers* contains a provision under which EU member states may choose to require broadcasters to spend a minimum of 10 per cent of their programming budget on independent European productions. The French Pay TV operator Canal+ is obliged to spend at least 45 per cent of its programming budget on the acquisition of cinematographic works produced in French.

If no public money is available, funding may be raised from *third parties* or from the audiovisual industry itself. In France, for example, a tax is levied on the sale of theatre tickets, and there is an additional special tax on video rentals and television channels.[14] The proceeds are used to provide automatic subsidies for filmmakers.

Since 2003, Mexico has pursued a similar approach by imposing a levy of one peso on each theatre ticket sold. However, this measure has led to the filing of petitions for injunction by distributors, and exhibitors have raised ticket prices by the same one peso amount.[15] Brazil appears to have introduced its new levy on film distributors in 2002 with greater success.[16] The United Kingdom raises money in support of its audiovisual industry from the National Lottery.[17]

Typically, subsidies for the audiovisual sector are administered by film foundations or institutes rather than directly by cultural ministries, which may lack the necessary expertise. For example, France has established the Centre National de la Cinématographie (CNC), which decides how to allocate subsidies for the production, distribution and exhibition of films, as well as television and video productions. The Australian Film Commission, in addition to making funding decisions, also promotes international co-productions and provides a central information resource.[18] India's National Film Development Corporation grants loans and promotes film distribution domestically and abroad.

Content quotas

Content quotas prescribe a certain percentage of local programmes that must be displayed as part of the overall programming of a broadcaster. Such quotas are intended to guarantee access to local content via domestic television channels, thus providing a domestic market for such productions and preventing broadcasters from filling their programme schedules exclusively with foreign content.

The European Union applies a content quota to all broadcasters operating in EU member states. It requires that a majority of all television programmes comprise European audiovisual works. Australia requires its commercial television channels to programme 50 per cent domestic content over the day. Canada has a 60 per cent local content quota for television, while South Africa maintains a content quota system of 30 per cent for terrestrial free-to-air channels, 50 per cent for its public broadcaster, and 5 per cent for terrestrial pay television channels. Malaysia has set a target of 80 per cent local content, and Singapore 55 per cent of the total programme schedule. China's content quota requirement is set at 90 per cent.[19]

Korea has actively implemented a screen quota system for its cinemas since 1993.[20] At that time, the market share of Korean films had shrivelled to 15.9 per cent of domestic cinema audiences. Under the original 1993 scheme, cinemas were required to show Korean movies on 146 days each year. Today, this 40 per cent quota has been effectively reduced to 106 days or 29.4 per cent. Still, the effect has been that in the ten years since 1993, the market share of Korean films has risen to 46.9 per cent.[21] However, Korea is facing strong pressure from the United States in bilateral trade negotiations to abolish the screen quota system on the grounds it is a barrier to market access for Hollywood film studios.[22]

In the debate at UNESCO level about a convention on cultural diversity, there is an increasing awareness that such an instrument, while useful to recognise the legitimacy of cultural policies to foster domestic creation, should also recognise the need to balance these policies with policies of openness to other cultures. Content quotas going well beyond the 50 per cent margin may be considered problematic under the principle of openness and balance foreseen in the

UNESCO draft convention on the protection and promotion of the diversity of cultural expressions. Article 2 para. 8 of the draft text (version 2 June 2005) provides that states that adopt measures to support the diversity of cultural expressions should seek to promote, in an appropriate manner, openness to other cultures of the world. The Chinese content quota of 90 per cent is not only highly questionable from the perspective of cultural diversity, it suggests political censorship.

Developing audiences

Developing countries often suffer from a severe lack of infrastructure for the distribution of cinema films. Under such conditions, television programmes may be the best way to promote local content and cultivate taste for local productions, even though television itself is not always widely available. At the same time, in at least some developing countries, the economic potential exists to create distinct markets for cinema and video distribution.

South Africa, for example, has created video resource centres in rural areas such as Lesotho and Swaziland. Funded by the government, they are used as screening venues in order to familiarise rural audiences with local productions, create demand for such programmes, and educate the people about different styles of storytelling. This strategy is reinforced by using the resource centres as video libraries where videos can be watched and rented. Indeed, video projections in informal settings in rural communities across Africa have given new life to the African film industry, and a new generation of African filmmakers has responded by adapting film-making to the special conditions of the continent. Especially in Nigeria, but also in Ghana, films are made from the outset primarily for video distribution.[23]

Music

With a rich and diverse heritage from which to draw, music is one of the key creative sectors of developing countries with the potential of establishing a thriving industry sector with export possibilities. However, very few musical artists make their way into the international market.[24] Jamaica stands out as an example of a developing country which to some extent has realised its high potential. It enjoys an enormous creative reservoir in the music sector typified by reggae, yet most of the economic and export potential of Jamaica's music sector remains untapped.[25]

Policy overview

Digital technology is radically changing not only the way music is created and produced, but, even more importantly, the manner in which it is distributed. Business via the Internet permits the offer and sale of music without recourse to traditional distribution channels and without the need physically to ship a record or disk to the buyer. Instead, the user can simply download the song directly from the Internet using his personal receiving equipment with MP3 technology.

From the perspective of developing countries, music and e-commerce are the fastest and most efficient means of penetrating global markets.[26] Yet developing countries face a daunting challenge in the context of new technologies. For them, access to the Internet, the necessary infrastructure and the know-how, are still very limited. UNCTAD has already identified many of the policy issues that they must address, including copyright legislation, universal access to the Internet at affordable cost, appropriate payment systems to support credit card transactions, regulations of banking transactions, security and data protection, financial and fiscal policies, contract laws applicable to e-commerce transactions and their enforcement, insurance issues, currency conversions, and the like.[27]

Some essential policies to protect the public interest, for example *must carry* rules – which ensure that certain cultural content is carried on all relevant electronic networks, such as cable networks – may in future need to be extended to dominant Internet portals and search engines. The purpose would be to ensure that users are not only able to access content that is sponsored by the company operating the portal or search engine.

Subsidies

France stands out among European countries for its strong support of the music sector. In addition to music quotas, France actively supports the export of French music through its export office *Bureau Export de la Musique Française*. The office provides information to the French music industry and promotes the participation of French music at international fairs and festivals. With the assistance of an Export Commission composed of professionals of both the music majors and the independent music distributors, it also provides funding for artists and music publishing houses for participation in festivals. The Export Office operates branch offices abroad with the aim of organising local concerts showcasing French musicians and exploring market opportunities for French labels and musical tours. When the Export Office was first created in 1993, French artists sold four million recordings per year abroad. Ten years later, annual sales had reached 34 million recordings.

Developing countries often lack the infrastructure to produce recordings, and CDs in particular. As long as the production facilities needed to produce physical product are located abroad, marketing and sales activities are likely to be based there as well. Consequently, a significant part of the added-value in the chain of production and distribution in the music industry goes to countries with superior production facilities. To address this shortcoming, industrial policy measures, such as facilitating the construction of the necessary production base, are essential.

Governments may also want to fund Internet portals to promote specific domestic content including content in local languages. In Canada, for example, the government of Québec has established such a cultural web-portal in cooperation with the private sector devoted to Canadian film, television and multimedia productions.[28] The site of the Canadian Cultural Catalogue is operated by an independent Québec publisher – an example of a successful public–private partnership. Publicly funded portals already exist in the music sector in countries such as the Netherlands and, more recently, Germany to promote exports.

Subsidies can also include the financing of skills acquisition and training in the music sector should be seen in a broad context, including cultivating business acumen in production and marketing techniques, in addition to transmitting artistic skills. For example, the Jamaican government offers training courses in basic copyright law and its application to the music sector.[29] The Reggae Studies Unit, established as a division of the Institute of Caribbean Studies of the University of the West Indies, may serve as a best practice example in this context. It operates on a multidisciplinary basis and targets such varied subjects as technical studies in music, sound synthesis and reproduction, as well as business, management and legal aspects of the reggae music industry.[30]

Music quotas

Music quotas are designed to promote domestic music. They apply to radio channels in much the same way as audiovisual quotas apply to television. As such they are subject to the same policy reservations as the latter, because they represent an interference with the programming freedom of broadcasters. Tanzania introduced music quotas as early as the mid-1960s. The original proposal for the new law envisioned a total ban of all foreign music on Tanzania's broadcasting channel Radio Tanzania Dar Es Salaam (RTD). Ultimately, it was decided that foreign music would be phased out over a period of time. As a result, foreign music could only be played on the radio at the direct request of a listener, and even then could not exceed 30 per cent of all music played.[31] It is claimed that this policy has had a very beneficial effect on the Tanzanian music sector, because RTD, in order to meet its domestic music quota, had to send staff to the most remote villages to record local music, guaranteeing access of local artists to the airwaves and in turn strengthening the domestic production base.[32] However, such a policy also comes at the expense of freedom of information, freedom of speech, and cultural diversity.

Broadcasting

Policy overview

There are three basic models for broadcasting. The first is the market model. When broadcasting was first introduced in the United States in 1912, the Radio Act treated it as a commercial activity to be financed by advertising. The next broadcasting model to emerge was the state- and party-controlled radio broadcasting system launched in 1917 by Russia's Communist Party and funded by the government. Public service broadcasting as a third model independent of the government and financed by the public through taxes on the sale of radio receivers started in 1922 with the establishment of the British Broadcasting Corporation (BBC). In those days, broadcasting existed only as radio services.

Evidence suggests that a dual broadcasting system in which public and commercial broadcasting coexist and in which their market shares are more or less evenly balanced, will ensure a strong basis for a country's creative audiovisual industries. In the United Kingdom, for example, the public service broadcaster BBC, with some 39 per cent TV market share, commands a strong position, and competition between public service and commercial broadcasting has always been intense. The BBC provides about 40 per cent annually of all UK investment in the domestic television industry. At the same time, the range of television programmes is considered broad and the quality high.

Three key factors contribute to this success.[33] First, market entry of broadcasters is controlled though a licensing system. Second, all broadcasters, both public service and commercial, are specifically required to broadcast a substantial amount of domestic content – although the programming obligations of public service broadcasters are more comprehensive as far as quality and range of programme genres are concerned. Third, because of the large domestic market, both pillars of the dual broadcasting system command large revenues: in the case of commercial broadcasters stemming from advertising and subscription, and in the case of public service broadcasting, largely and typically from a public licence fee paid by viewers and listeners. As the US free-to-air broadcasting market suggests, with four commercial networks and a weak or non-existent public broadcasting system, a model based on commercial broadcasting alone may not be optimal. Such a model tends to force commercial broadcasters to compete with one another to the extent of focusing their programming on a relatively few programme genres with the greatest mass appeal, such as sit-coms and similar entertainment, sports and local news, without regard to diversity, the public interest or, in the final analysis, quality.[34]

The Central and Eastern European countries illustrate yet another approach. Competition in their television markets started with the licensing of commercial broadcasters after the fall of the Berlin Wall. This has not led, however, to more content diversity or higher quality programmes. Commercial broadcasters offered diversion by filling their programming schedules largely with entertainment programmes of US origin. Nor did the former state broadcasters fill the vacuum – they were largely discredited due to their record of having served as propagandists for the status quo over the preceding decades.[35] Because clear, long-term government policies to ensure the availability of quality domestic programming were neglected, television channels tended to adopt simple programme formulas aimed at maximising audience share and little else. They discarded cultural, educational and journalistic programmes in preference to soap operas, often banal feature films, and low cost talk and quiz shows.[36]

Public interest programming obligations

Programming obligations are essential to ensuring that broadcasters fulfil their promise as an engine of domestic creative industries. The United Kingdom government has entered into an agreement with the BBC, requiring it to (i) stimulate, support and reflect, in drama, comedy, music and the visual and performing arts, the diversity of cultural activity in the United Kingdom; (ii) offer comprehensive, authoritative and impartial coverage of news and current affairs in the United Kingdom and throughout the world to support fair and informed debate at local, regional and national levels; (iii) provide wide-ranging coverage of sporting and other leisure events; (iv) offer programmes of an educational nature (including specialist factual, religious and social issues programmes as well as formal educational and vocational training programmes); (v) set a high standard of original programmes for children and young people; and (vi) offer programmes which reflect the lives and concerns of both local and national audiences. In addition, BBC programmes are required to maintain 'high general standards in all respects (and in particular in respect of their content, quality and editorial integrity) and to offer a wide range of subject matter (having regard both to the programmes as a whole and also to the times on which the programmes are shown)'.

The British *Channel 4* presents another interesting case study. It is a publicly owned corporation with far-reaching programming obligations, but is entirely advertising financed. The channel is explicitly prohibited from producing its own programmes and is required to commission or purchase content on the market, particularly from independent producers. Its programme mission requires Channel 4 to demonstrate innovation, experimentation and creativity, appeal to the tastes and interests of a culturally diverse society, and to include programmes of an educational nature.[37]

The bilingual German–French cultural channel *Arte* is another example of a public service broadcaster with a special remit. *Arte* shows how public service broadcasting can be used as a tool to foster the exchange of cultural content between countries and to promote audiovisual productions from one country to another. Developing countries may want to consider how such a model could be adapted to their circumstances, for example in the creation of a multinational television channel with a special remit, such as education or the promotion of local productions. Such a project would be less costly if the channel could broadcast in a common language.

Some developing countries comprise hundreds of different tribes speaking many different languages and dialects. In such circumstances, the challenge is to ensure that broadcasting contributes both to unifying the country while also reflecting its different cultures. The programming remits of public service broadcasters and their organisational structures need to be flexible enough to accommodate such potentially conflicting goals. For example, a national public service broadcaster can be divided into independent regional broadcasters each serving different ethnic groups. At the same time, as in the case of ARD, the German public service broadcasting system, the regional broadcasters can be required to contribute to a national broadcasting channel, be it radio or television, with a view to conveying both the cultural diversity of the country as well as its national identity.

Structuring public service broadcasting

Given the role that public service broadcasting can play to promote cultural diversity, and its potential as a model for developing countries, it is useful to consider how such broadcasters are structured to fulfil their mission. The European Broadcasting Union (EBU), the European association of public service broadcasters, has published a model law for public service broadcasting on its web site.[38] As explained in the model law, the first prerequisite of public service broadcasting is its independence from government. This is best secured by an independent authority overseeing the broadcaster and composed of representatives of a broad range of civil society. Their task is to ensure that the broadcaster meets its programming obligations and is insulated from political interference.

Independence also requires autonomous funding resources, such as licence fees paid by citizens on television and radio receiving equipment, and complemented by advertising and sponsorship revenues. At the same time, over-reliance on advertising revenues is likely to threaten the long-term viability of public service broadcasters.

Another key feature of public service broadcasting is its obligation to reach the entire population in terms of technical availability – the so-called universal service obligation. This is essential because public service broadcasting can only fulfil its integrative, informational and educational functions if all citizens have equal and open access to it, irrespective of their place of residence. At a practical level this tends to mean 'free-to-air' television, and ensuring that signals are transmitted to remote or inaccessible areas.

Community broadcasting

Community broadcasting can be defined as non-profit broadcasting based on citizens' initiative and a focus on local issues. Its strength lies in the production of local news and programmes of general interest to the community it serves. It provides a platform for different voices that would not be heard on commercial and national channels. However, community broadcasters typically operate without any broadcasting licence from the government as so-called pirate stations, making them both vulnerable and often politically suspect to the establishment. Some channels are owned by non-profit groups or by co-operatives whose members are the listeners themselves. They may also be operated by universities, ethnic groups, churches or trade unions. Channels are usually financed by donations from listeners. In some cases, international development agencies and advertisers, or even public authorities, may provide limited funding. Despite chronic lack of financing, their popularity has ensured that, notwithstanding often limited audience reach, they have established themselves in a number of countries as a third pillar of broadcasting, alongside public service and commercial broadcasting.

Community broadcasting has had its greatest success in the developing world. It is widespread in Latin America, and, more recently, has also been introduced in Africa and other parts of the world, such as the Philippines and India. Community radio in Brazil is particularly popular. There exist over 15,000 community radios across the country. Their success began in 1989 when a nationwide civil society movement called for commercial stations to be transformed into community radios featuring local reporting, local artists and local events.[39]

Evidence suggests that community radio may not only be an instrument to promote democratic dialogue, but to reduce poverty. A case study on community radio in Uganda showed that it helped improve agricultural production, increased turnout for immunisation, stimulated higher voter participation in elections, reduced corruption and improved security.[40]

Governments on occasion have embraced initiatives to support community broadcasting. For example, in 2003, the Brazilian government adopted a broadcasting initiative dedicated to the Caiapo Indian tribe in the state of Mato Grosso. For decades, the Caiapos, an indigenous tribe of some 15,000 people, produced their own films of such quality that they won prizes abroad. The government has now agreed to broadcast these programmes on a new channel *Aldeia Virtual* (Virtual Village), initially on the national educational channel *TV Educativa*, and ultimately on a special frequency granted to the Caiapos. The latter move is significant, because in addition to funding shortages, community broadcasters typically suffer from a lack of access to frequencies. The example of the Caiapos Indians shows the extent to which community broadcasting can become a medium to promote the local audiovisual creative sector with the potential of strengthening the cultural identity of different peoples.

New technologies have tremendous potential to enable the proliferation of community radios in developing countries, to provide new means of addressing their special needs, and to reduce both their production as well as their distribution costs.[41] A good example is the interface between the Internet and community radio provided by *Radio Viva Rio* in Rio de Janeiro.[42] From the outset, *Radio Viva Rio* has transmitted programmes via the Internet in order for other community radios to access and retransmit them seamlessly. The idea is to share content and information among community radios with a view to improving the overall quality, geographic scope and diversity of what is offered.[43]

More recent Internet developments, such as podcasting, – the provision of professional as well as private radio programmes for downloading on MP3 players – also have the potential to change significantly the availability of audio and video – programmes to the general public.

The international framework

A number of international strategies are available to policy-makers seeking to promote their domestic creative industries. Two strategies in particular stand out. First, policy-makers can adopt measures directed at strengthening cultural ties between or among countries. Second, they can target support programmes of key international organisations that are active in the cultural field.

Co-production agreements

Co-production agreements between countries ensure the access of each country's filmmakers to the public funds of the other country. Such agreements are designed generally to foster mutual understanding of the respective cultures of the countries involved. But they may also specifically aim at increasing the mutual exchange of audiovisual works with a view to enhancing their international competitiveness. They grant national treatment to filmmakers on a reciprocal basis, thus ensuring they have full access to the national public film funding schemes of each signatory country.

The European Convention on Cinematographic Co-production is an example of a multilateral agreement to enable filmmakers from an entire geographic region, in this case the 45 member states of the Council of Europe, to participate in each others' audiovisual support schemes. In addition, the Council of Europe's *Eurimages Fund* provides financial support to European co-productions and the distribution, broadcasting and exploitation of feature films and television programmes across European borders.[44] The decision to provide aid is based on an assessment of the quality of the work and whether it is likely to reflect and promote the contributions of diverse national aspects of Europe's cultural identity. Funding is available for works of co-producers from at least three of the fund's participating member states.

International and regional support schemes

Developing countries may choose to encourage and engage in international and regional support programmes. For example, through its knowledge portal, UNESCO offers web-based computer music tutorials aimed at fostering innovative uses of digital technology in music.[45] With the participation of the International Radio and Television University (URTI), UNESCO is also implementing the *Screens without Frontiers* project.[46] It is developing a worldwide database of audiovisual programmes in the genres of fiction, documentaries and magazines, for use by public television channels in developing and transitional countries. The project has the twin aims of facilitating the North–South flow of information and encouraging creative industries in the developing world to become producers and distributors of information themselves. It also seeks to improve the quality of cultural and educational public service broadcasting, including the use of new technologies, and to safeguard cultural productions.[47]

The EU makes available grants to directors and producers in the film and television sectors in countries of the African, Caribbean and Pacific (ACP) region which are signatories to the Cotonou Accord of 2000 (formerly the Lomé Convention). The aim is to develop cultural industries and to improve market access for cultural goods and services. Technical assistance for film theatres in ACP countries is also available, as is funding to facilitate access of artists from ACP countries to Europe.[48] It has been reported that the aid is so comprehensive that African film-making is largely financed through this programme.[49] The francophone countries, co-operating through the *Agence Intergouvernmentale de la Francophonie*, have created a guarantee fund for the benefit of cultural industries of the francophone countries of the South.[50]

Another model is provided by the Asia-Pacific Institute for Broadcasting Development (AIBD)[51] based in Kuala Lumpur. It is a regional intergovernmental organisation tasked with assisting its 26 member countries in the Asia-Pacific region to improve the professional capabilities of their broadcasting systems. The Institute offers training courses and seminars for broadcasting personnel from member countries.

Public–private partnerships

Partnerships between government and the private sector can also help developing countries raise the capital necessary to invest in domestic creative industries and gain access to expertise and information. There are numerous well-funded private foundations with cultural agendas, some of them specifically dedicated to assisting the development of the audiovisual sector worldwide. For example, the Thomson Foundation[52] has provided training and development assistance for broadcast media worldwide, with a special emphasis on developing countries. The Friedrich Ebert Foundation[53] has also been advising governments and non-governmental organisations worldwide on, among other matters, strategies to strengthen their public service broadcasting systems and to create networks of media professionals for mutual support. As mentioned above, the Canadian Cultural Catalogue is another example of a public–private partnership. In this case, the Cultural Ministry of Québec co-operates with partners from the film and telecommunications industry as well as from the publishing business to run the cross-referenced database on Canadian films, television and multimedia productions and their creators. Along the same lines, a group of cultural experts advised the South African government as early as 1998 to consider a 'Cultural Industry Development Agency'[54] as a public–private partnership agency tasked with knowledge and information management, human resource management, strategic investment, grant funding and advocacy on behalf of the cultural industry sector.

Investment capital for emerging cultural industries can also be made available by large globally operating private companies. Given the growing importance for companies to demonstrate not only that they respect the law, but that they also embrace principles of 'corporate social responsibility' (CSR), a number of them could be interested in supporting projects to help creative industries in developing countries. Multinational companies frequently assert that they are eager to 'give something back' to the local communities in which they operate. The potential to elevate cultural diversity and support of indigenous cultural industries on the CSR agenda has not been fully explored and its viability remains unclear.

The potential of public–private partnerships is suggested by the *Global Alliance for Cultural Diversity*, a project aimed at connecting people in the private, public and not-for-profit sectors with the goal of fostering economic development in developing countries worldwide. It focuses on knowledge sharing, copyright enforcement, and the development of infrastructure adapted to the needs of cultural enterprises.[55] Launched in January 2002 by UNESCO, the Alliance within two years had 22 pilot projects with funding totalling US$170,000, including corporate contributions. An illustrative project involves a training course for 12 music industry professionals in Africa to prepare their participation in the international music fair MIDEM in Cannes in 2004. The course includes professional skills training in marketing and commercial communications.

This latter example suggests that public–private partnerships may have their limits. To the extent that they key into viable strategic business models for the private partners involved, such as in the case of the Canadian Cultural Catalogue, they may have much greater potential in future. However, where such funding mostly serves as a short-term goodwill gesture with public relations value, its contribution is likely to remain modest and should not be regarded as a substitute for sustained public funding. As a bottom line, private investment is often linked to clearly defined business interests of the sponsors, and indeed may be most effective if it is. Commercial considerations circumscribe the range of public interest activities that corporations are prepared and willing to underwrite. Public–private partnerships may, therefore, supplement government policies and funding in the cultural sector, but cannot replace them.

International trade law

Government strategies to promote domestic creative industries must take account of international trade law – and visa versa. Depending on the extent of a country's trade liberalisation commitments, it has more or less flexibility to choose from the palette of legal instruments available to policy-makers in the cultural sector.

In many cases, the application of WTO legal principles would render cultural policies – in particular policies to foster creative industries in the developing world – flatly illegal and open countries adopting them to claims for compensation. Such risks are hardly theoretical, as the experience of New Zealand demonstrates. In the WTO negotiations on services concluded in 1995, New Zealand agreed to refrain from quantitative restrictions on the import of audiovisual services. A few years later, in 1999, the country's authorities were disturbed to learn that its broadcasting channels transmitted only 24 per cent of local content. They sought to introduce a quota system comparable with those widely employed in Europe and Australia. New Zealand was forced to abandon these plans, however, when the United States Trade Representative made clear it would take the matter to WTO dispute settlement.[56]

The most pertinent WTO rules for the audiovisual sector are those contained in the General Agreement of Trade in Services (GATS). The GATS covers all internationally traded services except those provided in the exercise of governmental authority. Since there is no 'cultural exception' in the GATS, all audiovisual services are covered by it. However, with the exception of the Most Favoured Nation (MFN) clause, the trade liberalising principles of GATS apply only to the extent that a member state has entered into specific commitments.

The potential impact of GATS on cultural policy can best be understood by considering the principle of 'national treatment'. It provides that WTO members must treat the services of foreign suppliers no differently than it treats its own domestic suppliers of those services. Thus, if a country were to commit itself to apply GATS to the audiovisual sector, it would in effect be committing to abandon any cultural policy that favoured its domestic creative industries over their foreign counterparts. It could no longer provide subsidies for the benefit of its domestic film, television or music services, unless it was prepared to grant the same benefits to all their foreign competitors. Nor could it apply domestic content quotas or maintain foreign ownership restrictions.

Meanwhile, more and more bilateral trade and investment agreements also target the audiovisual sector and are setting precedents in international trade law as to the legal treatment of audiovisual services. For example, under the US–Chile Trade Agreement of 2003, Chile has reserved the right to take certain measures in relation to its domestic film industry.[57] But the agreement also subjects all online and Internet services ('digital products') to the full force of trade liberalisation. In contrast, New Zealand's 2001 bilateral trade and investment agreement with Singapore contains a broad cultural exception in favour of the Maori people, an ethnic minority, to the effect that 'nothing in this Agreement shall preclude the adoption by New Zealand of measures it deems necessary to accord more favourable treatment to Maori in respect of matters covered by this Agreement including in fulfilment of its obligations under the Treaty of Waitangi'.[58]

In what may become a model clause for such bilateral trade agreements, the treaty text (Art. 74, para. 2) goes on to provide that 'the Parties agree that the interpretation of the Treaty of Waitangi, including as to the nature of the rights and obligations arising under it, shall not be subject to the dispute settlement provisions of this Agreement'. This clause avoids the risk inherent in all cultural exemption clauses that the scope of the exemption itself is subject to the rules of the agreement. Canada's experience is instructive in this respect. Its measures in support of domestic magazine publications were struck down in two consecutive decisions of a WTO dispute settlement body as violating Canada's free trade obligations under GATT.[59]

This is the background of the mandate given to the UNESCO Secretariat by the 32nd General Assembly in October 2003 to draft an international standard-setting instrument on the protection and promotion of the diversity of cultural expressions. The mandate is based on the 2001 UNESCO Universal Declaration on Cultural Diversity. It states that cultural diversity is as important for mankind as biodiversity is for nature (Art. 1). It also recognises that cultural goods and services are carriers of identity, values and meaning, and therefore must not be treated as if they were no different than other products or consumer goods (Art. 8).

Outlook: the way forward

Cultural policies to foster domestic creative industries cannot be taken in isolation. They must form part of a comprehensive national approach. Apart from a wide range of specific cultural and audiovisual measures, these policies need to cover such broad horizontal issues as freedom of speech, media pluralism, intellectual property rights, access to information and communication infrastructures and international trade law. Where cultural policies are concerned, there are no 'one-size-fits-all' solutions.

Developing countries interested in building and promoting their own domestic creative industries must undertake in-depth analyses of the strengths and weaknesses of their respective domestic cultural sectors. Support for content production alone is not enough for sustained creative industries. Structural support is also needed. All relevant ministries and government departments need to co-operate closely on the national level in the design and implementation of these policies. The private sector should also be consulted and their involvement encouraged. These policies should include artistes, producers, distributors and consumers, but they should also explore the possibilities of public–private partnerships, keeping in mind that their success will probably be a function of their links with the strategic business goals of the private partners involved.

A threshold issue for governments committed to pro-active policies in the cultural field is the collection of essential data and information needed to begin the process of analysing and choosing policies best suited to their particular circumstances. A related issue is securing the necessary support, in terms of best practices, lessons learned from other countries, and funding. Developing countries need not stand alone in facing these challenges. The international community can and should provide valuable assistance in the interest of fostering cultural diversity worldwide.

Finally, increased regional co-operation among developing countries appears to be a promising strategy. Such co-operation enables participating countries to share costs, administrative burdens, expertise and experience. Co-operation can extend to a wide range of activities, including co-production, joint marketing, shared training, databases and research facilities, and collaborative promotional efforts, including trade fairs and festivals. Resource constraints are probably the greatest single challenge that developing countries face in promoting their creative industries. It is common sense to pool such limited resources on a regional scale to leverage the best returns. Equally sensible are measures to foster the exchange of cultural productions across borders within regions.

Notes

1 See Rhonda Griffiths, Protection et promotion de la culture dans le Pacifique, 194 Le Courier ACP-UE, 64 ff. (2002).
2 Cine Artistes Welfare Fund of India (NFDC), at www.nfdcindia.com/cawfi.html.
3 Disinvestment Commission, Report XXI, New Delhi, July 2003.
4 Under a co-financing scheme, several investors join together to finance an audiovisual production.
5 European Commission, Media Programme–development, At europa.eu.int/comm/avpolicy/media/devel_en.html.
6 www.afc.gov.au/funding/fd/default.aspx.
7 In Germany, due to the competence of the individual states (Länder) for audiovisual policies, numerous public support schemes are available at the regional in addition to the national level. In the German states of Berlin and Brandenburg, for example, film categories eligible for this kind of funding comprise not only feature films, animation and documentaries, but also films for children and 'arthouse' films. The public loans for script and project developments usually must be paid back at the start of the production. Medienboard, Vergaberichtlinien für die Filmförderung (2002), at www.filmboard.de/fbb_d.htm.
8 For example, the film foundation of the German state of North Rhine Westphalia requires producers to spend at least one and a half Euro in that state for every Euro of funding they receive. Under these conditions, the film foundation funds not only German productions, but also international feature films which can be expected to be successful with cinema audiences. The film foundation also supports high quality films for television that are produced as international co-productions and are deemed to be in the special interest of North Rhine Westphalia, at Filmstiftung Nordrhein-Westfalen; Produktionsförderung (2004); at www.filmstiftung.de/Foerderungen/Produktion/main_produktion.php.
9 European Commission, Audiovisual Policy, Media (2004), at europa.eu.int/comm/avpolicy/media/distr_en.html
10 See Ivan Bernier, *Chronique 5, For Better Access to the Diversity of Foreign Film Offerings*, 6 (undated), at www.screenquota.org.
11 The Council of Europe comprises 45 member states, ranging from, for example, Albania, Armenia and Azerbaijan to all 27 member states of the European Union, all the way to the Russian Federation, Switzerland, Turkey and the Ukraine.
12 Such box office rebates are used by France and Spain, for example, see Tim Johnson, General Overview, in *The European Film Companies Alliance, Creative Financing For European Films*, 8 (2002).
13 Johnson, ibid. note 56, at 8.
14 Ibid. at 11.
15 European Audiovisual Observatory, Focus 2003, *supra* note, at 16.
16 Ibid.
17 Nesta Creative Investor, Background: Financials (2003), at www.nesta.org.uk/insidenesta/financials.html
18 Australian Film Commission, Afc Profile, Film Development (2004), at www.afc.gov.au/profile/about_us/filmdevelopment.aspx.
19 See overview in The South African Film and Television Industry Report, *supra* note 12, at 33.
20 Coalition for Cultural Diversity in Moving Images, The Screen Quota System in Korea and Cultural Diversity in Moving Images (2003), at www.screenquota.org.

21 Ibid.
22 Ibid.
23 Ledan, *supra* note 49, at 63.
24 Douglas B. Paterson, *Trends in Kenyan Popular Music, The Best Kept Secret in Africa?* (1996), at members.aol.com/dpaterson/trends.htm.
25 UNCTAD, *Electronic Commerce and Music Business Development in Jamaica: A Portal to the New Economy?*, 13 (2002); Zeljka Kozul-Wright and Lloyd Stanbury, *Becoming a Globally Competitive Player: The Case of the Music Industry in Jamaica, 138 UNCTAD Discussion Papers*, 16ff. (1998).
26 UNCTAD, *Electronic Commerce*, *supra* note 79, at 4.
27 Ibid. at 8–9.
28 Catalogue Culturel Canadien (2003), at www.catalogueculturelcanadien.com/index.4d.
29 Ibid. at 14.
30 Ibid. at 19.
31 Don Moore, Reaching the Villages: Radio in Tanzania, *The Journal of the North American Shortwave Association* (1996), at www.swl.net/patepluma/genboard/tanzania.html.
32 Ibid.
33 Ibid. at 5.
34 Ibid. at 12.
35 Youri Khiltchevski, *The Situation in Eastern and Central Europe*, *in* UNESCO, Public Service Broadcasting, *supra* note 113, at 132.
36 Ibid. at 131 f.
37 Channel 4 Programme Policy 2003, at www.channel4.com/about_c4/programme_policy_2003/policy_licence.html.
38 European Broadcasting Union, *Model Public Service Broadcasting Law, Handbook*, rev. edition (2003), at www.ebu.ch.
39 Bernardo Sorj, brazil@digitaldivide.com – Confronting Inequality in the Information Society, 124 (2003).
40 Richard Gerster and Sonja Zimmermann, *Information and Communication Technologies (Icts) and Poverty Reduction in Sub-Saharan Africa, a Learning Study (Synthesis)*, Building Digital Opportunities (Bdo) Programme 2003, 68 (2003).
41 Ibid.
42 RádioViva Rio, at www.radiovivario.com.br/site1/frame.asp; See also www.favelatemmemoria.com.br.
43 SORJ, *supra* note 128, at 124–125.
44 Council of Europe, Eurimages Europa Support Fund, at www.coe.int/T/E/Cultural_Co-operation/Eurimages.
45 UNESCO, Culture, at portal.unesco.org/culture/en/
46 UNESCO, Screens Without Frontiers, About SWF (2004), at webworld.unesco.org/screens/html/about.html
47 This latter goal is also being pursued by UNESCO's pending project to prepare a *List of Representative Works of World Cinema*: UNESCO, CICT, IFTC, List of Representative Works of World Cinema (2004), at www.unesco.org/iftc/r_files/r_lists.htm
48 For more details see, Korda Database on public funding for the film and audiovisual sector in Europe (2004), at korda.obs.coe.int/web/en.
49 Zeljka Kozul-Wright, From Culture to Cultural Industries – Policy Challenges for Cultural Industries in Developing Countries, in *Culturelink*, Special issue, 141, 147–148 (2002/2003).
50 Secrétariat International du Forum Francophone des Affaires, Les Industries culturelles, 19 Fiches Techniques (undated).
51 www.aibd.org.my/profile.htm.

52 www.thomsonfoundation.co.uk.
53 fesportal.fes.de.
54 The Cultural Strategy Group, Creative South Africa, *A Strategy for Realising the Potential of the Cultural Industries*, A Report to the Department of Arts, Culture, Science and Technology, November 1998, p. 5 at: www.dac.gov.za/reports/creative_SA_report/csa1.doc
55 UNESCO, Culture (2004), at portal.unesco.org/culture/en/
56 Ivan Bernier, *Developing Countries and the Plan for an International Convention on Cultural Diversity, Chronique 4*, 8–9 (undated) with further references, at www.screenquota.org/epage/default.asp.
57 United States–Chile Free Trade Agreement, signed 6 June 2003, at www.ustr.gov/new/fta.Chile/final/index.htm.
58 Text made available to the author by courtesy of Professor Jane Kelsey, University of Auckland, NZ, Faculty of Law.
59 Appellate Body Report, Canada – *Certain Measures Concerning Periodicals*, 30 June 1997, WT/DS31/AB/R.

11 Targeting creativity through the intermediary

Regional and local approaches in the UK and beyond

Tom Fleming

Introduction

> The real assets of the modern economy come out of our heads, not out of the ground: imagination, knowledge, skills, talent and credibility.
>
> (Leadbeater and Oakley 1999)

> These are industries that have always lived by their wits and by their inventiveness.
>
> (DCMS 2002, p. 10)

High stakes and high expectations

The last decade has seen the rapid rise of the *cultural and creative industries*[1] in the UK and other parts of the northern hemisphere:[2] as a recognised major growth sector with enormous significance for employment, productivity and the balance of trade (DCMS 1998, 2001; GLA 2002); as a construct for redefining and re-visioning places and even nations (Pine and Gilmore 1998); as a progressive sector with huge scope for advancing social agendas (UK Social Exclusion Unit 1999); and as a tool for regeneration and renewal, where 'creative places' are the most successful in attracting and retaining highly skilled, ambitious and entrepreneurial workers (Landry and Bianchini 1995; Verwijnen, 1999). This embrace with the 'creativity agenda' is thus in part a direct response to economic development opportunities, configured through interventions that focus on supporting businesses to maximise their growth potential; and in part a recognition of the broader value of creativity (or at least the perception and presentation of creativity), where palpably 'creative places' are more likely to be inclusive, innovative, forward-thinking and thus attractive locations in which to invest, live and work (Landry 2000; Florida 2002; Pratt 2002).

Over the past 20 years, the disappearance of local manufacturing industries, periodic crises in government and finance, and an increasing realisation that the convergence of technology and content provide high growth and distinctively competitive market positions, have made culture and creativity an increasingly key focus for UK and other northern hemisphere regions and cities. They are seen as providing the leading edge for national tourist industries; as offering a 'creative brand' to attract inward investment; and as providing new skills and identities that are hoped will bring with them a unique, competitive edge (Zukin 1995; Boyle 1997; Evans and Foord 2000). This creative focus accelerated during the 1990s, and terms such as the 'network society', 'experience economy', 'creative cities' and 'globalisation' were used to define the new modes of production and consumption within the 'new economy' (Kelly, 1998; Saxenian 2000; Yusef and Nabeshima 2003). A new emphasis was put on the interplay between the economy and culture, as well as on creating cross-overs between the generation of new content and new media technologies (Amin and Thrift, 1994; CIM 2004). The outcome for urban and some rural policies was that, rather than selling just goods or services, even very small places have the potential to mobilise cultural tourism, a diverse retail offer, distinctive architecture and new synergies in cultural and creative production and consumption. Small-scale, independent creative businesses and practitioners can lead the way in building a strong 'creative economy' and transforming the image, confidence and experience of places that might otherwise be languishing at the margins of global flows (Crewe and Forster 1993; O'Connor and Wynne 1996).

This broad conceptual and practical engagement with what might be termed a 'creativity agenda' was given a high profile and strategic legitimacy in the UK by the new Labour Government in 1998 – less than a year after coming to power. The government effectively raised the stakes by seeking to measure directly the size and economic impact of a newly defined complex of creative activities or 'sub-sectors': the creative industries sector. The significance (both real and potential) of the creative industries was heralded in 1998 by the Government's Department of Culture, Media and Sport (DCMS) through the publication of a high-profile Creative Industries Mapping Document, which provided estimations of the size and growth potential of the sector and its sub-sectors. This was accompanied by the launch of the specialist Creative Industries Task Force,[3] and an ongoing panoply of national initiatives that have focused most intensively on advancing intelligence and sector mapping tools,[4] promoting the nation's creative identity,[5] targeting ideas generation and innovation,[6] resourcing specialist sub-sector development programmes,[7] and advocating to other government departments – notably the Department of Trade and Industry – the significance of the sector and thus the need to develop specialist interventions to maximise its potential.

However, it is on a regional and local level (using national policy to legitimise intervention) that the creative industries has been prioritised most emphatically as a 'key driver' in the economic, social and definitional transformation of specific spaces and places. The DCMS – through its mapping and advocacy approach – helped to inform a wider audience of policy-makers of the significance, value and potential of the sector. In response, regional and local level decision-makers have been keen to attract creative industries activity and to add value to existing creative assets. Newly established English Regional Development Agencies (RDAs) offered for the first time clearly accessible resources for economic development that could be drawn-down with a level of regional autonomy. This allowed for the introduction of dedicated regional and local mapping studies to test the size and potential of the sector; followed by multiple initiatives determined to maximise the potential of a sector that offers employment opportunities alongside innovative approaches to physical gentrification; and new identities alongside alternative ways of (re)imagining places after decades of economic restructuring and cultural change (Comedia 1992; Scott 1997). Today, in the UK and much further a field, many regions and places are re-focusing their economic development policies through a 'creativity lens', many of which are directly embracing creative industries development programmes (Evans 2001; Ash 2003; Hesmondhalgh 2002), often through innovative approaches.

Limitations and doubts

However, though the importance of creativity as a generator of prosperity is acknowledged at the heart of government, across many areas of regional and local government, and increasingly by vital partners such as in the education sector, the growth potential of parts of the creative industries sector is being questioned by some private and public sector interests, with cross-sub-sector approaches to sector development seen by some as lacking in sophistication given the uneven growth patterns of different parts of the sector. For example, it is argued that intervention to support high-growth digital-content industries should differ from approaches to support more traditional and lower-growth visual arts activity (FSE 2005), though it is acknowledged that relationships do exist between these 'creative disciplines'. The essential limitations of the creative industries, as a policy construct, are being uncovered.

Moreover, some policy-makers and analysts rightfully question how intervention can simultaneously satisfy social, growth and cultural agendas, and point to the need for a clear rationale for each intervention, with interventions positioned to complement each other within a broader strategy capable of traversing different policy areas. For example, the RDAs in England[8] have commonly adopted 'catch-all' approaches that seek to maximise the potential of the creative industries across a range of strategic agenda – such as 'social inclusion', cultural tourism, regeneration and economic development. Such differing agendas require in most cases divergent approaches to support and development. This makes coherent and effective delivery through catch-all approaches a very difficult task, which in turn affects the quality and impact of intervention.

Others question the extent to which the creative industries differs substantially from other sectors and thus contest its 'special case' status (CFNW 2004; NESTA 2004). This is of importance, because issues that are often cited as specific to the Creative Industries sector – such as low level business skills or a lack of capital and barriers to accessing finance – are common to the small business sector as a whole.[9] Undoubtedly, many areas of the sector are distinctive and at variance with other sectors, but it is important that points of convergence are noted alongside points of divergence if intervention is to avoid an overplaying of the 'exceptionalism' of the creative industries (NESTA 2005).

Creative intermediaries and lessons of best practice

This chapter is therefore timely because the last ten years can be seen as an experimentation phase in creative industries intervention, with a myriad of differently targeted and mixed approaches introduced and variously reformed, refocused and adapted or rendered unworkable. This chapter provides a short review of good practice approaches to creative industries policy and intervention in the UK, focusing on the significance of specialist intermediaries advancing support across two *main agenda areas*: clusters/property development and business support (common intervention themes in the UK). Examples of innovative and effective intervention are given, culminating in an emphasis of the crucial significance of connecting intervention themes and ensuring that catch-all 'single instrument' intervention is avoided.

Here, the establishment of a *coherent landscape of intervention* is key: linking agendas and different parts of the sector to support a complex local, regional or national *creative ecology*: where value chains are efficient, interactive and allow for multiple processes of innovation across different creative activities; where new talent and ideas are given the space to grow and cross-fertilise; and where places and communities are able to support this transforming sector and in turn be transformed by it.

The role of the *creative intermediary* is vital: coordinating differently targeted intervention to ensure a clear and coherent landscape of provision is assembled, building relationships with the sector to ensure intervention flexibly embraces sectoral change, and advocating to policy-makers required new approaches capable of enhancing sector development. A creative intermediary operates, variously, as a gatekeeper (an access point offering generic and specialist support and advice); a broker (between practitioners and providers as a kind of 'dating agent'); an information resource (providing access to knowledge concerning education and training opportunities, employment initiatives and market opportunities); an initiator (calling for gaps in existing support to be filled and defects in provision to be eradicated); a provider of business support (offering planning advice and signposting); and an advocate (operating as a voice for the diverse activities, networks and enterprises of the creative sector in the locality and beyond) (Fleming 2004).

Creative intermediary models offer a way of connecting grassroots activity to high growth business agendas, of raising the profile of the potential benefits of creative activity to audiences that range from marginalised youth to corporate venture capitalists, and of checking interventions for their effectiveness as tested against their rationale. The creative intermediary maintains and navigates through the creative industries support landscape and works to ensure that it contributes effectively to a broader ecology.

Correspondingly, the chapter concludes by showing how creative intermediaries can lead processes of creative change in developing economies – building a creative ecology – while warning of the limitations of their role and impact. In contexts where resources are particularly limited and where sector intelligence/information is underdeveloped, the role of specialist intermediaries in representing the sector, encouraging partners to support its development needs, and constantly learning more about the sector (such as through mapping exercises) and projecting this knowledge to lever resources and support, is the most vital in creative industries development. Indeed, it represents a strategic priority (and a relatively low cost first-stage intervention) if aspirations for a successful creative economy are to be productively pursued. In developing contexts, intermediaries are likely to emerge from education institutions, economic development non-governmental organisations (NGOs), even government: key is their capacity to move freely and flexibly to uncover opportunities and build partnerships to pursue those opportunities. This introduces the critical sequencing approaches that can be adopted in developing contexts by key institutions to support the development of intermediary-led creative industries intervention.

Creative clusters and the role of creative intermediaries

> (T)he conscious creation or nourishment of cultural sites, clusters or 'milieus', is rapidly becoming something of an archetypal cultural planning instrument in the cultural planning tool box.
>
> (Mommaas 2004)

Creative businesses and practitioners like to cluster. They are knowledge-reliant, gaining their strength (often their intellectual property) through creative and practical exchange with other creatives; and enhancing their visibility, voice and spending power by collectivising – towards the costs of workspace, for showcasing and events (such as 'open studios'), to share a range of platforms, and to make the case for support (Jayne and Bell 2004). The need to cluster, and the need to cluster *affordably*, has contributed to the transformation of the urban landscape in many towns and cities in the UK and beyond, with creatives often acting as the 'pioneers', developing clusters of activity in old industrial (or other) buildings, attracted by the affordability, flexibility and ambiance of these 'unlikely' locations.

Historically, visionary property developers and land-lords have responded to (and in many cases driven) the demand for proximity and affordability by creatives – at first through the provision of affordable studio complexes for artists (capitalising innovatively in disused, under-used, even condemned space); and more recently through the provision of studios and managed workspaces developed with the specific space and support needs of the local sector in mind (such the increasing need for high bandwidth provision, specialist training and business support, or differently layered renting systems to encourage growth through laddered approaches to affordability that encourage different types of creative activity to congregate).[10] Companies such as ACME and ACAVA in London, Wasps in Scotland and Urban Splash in Manchester are employing diverse models of public/private sector partnership to develop properties concentrated with creative industries activity. Such companies – *creative property intermediaries* – are increasingly recognised as supporting agents of both the creative economy and the beneficiaries of a strong local creative industries sector – local communities, businesses and (if managed appropriately) those seeking to invest in an area: the private developers and the public sector managers of space.

What is clear is that studio complexes, creative managed workspaces, formal and informal physical clusters of creative practitioners and businesses, can lead the transformation of an area, giving it credibility, a new sense of life, by creatively utilising the spaces others – uncreatively – have left behind. Developers are moving ever deeper into the slipstream of creatives, recognising areas that creatives invest in as having commercial development potential. This presents a significant challenge, with the familiar pattern of creative practitioners and businesses being displaced by property prices inflated by the very presence of creatives a common concern. However, new approaches to planning are being developed that recognise the need for depth and breadth in the urban landscape, and that the increased sustainability and long-term vivacity of communities is often dependent upon the presence of creative businesses and practitioners.

In addition to the impact of the creative industries sector on re-utilising buildings or in some rare cases levering the development of new buildings,[11] the sector is now widely acknowledged as making a significant contribution to the regeneration of the physical environment through design quality and innovative approaches to planning and visioning where creative production and consumption activities offer depth and breadth to a landscape and milieu. In the UK, national and regional government has responded accordingly, with an emphasis on promoting or securing the development of creative industries workspace, showcase space and consumption space. For example, the UK Government's Urban and Rural White Papers[12] reflect on the work of Sir Richard Roger's Urban Task Force,[13] in which '*getting the design and quality of the urban fabric right*', is one of the four key steps to Urban Renaissance. Oxford Brookes review for DTLR[14] and the Bartlett's Study for CABE '*The Value of Urban Design*' establish the economic linkages in this context.

At a regional level, different RDAs are responding to this agenda. For example, the East of England Development Agency's (EEDA) commitment is reflected in its Urban Renaissance Strategy in which 'Good Design and Planning' is one of the six strategic objectives, with an emphasis on a mix of creative-led production and consumption spaces a key aim.[15] The London Development Agency, through its Creative London[16] Programme places securing accessible and affordable property as a prerequisite for a sustainable Creative Industries sector. This is based on a recognition that many creative businesses are relatively small and thus unable to pay the high property costs that in many cases have increased because of the inflationary influence of creative businesses on an otherwise 'unlikely' area. Securing property is the only guaranteed way of sustaining creative activity and avoiding the disruption and ultimate decimation of the sensitive creative ecology due to the displacing influence of incoming businesses capable of paying much more for property.

Led by creative intermediaries determined to stimulate creative activity in an area and then protect that activity, the public and private sector are ensuring that intensive processes of creative industries property development are at play in UK and other Northern hemisphere cities, attaching 'old' places[17] with new meanings, often going as far as to allocate (often falsely) an area or development with 'cultural quarter' status. They achieve this by utilising the opportunities provided by diverse, unconventional and relatively affordable building stock; and levering new opportunities offered by public and private finance to position buildings and clusters of buildings as central or relevant to evolving 'discourses of the city' (from publicity information to multiple senses of place) and to the physical core of the city (disconnection and isolation are not desirable if a cultural quarter is to 'succeed' and grow) (see Boyle 1993, 1997; Gomez 1998).

Some initiatives attend to the multidimensional, place-specific, yet trans-local focus of the creative industries sector to establish dynamic, sustainable, business-focused environments that offer development opportunities for the sector in ways that enhance the comparative advantage of the entire city. These include incubation initiatives (often in partnership with Higher Education institutions), where there is a real commitment to connecting very specialised support services (such as seed-funding for creative prototypes and intensive market development advice). At present, the most interconnected and value-adding physical developments that contain creative industries activity are those incubation spaces which genuinely connect learning and skills spaces to commercial and community spaces, allowing ideas and intelligence to flow, aspiration to be matched with opportunities and ideas to be met with investment.

A concentration of creative industries activity provides excellent opportunities to introduce network-based specialist support initiatives – from specialist seminars to showcase events, value-chain projects (connecting complementary businesses to each other) to investment programmes. This is most often led by intermediaries – often the same intermediaries who supported and levered support for the concentration of creative activity in the first place. Spatial concentration allows for efficient delivery and for a 'critical mass' of support services and business development opportunities to be introduced. For example – Kulturo in Turku, Finland – shows how the provision of affordable, flexible workspace is used to provide the basic infrastructure into which a range of specialist, growth-orientated support services are introduced, leading ultimately to the leverage of private sector investment in creative businesses 'incubated' through the process.

Kulturo is the creative industries incubation, investment readiness and investment vehicle of the Turku Science Park in South-West Finland. The Science Park offers over 200,000 square metres of space and specialist services for graduates from the three local universities – University of Turku, Åbo Akademi

University and Turku School of Economics and Business Administration. Creative graduates are signposted to Kulturo, which has been given 'Centre of Expertise' status by the Finnish Government, which provides it with additional resources and, significantly, a type of 'quality kite mark'. It operates as a not-for-profit limited company, with 96 per cent owned by the City of Turku and 4 per cent by the private sector. The Kulturo approach is to establish a comprehensive pre-investment to high growth investment support and development service to creative businesses, combining specialist support, advice, investment and workspace. This is conceptualised in terms of *a 'development tube'*, cradling a start-up business until it has the capacity and commercial partners to 'go it alone'.

The Kulturo Creative Development Tube (Figure 11.1) offers a coherent, dedicated, specialist approach to specialist support, seed investment, investment readiness and the leverage of investment for high growth creative companies. Although the Finnish context is very different from many others, including the UK, it is the extent of partnership and 'joined-up' development intervention (from the national to the local) that shows what can be achieved in other locations that have some resources for specialist sector support and a relatively healthy private investment market. Key to the success of this model is the provision of a broad *landscape* of support – allowing creative businesses to explore a range of development opportunities, providing connection to non-sector-specific intervention, and connecting through network initiatives different parts of the creative industries value chain (such as artists to animators, and animators to technology providers).

It is clear that securing property in which small and emergent creative businesses can grow is vital to ensure creative industries activity can prosper and grow in a location where – it is hoped – a successful economy will drive property prices upwards. It is equally important that the presence of concentrated creative industries activity is supported in ways that maximise its growth potential and ensure that it 'adds value' for the city or region across a range of agendas. For example, a concentration of creative industries activity can significantly enhance the image of a district or a city, providing it with a new energy as a distinctive 'creative sense of place' (Evans 2004).

However, it is important that it is not marketed in a way that proclaims an identity for the sector that is not shared by the businesses in the sector: too often, authorities overplay the significance of a concentration of activity and brand it as something unrecognisable to the businesses. Too many small-scale creative property/clustering initiatives are overplayed and oversold. Rather than becoming the first stage in a long-term strategy to secure a greater density of creative industries activity – towards a critical mass of interconnected activity as a *creative ecology* – they become the playthings of overly avaricious civic boosterism initiatives, heralded as 'quarters' before they are more than an assemblage of workspaces or buildings. City planners and marketers need to take care when promoting their emergent creative industries assets: to promote these assets as markers of identity for the district or city risks antagonising the creative practitioners upon which the success of the scheme depends.

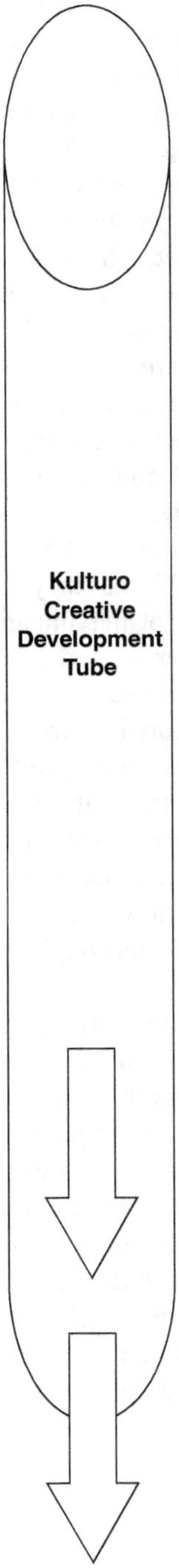

1. Pre-start-up specialised creative industries business advice, focusing on 40–60 businesses per year. This includes advice on recognising the commercial value of a company. Three specialist consultants undertake this role.

2. Funding is secured through Tekes – the main public funding organisation for research and development in Finland. A maximum of 10,000 euro per business can be used to undertake a business development diagnostic and formulate a provisional version of the business plan.

3. 'Liksa' funding is provided for next-stage business plan development (a maximum of 43,000 euro per business) This is provided by Sitra (Finnish National Fund for Research and Development), the main provider of public sector investment into independent creative companies in Finland (providing a comparable function to NESTA), with Tekes. The main function of this business plan is to develop an approach that is likely to appear attractive to the next-stage equality investors. Support may be provided here by a 'DIILI' consultant – who provides support and advice through the form of sweat equity as a 'knowledge capital investment' (paid for by Sitra). This introduces an expanded team with significantly greater chance of attracting investment.

By approving and receiving LIKSA funding, the recipient grants Sitra the right to engage in negotiations regarding an optional venture capital investment in a limited liability company utilising the business idea, entitling to a share of ownership subject to separate agreement. The crucial objective of LIKSA funding is to accelerate the enterprise's eligibility for capital financing in the start-up phase.

4. Incubation provision: facilities, ongoing consulting services and continued investment is levered-in by Kulturo to a total of 45% business costs for Year 1 (to include salaries and expenses). Incubation facilities are offered for 3–4 years, taking businesses over the 'death valley' of Years 1–2. Additional network support is provided (such as with co-locating businesses and locally based technology companies, including Nokia). This incubation 'cradle' for creatives increases investor confidence; 90% attract investment and continue to grow.

5. Business accelerator services, with leverage of next-stage investment vital. Services such as the SITRA-managed 'Intro' are available here, offering a mix of brokerage and introductory services as a specialist approach to investment readiness. Intro also provides an investment screening process to ensure deal flow is rapid. Additional public sector investment is also available at this stage, including low interest loans from Finnerva, and project funding from Tekes.

Webography:
Tekes: www.tekes.fi
Sitra: www.sitra.fi

Figure 11.1 The Kulturo Creative Development Tube.

Key here is working with the creatives (practitioners, businesses, etc.) and their intermediaries (these can be the same people), to ensure that a development is promoted to complementary creative businesses (establishing operable value chains), and that the identities promoted to wider audiences (such as to cultural tourists, inward investors, competitor cities, etc.) do not damage the identities being projected by tenant creative businesses. This is because creative businesses deal in meaning-laden goods where the 'meaning' of the product or idea is as informed by the cultural currency of where it is produced (the type of development, the district, the city, how it is marketed), just as much as it is by other determinants of taste – such as quality and the community in which it is consumed (Bourdieu 1984; Crewe 1996). To promote a creative industries workspace or district inappropriately could threaten the success of a product and therefore business. The work of creative intermediaries is therefore crucial: working for creative businesses to ensure they are positioned and presented appropriately within discourses of the development, district or city.

In some cases it might be argued that the public sector is trying too hard to identify concentrations of creative industries activity or 'clusters',[18] that they are being overly instructive in trying to create them, that they are not maximising the potential of the cluster as a prominent feature within a broader support landscape, or that they are ignoring the ways clusters might cross-over regional boundaries.[19] This has implications for creative industries support in terms of rationale, strategic position and anticipated impact. Likewise, too often private developers overplay the significance of creative activity to maximise its influence on the brand of a development. Examples of good practice – such as a managed workspace initiative or a new 'cultural quarter' – are too often operating 'out of position' (they may be isolated from or in competition with other intervention), are frequently piecemeal in their delivery function, and might be more effective operating across regional or sectoral boundaries.

Where they work most effectively – such as the Media Centre in Huddersfield, the Chocolate Factory in north London, the Custard Factory in Birmingham or the Broadway in Nottingham – they are embedded within a broader landscape of support and city discourses, and public and private sector partners are working together in ways that complement their strengths. Successful developments are locked into flows and networks facilitated by skilful intermediaries working to build complementary goals between businesses 'on the ground' and public and private institutions with the power to support the appropriate growth of the creative industries sector. This is because intermediaries are working to ensure creative clusters or places are conveyed appropriately, and that the maximum value of the cluster is extracted through the targeted and efficient allocation of specialist business support services and investment.

Specialist business support and cultural intermediaries

The provision of specialist business support – such as advice services, network development and showcasing – is the most frequently requested intervention for the creative industries in the UK and most of the northern hemisphere. The allocation of resources for specialist support is predicated on an assumption that the sector is an 'exceptional case' that differs sufficiently from other sectors and/or is of such importance that it requires specialist attention if it is to reach its growth potential and provide maximum positive externalities (Pratt 2004a). Crucially, it is the creative intermediaries – such as specialist development agencies, accountants or dedicated officers in local and regional authorities – that lead the coordination and development of specialist approaches to sector support.

Yet, the degree to which the creative industries might be considered 'exceptional' is contested by policy-makers, businesses in other sectors and in many cases the creative businesses themselves. This is because many creative businesses share characteristics common to other (mostly small) businesses, in particular those fleet-of-foot 'gazelles' that populate burgeoning technology sectors and the wider knowledge economy (Crone 2004). These include having a project-to-project existence, low levels of capital assets, a weak awareness of markets and low-level business planning skills. In addition, some creative businesses argue that by making a special case of the sector, investors (such as banks and business angels) are dissuaded from investing in a sector towards which they may already hold reservations – such as a sense that the sector is too closely connected to the 'arts subsidy system' and therefore not a true commercial proposition. This is especially the case for 'specialist support services' that attempt to juggle the agendas of high growth creative businesses with low growth sole traders through exactly the same support instrument.

However, despite the loose configuration of activities that make up the creative industries, despite overlaps with other sectors and despite the dangers of overemphasising its distinctiveness, there is a strong case to be made that enforces the true exceptionalism of the creative industries and thus the rationale for specialist sector support. The exceptionalism of the sector lies in both its practice/structure (i.e. how it operates) and how it is perceived (i.e. how perceptions of the sector affect its growth opportunities despite the reality of the practice/structure). In this sense, a creative business with excellent management systems and huge market potential may not reach its potential because it is viewed negatively (for example, it may be viewed as 'high risk') by support agents, investors and markets. Correspondingly, a creative business may have huge potential due to the high quality and originality of its creative ideas, but it does not have the expertise, infrastructure, networks, capital, and so on, to maximise this potential.

NESTA (2005) gauge that 80 per cent of a typical small and developing creative industries business shares exactly the characteristics of a small and developing business from another parallel sector (such as in technology). This leaves 20 per cent of a creative business that can be viewed as distinctive and thus requiring specialist support. This 20 per cent can be reduced to three main areas:

1 Many creative businesses are content producers. Newly created content might not have an obvious market or route to market; it may be difficult and

expensive to evaluate and protect; and opportunities to translate it into scalable business development opportunities might be very time-limited yet – if 'timed-right' – it can be hugely rewarding. Specialist approaches might therefore be required to locate the value of content in a creative business, build distribution platforms and markets, and allow for flexible responses to market opportunities.

2 Many creative businesses maintain approaches to 'doing business' that rely on creative passion, lifestyle aspirations and thus value systems that may place creativity ahead of entrepreneurialism (O'Connor and Wynne 1996; Leadbeater and Oakley 1999). This is in part a legacy of the under-provision of business development support in education institutions and in part due to a dependence for many creatives on the subsidised arts funding system. Many creative businesses are thus inappropriately geared and focused to build businesses with growth potential. They therefore require targeted, intensive support services to break down some of the cultural barriers to growth – such as a focus on 'extracting value' through specialist support in identifying, protecting and then selling intellectual property rights (IPR).

3 Creative businesses are 'value-adders': adding value to a wide variety of down-stream users. These include other businesses (improved design, enhanced brands, content to 'fill' new technology platforms), places (creative cities, regions and nations are more competitive, attract more tourists, have stronger identities) and people (creative communities are more inclusive, confident and innovative). The sector is thus 'deserving' of special attention because it is a growth sector in its own right and it is a value-adding sector across other sectors and strategic agendas.

Correspondingly, across the UK and beyond a range of specialist support services have been established to attend to the exceptionalism in profile and potential of the creative industries. These include the following.

Specialist business advice

This is a response to the widely accepted shortcomings in business and management skills in creative businesses – especially small-scale and early stage businesses. Interventions include advice surgeries on market development (including exporting), on securing intellectual property rights and maximising their value, or on the rudiments of business planning (which has historically been neglected by education institutions specialising in creativity, though this is changing). The UK and beyond is peppered with specialist creative industries advice services – some delivered through mainstream cross-sectoral business advice providers,[20] some through free-standing schemes initiated by regional or local authorities and then contracted out to bidding agencies,[21] and others through specialist sub-sectoral schemes such as those focusing on skills development delivered by the UK sector Skills Councils[22] or by local bodies such as Creative Skills in Cornwall.[23] Such schemes and interventions rely on high quality networks to ensure they reach target businesses and to guarantee that they are connected to complementary support services (which may be delivered locally, regionally or nationally). However, they too often operate in isolation, responding to a specific business support need, but lacking the flexibility to change to new needs or the connectivity to ensure they are operating within a broader landscape that, overall, provides a coherent and comprehensive package of support. In short, creative intermediaries are often underused, their potential for connecting complementary services and facilitating networks overlooked.

Facilitating networks, identifying value chains and showcasing services

The creative industries sector is dependent upon and re-articulated through networks (see for example Crewe 1996; Purvis 1996). It is a sector that flourishes through connectivity, whether formal or informal. This is because at a local level it is a sector made up of many individual sole traders, small companies and organisations, and larger companies dependent upon smaller companies through creative value-chain relationships. The sole traders and smaller companies rely on each other to enhance their visibility and voice, to share knowledge and thus improve competitiveness, to develop partnerships for the pursuit of specific creative projects/products, to raise their profile en masse and to improve confidence by reducing isolation. The larger (often non-creative industries) companies rely on the sole traders and smaller companies for specific creative services (an increasingly common requirement with the growing appreciation of creativity-led products and services, and the severance of in-house creative teams), and for enhancing the locality in which they are based (such as through out-of-office services and the 'ambiance' they bring) (Pratt 2004a).

In addition, the creative industries sector is founded on often jarring processes of risk and trust. It is a sector familiar with the notion of 'risk' (Raffo *et al.* 1999) because the development of an idea into a product or service is inherently a risky proposition. Yet exercised risks are too often extended into business strategies, partnership arrangements and non-contractual relationships. The informal, often social-driven networks that are so important for the knowledge systems of the creative industries sector are carried into transactions and deals. The provision of suitable networks and assistance in navigating those networks can therefore play a crucial role in diminishing senses of risk by allowing businesses to test propositions through the dynamics of creative exchange.

Correspondingly, the public sector in the UK and elsewhere has been very active in facilitating networks – from informally connecting creative practitioners to one another, to more instructive network initiatives such as 'creative industries databases', face-to-face networks, web portals, creative chambers of commerce, showcasing 'meet the buyer' or 'meet the investor' events, or even international trade missions. Initiatives stretch from the local (such as the Bristol Creative Technology Network),[24] to the regional (such as the South-East Media

Network),[25] to the highly specialised (such as the London Fashion Forum).[26] Network initiatives are increasingly sophisticated and bespoke to the development needs of creative businesses, often combining new media interfaces with face-to-face interaction opportunities, or mixing social and creative exchange opportunities with more stage-managed programmes. In addition, the most effective networks are those that are used to carry intelligence on creative and/or business development opportunities and are used as the channel for dedicated business advice and skills development programmes – such as those managed by the Cultural Industries Development Agency (CIDA)[27] in East London or the Cultural Industries Development Service (CIDS)[28] in Manchester, balancing specialist advice services with the coordination of networks and information on specialist support offered by a range of partners.

By contrast, the least effective networks are those established by the state without close collaboration with the sector they are seeking to serve. The creative industries is a networked economy and forges ahead with its own informal and more formalised networks regardless of the role of state support. This means that it is the task of the state – led by its intermediaries – to lock into and add value to existing networks, to ensure that networks connect to each other and, where identified *through collaboration* as necessary, to introduce new complementary network initiatives (which are often more instructive and targeted – such as trade portals or missions). Just as with the development of dedicated creative industries property or workspace, network intervention requires legitimacy and ownership from creative businesses and communities; they need to make sense to them. Too often, network initiatives in the creative industries take ownership away from creative businesses, supplanting the identity or purpose of the network with a well-intentioned though misinformed intervention.

Once again, the role of the creative intermediary is critical in ensuring *networks work* for the creative industries sector. The task for the creative intermediary is to 'make sense' of existing networks, identify the key components of value chains, and provide opportunities and initiatives that add resources and infrastructure to existing networks, make connection between those where it is productive to do so, and work in partnership with the sector to facilitate new ones, but only where a sector-led desire exists. This is a role intrinsic to the intermediary's broader task of 'creative place-building' (Crewe and Beaverstock 1998; Goodwin 1993): infusing a set of broad interdependencies that collapse the social and commercial so that a business begins to see the location and the meanings and resources it has to offer as being a key factor in creative opportunity and economic comparative advantage. Agencies such as CIDA and CIDS are leading this process.

Enabling investment

It is clear that many creative industries businesses are relatively 'under-invested', especially start-up and early-stage businesses (NESTA 2004, 2005;

FSE 2005). A combination of their distinctive attributes, their difficulty in gaining attributes that are shared by businesses from other sectors (such as clear management systems and recognisable and valuable assets) and, relatedly, significant qualitative evidence that persistent informational asymmetries exist between investors and investees (LDA 2003; CFNW 2004) point to the need for a dedicated and bespoke approach to investment and support. As introduced above, dedicated approaches to creative industries business support and cluster/network development are reasonably established in the UK and elsewhere. However, it is clear that they have made little impact on increasing or improving investment in start-up and early stage creative businesses (NESTA 2005). When seeking investment in order to grow, such businesses are faced by issues of market failure that are both generic to all small businesses and specific to the creative industries. It therefore follows that it makes clear strategic sense for the state to devise ways to address such market failure through both generic (cross-sectoral) intervention and bespoke intervention (that is connected through partnership and strategy to the generic intervention). It makes sense to intervene, but to do so in a very nuanced, collaborative and coherent way.

Several initiatives are emerging in the UK. Some focus on the provision of new money to bridge a perceived or tested gap in investment flowing from existing private investment markets (such as the Advantage Creative Fund in the West Midlands);[29] some provide small amounts of investment more to lever private sector investment than to bridge any defined gap in provision (such as the services of Culture Finance North West);[30] others focus solely on 'investment readiness' and 'investor readiness' – enhancing the business models and management capacities of creative businesses, brokering relations with investors and educating investors of the commercial potential of investing in the creative industries (such as through the Ready 4 Investment scheme piloted across the UK).[31]

Investment in a creative business requires that the investee is able to identify value in the business that can be extracted as value for the investor. Therefore, if a business is to come into contact with a specific type of investment opportunity, it is imperative that the business has the potential to provide the types of investment outcome required by that opportunity. This requires a clearly defined and coherent approach to creative industries investment and support, strategic connection and partnership with other vehicles and initiatives, and the flexibility to focus on specific business profiles and the investment opportunities they might spark. Few approaches to supporting investment in the creative industries succeed in brokering a coherent relationship between these different factors. Initiatives are frequently piecemeal (for example, they offer new investment opportunities without attending to issues of investment/investor readiness, and thus ignore long-term structural and cultural barriers to investment); under-co-ordinated (for example, they lack connectivity with the range of business support services available to the creative industries which, collectively, could advance investment opportunities) and are often competing (for example, a new creative industries fund may actually compete with a non-sector-specific fund). Other initiatives attempt to reach too many goals at once.

The connectedness of intervention is key: a fabric of initiatives, laid out across a consistent and navigable support and investment landscape, offers real potential for developing increased and improved investment in start-up and early stage creative industries businesses. A much stronger partnership is required that relies on a clear understanding by the state of why it is seeking to invest in or support early stage and start-up creative businesses; a coherent definition at the outset of the types of creative business that are being targeted for support, such as sub-sector or location in the value chain, business size, 'high growth' or other; anticipated geographical remit of intervention and justification of this approach; and a comprehensible definition of the anticipated outputs and outcomes of this intervention – from increased and improved investment criteria to the brokerage of coherent investment-driven partnerships. Specialist creative intermediaries – such as lawyers and accountants with expertise in creative intellectual property rights, and business advisers working directly with the sector – play a crucial role in ensuring an effective creative investment landscape is introduced and managed.

Ensuring a coherent approach and the role of the creative intermediary

The creative intermediary can play the lead role in working with partners to establish a coordinated approach to delivery, persuasively brokering initiatives that have a clear rationale and occupy a widely agreed and appreciated location within a broader landscape of creative industries support. For example, there are many challenges and dilemmas faced by the state as it seeks to bridge perceived investment gaps – to 'overcome the barriers' – for creative businesses. The state is required to consider issues that range from where in the value chain to target investment, what the key support and investment needs might be for such creative businesses, how to build partnerships within the state and with private sector communities, and thus how to work towards locating discrete investments within an increasingly coherent support and investment landscape. Similar challenges persist when considering the focus of 'specialist' business advice and support.

The state is also required in many instances to consider issues beyond pure economics: approaches to creative industries intervention may also contain aims and objectives that overlap with agendas in skills, education, social inclusion, regeneration and cultural development. Rarely – whether in developed or developing world contexts – can a state-led creative industries investment initiative focus singularly on the economic impact of investment and investment support. This introduces tensions and contradictions that can only be resolved through the close supervision and support of dedicated intermediaries – to include a combination of investment savvy creative businesses, lawyers and accountants specialising in creative intellectual property, and dedicated public sector employees who have worked intensively to occupy the spaces between small businesses, large corporations and the state.

The Creative London[32] programme of the London Development Agency provides an example of how creative intermediaries have led the way in shaping investment and support programmes in the creative industries. By consulting with the full range of sector support bodies, initiatives and intermediaries across the UK capital, *and by continuing to consult*, an 'aerial' and 'underground' view of support was established, allowing Creative London to identify weaknesses and gaps in support, as well as where strong points could be connected to benefit a wider geography and sector profile. A series of ten creative hubs was identified across London – each an existing or emergent cluster of creative industries activity and each with a strong on-the-ground presence of intermediary support (often through a dedicated Creative Industries Development Agency). The key aim of the Creative London programme is to connect each of these ten hubs so that they contribute collaboratively towards the greater good of the creative economy of London (measured in terms of growth and value-added). This is channelled through four themes: property (increasing the concentration of affordable, networked, appropriately supported space), enterprise (supporting growth through dedicated support services), talent (providing opportunities for new entrants to the sector – especially for talented individuals otherwise marginalised) and showcasing (raising the profile of a 'Creative London' to creative businesses and to a range of audiences that includes inward investors and cultural tourists).

Each hub has written an investment plan that outlines how existing support provision can be complemented by provision based in the other hubs, and how in turn this combination of services can operate within a coherent landscape of city-wide creative industries support services. In addition, Creative London has introduced four pan-London specialised services that would not work effectively or efficiently if sub-divided into each hub. First, Creative Match[33] – a brokerage agency working as a pan-London intermediary service to connect creative businesses to appropriate property, focusing particularly on building critical mass in the ten hubs through an emphasis on finding temporary creative uses for buildings. Second, the Creative London 'Creative Business Accelerator' service, designed to fast-track investment to high growth creative businesses through specialist advice and support offered by expert intermediaries, in partnership with overseeing networks of private sector investors (such as banks and business angels) and state-led funds. These include the third intervention – the Creative Seed Fund, designed to bridge the gap in early stage investment in the creative industries and to lever additional investment. This will in turn complement and be complemented by the fourth intervention – 'Own It',[34] which provides a free IPR rapid response support mechanism and advice facility to creative people across London. Own It relies upon an extensive network of sector specific and legal experts, subsidised to offer their services. Services include on-line news and features, specialist seminars and one free legal advice or intervention session.

Crucial are the strategic relations between these programmes, with intermediaries working 'on the ground' in the ten hubs as gatekeepers and conduits of information, ensuring that pan-London initiatives are profiles in local and sub-sectoral networks, that business support gears businesses to benefit from these initiatives, and that there is a collective drive towards the wider goals of increasing the productivity and growth of the creative industries sector for the entire city.

This is a substantial undertaking that is already showing signs of weakness – where for example pan-London opportunities are not filtered down to the appropriate businesses within the hubs, or where hubs are unnecessarily competing for resources. However, the overall schematic correctly merges local and regional provision to cross-sectoral and sub-sectoral provision, to provision that focuses on high growth and on lower growth, and so on. In other words, the Creative London programme is based upon a commitment to establish a coherent landscape of support that is modified on the ground and within niche activities by intermediaries who know their sector or their locality best, have established trust in these contexts, and are committed to extending opportunities to these contexts through connectivity with other contexts and with city-wide programmes.

Best practice lessons: sequencing issues and key interventions in developing country contexts

This chapter, through northern hemisphere examples, has introduced the challenges of locating and justifying the rationale for public sector intervention in the creative industries, of connecting discrete interventions so that they complement each other, and of better preparing businesses and locations to work as successful teams as part of a wider creative ecology. For support services to combine an often very nuanced and targeted approach with a broader strategic relevance, sector development challenges are best faced within a coherently devised, mapped and agreed creative industries support landscape that is managed by networks of active, trusted, flexible and fast-moving creative intermediaries. These may be in dedicated creative development agencies or they may be small law firms; crucial is their connectedness to each other and their commitment to making the landscape both navigable and replete with sector development opportunities that make sense as a whole.

This chapter distances itself from catch-all or simple ‘fix-it’ approaches based on simplistic reform and inflexible tools. Such approaches can only result in inappropriate businesses reaching the shop windows or computer screens of inappropriate markets, high growth support mechanisms wrongly deployed on stable yet low growth businesses, and other instruments ill-equipped to connect the right types of businesses to the right types of support and investment. Opportunistic, proactive and responsive, the task of the creative intermediary is to identify, pursue and implement projects and programmes that are absolutely ‘in tune’ with the development needs and potential of the local creative industries sector, while complementary to and accessible within the wider support and development landscape.

This requires (and explains) the divergent models, structures and sub-sectoral emphases of creative intermediary services in different places. Indeed, the manifold and diverse roles incumbent on a locally sensitive and tailored creative intermediary service require that the service look as carefully at 'itself' as the sector it is seeking to serve, because without this matching of structure and delivery with need, the local creative industries sector will be inappropriately supported, under-supported, even harmed. This is a cultural process as much as it is structural, because for a creative intermediary service to gain the trust of creative businesses and organisations (and thus be in a position to offer support), it must be able to operate across a range of cultural paradigms and maintain a cultural credibility across different creative communities.

The challenge in developing contexts is to establish appropriate support – towards a landscape of support – that emerges naturally and effectively from existing institutions, and that makes large strides with relatively small resources. The following four issues are key here:

Utilising the existing capacity and expertise of existing institutions

Unlike in developed contexts where the introduction of a new specialist creative industries development agency might be the first intervention undertaken, in developing contexts intermediaries will in most cases be required to emerge from existing institutions. The higher education sector can provide a vital role here: it is a major land-owner (which advances opportunities for clustering), it is often the major centre of expertise and robust economic intelligence and it is the provider of skills and talent to the (creative) economy. For example, the role of the American University of Beirut (AUB) is providing significant expertise and in-kind resources to support the Creative Futures Programme[35] – a creative industries development programme led by the NGO L'Agenda Culturel, with the support of the British Council. AUB is supporting a mapping project, which will reveal the size and scope of the sector and thus establish the case for state resources to support sector development (see below). AUB is therefore giving knowledge and critical sector intelligence to intermediaries working through L'Agenda Culturel and partners, utilising its in-house expertise and capacity, with a low-level financial burden. This 'early stage' partnership-driven intervention will seek gradually to lever support directly from the state while absorbing costs as much as possible within existing institutions. This slow-build approach also helps to establish a very nuanced and sensitive approach to sector support because expensive and intensive intervention can only be introduced after a long period of concept development and advocacy to a sceptical and resource-limited state. Significantly, advocacy will focus primarily on the Ministry of Finance, rather than the Ministry of Culture; highlighting the economic importance of the sector levers more support and investment than a focus on its cultural or social significance. Indeed, it should be presented as the responsibility of Ministries of Finance, Economy and Trade to take a lead on creative industries policy if the sector is to avoid being placed into an 'arts and culture subsidy silo'.

Mapping and 'intelligence' are primary

In the UK, initial mapping work undertaken for the DCMS was key in establishing an understanding of and appetite for a more dedicated approach to creative industries development and support. Similarly, on a regional and local level, mapping has provided the spur for political support and stronger sector-focused partnerships. This is of equal, if not greater significance in developing contexts: without some baseline mapping, knowledge of sector size and scope remains guess-work; intelligence relating to sector profile (such as trading patterns and barriers to growth) is scarce; and the argument for sector investment and support cannot be effectively made. Beyond linking key institutions (as above), the crucial early stage intervention in developing contexts must be to undertake an exercise in sector mapping. In Colombia, Los Andes University and the City of Bogota are working in partnership to undertake a creative industries mapping exercise;[36] basic sector mapping is underway in south-eastern European states (or parts of states) such as Bosnia and Herzegovina and Albania; and local to national mapping activities are commonplace in South-East Asia. The best approaches to mapping do not simply 'count' activity (such as in numbers of business or sector gross value added); they supply intelligence on how the sector operates, its support needs, and how related support can advance sector growth and maximise its positive externalities (such as to social agendas or to other economic activities such as cultural tourism). These approaches provide the material for advocacy – towards the leverage of resources for specialist support; and the intelligence required to respond (through limited resources) in appropriate and effective ways.

Catalysing networks of intermediaries

Mapping work is stimulated by the efforts of intermediaries keen to maximise the potential of their creative economy. In some cases, it will be creative businesses (and networks of businesses) that provide the intermediary function, pressurising public sector partners to take their sector seriously and start by undertaking some mapping. In other cases, NGOs working in the sector (such as arts organisations) will take a lead, using their role as unofficial sector representatives to broker relations with institutions such as universities, even city governments. These are crucial pioneer intermediaries, taking the first step towards sector support. However, for support to progress from mapping requires that intermediaries take the information and intelligence of the mapping and translate it effectively to decision-makers and funders. It is important here that intermediaries work together through networks to show that the creative industries sector is not a marginal or minority activity but one shared by stakeholders across a wide range of development areas. For example, the mapping work undertaken in Lebanon will be utilised and *carried forwards* by a network of intermediaries that includes, as expected, arts and cultural organisations and the creative businesses themselves, but also banks that would like to invest in creative businesses but are unable to because the businesses require specialist support to improve their commercial capacity and reduce risk; tourist agencies eager to attract cultural tourists and related creative consumption opportunities; and education institutions determined to increase graduate retention rates in the city/country and to allow creative graduates to develop creative businesses and careers. Such networks have a larger voice and higher profile than individual intermediaries, and they have the capacity to pool resources and expertise that can lead to the introduction of specialist support services with or without direct investment from the state (e.g. for a small resource, institutions with creative intermediaries can co-invest in the basics of a creative industries development agency and/or specialist projects such as showcase events).

Allowing businesses to take a lead

Where resources are limited, it is of even greater importance that intermediaries work to engage the private sector, and in turn stimulate intermediary activity from businesses. Private sector leadership of creative industries intervention is not widespread or advanced in the northern hemisphere – other than the role of multinational creative businesses in negotiating legal frameworks for creative products (such as in relation to IPR). At a local level, some success has been achieved in establishing specialist sector networks to drive the intervention agenda.[37] However, businesses too often feel alienated from the support process because of the perceived irrelevance of previous support services, a perception that the state cannot respond to distinctive sector needs, and because businesses are time-poor and therefore find it difficult to justify intensive engagement with the public sector. By contrast, in a developing context, where state resources are relatively small, institutions are underdeveloped and the track record of specialist support is negligible, creative businesses can and must play a much more prominent role. Specialist business-led consortia, networks and project partnerships can play a leading role provided they are convinced of the commercial impact of participation

Figure 11.2 provides a basic schematic for creative industries support in a developing context, showing how the most basic commitments can lever long-term sustained sector support and investment:

Conclusion: moving forward, with some difficult questions

Creative intermediaries, in their efforts to influence, coordinate and deliver intervention in creative industries development, face a series of implicit and explicit inconsistencies and dilemmas. These are as relevant in developing world contexts as they are in the northern hemisphere (Wiedemann 2004). These are issues of *definition*, *differentiation* and *direction*; each of which impacts upon how the creative industries are understood, presented and supported.

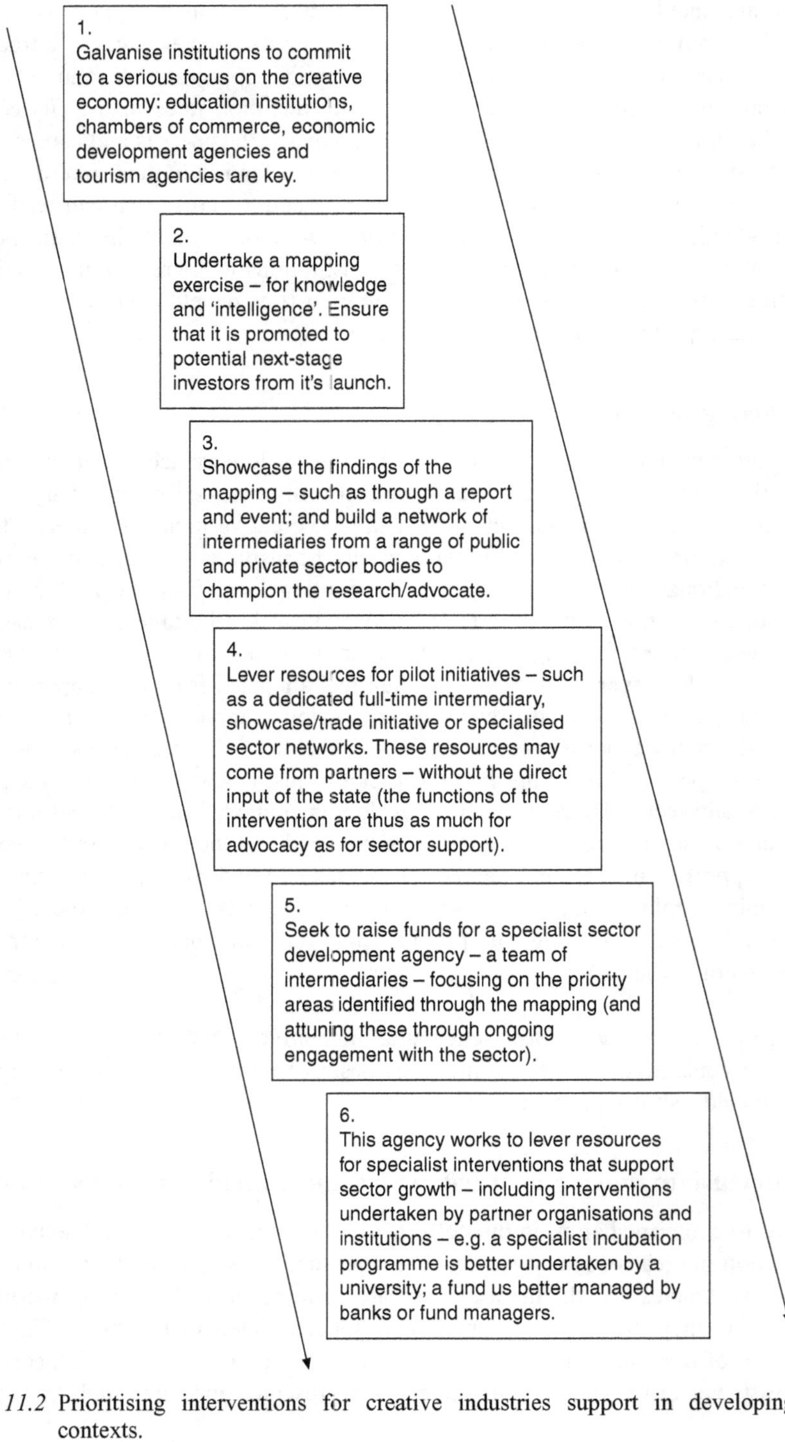

Figure 11.2 Prioritising interventions for creative industries support in developing contexts.

Definition

Ask whether the creative industries in a specific locality really requires specialised, dedicated support and investment. This may marginalise the sector, distort the investment market and overplay the differences between the sector and other sectors. Specialised intervention might disadvantage the sector if it doesn't strategically complement other more 'mainstream' intervention, or it may cause confusion and ill-feeling if it only targets a specific part of the sector despite adopting a general 'creative industries brand and approach'. It is vital therefore to establish at an early stage the desired/required definition of the creative industries to suit the specific development context and to map the sector on these terms. This should be based on a partnership approach to sector development, where the private sector plays an active part in 'self-definition'.

Differentiation

Ask whether, given that only parts of the creative industries have high growth potential, policy-makers and intermediaries should employ different approaches to investment and support for different parts of the sector. Most creative businesses in specific sub-sectors (such as in graphic design and furniture design) operate under a seemingly 'natural' and accepted size limit, whereas other types of creative business (such as in software design or computer games) in a greater number of cases have the potential – should they wish – to develop businesses that are scalable even to global markets. Different types of creative business therefore require different types of support and different sizes of investment. The task for the state and intermediaries is to make policy decisions regarding the relative importance they hold for certain types of creative businesses (this may include non-economic factors such as cultural and social value), and thus where to target support, how to present it and how to connect it to non-targeted support. Processes of mapping should help to prioritise actions and regulate emphasis, as well as to make the case for support for areas of the creative industries that might lack growth potential, but play an important part in supplying talent and ideas to the rest of the sector (the visual arts and crafts are common examples here).

Direction

Decide whether to focus on specific geographical areas. High growth creative businesses increasingly operate across geographical boundaries, with scalable businesses requiring distributors and markets that operate internationally (Pratt 2004a). Support for and investment in early stage and high growth creative businesses may therefore allow such businesses to build a position in creative value-chains that ultimately requires them to locate their growth elsewhere. Local support for the creative industries may consequently result in 'leakage' of creative assets to competitor cities, regions, even nations. Intermediaries may therefore work to target intervention in ways that make location a vital asset for business growth, while accepting that the location operates as a node in a value-chain that is often necessarily trans-local. Alternatively, intermediaries may seek to introduce interventions that target the more numerous smaller creative businesses that are likely to remain small but on aggregate offer a great deal to local and regional economies, cultures, networks and senses of place (Jeffcutt 2004). Key is establishing effective partnership that communicates effectively with a mix of business-led networks to ensure that interventions support the commercial interests of the sector (whether these be local or global), in ways that make activity and a base in the locality a key factor in comparative advantage.

A parable for creative industries intervention

An old Greek story tells of a merchant ship that gets thrown into a storm. As the storm worsens, the captain demands that all passengers throw their belongings overboard. As the merchants lament losing their valuable goods, one man calmly throws all of his possessions into the sea. The captain asks him why he is not upset. The man replies: 'These are things, but everything of real value I carry in my head.'[38] This represents both the curse and the blessing of creative businesses – creative people – as the 'subjects of intervention'. They hold so much value, they constantly produce so much of value, but unless it can be accessed, touched and measured, the value will not be appreciated. The challenge remains in creative industries intervention to extract as much value as possible, seek ways to protect it and translate it, allow decision-makers and investors to see it, feel it, weigh it, and then use further support and investment to go on creating more value. The challenge is increased because values vary for different consumers, investors and decision-makers – Is the aim for a 'creative city' or 'creative nation', a creative industries sector made up of high growth businesses, or a sector that provides opportunities to the marginalised and disenfranchised? The challenge should be for the conflation of each of these aims – maximising the value of the creative industries *across the board*. This requires immense dedication and a very strict commitment to coordinating a coherent landscape of intervention where intervention is introduced precisely in relation to specific strategic rationale. Only creative intermediaries – those that know the sector and can express the value of the sector – are in a position to plot this landscape.

In developing contexts – where resources are less available, institutions often weaker, legal frameworks sometimes less refined – the importance of intermediaries is even greater. Without committed networks of intermediaries, working to unite private and public sector interests and to strengthen sector support through the leverage of partnership-driven approaches, the creative industries will inevitably flounder and talent will inexorably 'leak' to locations with strong partnerships, committed institutions and a state that tries to maximise the use its resources – however scarce. In an increasingly globalised world where developing nations are losing talent and skills at great magnitude, the creative economy offers a way forwards to retain talent and attract talent from places that neglect the value (real and potential) of their creative economy. By supporting and listening to the creative intermediaries, developing nations can take a huge first step in maximising the potential of this creative value.

Notes

1 Referred to in this chapter as the 'creative industries' for reasons of continuity. The creative industries sector is an aggregation of a complex collection of industrial and creative sectors and sub-sectors, and its 'boundaries' are thus often contested. The term used here is based on the definition employed by DCMS Creative Industries Task Force (1998):

> Those activities which have their origin in individual creativity, skill and talent, and which have their potential for wealth and job creation through the generation and exploitation of intellectual property. These have been taken to include the following key sectors: advertising, architecture, art and antiques, crafts, design, designer fashion, film, interactive leisure software, music, the performing arts, publishing, software and television and radio.

2 Plus considerable policy activity in Australasia and South Africa.

3 The Task Force was composed of leading industry figures and charged with an advisory and advocacy remit. One of its key recommendations was for the production of a document that provided an initial overview of the sector: the Creative Industries Mapping Document.

4 The creative industries sector is to an extent being reconceptualised – especially in terms of how it is measured and how intervention should be targeted. The DCMS Data Evidence Toolkit (2004) focuses on an understanding of the creative industries value-chain as the first step towards a more rigorous approach to measurement, including the measurement of growth. This is based on a 'Creative Industries Production System' approach, as introduced by the London School of Economics. This approach offers a departure from segmenting the sector into specific sub-sectors, instead laying emphasis on the significance of 'activity type' in terms of position on the production chain – from ideas generation to distribution and retail (also see Pratt 2004a, 2004b).

5 Such as through the activities of the British Council Creative Industries Team: highlighting the strength and quality of the UK's creative industries to project a forward-thinking, innovative and rich identity for a nation often understood as anachronistic and dependent on 'old culture' (see British Council 2004).

6 Led by the launch of the National Endowment of Science, Technology and the Arts (NESTA). NESTA's purpose, as set out in the National Lottery Act (1998), is 'to support and promote talent, innovation and creativity in the fields of science, technology and the arts'. See www.nesta.org.uk for an overview of the range of activities it undertakes to encourage and support innovation and creative practice.

7 Such as through the activities of the Film Council (www.ukfilmcouncil.org.uk) or Design Council (www.designcouncil.org.uk).

8 RDAs are not active in Scotland, Wales and Northern Ireland – although similar economic development bodies exist, such as Scottish Enterprise (see www.scottish-enterprise.com).

9 See for example the Small Business Service 'Comprehensive Strategy for Start-ups', 2002. This provides a profile of key barriers to growth for small, start-up companies. Each of the barriers is applicable to the creative industries sector.

10 See ACE (2003a) and Hadley (2004), for a detailed introduction to the roles of

different studio providers (encompassing many different models, approaches and ethics) as key pioneers in urban regeneration.

11 This is most common in sub-sectors such as media, film and design (with media centres and incubator spaces increasingly widespread in the 'urban landscape'). However some examples of new build do exist in other sub-sectors – notably Yorkshire Artspace, a major new studios complex in Sheffield supported by a range of funds that included a large contribution from the National Lottery. This funding resource is unlikely to be available for future creative workspace developments.

12 *Our Towns, Our Cities: The Future and Our Countryside, the Future*, 2000, Office of the Deputy Prime Minister (ODPM).

13 *Towards an Urban Renaissance the Report of the Urban Task Force*, 1999, ODPM.

14 *Literature Review of Public Space and Local Environments for the Cross Cutting Review*, 2001, Department of Transport, Local Government and the Regions (DTLR).

15 *Towns and Cities Action Plan Urban Renaissance in the East of England*, 2003, East of England Development Agency (EEDA).

16 See www.creativelondon.org.uk

17 And some rural areas – see for example Wysing Arts – a complex of artists' studios in rural Cambridgeshire: www.wysingarts.org

18 See Pratt (2004a, 2004b) for a critical overview of the value of cluster theories and methodologies for the creative industries – a sector embedded in value-chains that stretch from the local to the global and back again.

19 Each of these points was introduced by the Select Committee on Trade and Industry in July 2004 in its appraisal of RDA cluster policy. They are points made with regard to any type of cluster policy, rather than those that exclusively prioritise the creative industries. Also see DTI (2004).

20 Such as the Business Link Network in England (see www.businesslink.gov.uk) and through Local Authority business support teams.

21 Such as Creative Herefordshire: an initiative established by the RDA – Advantage West Midlands, with the support of the local authority and Business Link, funded through European Union Structural Funds. It provides services in advice, training and networking (where an online database of local creative businesses provides the 'network engine'). See www.creativeherefordshire.co.uk

22 Such as the range of professional development courses provided across the UK by Skillset – the Sector Skills Council for audio-visual activities, set up by the Government as part of its commitment to skills development generally and the creative economy in particular (see www.skillset.org).

23 See www.creativeskills.org.uk – a specialist skills development initiative for the creative industries in Cornwall, funded through a range of European and regional monies.

24 An ATM network connecting local traditional and new media content producers, facilities houses, broadcasters, art and exhibition centres and the University of Bristol. It is used for the transmission of pre- and post-production and interactive material, and to provide access to shared media servers. See www.cs.bris.ac.uk/Research/Digitalmedia/medianetwork.html

25 See www.southeastmedianetwork.co.uk This is a collective network of six regional organisations supporting media and communication companies in the South East of England. The network acts as a gateway to over 3,000 media businesses in the South East.

26 See www.lffonline.com – a news, showcasing and information service funded by the London Development Agency. This is complemented by Fashion Capital – also supported by the London Development Agency – an online portal that provides information and advice for fashion companies seeking suppliers, manufacturers, retailers, and so on, plus information on key sector trends. See www.fashioncapital.co.uk

27 See www.cida.co.uk – a specialist not-for-profit agency established as an 'arm's-

length' intermediary service by the local authority to deliver specialist business advice, network support, information services and training to the burgeoning creative industries sector of the East End.

28 See www.cids.co.uk – the specialist not-for-profit agency established to support the development of the Creative Industries in Manchester and some neighbouring boroughs through advice, information, network development and advocacy/brokerage services. These include an online information portal for the local sector and a range of very targeted initiatives, such as trade shows and missions.

29 The Advantage Creative Fund has moved beyond its 2000–2001 pilot stage, relaunched as a £5 million venture capital fund that targets creative industries businesses. The target is to invest in 60–80 companies by 2008, with investments ranging from £25,000 to 100,000. The Fund is managed by a not-for-profit company, supported through Advantage West Midlands (the RDA), Arts Council England and European Structural Funds. As with any venture capital programme, the aim of the Fund is to realise a commercial return. See www.creative-advantage-fund.co.uk

30 Culture Finance North-West was established as a 2-year pilot project between January 2003 and December 2004, to test the potential market for micro-credit for creative businesses and assess the viability and capacity of an agency that works to broker 'creative investment' from other sources. It is funded and supported through a partnership of the Arts Council of England (North West) and the North West Development Agency. It has three main functions: it is a creative investor, providing unsecured micro- and medium loans of between £1,000 and 20,000; it is a creative investment advocate and broker, building partnerships with other lenders towards direct co-investment, or raising the profile of creative industries propositions to a range of investors; and it is a sign-poster, hand holder and matchmaker, connecting applicant businesses that seek to raise more finance. See www.culturefinance.co.uk

31 Ready 4 Growth is an initiative part-funded under the European Commission Information Society eContent programme. It was launched in 2002 to provide practical guidance on critical growth issues for start-up and early stage eContent businesses (which includes some creative industries content businesses), to directly assist 450 European beneficiary businesses to access investment, to inform other businesses and investors of practical approaches to investment, and thus to symbolise the investment potential of this emerging sector. The programme is managed by Greater London Enterprise and delivered in the UK by oneLondon and London Business Angels. See www.ready4growth.com

32 See www.creativelondon.org.uk

33 See www.creativespaceagency.org.uk

34 See www.own-it.org

35 See www.britishcouncil.org/lebanon-arts-and-culture-creative-industries-page.htm

36 With support from the British Council – which is funding British experts/intermediaries to provide advice.

37 Such as the Manchester Music Network (www.manchester-music.org.uk/default.asp) or the 'Cluster Group' media network of the City Fringe Partnership in inner-east London (www.thecluster.net/).

38 Adapted from CIM: www.cimfunds.com

Bibliography

ACE (2003a) *Artists Workspace Internal Advisory Paper* (ACE, London).

Amin, A. and Thrift, N. (1994) *Globalization, Institutions, and Regional Development in Europe* (Oxford University Press, Oxford).

Ash, C. (2003) 'Inner city inspiration', *Arts Professional*, Issue 42: 5.

Bianchini, F. and Parkinson, M. (eds) (1993) *Cultural Policy and Urban Regeneration* (Manchester University Press, Manchester).
Bianchini, F., Fisher, M., Montgomery, J. and Worpole, K. (1988) *City Centres, City Cultures: The Role of the Arts in the Revitalisation of Towns and Cities* (Manchester Free Press for the Centre of Local Economic Strategies, Manchester).
Bourdieu, P. (1984) *Distinction* (Harvard University Press, Cambridge Massachusetts).
Bovane, L. (1990) 'Cultural intermediaries: a new role for intellectuals in the post-modern age', *Innovation*, Vol. 3(1) (Interdisciplinary Centre for Comparative Research in Technology and Social Policy).
Boyle, M. (1993) 'Leisure, place and identity: Glasgow's role as a European City of Culture' (PhD thesis, The University of Edinburgh).
Boyle, M. (1997) 'Civic boosterism in the politics of local economic development: "institutional positions" and "strategic outcomes" in the consumption of hallmark events', *Environment and Planning A*, 29(11): 1975–1998.
British Council (2004) *Creative Industries* (British Council, London).
Castells, M. (1996) *The Rise of the Network Society* (Blackwell, Oxford).
Comedia (1992) *The Importance of Culture for Urban Economic Development* (Comedia, Stroud).
Comedia (1997d) *A Cultural Industries Strategy for Tower Hamlets* (Comedia, London).
Creative Industries Management (2001) *Content – Europe's New Growth Engine* (CIM Finland).
Creative Industries Management (2003) *Deal flow Analysis Report* (Confidential Report, CIM, Helsinki).
Creative Industries Management (2004) *Venture Fund for Creative Industries and Creative Industries Markets* (CIM, Helsinki).
Crewe, L. (1996) 'Material culture: embedded firms, organisational networks and the local economic development of a fashion quarter', *Regional Studies*, 30(3): 257–272.
Crewe, L. and Beaverstock, J. (1998) 'Fashioning the city: cultures of consumption in contemporary urban spaces', *Geoforum*, 29(3): 287–308.
Crewe, L. and Davenport, E. (1992) 'The puppet show: showcasing buyer–supplier relationships within clothing retailing', *Transactions of the Institute of British Geographers*, New Series 17.
Crewe, L. and Forster, Z. (1993) 'Markets, design and local agglomeration: the role of small independent retailers in the workings of the fashion system', *Environment and Planning D: Society and Space*, 11: 213–229.
Crone, M. (2004) *Celtic Tiger Cubs: Ireland's VC-Funded Software Start-ups* (Economic Research Institute of Northern Ireland, Belfast).
Culture Finance North-West (2004) *Finance and the Creative Industries in England's North-West: Supply and Demand Side Issues* (CFNW, Manchester).
Culture Finance North-West (2004b) *Review Paper* (CFNW, Manchester).
DCMS (1998) *Creative Industries Mapping Document* (Department for Culture, Media and Sport, London).
DCMS (2001) *Creative Industries Mapping Document* (Department for Culture, Media and Sport, London).
DCMS (2002) *Report on the Creative Industries Finance Conference* (DCMS, London).
DTI (2004) *A Practical Guide to Cluster Development* (DTI, London).
Evans, G. (2001) *Cultural Planning: an Urban Renaissance?* (Routledge, London).
Evans, G. (2004) 'Cultural Industry Quarters: From Pre-Industrial to Post-Industrial Production', in Jayne, M. and Bell, D. (eds) *City of Quarters* (Ashgate, Aldershot), pp. 71–92.

Evans, G. and Foord, J. (2000) 'Landscapes of cultural production and regeneration', in Benson, J. and Rose, M. (eds) *Urban Lifestyles: Spaces, Places, People* (A.T. Balkema, Rotterdam): pp. 349–356.

Featherstone, M. (1991) *Consumer Culture and Postmodernism* (Sage, London).

Finance South-East (2005) Creative Industries Fund for the South-East (FSE, Crowthorne).

Fleming, T. (2004) 'Supporting the Cultural Quarter? The Role of Creative Intermediary', In Jayne, M. and Bell, D. (eds) *City of Quarters* (Ashgate, Aldershot), pp. 93–108.

Florida, R. (2002) *The Rise of the Creative Class* (Basic Books, New York).

Foord, J. (1999) 'Creative Hackney: reflections on 'Hidden Art', London', *Rising East*, Autumn edition.

Giddens, A. (1990) *The Consequences of Modernity* (Polity/Blackwell, Cambridge).

GLA (2002) *Creativity – London's Core Business* (GLA, London).

Gomez, M. V. (1998) 'Reflective images: the case of urban regeneration in Glasgow and Bilbao', *International Journal of Urban and Regional Research*, 22(1): 106–121.

Goodwin, M. (1993) 'The city as commodity: the contested spaces of urban development', in Kearns, G. and Phlo, C. (eds) *The City as Cultural Capital, Past and Present* (Permagon, Oxford).

Griffiths, R. (1998) 'Making sameness: place marketing and the new urban entrepreneurialism', in Oakley, N. (ed.) *Cities, Economic Competition and Urban Policy* (Paul Chapman Publishing, London).

Hadley, J. (2004) *Supporting Artists' Workspace – Three Arts Council Funded Studio Conferences* (ACE, London).

Hesmondhalgh, D. (2002) *The Cultural Industries* (Sage, London).

Jayne, M. and Bell, D. (eds) (2004) *City of Quarters* (Ashgate, Aldershot).

Jeffcutt, P. (2004) *Knowledge Relationships and Transactions in a Cultural Economy: Analysing the Creative Industries Ecosystem* (Media International, Australia).

Kelly, K. (1998) *New Rules for the New Economy: 10 Radical Strategies for a Connected World* (Fourth Estate, London).

Landry, C. (2000) *The Creative City; a Toolkit for Urban Innovators* (Earthscan, London).

Landry, C. and Bianchini, F. (1995) *The Creative City* (Demos, London).

LDA (2003) *The Creative Business Accelerator* (LDA, London) – Confidential.

Leadbeater, C. and Oakley, K. (1999) *The Independents: Britain's New Cultural Entrepreneurs* (Demos, London).

MIPC (1999) *ICISS Report – Local Cultural Industries Support Services in the UK: Towards a Model of Best Practice* (MIPC, Manchester).

Mommaas, H. (2004) *Cultural Clusters and the Post-industrial City: Towards the Remapping of Urban Cultural Policy*, Urban Studies, 41(3): 507–532.

NESTA (2004) *Forward Thinking – New Solutions to Old Problems: Investing in the Creative Industries* (NESTA, London).

NESTA (2005) *Creating Value – How the UK can Invest in New Creative Businesses* (NESTA, London).

O'Connor, J. (2004) *'A Special Kind of City Knowledge': Innovative Clusters, Tacit Knowledge and the 'Creative City'* (MIPC, Manchester).

O'Connor, J. and Wynne, D. (eds) (1996) *From the Margins to the Centre: Cultural Production and Consumption in the Post-industrial City* (Ashgate Publishing, Aldershot).

Pine, J. and Gilmore, J. H. (1999) *The Experience Economy: Work is Theatre and Every Business a Stage* (Harvard Business School Press, Boston).

Pratt, A. (1999) 'Cultural Industries: the First steps, and the roads ahead' (Paper presented at the *Cultural Industries and the City Conference*, Manchester Metropolitan University, 14.12.99).

Pratt, A. (2002) 'Hot jobs in cool places. The material cultures of new media product spaces: the case of south of the market, San Francisco', *Information, Communication Society*, 5(1): 27–50.

Pratt, A. (2004a) *Creative Clusters: Towards the Governance of the Creative Industries Production System?* (Media International Australia).

Pratt, A. (2004b) *Cultural Industries: Beyond the Cluster Paradigm?* (LSE, London).

Purvis, S. (1996) 'The interchangeable roles of the producer, consumer and cultural intermediary: the new "pop" fashion designer', in O'Connor, J. and Ynne, D. (eds) *From the Margins to the Centre: Cultural Production and Consumption in the Post-Industrial City* (Ashgate Publishing, Aldershot).

Raffo, C., O'Connor, J., Lovatt, A. and Banks, M. (1999) 'Risk and trust in the cultural industries', *Geoforum*, 31(4): 453–464.

Robertson, R. (1995) 'Glocalisation: time-space and homogeneity-heterogeneity', in Featherstone, M., Lash, S. and Robertson, R. (eds) *Global Modernities* (Sage, London).

Ryan, B. (1992) *Making Capital from Culture* (Walter de Gruyter, New York).

Saxenian, A. (2000) *The Bangalore boom: from brain drain to brain circulation?* In Kenniston, K. and Kumar, D. (eds) *Bridging the Digital Divide: Lessons from India* (National Institute of Advanced Study, Bangalore).

Scott, A. J. (1997) 'The cultural economy of cities', *International Journal of Urban and Regional Research*, 21(2): 323–339.

SBS (2002) *A Comprehensive Strategy for Start-ups – A Consultation Document.*

UK Social Exclusion Unit (1999) *The PAT 10 Report* (PAT – Policy Action Team, London).

Verwijnen, J. (1999) 'The creative city as a field condition: can urban innovation and creativity overcome bureaucracy and technocracy?', *Built Environment*, 24(2/3): 142–154.

Verwijnen, J. and Lehtovuori, P. (1999) *Creative Cities: Cultural Industries, Urban Development and the Information Society* (University of Art and Design Press, Helsinki).

Wiedemann, V. (2004) *Promoting Creative Industries: Public Policies in Support of Film, Music and Broadcasting in Developing Countries* `

Yusef, S. and Nabeshima, K. (2003) *Urban Development Needs Creativity: How Creative Industries can Affect Urban Areas* (World Bank Group, Washington, DC).

Zukin, S. (1995) *The Culture of Cities* (Blackwell, Cambridge MA).

Zukin, S. (2001) 'How to create a culture capital: reflections on urban markets and places', in Blazwick, I. (ed.) *Century City: Art and Culture in the Modern Metropolis* (Tate Publishing, London): pp. 259–264.

12 The policy parameters

Anna Jaguaribe

Introduction

This chapter discusses how economic and social factors, such as the intangible nature of creative production, traditions in public financing for culture and social patterns of consumption of cultural goods and services, condition public policy for creative industries with special relevance for developing countries.

Creative industries are a dynamic and expanding cluster of economic activities, which are estimated to account for more than 7 percent of the world's GDP and are forecasted to grow on average by 10 percent a year (UNCTAD 2004).[1] They are knowledge and creativity based activities which cut across traditional divides in manufacturing, arts and high technology. The activities comprising the core cluster of creative industries – audiovisual production, publishing, music and software – are in themselves not new, nor do they form an organic industrial sector in the traditional sense. They have in common the fact that they are creativity based, operate in the frontiers of technology, are protected by copyright legislation and are distributed by an extremely competitive market dominated globally by large oligopolies. The economic weight and social dimension of this new cluster of activities gives credence to the rise of a new paradigm or frontier of creative economy.

Because they produce and circulate texts, images and symbols, creative industries are at once a trade product, an instrument of communication and socialization, and a form of social consumption. They are an intrinsic part of what Jameson refers to as the cultural turn of contemporary capitalism; the transformation of culture into a social and economic resource. (Jameson 1998, 1992). A turn which has given a new political angle to the discussion of the social role of culture and shifted the parameters of the debate from a discussion on the commercialization of culture to a debate over the political management and appropriation of cultural goods and services.[2]

The global economic dimension of creative industries has generated a new urgency with regards to policy-making in the area. Assessing the economic and development impact of creative industries is a new challenge for political and economic analysis and the industry is at the center stage of international debates concerning access to knowledge, preservation of cultural diversity and international trade rules.

The appeal of creative industries to policy-makers comes from the many externalities which creative industries can produce, but also from the fact that the consumption of creative goods and services has become a form of social participation with particular appeal to the various cultural Diasporas of the globalized economy.

This chapter will analyze different patterns of policy-making in this field. It will discuss the role of different stakeholders from the public, private and non-profit sector in policy-making. It will argue that the policies geared towards creative industries have evolved from a generalized acceptance of culture as a public good to the pursuit of creative industries as purveyors of economic value added and the aggressive search for advantages in a skewed international distribution market.

It will point out that independently of past practices and models of public policy there is a certain convergence in what concerns the use of mixed financial incentives for creative industries. In fact, policies for creative goods and services are wide in scope ranging from measures to support individual talent to trade promotion; they are innovative, in terms of financial support and incentives and afford special opportunities for collaboration between the private, public and non-profit sectors.

There are no "ideal type" policy models for promoting creative industries and results can be measured when viewed in the context of specific market and industrial structures. There are, however, several common parameters, which condition policy, and derive from the economic uncertainties associated with the creative process. This chapter will review how the unique characteristics of creative goods and the particular ways in which they are produced influence the design of public policy and open up economic opportunities and challenges for developing countries.

The special characteristics of creative goods and services

Defining creative industries and its economic impact

The term creative industries is a relatively new concept used to represent a cluster of activities which have creativity as an essential component, are directly inserted into the industrial process and subject to copyright protection. Creative industries are distinguishable from the world of cultural heritage and applied arts and crafts in that they are innovative and unique, but also reproducible in an industrial scale. Although not interrelated in the traditional sense of an industrial sector, these different economic activities have in common the fact that they are all producers of texts, images and symbols.

There is still a great deal of statistical imprecision regarding the contribution of creative industries to GNP, as well as to trade and employment, in developed and developing countries alike. This is in part explainable by the fact that there is no consensual or tight definition of what activities should form part of the creative industries cluster. But it is also due to the difficulty of establishing criteria to distinguish the tangible from the intangible components of creative goods and services: music from the CD hardware, design from fabric and film content from the actual celluloid reel. To this should be added that in the case of developing countries, creative industries are often informal industries with seasonal employment patterns

A lot of research is still required for valid international data comparisons. Still, it is possible to evaluate on the basis of copyright data, selected national and regional statistics and data gathered by international organizations such as UNESCO, UNCTAD, OECD and the World Bank, the economic growth opportunities generated by creative industries and the options open for public policy.

In the United States, the copyright sector as a whole, but in particular the audiovisual and musical sectors, accounts for 6 percent of the national GDP and employs about 1.5 million people. Music industry exports alone are the second largest source of external trade revenues in the United States, coming immediately after the space industry. In France, the United Kingdom, Germany and Spain, the cultural sector accounts for over 3 percent of the GDP (OAS Culture Series 2003). In New Zealand, the creative sector has grown from 2.6 percent of GDP in 1996 to 3.1 percent in 2000 and its share of employment has risen from 3.0 percent to 3.6 percent in the same period (Creative Industries, New Zealand Institute of Economic Research 2002).

A few governments sponsoring the development of creative industries have attempted to map the economic impact of these industries in the national GNP. Some such as the United Kingdom, which has a specific ministry for creative industries, have succeeded in including these industries into the national accounts and determining the impact of each individual industry to the overall GNP. The 2001 mapping document on creative industries in the United Kingdom reveals that creative industries generated £112.5 billion in revenue, accounted for £10.3 billion in exports, 1.3 million jobs and contributed over 5 percent to GDP (Creative Industries Economic Estimates, DCMS, 2003).

Statistics on cultural industries collected by UNESCO, which are constantly being updated, show that overall culture trade as a percentage of GNP from 1980 to 1991, grew from 0.2 to 0.8 percent in developing countries and 0.8 to 1 percent in the industrial world.

From 1980 to 1998, the annual world trade of print, literature, music, visual arts, cinema, photo, radio and TV games, amongst others, surged from US$95.340 million to 387.927 million (UNESCO Culture Trade and Globalization 2004).

The economic potential of creative industries is not exclusive to developed economies or restricted to technologically intensive areas of the knowledge economy. Existing data show that in the last decade the performance of Latin American countries in creative industries has not been negligible. In Brazil, Mexico, Colombia and Argentina, creative industries have achieved almost 3 percent of GDP. (OAS Culture Series and Andres Bello Cultural Agreements 2003).

Studies carried out in Brazil show a historical trend; already in 1994, creative industries accounted for 1.0 percent of the GNP compared with 0.4 percent for manufacturing in electric and electronic equipment and 0.6 percent for manufacturing of automobiles, trucks and other vehicles (IPEA 2000), and generated 0.84 percent of overall employment of which 76.8 percent was in the private sector in contrast to 0.44 percent of the industry of electric and electronic materials and 0.55 percent of the automotive industry (Fundaçao João Pinheiro 1998).

Given this performance, creative industries have come to be accepted as a dynamic new source of growth, but also somewhat as a socio-economic promise; generating added value in times of slow growth, employment outside of the public sector and opening up opportunities for trade. The various subsectors of the industries in which small and medium sized businesses predominate are highly labor intensive and tend to be firmly embedded in local milieus and regional networks, with the additional benefit of having fewer formal barriers of entry into the labor market and a high level of on the job training (Essen Declaration 1999).

Yet, creative industries are not the latest version of a development panacea. They share a set of characteristics which distinguishes them from other economic goods, with significant implications for their economic performance, particularly in developing countries. In so far as they are ideas and creativity based industries, they pose few entry requirements and constitute open entrepreneurial opportunities for developing countries. Moreover, creative goods and services have both tangible and intangible elements (form and symbolic content) and as such share many of the characteristics of "public goods," non rivalry in consumption (one person's use does not detract from another) and non exclusivity in benefits (consumption cannot be singularly appropriated). These characteristics in part explain the risky and unpredictable nature of the industry, but also imply that competitive market forces alone will not guarantee the efficient supply of these goods, and that various forms of institutional coordination, public policy intervention and regulation will be required in order to guarantee appropriate conditions for creative industries to prosper. (UNCTAD 2003).[3]

Creative industries and market organization

Creative production is based on talent and innovation but also depends on manufacturing and entrepreneurial skills. This double requirement of creativity and capital makes creative firms flexible in organization and management but also financially challenging. Creative industries can range from small independent enterprises to major international conglomerates. In fact, what mostly seems to characterize the development of creative industries is the constant rise and fall of small and medium sized enterprises. Size and flexibility are in part dictated by the importance of creative talent and the relative ease by which technological innovations can be adopted, but financial sustainability and the capacity to withstand losses are important countervailing forces to size and flexibility. This is particularly significant for developing countries where high interest rates make commercial borrowing hazardous and venture capital is rarely available. The ups and downs of producers of independent labels in music in Latin America are a case in point.

Moreover financial opportunity is not the sole determining factor for success. Even where large monopolies command the market, as in the case of American audiovisual industries, the dependency of the industry on creativity and freedom (often associated with independent production) will dictate the organizational format of the most successful firms. The success of HBO in contrast to more traditional firms such as Disney is a case in point. While part of the large AOL Time Warner Empire, HBO employs 1,770 people, roughly 2 percent of the labor force of the conglomerate, operates in a geographical site of its own disassociated from the rest of the conglomerate, works on the basis of subscriptions rather than advertisements and places a premium on individual creativity. This level of organizational independence has in the last years given the firm a creative edge over its competitors. Moreover the fact that it belongs to a large distribution empire guarantees a cushion of financial and risk protection not associated with independent firms with similar organizational characteristics. (*The Economist* 2003).

Creative goods and services have in common the fact they are shaped and transformed by information technology and protected (and sometimes limited) by copyright legislation, but they are not an organic industrial sector in the traditional industrial sense.

In principle, the absence of technological and organizational prerequisites should offer better entry opportunities for developing economies. Most countries independently of their level of industrialization can develop one form of creative industry or another. But, while some creative industries such as music, fashion and design have few entry prerequisites, distribution subjects them to harsh competition.

Because creative goods and service have high components of risk and unpredictability, firms will attempt to gain command of the market in order to even out the imponderables associated with the creative process (variations in taste, fashion, cultural diversity) and this can in part be achieved by controlling distribution. Thus while creative industries in principle do not have particular technological entry requirements and favor flexible organization, in practice the risks associated with the market for creative production pushes the industry in the direction of concentration, oligopolies and internationalization. Concentration works to instill a measure of scarcity in the market, tame competition by co-opting potential independent talent and imposing price structures, which minimize the cost variation between production and reproduction. Concentration is also a way of achieving some protection against losses. The ratio of fixed costs to variable costs in the cultural industries means that big hits are extremely profitable. Beyond the break-even point, the profit made from the sale of every extra unit can be considerable and can compensate the inevitable losses, which derive from the elusive nature of big hits and the unpredictable nature of demand. (Hesmondhalgh 2002).

The tension between independent producers and large distribution firms, characteristic of creative industries, exists in developed and developing countries alike. Most developing countries with successful audiovisual productions, such as Brazil, Mexico, India and China, have developed a large national monopoly which both produces and controls the national distribution of audiovisual services, in particular for the TV market. Globo TV, Z TV and Televisa are cases in point. Often these firms will also act as the intermediary of international distribution monopolies, as is the case of Globo TV. In this context, the range of options open to the independent producer will in large part depend on the financial and regulatory support of public policy and the capacity of individual entrepreneurs to harness creative talent and exploit entry opportunities afforded by technological innovation.

Creative industries and the knowledge economy

Creative industries are information-producing activities prone to the innovations of information technology, in particular digitalization. They share many of the peculiarities of the post-fordist economy, but, unlike IT based firms, creative enterprises are not dependent on the accumulation, development and transformation of knowledge paradigms. This distinction is particularly relevant for developing economies struggling with technological modernization. While it is not possible to have a knowledge economy without scientific and technological accumulation, it is possible to have a creative economy and creative industries which benefit from technological innovations but do not depend on the formal accumulation of scientific and technical knowledge.

Technological innovations push the production frontiers of creative goods and services, shaping performances and setting standards of production, and some industries such as the audiovisual sector thrive on technological creativity. Software development was indispensable for the development of video games, architectural design and cheaper editing. Digital technologies have made audiovisual production not only cheaper but also feasible on a smaller scale of production.

Further parallels can be traced between the building of an innovative economy and creative development strategies. The possibility of leapfrogging into certain technological innovations in moments of paradigm change has greatly altered development prospects. Thus mobile telephones have come to compensate deficits in fixed communication, access to the Internet is now possible in worlds where a telephone call used to be an impossible technological adventure and credit card formats can be used for basic services while sidestepping bank accounts.

Creative industries can also grow through the pursuit of technological niches. Countries with a very high production of communication technology such as Korea can be less active in electronic commerce, whereas countries with no domestic production of information technology such as Australia are on the forefront of electronic business. India's success story in developing software is another case in point. In the case of creative industries, technological innovation is not the exclusive priority of large firms, it pushes the frontiers of creativity, diminishes costs and offers alternative solutions to distribution, characteristics which have a particular appeal for developing countries.

The audiovisual and media sector are a good example of the complex interplay between technological innovation and traditional market influences. Concentration and internationalization have accompanied the development of these industries from an early stage. This tendency has not been dictated by the pressures, cost and influence of technological innovation, but is a reflection of the risky nature of the commodities produced and the costs and economy of scale which became associated with movies at an early stage. In the audiovisual sector, large conglomerates coexist with a permanent proliferation of small and medium enterprises. Large conglomerates attempt to control the market by determining taste in order to guarantee demand and in so doing progressively diminish diversity in market choices. Still, there is a limit up to which imposed taste brings economic assurance and novelty, and often, big hits originate in creations from independent producers operating outside the schemes of predetermined taste. It is in this uneasy tension between innovative initiatives and forces of concentration that the opportunities for entry into the market can be found.

The formation and development of Hollywood conglomerates is a good example of this tension between independent creativity and market control. The early Hollywood studios operated with the logic of concentration traditional of the 1930s. The big studios controlled all forms of film production, script, actors, distribution and publicity all the way to the movie theaters themselves.

Although foreign revenues made up over 30 percent of the total international gross revenues of Hollywood, production, scripts, and market orientation were mostly national in orientation (Seagrave 1997). Internationalization became an objective for the Hollywood studios after US courts obliged them to end their vertically integrated control of the US market (Hesmondhalgh 2002).

A new market strategy will emerge following the wave of capital internationalization of the 1960s and the technological innovations of the 1970s. As films become more technologically intensive and with greater special effects, costs weigh down the big studios, which begin to subcontract parts of this former value chain. At the same time, new major players enter into the competition; film loses some of its exclusivity and becomes part of polyvalent organizations. With the advent of mega-media groups in the 1980s and 1990s, the audiovisual sector comes to be absorbed into the competitive game for media control.

The global reach of the US film industry increases exponentially during the 1980s with its share of global receipts arriving at 41 percent in 1999. The rate of domination of specific markets vary. Across the European Union Hollywood shares of box office receipts rose from 60.2 percent in 1984 to 71.7 percent in 1991. In the United Kingdom, Hollywood had 93 percent of the market, but in France its share was significantly lower at 58 percent. (Held 1999; Hesmondhalgh 2002).

Moreover, Hollywood is not the sole example of success in film production and distribution. The world market of film production is varied with India heading the market with a production of 839 films a year, followed by China and Hong Kong with 456 titles, the Philippines with 456 and the United States with 385 titles.

Into the 1930s and 1940s, most European countries which are now behind Hollywood in film production had an active, private, very little sponsored, film industry. In Latin America, Brazil, Argentina and Mexico produced for important segments of the national market. The same holds true for Egypt and China.

The films produced in developing countries were comic and romantic melodramas, targeted to a very general public, with uncomplicated scripts and no special technological effects. Although featuring popular actors, they did not create a grand star system. This budding but promising industry comes to a decline during the 1950s and 1960s with the advent of national TV and the internationalization of Hollywood. It will begin to re-emerge only in the late 1980s. Income from the audiovisual industry in Brazil in 1997 was around 1 percent of the GNP, 0.5 percent for Mexico, 1 percent for Argentina, 1.1 percent for Europe and 2.7 percent for the United States (Reis 1999).

The 1990s and the first years of the twenty-first century seem to bring a consolidation to those national markets which have survived the travails of the 1980s and in the case of the developing world survived the competition of television in the national markets. Brazilian films are a case in point, nationally produced features, in spite of a policy of quotas favoring national production, had never more than 8 percent of the national audience throughout the 1970s and 1980s. The spread of new production firms, increased market incentives and the benefits of digitalization have increased the number and quality of films available and in 2003, national films have arrived at almost 20 percent of the national market.

Furthermore, digitalization and the lowering of production costs that comes with it is now allowing the production of relatively high quality and low cost films capable of competing in quality, although not in marketing and distribution, with films produced by larger studios.

Globalization and consumption in creative industries

Traditional sociological analysis contends that an increase in cultural consumption is part of the package of industrial modernization. In service economies, diminished hours of labor increase leisure activities and this in turn leads to a greater demand for entertainment. The diffusion of private TV is a case in point. In 1950 only 9 percentof American households had a television set; by 1960 the proportion had risen to 87 percent reaching 98 percent in 1990 (Heilbrun 2001).

The diversification of the service industry in the 1970s and the ensuing deregulation of the market expanded the offer of cultural services and further increased the potential for consuming culture as leisure. Cable TV is a case in point.

In this paradigm of modernization, the consumption of culture is tied to economic achievements. Increased income brings about increased service consumption. Higher income countries produce more diversified service sectors, which in turn increase the demand for cultural goods. Expanded cultural consumption consolidates the mass markets for creative goods and reiterates the trend toward the transformation of culture into tradable commodities.

The development of the audiovisual industry exemplifies this paradigm of modernization. Audiovisual is the perfect answer to the mass entertainment of the industrial age in so far as it is a collective consumption which is repetitive but individually enjoyed. It is urban, not subject to major seasonal variations and appropriate to all age groups, levels of education and income.

When cultural consumption is viewed in the context of this modernization paradigm, developing countries are usually relegated to the position of consumers of imported cultural goods and services and producers of folklore. A more discriminating analysis of the service sectors in developing countries shows that the expansion in the supply and demand in services, in particular with regards to information, is more complex than presumed by theories which link consumption of creative goods and services to levels of industrial development.

Just as service sectors expand in economic downturns and in riches, giving rise to informal and formal employment, so does the consumption of cultural goods in cash poor economy. In contrast to traditional economic goods, creative industries produces goods and services which are bought and sold but also shared. The widespread audience of television soap operas throughout Latin America and Asia is only one of the many forms in which this takes place. While leisure accounted for only 3.5 percent of the total expenditures of Brazilian families in 1996, statistics for the same year reveal that 91.3 percent of urban households and 54.3 percent of rural households had TV sets and spent over four hours watching national programs (Reis 1999).

The shortcomings of determining cultural consumption strictly by levels of income is that it neglects the role of culture in the present process of capital accumulation and the importance of media industries in the process of socialization. Disciplinary institutions, such as the school, church and public ordinances, which were the basis of nineteenth-century socialization, are no longer the sole purveyors of rules and social conduct and socialization is increasingly carried out through media exchanges and consumption of symbolic creative goods and services.[4] Globalization as noted by Appadurai creates communities with no sense of place tied together by mediatic exchanges of "culture." (Appadurai 1997). Cultural identities are more fragmented and lack a precise geography making cultural exchanges dependent on the "mediatic" circulation of texts, images and symbols.

Once again the audiovisual sector is the best example for this new form of cultural consumption. The highest number of film titles produced in the world comes from India, consumed locally and throughout the Indian Diaspora across the globe. As with India, most developing countries with large migrant populations, such as the Philippines and China, will have extremely active audiovisual sectors.

The phenomenon is not limited only to large countries or migrant populations. The consumption of TV by developing nations has grown in a proportion that is not related to the rise in income level or increase in leisure time. Thus it is not solely "increased riches" which leads to the consumption of culture but also the transformation of cultural consumption into a tangible form of social identification.

Globalization and cultural diversity

The idea that the economic production and consumption of culture increases the danger of cultural homogenization is of course not new. The concept of reification or "commodification" of culture has been exhaustively debated by authors of Marxist tradition, from Lukacs to Adorno. What distinguishes the work of these authors from contemporary analyses, even those belonging to a Marxist theoretical tradition, is the emphasis on the democratization of culture. Contemporary approaches to culture will stress the fact that culture, because it has been extensively democratized, is no longer an isolated creation but an element in a flux of information. In this context the distinction between high culture and mass culture becomes less relevant than the fact that cultural activities in general are inserted within a system of communication that has become affected by media and globalization.

Globalization affects creative industries by increasing cultural and creative exchanges and expanding trade, investments and production in goods and services. It also reinforces the market domination of a small number of megacorporations with control over packages of distribution. This geography of distribution lends a new turn to the debate on the "massification" of culture. In question is not the transformation of creativity into mass entertainment and consumption, but the preservation of diversity increasingly menaced by the appropriation of cultural industries by the global mass media. In the era of liberalization and privatization cultural production becomes the province of global electronic mass media and the frontiers between culture as identity and as entertainment become porous.

The menace of cultural homogenization applies equally to rich and poor countries and transforms culture into a central political issue. The small number of media conglomerates controlling the global market has reduced the offer of television products throughout the world in such a manner that Italians, British, Australian and Asian audiences have the same identical samples of TV products at their disposal. The audiovisual industries of Hollywood earn the greatest part of their revenue through exports. However, notwithstanding the increase in the global production of audiovisual products, the exposure of the American public to diversity in audiovisuals is limited, and the percentage of foreign films in circulation in the USA is no higher than 3 percent.[5]

The instruments available for creating defenses against cultural homogenization are of course different for countries in the developing world. Large sectors of the world's population have been completely disenfranchised from the production of culture and turned into either voyeurs of high-level cultural spectacles or into objects of cultural voyeurism themselves (Appadurai 1997).

But the problem cannot be simply reduced to one of domination by powerful countries and/or corporations. Globalization has blurred the frontiers of local versus international cultural creations, partly because the market, distribution chains and copyrights legislation operate on a global scale, but also because creators do not produce in self-enclosed national cultural contexts. The world of music production provides a good example. At present, a large number of countries in the world produce some variation of rock and roll that in fact has mainly local meaning and children across the globe play with Japanese video games that have been extirpated of any Japanese characteristics.

This interplay of influences does not globalize market opportunities. In fact, these diversified products with very few exceptions will most probably remain local creations, as the control of distribution is the most important instrument of domination of media conglomerates.

Still, there are important mitigating circumstances that favor the production of creative industries in local markets. Comparative studies of audiovisual production in developing and developed countries have shown that audiences have a preference for local content. In fact, it may very well be that the future of television might be regional rather than global as, in spite off the impact of blockbuster films produced by the media conglomerates across the globe, there is a net preference in the case of television for local content products.

The cost of imported television drama can be less than on-tenth of the cost of creating an original production, yet Mexico's Televisa, its leading exporter of Spanish language programs, sells its products to over 128 countries in the world (Paxman 2003). Similarly Zee TV in India is now the world's largest Asian television network, covering Asia, Europe and the United States and catering to 24 million people of the Indian Diaspora around the world (Thussu 1998).

What this seems to indicate is that cultural globalization gives rise to contradictory tendencies. On the one hand, international media conglomerates extend their influence by controlling the production and distribution of news and services both abroad and at home. On the other hand, regions exhibit sub-networks and connections within this global network giving rise to or reinforcing regional cultures within global cultures (Crane 2002).

The interplay between the global and the local is complex because not only are global products often nationalized, but national products can also be created as global hybrid products. Cricket has been transformed into a most successful Indian and Pakistan sport giving rise to a super-specialized culture of transmission of sports events (Appadurai 1997). Britain's Channel 4 and the Italian TV are now joining forces to produce television serials geared to the adolescent audience, with English actors, Italian directors and American inspiration.

One of the many arguments for the global success of Hollywood films is that Hollywood produced the first really universal media product. Semati and

Sortirin (1999) argue that, from the very start, Hollywood films were international. They were produced by immigrants and reflected a scale of values, esthetic and language, which did not reflect everyday common life in America. Likewise, present Hollywood while emphasizing idealized American attributes, such as individual worthiness and opportunity, self-empowerment and the magical virtue of consumerism, is also symbolically organized as a global product. Different cultures can have different readings of the Hollywood narrative and still develop a direct relationship with the text. The film then becomes something of a "fordism" of the imaginary.

Hollywood is not just a model and a powerful industrial force to contend with, but it influences and shapes the chances for the globalization of creative goods and services produced with alternative codes and values outside of the Hollywood scenery. The larger part of successful films produced in the developing world is made for the national market and/or the Diaspora abroad, a choice which has very often been at the expense of quality and complexity of narrative, and the few "global" products coming from developing countries have been produced, financed and distributed by major corporations and often with actors internal to the Hollywood network. A vital audiovisual production sector must go beyond the limits of the social segmentation of the market and reflect cultural alternatives, which bring together the diversity of various national social imaginaries. Until now, models of mass production in the audiovisual industries have been limited to Hollywood or mass markets of ethnic origins. Globalization and new technologies open possibilities for alternative and more innovative forms of mass production which put a premium on variety without dismissing text. China, India, Brazil and many other mass markets with increasing consumption of audiovisuals have the opportunity to face this challenge of variety and innovation versus content.

Digitalization, market structures and creative industries

Technological innovation affects creative industries in a variety of manners. As producers of texts, images and information creative industries benefit from the technological innovations related to the circulation of information, in particular digitalization, but while technical innovations may enhance or facilitate creativity they do not originate it. Thus, computer-aided designs have altered the practice of architectural design but have not augmented the supply of architectural talent.[6]

The new digital paradigm is still in the process of being consolidated and its impact on creative industries seems to be a mix of constraint and revolution. Digitalization means different things to different industries. Evaluating its impact is still difficult as the technology is unevenly distributed and most countries have yet to set in motion the infrastructure required for the large-scale diffusion of the new paradigm. That notwithstanding, the new technology has already had definitive impact on the audiovisual sector. Music, film and editing in general have been transformed and whole new sectors of production responsible for sharp increases in trade, such as video games, have appeared.

Digitalization opened new avenues for distribution of creative goods and services and has in general worked to lower costs and production time, and increase work efficiency and quality of production. The advent of computer samplers and sequencers has allowed for swifter production in the music industry and the elimination of a series of intermediations between the creation and the production and circulation of records. The consolidation of an Internet economy has also afforded increased reduction of cost in music circulation.

Studies by the International Telecommunication Union regarding the comparative speed in which certain key technologies have been diffused show that while the telephone has taken 74 years to arrive at 50 million users, the radio 36, television 13 and the Internet four, the software Napster has reached 50 million users in only one year (ECLAC 2004).

In the case of the film industry, digitalization has bridged the gap between professional high cost productions and independent low cost films allowing for the production of top scale films with significantly diminished production costs. In the world of editing, digitalization has made possible the creation of quality products by independent producers, shortened the process of text editing and placed graphics, in general, at the disposal of all.

Digitalization and the Internet have without doubt increased the empowering of individual creators. The "doing it yourself" potential of the technology has shortened the gap between the professional and the dilettante and increased the competitive potential of small and medium enterprises. But digitalization has not made creative industries immune from the pressures of the market, nor has it altered the manner in which major distributors operate.

Viewed from the development angle, digital goods have the potential to integrate disparate geographical worlds better and greatly diminish the information divide, but they also break down informal industrial protection which until now sheltered local industry in the developing world (ECLAC 2004).

Digitalization is also a somewhat complex technological instrument requiring certain levels of specialization and standards of quality which impose new difficulties to the creative process. While having significant effects on the production and consumption of creative industries the new technologies have not brought about a new era in cultural production. New industries such as digital television, Internet service provision and computer games all carry strong inheritances from relatively stable ways of organizing cultural production and the fundamental characteristic of contemporary media: big business in a constant search for monopoly positions and minimal regulations (Hesmondhalgh 2002). Most developing countries have adopted policies dedicated to bridging the digital divide; international organizations such as UNESCO, UNDP, UNCTAD and the World Bank have developed programmes and projects in this area, most often in conjunction with the communications ministries in developing countries. Creative industries are primary beneficiaries of these policies and more than most sectors can contribute to diffuse training in digital technologies. It is in this regard vital that the promotion of creative industries succeeds in becoming a horizontal policy objective between the cultural, planning and communications ministries.

Policies for creative industries: an evolving institutional framework

Policies in support of creative industries come from a multiplicity of interventions that are public and private in nature, as well as federal or local in origin. Globalization has ensured that cultural policy while domestic in application can no longer be solely national in perspective. The distribution of creative goods operates by global rules of competition and production, while taking place in the domestic market it is also global in scope and perspective.[7]

Creative industries have many different sources of financing, but they are also beneficiaries of a consolidated tradition of public financing for culture, which in many OECD countries reached its high point in the 1970s, when the association of culture with democratic values lends political legitimacy to public spending. As the distinction between commercial art and non-commercial art became progressively blurred, particularly in what concerns the audiovisual sector, creative industries came to benefit in direct and indirect ways from overall public spending on culture.

The economic downturn of the mid 1970s and the advent of a neo-liberal paradigm will change this perspective on public spending and lead to the new emphasis on privatization of culture.

Traditions in public financing

The motivations for adopting public policies in favor of creative industries do not differ from that of cultural policy in general: support for public goods and insurance against market failure. Most countries have one form or another of cultural policy in support of the arts and incentives or subsidies for creative business. Moreover it is the manner in which creative industries as an activity is perceived that will in part determine the policy line adopted.

Although there are no pure policy ideal types it is possible to single out a series of characteristics which when stressed can approximate policy models.

- In general terms most countries have a federally financed institution responsible for supporting the arts. The economic strength of these institutions will in large part depend on the manner in which they guarantee their resources. That is, whether resources are ensured through permanent budget lines as in France, or through yearly appropriations, subject to economic and political circumstances, as in the United States. By and large, permanent budget lines ensure resource availability and allow for long range planning which often compensates for a relative shortage of resources.
- The crisis of the welfare state has led most countries with centralized budgets for culture to spread the federal responsibility with regional and municipal funds. With the same logic and with few exceptions, centralized governmental structures are being replaced by a system of grants and partnerships with foundations and the non-profit sector.

- Large cities, because they tend to be global financial hubs, can develop metropolitan public/private schemes of sponsorship that are additional to, and compensatory for failures in, funding by federal institutions.
- The sponsoring of the arts does not guarantee the sustenance of creative industries, special financial and industrial incentives are required to bridge the gap between the arts and the economy. Funding from the private and non-profit sector is central in bridging this gap and the importance and magnitude of this sector is directly related to the structure and system of taxation of revenues and the facilities existing within the law for income tax discounts.
- Private and commercial sponsorships are an additional instrument for financing creative activities which are increasingly more widespread and gain financial relevance depending on the size and structure of the markets in question. The structure of income tax deductions will influence the breakdown in the origins of private sponsorship, favoring either individual donations or corporate sponsorships.
- Market size is an important but not sufficient explanation for private sponsorship; equally relevant are the dimensions of the capital market and the availability of venture capital and investment options. Likewise public financing and centralized budgetary allocations alone do not determine the nature of financing for creative industries. Even when tax incentives and deductions play a small role in the overall financing, alternative forms of funding through taxes and special allocations are also present.

Public sponsorship and market incentives

In most OECD countries, national institutions for cultural financing have developed their contemporary features with the economic expansion of the 1960s. The modalities of funding adopted followed the movements of expansion and recession of the national economies, with waves of expansion and slumps in the 1970s and 1980s. Moreover the modalities of budgetary appropriation have also conditioned the degree to which these institutions were subject to economic and political downfalls. In the cases of Europe and the United States contrasting patterns evolved.

The United States is an interesting example of the relationship between centralized and federal approaches to the financing of culture. The two major national institutions which handle the financing of cultural activities, The National Endowment for the Arts and The National Endowment for the Humanities, were created in the 1965, and were preceded by initiatives at the state level, in particular the creation of the New York State Council for the Arts.

The argument for public financing of creative production is well described in the report of the President's Committee on the Arts in America of 1997, which states that the arts are an investment opportunity for government, offering high rates of return on investment in both economic and non-economic terms, low manageable risk, and sufficient and compelling opportunities for substantial investment. The same report advises that this opportunity evaporates without a minimum level of public funding. Private dollars cannot substitute for public dollars as each responds to distinct and critical funding requirements. Foundations, corporations and individuals have been generally unwilling to support several critical phases in the arts business system, including idea generation and development as well as distribution and marketing (President Clinton's Report 1997).

Although the case for the public financing of the arts is generally accepted, centralized forms of cultural financing have never had a stable life in the United States. The first debates concerning the funding of public television proposed a form of financing through a specific TV tax, a system similar to that adopted in Europe, but pressures towards local autonomy, the fears those central structures would gain political independence, moved against centralized policy options and in favor of financing through individual appropriations. National institutions such as the NEA and NEH lack the budgetary stability and political independence which equivalent institutions have in Europe, most notably France and England. In fact these institutions are vulnerable to alternative currents of power in the Congress and the Executive. The radical downsizing of the NEA in 1991 is a case in point. From 1992 to 2000 the budgetary allocations of NEA wavered from US$176 million to 105 million, reaching an all time low in 1997 with $99 million. By contrast, state allocations increased from $213 million to 447 million and local financing from $600 million to 800 million (US Executive Budget, 1999).

These figures are partial accounts of a larger reality. In fact, there are substantial levels of indirect public financing for the arts and the total direct spending at the federal level can be estimated to be many times higher than the reduced budget of the NEA. During the 1970s and in part of the 1980s declining federal funds have been compensated by rising state funds. This is particularly the case for states with international urban centers such as New York. In 1996, the Regional Planning Association established that the arts represented a $11 billion industry for the city (Martorella 2002). In fact, the city of New York has pioneered institutional support for the arts in America and hosts one of the most dynamic forms of public sponsorship: The New York State Council for the Arts, founded in 1960, and which preceded all federal organizations in the sponsorship of the arts. State funding operates through grants, foregoing of tax revenues and the allocation of non-profit status for specific organizations and private donors in exchange for funding of particular sectors. The philosophy of funding is as always couched in value terms as argued by the New York Alliance for the Arts: "a major reason for encouraging robust and reliable support for the arts is economic self-interest; to protect this major industry which by the year 2000 had passed the $12 billion level of economic impact in NYC" (Alliance for the Arts 2004).

A study on the non-profit industry in New York City conducted by the Alliance for the Arts has shown that the creative sector grew by 22 percent from 1995 to 1999. This growth was fueled by increases of 30 percent in earned income and by 21 percent in private contributions, which outweighed the decrease in governmental funding.

What this study also showed was that earnings were also proportional to the size of the organizations. Income growth between 1995 and 1999 was strongest for the larger organizations but did not filter down to the smallest organizations. The largest organizations, which earned the greatest share of their income, also enjoyed the most growth. Thus very large organizations derived 53 percent of their income from earned sources, large organizations 48 percent, medium organizations 44 percent and Small organizations 39 percent (Alliance for the Arts 2004).

What is equally important is that in matters of financing the boundaries between private, public, profit and non-profit, federal, state and local seem to be blurring, with all institutions facing similar challenges and differentiating lines becoming more dependent on the form of organization and market segment in which each institution operates. That is, large versus small organizations serving broad versus niche markets (McCarthy 2001).

During the 1990s, the combination of neo-liberal ideologies and the efforts towards streamlining the national budget led to a major downfall in public contributions, which was in part compensated by a rise in individual private donations. Giving USA indicates that, for the year 2000, $152 billion were allocated for cultural industries with 75 percent of the total coming from individual donors and many arts organizations benefited from the dramatic increase in new millionaires during the 1990s.

Corporate giving accelerated gradually throughout the decade, but the increase in foundation giving was even more dramatic. From 1990 to 1995 foundation giving increased by almost one-half and in the next five years it grew by more than 250 percent.

The financing schemes described are but a limited aspect of the financing of creative industries. In so far as they are also a commercial enterprise, albeit a special one, creative industries are also part of the overall system of market financing. In the case of the United States, they benefit from the competitiveness of financial capital and the increasing opportunities of the venture capital market.

The financing of creative industries in European countries presents a very different scenario. It is a generally accepted truism that European welfare economies offer a pattern of public policy and financing which relies in large part on the public sphere. While the market versus state duality has been somewhat present in most welfare and distributive economic policy, creative industries are a bit of a special case. This is so because even in cases where public funds have come to bear a large share of the culture budget as in France, a great deal of innovation exists in devising alternatives to direct public financing.

Amongst the European countries with big cultural budgets, the case of France is unique in that it combines a strong and constant flow of funds coming from the ordinary budget with a multiplicity of indirect schemes of financing. In the last years, changes in legislation have been under way to allow tapping of the private market for financing in schemes other than commercial sponsorships. Moreover these modalities of funds are still modest compared with the direct and indirect forms of public financing.

Public intervention in cultural development and institutions has been a feature of the French State since the seventeenth century. This long tradition has also been unique in that, since the onset, culture has not been treated solely as heritage preservation but also as creative opportunity. Throughout the 1980s and 1990s, when most central budgets for culture in Europe were severely diminished, France maintained a level of investment which reached almost 1 percent of the overall State expenditures and in 2000 the budget exceeded the 1 percent figure.

The Ministries of Culture and Foreign Affairs carry out financing at the central level, with funds also being allocated in smaller proportions by other ministries such as education and research. As early as the 1970s a Special Fund for Cultural Intervention was created with the joint participation of several ministries. The system provides that 1 percent of the construction costs of any public building be dedicated to the funding of art works.

At the regional level, Regional Affairs Directorates work in an autonomous manner in conjunction with regional, municipal and local authorities. This division of responsibilities creates a cross-pattern of funds and institutional frameworks which guarantees a great deal of stability to the financing of creativity. Particularly noteworthy in scope are the regional funds for museum acquisitions, the regional funds for library acquisitions and the regional funds for contemporary art. The devolution law of the 1980s has increased the level of participation of regional and local authorities, which now represent 60 percent of overall funding.

For the year 1996, the State covered 52.3 percent of the expenditures on culture and local authorities, were responsible for 47.7 percent. Within the central budget 20.5 percent of funds came from the Ministry of Culture, 28.6 percent from other ministries and 3.2 percent from special treasury accounts for the cinema and audiovisual sector. In addition to specific treasury allocations, the audiovisual sector also benefits from several other generic culture funds. The complexity of the financing schemes is a response to the growing importance of the sector, in 1980 France had three public TV networks; today it has over 100 networks.

Incentive schemes comprise a variety of methods ranging from tax incentives, deductions and exoneration for certain categories, reduction of value added tax, special financial accounts for film and TV, support accounts, taxes levied on theater and cinema tickets, taxes coming from the sales of TV and rentals of audiovisual materials, as well as a large gamut of quotas protecting independent film production, regional European products and French language creations.

Different kinds of quotas are applied to networks producing original works in French, a large share of which are devoted to independent productions. Canal Plus in exchange for the opportunity of presenting films a year after their release must devote 20 percent of its total annual resources for the acquisition of broadcasting rights for original European and French language productions. Rules and regulations also apply to prime time viewing; 60 percent of prime time must be European and at least 40 percent of French language content.

The United Kingdom presents a curious contrast to the cases of United Statese and France, in so far as its public policies for the arts had a modest beginning and it now represents one of the most flexible and active programs in support of creative industries. John Maynard Keynes created the Council for encouragement of music and the arts, now the Arts Council of Great Britain, in the 1940s, with a modest budget of £235,000. The resources available increased significantly throughout the 1960s reaching £7.2 million in 1968. The privatization drives of the 1980s also affected the cultural sector by placing emphasis on the policies of matching funds, pursuit of commercial revenues and sponsorships and the creation of bridging institutions between culture and trade. With the creation of the Arts Lottery in the 1990s a steady additional source of funds has been guaranteed. England is the sole European country to have a ministry devoted to creative industries and an Arts and Media Strategy which serves as a policy guide for arts funding and development combining creative industries with Export Promotion Initiatives. These more innovative policies coexist with more traditional quota systems for the media, which resembles in intent the policies adopted by France. Quotas of transmission time are reserved for European works and 10 percent of the transmissions are exclusive for independent productions. In this context, the BBC, ITV companies, Channel 4 and Channel 5 should in principle devote at least 25 percent of their quality programming time to a range of European independent productions.

Partnerships with the private and non-profit sector are actively sought. Creative industries are pursued as an economic value through trade promotion and incentives. As of now England remains the only European country to have included creative industries in its national accounts and made significant efforts to incorporate them into the standard industrial classification codes. These initiatives go beyond a mere branding operation and constitute an active economic policy.

In contrast to the American experience, the British policy for stimulating creative industries relies more on creating opportunities for investment than in tax exemption for the arts. Instruments such as increasing tax deductions, individual tax exemption schemes, private bequests and donations play a lesser role in sustaining creative industries in England than in the United States. There is in this regard no English model for sustaining creative industries.

In spite of different financing traditions and policy instruments, France, England and the United States all emphasize the export of national cultural production. In the case of the United States this is achieved through the work of the big distribution conglomerates with a helping hand of the State Department. In the cases of France and England, the promotion of national creative industries is an intrinsic part of the activities of the Foreign and Trade Ministries, the European Commission, the European Council and the OECD.

This interplay of policy instruments is with very few exceptions absent in developing countries, where cultural budgets are divorced from economic and export activities and foreign ministries and trade ministries do not consider creative industries a representative priority in international affairs. This is so, nothwithstanding the weight of creative industries in conflicting international trade negotiations.

Policy options for creative industries

The case for policies in favor of creative industries cannot rest alone on the competition for a new growth paradigm, but must refer to the importance of guaranteeing global opportunities for a more equitable production and circulation of creative goods and services. The notion of policies must also be revised as the objective is not limited to improving production of creative goods and services and devising instruments which can handle the complexities of the creative economy, but ensuring the economic conditions for creative innovation and nurturing the interplay between creative ideas, the production of goods and services and their circulation.

In most developing countries, policy options available for sustaining creative industries are scarce. With notable exceptions such as Mexico, China and India, where the promotion of national culture is a major, political option, cultural ministries still obtain the most meager portions of the national budgets, and public policy for the cultural sector is more a political tribute to national culture than an element of a development strategy. This perspective is often reinforced by the cultural ministries themselves, which tend to define their mandates in terms of heritage protection rather than as active promoters of innovation in the cultural field. Yet, the present development challenge is not to regard culture solely as a common inheritance, an attribute of the past to be revered and preserved, but also as a source of creativity, an instrument of social interaction and a means through which society represents itself.

The experiences reviewed show that creative industries have characteristics which condition policy and which emanate not only from the structure of the market but from the nature of the creative process. Thus, creativity and talent will not lead to the development of creative industries if not properly rewarded and protected. Creative industries require institutional frameworks which operate as a stimulant to creativity and act as bridging institutions, capable of providing links between the individual independent producer and the market. The market for creative industries in turn requires incentives, regulation and monitoring, as well as specific export promotion policies.

Globalization has made access to credit increasingly difficult for most developing countries. Scarcity of funds, uneven access to foreign direct investment and high interest rates have transformed the realm of public policy into a battleground for finance. In many countries private incentives for creative industries have come to compete with absent public funds for the most basic sponsorship of culture, further depleting the options of financing available to independent cultural producers. In this scenario, it is easy to relegate creative industries to the realm of the superfluous.

Still, the debate over public policy cannot be reduced to the struggle for public funds for culture and the protection of the cultural historical patrimony as an end in itself. Throughout the 1990s, most developing countries, in one way or another, have attempted to confront the challenges of globalization through adjustment policies, privatization and schemes of attracting greater levels of foreign direct investments. The balance of these efforts has been severely unsatisfactory and in most cases the combination of policies required resulted in a veritable straightjacket for development projects. Despite the narrowing of existing policy spaces, there are still important financial, fiscal and macroeconomic policy options available to developing countries which allow for viable choices in industrial policy. Globalization is not an autonomous and irresistible process driven by impersonal forces and technological progress (Kozul-Wright and Rayment 2004). As all complex processes it can also be understood as entailing predicament, strategy and opportunity. Investments in culture have significant externalities, creating added value and jobs outside the public sector. Although they depend on creativity, creative industries, particularly those associated with information and media, are not ephemeral economic activities and at the national level, supply is often a guarantee of demand.

The job market for creative industries is varied, comprising technologically intensive activities as well as activities with low training prerequisites. In many cases training for creative industries is a "learning by doing exercise" evolving from the creative process. But, while easy to stimulate, creative industries are difficult to sustain. They are part of complex distribution markets and networks of productive relations and services, which require regulation, stimulation and proper infrastructures; they are evolving economic activities, not mere recipients of state protection.

The operational environment of creative industries is characterized more by a constant movement of "creative destruction" than by incremental change, and the coexistence of small, medium and large enterprises is a constant struggle for entry opportunities and survival against takeover from large oligopolies. Developing countries do not escape this predicament. In fact, in most developing countries with economically significant audiovisual industries, large enterprises in the information sector are constantly co-opting potential new creators and undermining the economic potential of the independent creator, the production of "telenovelas" is a case in point. While generating exports and thereby bridging the gap between national production and international distribution, "telenovelas" have also stifled the development of audiovisual productions, in particular film, outside of the television market. Because international barriers for distribution are so strong, national production and distribution barriers are often disregarded to the disadvantage of national independent producers.

Successful film industries have emerged and became consolidated whenever market incentives for sustaining film production were combined, at least in the early stages, with an appropriate broadcasting policy, regulating the relationship between the various media and the independent producer. The fusion of audiovisual industries with major information conglomerates has increased the need for appropriate broadcasting policies, now aiming not only at guaranteeing a market for independent producers but also at preserving the diversity of information.

Policies for creative industries have evolved from different institutional traditions but converge in the need to provide two types of links: between the individual creators and the market and between the national and the global market. In the case of developing countries, good results have been obtained in the export of audiovisual materials at the regional level and to culturally linked communities around the globe. Still, a lot needs to be done to guarantee the internal sustainability of creative industries and to exploit further the possibilities of the export markets. The markets for creative industries are at once global and local and this places an onus on policy-making, which must attend to local requirements but also be global in perspective. Policy-making involves developing appropriate instruments of copyright protection, which are not merely formal extensions of legislations drafted to protect rents from distributors, but which can function within the existing market conditions of developing countries. It also entails formulating and implementing broadcasting policies which can protect as well as stimulate independent creation and, last but not least, it depends on appropriate economic analysis and research.

Policy-making in the area of creative industries is a new field, with best practices, but no standard policy model. Statistics regarding creative industries are scarce in developed countries, but even more so in developing economies. Lack of data leads to lack of research and the absence of economic analysis. Moreover, absence of data is only one aspect of the existing knowledge and conceptual gap. More needs to be done to define a research agenda for creative industries, which must include the areas of investment and financing, market distribution and trade, as well as technological innovation. Creative industries are content industries which utilize flexible manufacturing and high technology; they do not fit easily into traditional industrial firm models. Concerning trade and distribution, the existence of large oligopolies in distribution conditions, and what we know regarding competition in the global market, limits research into alternative modalities. Much still needs to be done to understand alternative forms of distribution for content industries. Serious economic research is necessary, as well as devising policy alternatives which guarantee that the disparities of the global market do not preempt developing countries from participating in the global exchange with their own creative products.

There are no ideal policy schemes for supporting creative industries and sound policies are often a virtue of recognizing and ceasing global opportunities. In the coming years the preservation of cultural and creative diversity and the economic rules guiding the trade of creative goods and services will increasingly be an important part of the international political debate. Developing countries should be prepared to deal with this challenge, not only to preserve the possibility of participating in what will likely become one of the most dynamic sectors of global trade, but also for the defense of their own global cultural diversity.

The arguments and policies in support of cultural diversity at a national and global level cannot be restricted or subsumed by a discourse of preservation, but must encompass creation, distribution and innovation. At stake is not the preservation of ethnicities, dying cultures or condemned languages, but the possibility of having access to diverse creative industries and more equitable rules for competing on the international market.

At the national level creative industries must be incorporated within the agenda of development and innovation. This implies moving away from the stalemate of public versus private financing and exploring alternative and decentralized instruments for financing creative industries. At the international level it implies targeting creative industries as an issue central to the trade, governance and access to knowledge debate. Unlike other international political challenges, the preservation of and access to creative diversity is not a challenge for selected individual countries, but a predicament with only global winners and losers.

Notes

1 Statistics regarding the contribution of creative industries to global GDP vary according to the range of industries covered by the definition. UNCTAD figures have been discussed in the High Level Panel on Creative Industries in São Paulo, Brazil 2004.

2 The notion of culture as a resource has been put forth by Yudice (2003). More recently, the role of creative industries in generating added value has opened a new dimension in the discussion of culture and capital accumulation, centered on the battle for copyrights and the privatization of the public space of cultural exchanges.

3 While the distinction between public and private goods goes back to Adam Smith, the analysis of efficiency in the production of public goods is undertaken by Samuelson (1954). At present, the concept and discussion of the role of public goods has evolved beyond the economic analysis of market efficiency to refer also to the provision and management of goods made public by the expansion of globalization. Stiglitz (1999) covers this issue.

4 A parallel is being made with the analysis of Foucault (1977) regarding the origins of institutions shaping socialization in early industrial societies. Rather than a change in language or institutional format, what seems to characterize the social use of creative industries in late capitalism is their capacity to bridge, simplify and condition cultural identities fragmented by globalization.

5 A distinction between the homogenization of culture and the globalization of creative industries is pertinent. The notion of cultural homogenization refers to the impact of the media on cultural productions worldwide; the imposition of styles, fashions and messages which derive from the mass products distributed and consumed. The globalization of creative industries refers to the system of distribution of creative goods and services. While the creative process often transcends the frontiers between national and international, the distribution of creative goods and services does not. The absence of cultural diversity in national markets is more often dictated by the operations of distribution cartels than by the homogenization of creative productions.

6 Competition on the Internet is a good example of the importance of creativity, notwithstanding advantages in technology. Lohr (2000) discusses how culture and not raw technology alone will determine whether the United States retains its status as the preeminent Internet nation (Yudice 2003).

7 The impact of globalization on national policy space and the increasing transnationalization of media companies often diminish the effectiveness of traditional policy instruments in support of national productions, such as quota systems, incentives and

import restrictions, as local industries merge or become attached to distribution packages which are global in nature.

Bibliography

Adorno, Theodor W., (1981) *Prisms*, MIT Press.

Alliance for the Arts, (2004) *Who Pays for the Arts?* Alliance for the Arts, New York.

Appadurai, Arjun, (1997) *Modernity at Large*, University of Minnesota Press.

Canadian Foundation for the Americas, (2004) *Culture Trade in the Americas*, Focal.

Crane, Diana, (2002) *Global Culture: Media, Arts, Policy and Globalization*, Routledge, Center for Arts and Culture, Cultural Policies Series, Washington DC.

Compendium, (2003) *A Compendium of Basic Facts and Trends of Cultural Policies in Europe*, Council of Europe.

Convenio Andres Bello, (1999) *Estudio sobre el Aporte de las Industrias Culturales y del Entretenimiento.*

ECLAC, (2004) *Building an Information Society: a Latin American and Caribbean Perspective*, ECLAC.

Economist, The, (2003) "Survey of the film Industry," 18 January.

Essen Declaration, (1999*) 10 Axioms for the Cultural Industries in Europe*, International Congress of Experts on Cultural Industries in Europe.

Foucault, Michel, (1977) *Discipline and Punishment: the Birth of the Prison*, Pantheon Books.

Fundação João Pinheiro, (1998) *Diagnosticos dos Investimentos na Cultura no Brasil* Fundação João Pinheiro, Brazil.

Garnham, Nicholas, (1990) *Capitalism and Communication*, Sage Publications.

Hallin, Daniel, (2000) Commercialism and professionalism in the American news media, in James Curren and Michael Gurevitch (eds), *Mass Media and Society*, Oxford University Press.

Heilbrun, James, (2001) *The Economics of Art and Culture*, Cambridge University Press.

Held, David, (1999) *Global Transformations, Politics, Economics and Culture*, Stanford University Press.

Hesmondhalgh, David, (2002) *The Cultural Industries*, Sage Publications.

Howkins, John, (2001), *The Creative Economy*, Penguin Books, London.

IPEA, (2000), *Seis estudos sobre a cultura e desenvolvimento*, Instituto de Pesquisa Econômica Aplicada, Brazil, September.

IDATE, (2001) *Survey on National Cinematography, World Film and TV Market.*

Jameson, Frederic, (1992) *Postmodernism or the Cultural Logic of Late Capitalism*, Duke University Press.

Jameson, Frederic, (1998) *The Cultures of Globalization*, Duke University Press, *The Cultural Turn: Selected writings on the postmodern*, Verso.

Kozul-Wright, Zeljka, (2001) *Challenges and Prospects of the Music Industry for Developing Countries, Music Industry Workshop*, European Parliament, Brussels.

Kozul-Wright, Richard and Rayment, Paul, (2004) *Globalization Reloaded: An UNCTAD Perspective*, UNCTAD Discussion Papers 167, January.

Leclerc, Jean Pierre, (2003) *Reflexions sur le Dispositif Francais de Soutien a la Production Cinematographique*, Special Report for the Ministry of Culture and Communication France, January.

Lohr, Steve, (2000) "Welcome to the Internet the first Global Colony," *New York Times*, 9 January.

Lukacs, Georg, (1971) *History and Class Consciousness*, Cambridge University Press.
Martorella, Rosanne, (2002) "The Economic Consequences of Cultural Tourism in New York City," in D. Crane, N. Kawashima and K. Kawasaki (eds), *Media Arts, Policy and Globalization*, Routledge, London.
Mackay, Donald, (2004) *Culture and Trade in the Americas*, FOCAL, Canadian Foundation for the Americas.
McCarthy, Kevin, (2001) *The Performing Arts in a New Era*, Rand, Santa Monica, CA.
Mckinsey Rapport, (1997) *You've Got to Have Art*, Mckinsey, New York.
New Zealand Institute of Economic Research, (March 2002) *Report to Industry* New Zealand.
Organization of American States, (2003) *Cultural Industries in the Latin American Economies.*
Paxman, Andrew, (2003) "Hybridized, Glocalized and Hecho en Mexico: Foreign Influences on Mexican TV programming since the 1950s," *Global Media Journal*, 2 (2).
President Clinton's Report, (1997) *Creative America*, Committee on the Arts and Humanities.
Reis, Eustaquio, (1999) *A Economia do Cinema no Brasil*, Ministerio da Industria e Comercio Brazil.
Samuelson, Paul, (1954) "The Pure Theory of Public Expenditures," *Review of Economic and Statistics*, 36: 387–389.
Seagrave, Kerry, (1997) *American Films Abroad*, McFarland and Company, Jefferson, NC.
Seaman, Bruce, (2002), *National Investment in the Arts*, Center for Arts and Culture, Washington, DC. March.
Semati, Mendi and Sortirin, Patty J., (1999) "Hollywood's Transnational Appeal," *Journal of Popular Film and Television*, 26 (4).
Smith, Adam, 1994 (1776) *The Wealth of Nations: An Inquiry into the Nature and Causes*, Modern Library.
Stiglitz, Joseph, (1999) "Knowledge as a Public Good," in Inge Kaul (ed.), *Global Public Goods*, Oxford University Press.
Thussu, Daya, (1998) "Localizing the Global: Zee TV in India," in D.K. Thussu (ed.), *Electronic Empires, Global Media and Local Resistence*, Arnold, London.
UNCTAD, (2003) *Music Industry Workshop*, European Parliament, Brussels, Belgium, May 2001.
UNCTAD, (2004) *Creative Industries and Development*, TD8XI9/BP13.
UNESCO, (2000) *World Culture Report.*
UNESCO, (2004) *Culture Trade and Globalization.*
United Kingdom, (2003) *Creative Industries Economic Estimates Statistical Bulletin*, July.
Venturelli, Shalini, (2003) *From the Information Economy to the Creative Economy; Moving Culture to the Center of International Public Policy*. Cultural Comment Series, Center for Arts and Culture.
World Bank, (2003) *Development Outreach*, November.
Wyszomirsky, Margaret, (2003) *Creative Industries and Cultural Professions in the 21th Century*, Barnett Symposium on the Arts and Public Policy.
Wyszomirski, Margaret and Clubb, Pat, (1989) *The Cost of Culture: Patterns and Prospects of Private Arts Patronage*, Aca Books.
Yudice, George, (2003) *The Expediency of Culture*, Duke University Press.
Yusuf, S. and Nabeshima, K., (2003) *How Creative Industries can Affect Urban Areas*, World Bank Development Outreach.

Index

www.ingramcontent.com/pod-product-compliance
Lightning Source LLC
LaVergne TN
LVHW011111300926
849160LV00008B/344
9780415512466